CAMBRIDGE
UNIVERSITY PRESS

CAMBRIDGE EN
Language Assessment
Part of the University of Cambridge

MW00332600

Cambridge English

Objective
First

Student's Book
with answers

Annette Capel   Wendy Sharp   **Fourth Edition**

CAMBRIDGE
UNIVERSITY PRESS

University Printing House, Cambridge CB2 8BS, United Kingdom

Cambridge University Press is part of the University of Cambridge.

It furthers the University's mission by disseminating knowledge in the pursuit of education, learning and research at the highest international levels of excellence.

www.cambridge.org
Information on this title: www.cambridge.org/9781107628304

First edition © Cambridge University Press 2000
Second edition © Cambridge University Press 2008
Third edition © Cambridge University Press 2012
Fourth edition © Cambridge University Press and UCLES 2014

First published 2000
Second edition 2008
Third edition 2012
Fourth edition 2014

Printed in Italy by L.E.G.O. S.p.A

A catalogue for this publication is available from the British Library

ISBN 978-1-107-62830-4   Student's Book with answers with CD-ROM
ISBN 978-1-107-62834-2   Student's Book without answers with CD-ROM
ISBN 978-1-107-62835-9   Teacher's Book with Teacher's Resources CD-ROM
ISBN 978-1-107-62854-0   Class Audio CDs (2)
ISBN 978-1-107-62839-7   Workbook without answers with Audio CD
ISBN 978-1-107-62845-8   Workbook with answers with Audio CD
ISBN 978-1-107-62856-4   Student's Pack (Student's Book without answers with CD-ROM, Workbook without answers with Audio CD)
ISBN 978-1-107-62847-2   Student's Book Pack (Student's Book with answers with CD-ROM and Class Audio CDs (2))
ISBN 978-1-107-29696-1   Student's Book ebook
ISBN 978-1-107-62857-1   Presentation Plus DVD-ROM

Additional resources for this publication at www.cambridge.org/elt/objectivefirstnew

Cover concept by Tim Elcock

Produced by Hart McLeod

Acknowledgements

The authors and publishers would like to thank the teachers and consultants who commented on the material: Brazil: Eliane Sanchez Querino (KNOW-HOW); Czech Rep.: Alês Novak; Hungary: Ildiko Berke; Italy: Robert Islam (British School of English), Fiona Line (Modern English); Mexico: Lizeth Jerezano Rodriguez, Graciella Toral Garcia; Poland: Dr Andrzej Diniejko (University of Warsaw); Russia: Tatyana Elistratova; Spain: Caroline Cooke, Nick Shaw (Cambridge English Studio), Leanne White; Switzerland: Allan Dalcher; UK: Kathryn Alevizos, David Jay, Julie Moore.

The authors would again like to thank Alyson Maskell for her many constructive suggestions, sensible solutions and meticulous editorial support on this edition. Thanks also go to Lynn Townsend, Lorraine Poulter, Joanne Hunter and Sara Bennett at Cambridge University Press, and to Hart McLeod for their creative work.

Development of this publication has made use of the *Cambridge English Corpus* (CEC). The CEC is a computer database of contemporary spoken and written English, which currently stands at over one billion words. It includes British English, American English and other varieties of English. It also includes the Cambridge Learner Corpus, developed in collaboration with the Cambridge English Language Assessment. Cambridge University Press has built up the CEC to provide evidence about language use that helps to produce better language teaching materials.

This product is informed by the *English Vocabulary Profile*, built as part of *English Profile*, a collaborative programme designed to enhance the learning, teaching and assessment of English worldwide. Its main funding partners are Cambridge University Press and Cambridge English Language Assessment and its aim is to create a 'profile' for English linked to the Common European Framework of Reference for Languages (CEF). *English Profile* outcomes, such as the *English Vocabulary Profile*, will provide detailed information about the language that learners can be expected to demonstrate at each CEF level, offering a clear benchmark for learners' proficiency. For more information, please visit www.englishprofile.org

The *Cambridge Advanced Learner's Dictionary* is the world's most widely used dictionary for learners of English. Including all the words and phrases that learners are likely to come across, it also has easy-to-understand definitions and example sentences to show how the word is used in context. The *Cambridge Advanced Learner's Dictionary* is available online at dictionary.cambridge.org. © Cambridge University Press, fourth edition, 2013, reproduced with permission.

The authors and publishers acknowledge the following sources of copyright material and are grateful for the permissions granted. While every effort has been made, it has not always been possible to identify the sources of all the material used, or to trace all copyright holders. If any omissions are brought to our notice, we will be happy to include the appropriate acknowledgements on reprinting.

The publisher has used its best endeavours to ensure that the URLs for external websites referred to in this book are correct and active at the time of going to press. However, the publisher has no responsibility for the websites and can make no guarantee that a site will remain live or that the content is or will remain appropriate.

Helen Storey for the text on p. 12, published by Faber and Faber;

Future Publishing Limited for the reviews on pp. 16–17 from PC Gamer, 1997. Copyright © Future Publishing Ltd;

Gary Stock for the text on p. 19 from www.googlewhack.com/stock.htm. Reproduced with permission;

Penguin Books Ltd and Random House Inc for the extract on p. 37 from *The Big Sleep* by Raymond Chandler (Penguin 1948). Copyright © 1939 by Raymond Chandler and renewed by Helga Green of the Estate of Raymond Chandler. Used by permission of Alfred A Knopf, a division of Random House Inc and Penguin Books Ltd;

Solo Syndication for the text on p. 40 adapted from 'British student, 19, becomes a Far East superstar after winning Chinese X Factor' by Liz Thomas, *Daily Mail* 18.1.10. Copyright © Daily Mail;

News Syndication for the text on p. 46 adapted from 'World features Direct' by Debbie Hall, *The Sun* 12.3.00, for the text on p. 47 adapted from 'Flying High' by Liz Gill, *The Sun* 19.7.03, for the text on p. 51 adapted from 'Fitness' by Cheryl Holmes, *The Sun* 21.5.05, for the text on p. 61 adapted from 'King of Madison Avenue' by Brian Schofield, *The Sunday Times* 8.2.09, for the text on p. 143 adapted from 'Glastonbudget' by Chris Catchpole, *The Sun* 1.6.10, for the text on p. 153 adapted from 'Zimbabwe Holiday' by Sean Newson, *The Sun* 2.6.02. Copyright News Syndication;

Telegraph Media Group Limited for the text on p. 80 adapted from 'Shops with the sweet smell of success' by Jacqui Thornton, *The Telegraph* 1999, for the text on p. 104 adapted from 'How sound and colour influence the taste of food' by Richard Gray, *The Telegraph* 30.5.08. Copyright © Telegraph Media Group Limited;

Immediate Media Company Bristol Limited for the text on p. 95 adapted from 'How to be an office god' by Jonathan Green, *BBC Focus Magazine*, sciencefocus.com. Copyright © Immediate Media Company Bristol Limited 2013;

HarperCollins Publishers Ltd, Houghton Mifflin Harcourt Publishing Company and Penguin Canada Books Inc for the extract on p. 116 from *The Hungry Tide* by Amitav Ghosh. Copyright © 2004, 2005 Amitav Ghosh. Reproduced with permission of HarperCollins Publishers Ltd, Houghton Mifflin Harcourt Publishing Company and Penguin Canada Books Inc;

David Higham Associates Limited for the text on p. 129 from *The Day of the Triffids* by John Wyndham, published by Penguin Books Ltd. Reproduced with permission;

Text on p. 133 © Crown Copyright;

The Guardian for the text on p. 141, text (a) adapted from 'Me and my car, Charlie Dark' by Donna McConnell, *The Observer* 5.6.05, text (b) adapted from 'Doh! James Wood Literary Critic' by Philip Olterman, *The Guardian* 3.2.07, text (c) adapted from 'Me and my car, Rachel Mari Kimber', *The Observer* 26.5.05, text (d) adapted from 'Me and my car, Sharon Nnatu' by Donna McConnell, *The Observer* 12.6.05. Copyright Guardian News & Media Ltd, 2005 and for the text on p. 161 adapted from 'Wrong number lands navy expert in Spielberg's war' by Nick Hopkins, *The Guardian* 6.8.98. Copyright Guardian News & Media Ltd 1998;

IPC Syndication for the text on p. 161 adapted from 'How to make a small fortune' *Woman's Weekly* 16.9.97. Copyright © IPC Syndication/Woman's Weekly;

Photo acknowledgements:

p. 10 (1a): iStockphoto.com/Justin Horrocks; p. 10 (1b): Annika Johnemark / photographersdirect.com; p. 10 (2a): DreamPictures/Getty Images; p. 10 (2b): itanistock/ Alamy; p. 10 (3a): DreamPictures/Shannon Faulk/Purestock/Superstock; p. 10 (3b): iStockphoto.com/ranplett; p. 10 (4a): Darren Baker/Alamy; p. 10 (4b): Sujata Majumdar/ photographersdirect.com; p. 19: F1 Online/Rex Features; p. 22 (1): Tetra Images/Superstock; p. 22 (2): Gavin Hellier/Alamy; p. 22 (3): John Dakars/Eye Ubiquitous/Hutchison; p. 22 (4): Hemis.fr/Superstock; p. 28 (1, 5): iStockphoto/Thinkstock; p. 28 (2): Nature Picture Library/ Rex Features; p. 28 (3): Masa Ushioda/Alamy; p. 28 (4): Jurgen & Christine Sohns/FLPA; p. 28 (6): K. Tornblom/IBL/Rex Features; p. 29: John Foxx Images; p. 33: imagebroker/FLPA; p. 34 (1): imagebroker/FLPA; p. 34 (2): Emma Wood/Alamy; p. 34 (3): iStockphoto/ Thinkstock; p. 34 (4): Mark A. Johnson/Corbis; p. 34 (5): Blend Images/Superstock; p. 34 (6): Mallaun Ludwig/Prisma/Superstock; p. 37: Warner Bros/The Kobal Collection; p. 40: Adrian Sheratt/Rex Features; p. 50 (l): Stefano Cavoretto/Shutterstock; p. 50 (r): Leo Mason/Getty Images; p. 50 (r): WestEnd61/Getty Images; p. 51: Photri Images/Superstock; p. 52: Popperfoto/ Getty Images; p. 54 (1): Imagebroker.net/Superstock; p. 54 (2): Hill Creek Pictures/Purestock/ Superstock; p. 54 (3): Jupiterimages/Thinkstock; p. 54 (4): ONOKY Photononstop/Alamy; p. 57: iStockphoto/Thinkstock; p. 60: Image courtesy of the Advertising Archives; p. 61: Topfoto/UPP; p. 63 (1): Helene Rogers/Art Directors & TRIP; p. 63 (2): Kathy deWitt/ Alamy; p. 63 (3): Stuart Kelly/Alamy; p. 63 (4): Peter Cavanagh/Alamy; p. 66 (t): Spyglass Entertainment/Ronald Grant Archive; p. 66 (b): Victor Habbick Visions/Science Photo Library; p. 68: NASA/ Science Photo Library; p. 69: Photosindia/ Alamy; p. 70: Jupiterimages/ Thinkstock; p. 72 (l): Evan Agostini/AP/Press Association Images; p. 72 (c): Henry Lamb/ Photowire/BEI/ Rex Features; p. 72 (r): Jeffery Mayer/WireImage/Getty Images; p. 73: age fotostock/Superstock; p. 78 (1): Jerry Amster/Superstock; p. 78 (2): Getty Images; p. 78 (3): Motoring Picture Library/Alamy; p. 78 (4): Neil McAllister/Alamy; p. 81: Ian McKinnell/Getty Images; p. 84: Warner Bros/Ronald Grant Archive; p. 85: Image courtesy of the Advertising Archives; p. 86 (l): Goodluz/Shutterstock; p. 86 (r): Alexander Caminada/Rex Features; p. 87 (Christie): AFP/Getty Images; p. 87 (Madonna): Matt Baron/BEI/Rex Features; p. 87 (Lennox): Ken McKay/Rex Features; p. 87 (Gauguin): Bettmann/Corbis; p. 87 (Cruise): Broadimage/Rex Features; p. 87: Socrates, marble head, copy from a bronze from the Pompeion in Athens, made by Lysippus, Classical Greek, c.330 BC, /Louvre, Paris, France /The Bridgeman Art Library; p. 90: Travel Library Ltd/ Superstock; p. 92 (l): Gianni Cigolini/Getty Images; p. 92 (r): Ukraft/ Alamy; p. 93 (A): Flirt/Superstock; p. 93 (B): Catchlight Visual Services/Alamy; p. 93 (C): Thinkstock; p. 93 (D): Christopher Robbins/Getty Images; p. 93 (E): StockLife/Shutterstock; p. 95: Popperfoto/Getty Images; p. 97: Bruno Vincent/Getty Images; p. 98 (1): Eye Ubiquitous/ Rex Features; p. 98 (2): Adrian Sheratt/Rex Features; p. 98 (3): Inter Vision Ltd/Travel Pictures Ltd; p. 98 (4): AFP/Getty Images; p. 101: Melanie Friend/Eye Ubiquitous/Hutchison; p. 102: Oliver Gerhard/Imagebroker/FLPA; p. 104 (Kunu): Lowell Georgia/Corbis; p. 104(Akiko): Lori Adamski Peek/Getty Images; p. 104 (Gayle): F1 Online/Thinkstock; p. 106: Chris Rennie/ Art Directors & TRIP; p. 110 (1): Thinkstock; p. 110 (2): Dave Thompson/PA Wire/Press Association Images; p. 110 (3): iStockphoto.com/Hans-Martens; p. 110 (4): Martin Black/ Imagestate; p. 111: M.Powell/The Times/Rex Features; p. 113: Helene Rogers/Art Directors & TRIP; p. 114: © warrensmith.biz; p. 116: © Amitav Ghosh, 2005, The Hungry Tide, HarperCollins Publishers Ltd.; p. 118 (A): *King Lear* by Shakespeare/Cambridge University Press; p. 118 (B): © Gerald Martin, 2009, Gabriel García Márquez - A Life, Bloomsbury Publishing plc; p. 118 (C): *Broken Angels* by Richard Morgan, Orion Publishing Group, London; Cover design © Orion Publishing Group, Jacket illustration © Chris Moore/Artist Partners; p. 118 (D): from *A Body in the Bath House* by Lindsay Davis, published by Century. Reprinted by permission of The Random House Group Ltd.; p. 118 (E): Designed by Brian Roberts/Guardian Books; p. 118 (F): *The Last Detective* by Robert Crais, Orion Publishing Group, London; Cover design © Orion Publishing Group, Cover image © André Burian/ Corbis; p. 122: MIRA/Alamy; p. 124 (t): Robert Stainforth/Alamy; p. 124 (b) IT Stock/ Thinkstock; p. 125: Andrew Cowie/Colorsport; p. 126 (t): TEK Image /Science Photo Library; p. 126 (b): Image Source/Rex Features: p. 127: Polka Dot Images/Thinkstock; p. 130 (1): iStockphoto/Thinkstock; p. 130 (2): Flirt/Superstock; p. 130 (3): Frederic Sierakowski/Rex Features; p. 130 (4): Helene Rogers/ Art Directors & TRIP; p. 130 (5): Charles Thatcher/Getty Images; p. 136 (1): Leslie Woodhead/Eye Ubiquitous/Hutchison; p. 136 (2): Julian Calder/Getty Images; p. 138: Jon Blau/Camera Press London; p. 139: eye35/Alamy; p. 140: Dennis Kitchen/ Getty Images; p. 142 (t): AFP/Getty Images; p. 143: Courtesy of Glastonbudget Music Festival, Mockstar Ltd, www.glastonbudget.org; p. 145: Everett Collection/Rex Features; p. 148 (1): Gerald Cubitt; p. 148 (2): iStockphoto.com/mashurov; p. 148 (3): Amy & Chuck Wiley/Wales/ Getty Images; p. 148/149 (4): iStockphoto.com/hepatus; p. 148/149 (4): iStockphoto.com/Beboy_ltd; p. 151: A.T. Willet/Alamy; p. 154 (1): © Universal/Everett Collection/Rex Features; p. 154 (2): Dreamworks/Aardman Animation/The Kobal Collection; p. 155 (3): Chuck Franklin/Alamy; p. 155 (4): KeystoneUSA-Zuma/Rex Features; p. 157: Morgan Creek/J. Farmer/The Kobal Collection; p. 158: PA Photos/Topfoto; p. 159: Danny Martindale/WireImage/Getty Images; p. 161 (tl): Bournemouth News; p. 161 (br): Lefteris Pitarakis/AP/Press Association Images; p. 162 (l): AlamyCelebrity/Alamy; p. 162 (r): Nicholas Khayat/Rex Features; p. 163 (l): Dr. Wilfried Bahnmuller/ Imagebroker/Robert Harding; p. 163 (r): Dreamtours/Imagebroker/ FLPA.

We are unable to trace the copyright holder for the photograph that appears on page 142 (b) and would appreciate any help which would enable us to do so.

Illustrator acknowledgements:

Laetitia Aynie pp. 13, 79, 80; Dominic Bugatto p. 132; Karen Donnelly p. 45; Nick Duffy pp. 31, 42, 95, 100, 119, 133; Federico pp. 16, 24, 51; Pablo Gallego pp. 11, 39, 47; Gemma Hastilow p. 67; Kevin Hopgood p. 37; Katie Mac pp. 48, 105, 151; Louise Morgan p. 137; Julian Mosedale pp. 65, 74, 75, 107, 112, 122, 142, 150, 156; Roger Penwill p. 86; Jorge Santillan pp. 34, 163; Jamie Sneddon p. 61; David Tazzyman p. 89

We are unable to trace the copyright holder for the illustrations that appear on pages 77, 116 and117, we would appreciate any help which would enable us to do so.

Recordings produced by Ian Harker and recorded at The Soundhouse Studios.

Picture research by Kevin Brown

Corpus research by Julie Moore

Map of Objective First Student's Book

TOPIC	EXAM PRACTICE	GRAMMAR	VOCABULARY
Unit 1 **Fashion matters 10–13** Fashion; describing people	Paper 4 Speaking: 2 Paper 3 Listening: 3 Paper 1 Reading and Use of English: 4	Comparison: adjectives and adverbs Adverbs of degree	APPEARANCE AND CLOTHING Phrasal verbs
Exam folder 1 14–15	Paper 1 Reading and Use of English: 4 Key word transformations		
Unit 2 **The virtual world 16–19** Computer games; the internet	Paper 1 Reading and Use of English: 7	-ly adverbs Review of present tenses	COMPUTERS Collocations Word formation
Writing folder 1 20–21	Paper 2 Writing: 2 Informal letters		
Unit 3 **Going places 22–25** Travel	Paper 4 Speaking: 2 Paper 3 Listening: 2 Paper 1 Reading and Use of English: 1 and 4	Modals 1: Obligation, necessity and permission Prepositions of location	TRAVEL AND HOLIDAYS Topic set – travel and holidays Phrasal verbs Collocations
Exam folder 2 26–27	Paper 1 Reading and Use of English: 3 Word formation		
Unit 4 **Endangered 28–31** Animals	Paper 1 Reading and Use of English: 7 Paper 1 Reading and Use of English: 4	as and like Compound adjectives	ANIMALS Word formation Topic set – parts of animals Expressions with time
Writing folder 2 32–33	Paper 2 Writing: 1 Essays		
Unit 5 **Mixed emotions 34–37** Describing frightening and positive experiences	Paper 3 Listening: Skills for Listening Paper 1 Reading and Use of English: 2	Review of past tenses: past simple past continuous present perfect past perfect Irregular verbs	EMOTIONS Collocations – adverbs of degree
Exam folder 3 38–39	Paper 1 Reading and Use of English: 2 Open cloze		
Unit 6 **What if? 40–43** Winning prizes and celebrity culture	Paper 1 Reading and Use of English: 6 Paper 1 Reading and Use of English: 1 and 3 Paper 4 Speaking: 4	Conditionals with if Conditionals with unless Parts of speech	WINNING AND CELEBRITY Phrasal verbs with keep Word formation
Writing folder 3 44–45	Paper 2 Writing: 2 Reports		
Units 1–6 Revision 46–47			
Unit 7 **Life's too short 48–51** Sport	Paper 1 Reading and Use of English: 3 and 4 Paper 3 Listening: 3 Paper 4 Speaking: 3	Gerunds and infinitives 1	SPORT Collocations – sports Expressions with do Word formation
Exam folder 4 52–53	Paper 1 Reading and Use of English: 1 Multiple-choice cloze		
Unit 8 **Growing up 54–57** Childhood	Paper 4 Speaking: 2 and 4 Paper 1 Reading and Use of English: 5 Paper 1 Reading and Use of English: 3	used to and would	JOBS AND WORK Collocations Phrasal verbs with get Word formation
Writing folder 4 58–59	Paper 2 Writing: 1 Essays		

TOPIC	EXAM PRACTICE	GRAMMAR	VOCABULARY
Unit 9 **The hard sell 60–63** Advertising	Paper 1 Reading and Use of English: 2 Paper 3 Listening: 4	Modals 2: Speculation and deduction Order of adjectives	PRODUCTS AND PROMOTION Adjective–noun collocations Expressions for discussing ideas
Exam folder 5 64–65	Paper 3 Listening: 2 Sentence completion		
Unit 10 **The final frontier 66–69** Space	Paper 4 Speaking: 2 Paper 1 Reading and Use of English: 6	Review of future tenses	SPACE Word formation Phrases with *at*
Writing folder 5 70–71	Paper 2 Writing: 2 Articles		
Unit 11 **Like mother, like daughter 72–75** Family	Paper 4 Speaking: 1 Paper 3 Listening: 4	Past and present participles *be like* and *look like*	PERSONALITY Adjectives describing personality Phrasal verbs and expressions with *take* Collocations – adverb or adjective?
Exam folder 6 76–77	Paper 3 Listening: 1 Short extracts		
Unit 12 **A great idea 78–81** Technology and inventions	Paper 4 Speaking: 2 Paper 1 Reading and Use of English: 7 Paper 1 Reading and Use of English: 4	The passive	INVENTIONS Word formation Collocations with *come*, *tell* and *fall*
Writing folder 6 82–83	Paper 2 Writing: 2 Reviews		
Units 7–12 Revision 84–85			
Unit 13 **Education for life 86–89** Education	Paper 4 Speaking: 2 Paper 3 Listening: 3 Paper 1 Reading and Use of English: 4	Reporting	SCHOOL AND EDUCATION Word formation Collocations
Exam folder 7 90–91	Paper 3 Listening: 3 Multiple matching		
Unit 14 **Career moves 92–95** Working life	Paper 4 Speaking: 2 Paper 1 Reading and Use of English: 7	Perfect tenses *all / whole*	THE WORKPLACE Word formation – negative prefixes
Writing folder 7 96–97	Paper 2 Writing: 2 Letters of application		
Unit 15 **Too many people? 98–101** The environment	Paper 4 Speaking: 2 and 4 Paper 3 Listening: 2 Paper 1 Reading and Use of English: 2 and 3	Countable and uncountable nouns *some*, *any* and *no*	THE ENVIRONMENT Topic set – the natural world Word formation Expressions of quantity
Exam folder 8 102–103	Paper 3 Listening: 4 Multiple choice		
Unit 16 **Eat to live 104–107** Food	Paper 1 Reading and Use of English: 6 Paper 4 Speaking: 3	The article Possession Prepositions of time	FOOD Collocations – food
Writing folder 8 108–109	Paper 2 Writing: 1 Essays		
Unit 17 **Collectors and creators 110–113** Hobbies	Paper 4 Speaking: 2 Paper 3 Listening: 1 Paper 1 Reading and Use of English: 2	Relative clauses Relative pronouns *who*, *whom*, *whose*	HOBBIES Phrasal verbs and expressions with *look* Word formation

Content of the Cambridge English: First

The *Cambridge English: First* examination consists of four papers. The Reading and Use of English paper carries 40% of the marks, while the Writing, Listening and Speaking papers each carry 20% of the marks. It is not necessary to pass all four papers in order to pass the examination. If you achieve a grade A in the examination, you will be awarded a *Cambridge English: First* certificate at C1 level. If you achieve grade B or C, you will be awarded a *Cambridge English: First* certificate at B2 level. If your performance is below B2, but falls within Level B1, you will get a *Cambridge English* certificate stating that you demonstrated ability at B1 level.

As well as being told your grade, you will also be given a Statement of Results – a graphical profile of your performance, i.e. it will show whether you have done especially well or badly on some of the papers.

Paper 1 Reading and Use of English 1 hour 15 minutes

There are seven parts to this paper and they are always in the same order. The first four parts test your grammar and vocabulary. The last three parts each contain a text and a comprehension task. The texts used are from newspaper and magazine articles, fiction and reviews.

Part	Task type	Number of questions	Task format	Objective Exam folder
1	Multiple choice gap-fill, mainly testing vocabulary	8	You must choose which word from four answers completes each of the eight gaps in a text.	**4** (52–53)
2	Open gap-fill, testing mainly grammar	8	You must complete a text with eight gaps.	**3** (38–39)
3	Word formation	8	You need to use the right form of a given word to fill the gaps in a text containing eight gaps.	**2** (26–27)
4	Key word transformations testing grammar and vocabulary	6	You must complete a sentence with a given word, so that it means the same as the first sentence.	**1** (14–15)
5	Multiple choice	6	You must read a text and answer multiple-choice questions with four options: A, B, C or D.	Fiction **10** (128–129) Non-fiction **12** (152–153)
6	Gapped text	6	You must read a text with sentences removed. You need to use the missing sentences to complete the text.	**9** (114–115)
7	Multiple matching	10	You must answer the questions by finding the relevant information in the text or texts.	**11** (140–141)

Paper 2 Writing 1 hour 20 minutes

There are two parts to this paper. Part 1 is compulsory, you have to answer it. In Part 2 there are three questions and you must choose one. Each part carries equal marks and you are expected to write between 140–190 words for Part 1 and 140–190 for Part 2.

Part	Task type	Number of tasks	Task format	Objective Writing folder
1	Question 1 Writing an essay	1 compulsory	An essay presented through rubric and short notes.	**2** (32–33); **4** (58–59); **8** (108–109)
2	Questions 2–4 • an article • a letter or email • a report • a review	One task to be selected from a choice of three	You are given a choice of topics and you have to respond to one of them in the way specified.	Informal letters and emails **1** (20–21); **10** (134–5) Letters of application **7** (96–97); Articles **5** (70–71); **12** (158–159); Reviews **6** (82–83); **9** (120–121); Reports **3** (44–45); **11** (146–147)

Paper 3 Listening about 40 minutes

There are four parts to this paper. Each part is heard twice. The texts are a variety of types with either one speaker or more than one.

Part	Task type	Number of questions	Task format	Objective Exam folder
1	Multiple choice	8	You hear short, unrelated extracts, each about 30 seconds, with either one or two speakers. You must choose an answer from A, B or C.	**6** (76–77)
2	Sentence completion	10	You hear one speaker and this part lasts about three minutes. You must write a word or short phrase to complete the sentences.	**5** (64–65)
3	Multiple matching	5	You hear five unrelated extracts with a common theme. Each lasts about 30 seconds. You must choose the correct answer from a list of eight.	**7** (90–91)
4	Multiple choice	7	You hear an interview or a conversation of about three minutes. You must choose an answer from A, B or C.	**8** (102–103)

Paper 4 Speaking about 14 minutes

There are four parts to this paper. There are usually two of you taking the examination and two examiners. This paper tests your accuracy, vocabulary, pronunciation and your ability to communicate and complete the tasks.

Part	Task type	Time	Format	Objective Speaking folder
1	The interviewer asks each candidate some questions.	2 minutes	You are asked to give information about yourself.	Speaking folder (162–163)
2	Each candidate talks to the interviewer for about 1 minute.	4 minutes	You have to talk about two pictures and then comment on the other candidate's pictures.	Speaking folder (162–163)
3	Candidates have to discuss a task together.	4 minutes	You are given some material in the form of a discussion question and five prompts, presented as a mind map, to discuss with the other candidate.	Speaking folder (162–163)
4	Candidates offer opinions relating to the task they have just completed.	4 minutes	The interviewer will join in with your discussion.	Speaking folder (162–163)

New for this edition of Objective First

2015 examination

All of the material in this Student's Book and in the other components of the course has been fully updated to reflect the new specifications of the *Cambridge English: First*. The revised examination comprises four papers (see Content of the *Cambridge English: First* on pages 7–8 for details) and is now slightly shorter at around 3.5 hours.

B2 English Profile **English Vocabulary Profile**

Objective First has been informed by the *English Vocabulary Profile*, which guarantees suitable treatment of words, phrases and phrasal verbs at B2 level. The *English Vocabulary Profile* is an online resource with detailed and up-to-date information about the words, phrases, phrasal verbs and idioms that learners of English know at each of the six levels of the Common European Framework – A1 to C2. The authors have used this rich and reliable resource to select vocabulary that is relevant to the B2 level. The course deals systematically with areas of vocabulary development that are important for the *Cambridge English: First* examination: topic vocabulary, common words with several meanings, phrases and collocations, phrasal verbs and word families.

CD-ROM

On the CD-ROM there are 96 exercises, eight for each pair of units, giving extra practice in vocabulary, grammar, reading, listening and writing. There are also additional resources for students including downloadable wordlists with and without definitions.

Webpage

The dedicated webpage is: www.cambridge.org/elt/objectivefirstnew
On this page you will find a number of useful resources for both students and teachers:
- Photocopiable *Cambridge English: First* Practice Tests with audio
- Photocopiable unit-by-unit wordlists

Presentation Plus

Presentation Plus interactive whiteboard software allows teachers to present and interact directly with the Student's Book, Workbook and Class Audio at the front of the classroom. With Presentation Plus you can highlight, write and erase; hide and reveal text and images; zoom in and out; create notes and save annotations; attach your own web links; display answer keys; play all Class Audio and display the listening scripts; and connect to Cambridge Dictionaries Online via the internet. Presentation Plus can be used with all types of interactive whiteboards or with a computer and projector.

Speaking

1. How important is fashion to you? What sort of clothes do you prefer to wear? Do you ever have to wear things you don't really like? If so, when, and why? Talk with a partner.

2. Describe what people in the class are wearing today. Then list topic vocabulary in sets like these.

   Clothes: *suit, sweatshirt,* ....
   Footwear: *boots, sandals,* ....
   Jewellery: *bracelet, earrings,* ....
   Headgear: *hood, helmet,* ....
   Materials: *woollen, leather,* ....
   Appearance: *casual, smart,* ....

3. Work in pairs. Choose a pair of photos, for example 1a and 1b. Describe what each person is wearing and say something about their appearance.

4. In the same pairs, compare the two people in your photos. These examples may help you.

   The one on the left is younger than the one on the right.
   This girl's clothes are not as stylish as the other one's.
   This man seems to be less serious than the man in the suit.

5. As a class, summarise what you said about the people.

Listening

6. **1 02** You will hear some short recordings, where five of the people in the photos talk about what they like to wear. Say who is speaking in each case.

   Here is an example. Speaker 1 is the man in photo 3b. Look at his photo as you listen.

   In this transcript of what Speaker 1 says, some words and phrases are highlighted. This is to show that parts of an exam recording may make you think that other answers are possible. This is why you must listen carefully and check when you listen a second time.

   I'm not a suit man. *Even for work, I can get away with casual stuff, though I still **like my clothes to look smart**. I love shopping – my favourite place is Paul Smith in Covent Garden. I bought a really nice woollen shirt there recently. Clothes are important to me, but they need to be comfortable as well as **stylish**.*

   1 03 Now listen to the other four speakers and match the correct photo to each speaker. Compare answers with someone else when you have finished.

   Speaker 2 ☐
   Speaker 3 ☐
   Speaker 4 ☐
   Speaker 5 ☐

Vocabulary

Phrasal verbs

Phrasal verbs are used in spoken and written English, especially in informal situations. You already know some basic phrasal verbs: for example, you *wake up* in the morning and *put on* your clothes. These phrasal verbs are at A1 and A2 level. However, the ones you will need to learn at B2 will be harder than these because their meaning will be less obvious. *Objective First* will give you regular help in learning phrasal verbs. In your vocabulary notebook you can organise them

- by topic, e.g. phrasal verbs for *Fashion and clothes*
- by main verb, e.g. phrasal verbs with *go*
- by particle (adverb or preposition), e.g. phrasal verbs with *out*

In the recordings there are several examples of phrasal verbs. For example, Speaker 1 says:
*Even for work, I can **get away with** casual stuff.*
Be careful with word order: three-part phrasal verbs like the example are never separated. Two-part phrasal verbs containing an adverb have a flexible word order when used with a noun object, but if the object is a pronoun, it always comes between the verb and the adverb.
EXAMPLE: *I tried on the red jacket. / I tried the red jacket on. I tried it on.*

7 Listen to Speakers 2–5 again and tick the phrasal verbs you hear. Then match them to definitions a–i.

add to	go out	save up
cut down	keep up with	slip on
dress up	pull on	stand out
fit in with	put together	take back

a be easy to see or notice
b create something by joining or combining different things
c return something
d wear smarter clothes than usual
e keep money for something in the future
f reduce
g put something on quickly
h go somewhere for entertainment
i understand something that is changing fast

Corpus spot

Many phrasal verbs contain irregular verbs. Be careful with past tense forms – the *Cambridge Learner Corpus* shows that exam candidates often make mistakes with these.

I **took off** my coat and sat down.

NOT I ~~taked~~ off my coat and sat down.

Phrasal verbs with *go*

8 Complete the sentences with a phrasal verb with *go*. Use the correct form of *go* and an adverb or preposition from the box.

go + | ahead   back   for   in   on   over   up

EXAMPLE: *That new shop has some great swimwear. I __went in__ there yesterday for the first time.*

a The prices of leather bags have .... a lot recently.
b Why are you looking at me like that? What's .... ?
c The design company .... the applicant with the best portfolio.
d I .... to the same shoe shop but there were no more pairs in my size.
e You'll need to .... all the figures in the report to check they're correct.
f Can I wear your necklace tonight? – Sure, ... !

9 Now complete this letter with some of the phrasal verbs from 7. More than one answer may be possible.

Dear Jayne

Last night, Maria, Sally and I **(1)** .... clubbing. I was late back from work, so I just **(2)** .... some black jeans and a sparkly T-shirt, but the other two really **(3)** .... ! Maria chose a stunning purple dress and sprayed her hair pink. Sally **(4)** .... the most outrageous outfit – red leather shorts, a bright green top and knee-length boots with stars on. When we got there, they both **(5)** .... on the dance floor and I looked very ordinary in comparison.

Honestly, I can't **(6)** .... them – they're so fashion-conscious. What would you do in my position?

10 What advice would you give the writer? Discuss in pairs.

Comparison

1 Read this short text about the fashion industry. Do you agree with its viewpoint?

> Why is it that fashion houses design their clothes for the youngest and skinniest men and women? We may not actually want to look like supermodels, but it is a fact that the most underweight models have dominated the world's catwalks for a very long time. It seems it is not in the interests of the fashion industry to represent an 'average' person. Although 'slimmer' may not always mean 'more desirable' in the real world, fashion succeeds because it carries with it that image of the least achievable figure.

2 These comparison structures are used with adjectives.

-er than	more … than	the most …
the -est	less … than	the least …

a Why do we say *younger than* but **less** *serious than*; and *the youngest* but *the **most** underweight*?

b Which common adjectives can we either add *-er/-est* to or use *more/most* with?

c What are the spelling rules for forming the comparative and superlative of words like *slim* and *skinny*?

Check the Grammar folder when you see this:

G → page 166

Corpus spot

Correct the mistakes that exam candidates have made with comparatives in these sentences.
a What are the better clothes to wear at the camp?
b He is famouser than all the others in the film.
c You look more tired and thiner.
d I would like to buy a much more better one.
e It's now more easy to get there.
f This is even worser than before.

3 Give the comparative and superlative forms of these adjectives.

bright	brighter	the brightest
big		
thin		
dirty		
casual	more/less casual	
outrageous	more/less outrageous	
good		the best
bad	worse	

4 Now complete the following sentences by using one of the adjectives in 3, choosing either the comparative or the superlative form.

a Have you painted this room recently? Everything's looking a lot .... than before.

b Out of all my friends, Jake wears .... clothes – take his handmade plastic coat, for example!

c Don't dress up for the club tonight – everyone's looking .... there nowadays.

d You can't put those disgusting jeans on again – they're .... pair I've ever seen!

e I'm a bit worried about Sally. She doesn't eat a thing and so she's getting .... than ever.

f My brother has .... taste in ties ever – awful designs in really odd colours!

g There's no way you can fit into my shoes – your feet are a lot .... than mine!

h Market stalls often offer slightly .... value for money than shops.

Grammar extra

Note the use of *a lot* and *slightly* in sentences *g* and *h*. These are adverbs of degree, which are commonly used with comparative adjectives. Some adverbs of degree are also used with superlative adjectives, as in this example:

*Chrissie is **by far** the most creative student on our design course.*

Put these adverbs of degree into the following sentences. Which one can be used with both comparative and superlative adjectives?

a bit   a great deal   much

a This ring is only .... more expensive and it's .... nicer than the others.

b Tracksuits may be .... warmer, but shorts are .... the best for running in, whatever the weather.

G → page 166

5 *not as … as / not so … as*

You used this structure to compare the people in the photos in the last lesson. Now compare these different types of footwear in the same way, choosing suitable adjectives from the ones below to describe them.

comfortable   elegant   practical   outrageous

EXAMPLE: *The high-heeled shoes don't look as comfortable as the flip flops.*

G → page 166

6 Identify the comparative adverbs in this short newspaper article and then explain how they are formed.

FASHION *KNOCK-OFFS*

Counterfeit consumer goods – more commonly known as 'knock-offs' – are imitation goods that are offered for sale at much lower prices than the genuine products, and they are a big problem for the fashion industry. Knock-offs are now far more readily available than they were a few years ago, both on the web and on market stalls worldwide. These fake designer goods damage the actual brands in more ways than one, reducing their sales and causing them to be regarded less exclusively, no longer the luxury items they once were. Some people view the matter less seriously, arguing that knock-offs offer a type of free advertising and promotion to the real designer labels. However, there is no getting away from the fact that this is an illegal activity, and the fashion industry is starting to fight back with high-tech solutions that will distinguish the real goods from cheap copies.

7 What do you feel about counterfeit goods? Would you buy them? Why? / Why not?

8 Practise comparison structures by completing the second sentences so that they have a similar meaning to the first. Use the word given.

0 Mary is shorter than her brother.
NOT
Mary is ..... *NOT AS TALL AS* ..... her brother.

1 These sunglasses cost a bit less than my last pair.
WERE
These sunglasses .... than my last pair.

2 Coco Chanel was an extremely talented designer.
MOST
Coco Chanel was one of .... in the world.

3 I preferred you with curlier hair.
STRAIGHT
I preferred your hair when it wasn't .... is now.

4 This shoe shop is the cheapest one I've found.
EXPENSIVE
This shoe shop is .... all the ones I've found.

5 Suzanne's host at the dinner party wasn't as elegantly dressed as she was.
MORE
At the dinner party, Suzanne was far .... her host.

6 It takes much less time to travel by train than by car.
LOT
Travelling by train .... travelling by car.

7 Harry wears smarter clothes now he has a girlfriend.
LESS
Harry dressed .... he didn't have a girlfriend.

8 That model is only 17 – I thought she was older.
AS
That model is not .... I thought.

Exam folder 1

Paper 1 Part 4 Key word transformations

In this part of the Reading and Use of English paper you are tested on both grammar and vocabulary. There are six questions and an example at the beginning.
You can get up to two marks for each question.

1   Read the Part 4 exam instructions below and then look at the example (0).

Complete the second sentence so that it has a similar meaning to the first sentence, using the word given. **Do not change the word given**. You must use between **two** and **five** words, including the word given. Here is an example (0).

0 Have you got a belt that is cheaper than this one? ← *first sentence*
   LESS ← *key word – this never changes*
   Have you got .... than this one?
   The second sentence must mean the same as the first when it is complete.

The gap can be filled by the words 'a less expensive belt', so you write:

Example: | **0** | *A LESS EXPENSIVE BELT* |

1 mark + 1 mark

Write **only** the missing words **IN CAPITAL LETTERS on the separate answer sheet**.

2   Think about what is important in this exam task. What advice would you give another student about answering Part 4 in the exam?

3   Now read the advice given in the bullet points.

EXAM ADVICE

- Read the first sentence carefully.
- Think about how the key word given is commonly used.
- Complete the gap with a possible answer. You can use the question paper for rough answers.
- Count the number of words you have used in the gap. You must use not fewer than two and not more than five, including the word in bold. Note that a contracted form such as 'don't' counts as two words.
- Read the completed second sentence to check it means the same as the first.
- Ask yourself whether the words in the gap fit the sentence grammatically.
- Transfer your answer (just the words in the gap) to the answer sheet.

4 Complete these key word transformations, using the instructions in 1.

1 'A club has just opened in Leeds,' said Maria to Sally.
TOLD
Maria .... club in Leeds.

2 I returned the dress to the shop because it was badly made.
TOOK
Because the dress was badly made, I .... to the shop.

3 Some shops try really hard to help you.
EFFORT
Some shops really .... to help you.

4 Fifty years ago, cars were slower than they are nowadays.
AS
Fifty years ago, cars .... they are nowadays.

5 It's a lot easier to learn a language by visiting the country where it's spoken.
MUCH
You can learn a language .... you visit the country where it's spoken.

6 For me, Stella McCartney is doing a lot more interesting work than other designers today.
FAR
For me, Stella McCartney is by .... designer working today.

2.1 The virtual world

Speaking

1 How far do you agree with the following statement? Discuss your ideas.

Computer games are anti-social and violent, and their users are mindless nerds.

> **nerd** /nɜːd/ *noun* [C] *informal* someone, especially a man, who is not fashionable and who is interested in boring things • **nerdy** *adjective informal* boring and not fashionable

2 What are the good things about playing games online? Are there any disadvantages?

3 In pairs, decide on the five most important features of any computer game, choosing from a–h below. What else do you look for in a virtual game?

  a fast pace
  b easy to get into
  c lots of action
  d puzzles to solve
  e single- and multi-player modes
  f suitable for all ages
  g great background music
  h sophisticated graphics

Exam spot

For Paper 1 Part 7 you need to match the questions to the texts in an efficient way. By **skimming** the text (reading it very quickly, not trying to understand every word but just trying to get a general idea of what it is about) and **scanning** it (running your eyes over it very quickly, just looking for particular words or information) you can find the answers more quickly. These are essential skills to learn.

Reading

4 Scan the four online reviews of computer games to answer a–d quickly.

Which game

  a is the cheapest?
  b gets the best review?
  c seems the least suitable for adults?
  d has the most impressive soundtrack?

Where did you find this information? How much text did you need to read?

1

The great thing about this game is that to get anywhere, you need to adopt its unique way of thinking – forget all normal rules. Reality is meaningless here, in a world where up can mean down, left becomes right, and everything feels remarkably weird. The puzzles can't be solved unless you are willing to spend sufficient thinking time – and you need to keep an open mind! Part of the game's charm lies in the almost complete absence of instructions, yet this can also be a drawback, leading to huge frustration. There are no set paths to wander down and you are very much guided by your own curiosity and imagination. And while you're gathering your thoughts, you can enjoy the background music, which is truly original and builds well in scary moments. Patience is definitely required for this game, but there's great satisfaction for those who rise to the challenge.

THE VERDICT

● *Expect the unexpected – and make full use of your brainpower!*
**** £39.99

2

This game's all about finding power for your ray gun, which you get by capturing tiny cartoon figures. The ray's pretty weak when you start – it needs electricity after all – so you only move small objects. This gives you enough power to turn on household appliances like fridges or vacuum cleaners, and locate the electrically charged critters hiding in them. You feel pretty hopeless to begin with, but ten minutes and several hundred hits later, you reach the point of feeling more like a superhero as the adventure develops. You overturn sofas, beds and other huge items, leaving rooms in a very messy state. And that's nothing! In higher levels, you walk the streets, so powerful that you can lift cars, trucks and eventually entire buildings. It's a shame that the gun resets to weak with each new level, but there are some impressive gameplay touches that stop you mindlessly breaking stuff – your grandma would approve!

THE VERDICT

● *A great sense of progression as you go from weak to strong – never thought electricity could be so much fun!* ****** £28.75**

5 In groups of four, choose one review each and skim the text to find out what sort of game it is. Then scan your review to find one good and one bad point, looking out for phrases similar to the ones below. Compare your findings with other groups.

Good points
The great thing about

Bad points
It's a shame that

3

Did you know that car games have a poor relation? Yes, it's their motorbike cousins! Somehow motorbike games never provide the same thrill as car games, but this version comes very close and is easily the best available. There are eight different bikes, nine long tracks and a choice of race styles: Grand Prix or the muddy scrambling type, which gets quite tricky. The intelligence and speed of your 23 computer opponents are high, and guarantee a game demanding enough for the most advanced racer. So get on your bikes and take control!

THE VERDICT

● *A super-slick bike racer that truly does not disappoint.* ***** *£27.50*

4

This game is not demanding, perhaps because it's primarily aimed at kids under ten, though with only six levels and no multi-player mode, it's likely to be a bit disappointing even for the youngest of players. The little guy jogs along endlessly at a slow rate, which gets extremely boring at times. Jumping works OK, with a nice double-jump facility for things that are out of reach. Graphically, the game looks good with its bright and colourful cartoony feel, and occasionally there's some really nice background animation too. It's just too bad there isn't more content – games of this type are becoming more and more complex, but not this one! Even kids will get through most of it in an afternoon, as the puzzles and tasks are far too simple.

THE VERDICT

● *Simplistic gameplay suitable for a very young audience* ** *£17.99*

Vocabulary
Collocations

Vocabulary development beyond topic sets is essential for B2 level. Word formation, phrases, phrasal verbs and collocations are all important areas.

Learn which words commonly go together – nouns after a certain verb, adverbs with adjectives, etc. Some words have a close association, for example *bitterly disappointed*. Strong collocations like these are tested in the exam.

6 Read reviews 1–3 and find the nouns that go with verbs a–d. Then choose two more collocates for each verb from the box.

a solve .... (review 1)
b spend .... (review 1)
c reach .... (review 2)
d take .... (review 3)

| advantage | conclusion | crime | fortune |
| goal | interest | money | problem |

G rammar extra

-ly adverbs

All the adverbs below were used in the reviews of computer games. Write down their related adjectives and then say what the spelling rules are for forming these adverbs.

easily endlessly graphically remarkably truly

Some adverbs do not end in *-ly*. The most common of these are *fast*, *hard*, *late* and *well*. Note also the adverbs *hardly* and *lately*, which have different meanings.

Explain the meaning of the adverbs used below.
a She hardly thought about work while she was on holiday.
b He thought hard before answering.
c There have been a lot of good films lately.
d We arrived late for the film, which had already started.

 G → page 166

Corpus spot

Correct any spelling mistakes that exam candidates have made with adverbs in these sentences.
a Unfortunatelly, I'm quite busy at the moment.
b If I were you, I would definitly spend my evenings reading by the fireside.
c You just have to say your name and the computer opens the door automaticly.
d Entering the restaurant, you immediatly feel comfortable.
e We realy started to work hard the morning before the show.
f You must adjust the laser extremily carefully to get it in the correct position.
g I would like more information, especialy about accommodation.
h The computer completly takes hold of our lives.

Review of present tenses

1 **Identify the underlined tenses in examples a–d. Then complete the grammar explanation below.**

a The little guy <u>jogs along</u> endlessly at a slow rate.

b While <u>you're gathering</u> your thoughts, you can enjoy the background music.

c It's a shame that the gun <u>resets</u> to weak with each new level.

d Games of this type <u>are becoming</u> more and more complex.

> The present .... tense is used for permanent situations (example ....) or to talk about actions which are habitual or repeated (example ....). On the other hand, the present .... tense is used for temporary situations (example ....), or for situations that are changing or developing (example ....).

2 **Explain the other uses of each tense that are illustrated in these examples.**

a <u>We're buying</u> a new computer next weekend.

b If <u>you finish</u> all the levels within an hour, <u>you get</u> extra points.

c Don't talk to me while <u>I'm playing</u>!

d Once <u>you decide</u> where to go, let me know.

e All the planets in our solar system <u>orbit</u> the sun.

G → page 167

3 **Correct any mistakes with tenses in these sentences. Some sentences are correct.**

a Electronic books are becoming more and more popular.

b This week only, the shop sells all software at 20% off.

c Don't shut down the computer as I'm downloading a film.

d As soon as you are playing this game, you realise the graphics are tremendous – everything is so realistic.

e My neighbour gives me access to his wifi this week but I'm planning to install my own on Monday.

f When you visit the website, you are getting a choice of free downloadable applications.

g Once I find a useful site, I'm bookmarking it for future reference.

4 **Choose the correct present tense for each of these sentences, using the verbs in brackets.**

a My new game is sensational – as soon as you .... a level, you .... something completely different to do. (finish, get)

b Generally, online customer support .... , though some computer manuals are still not accessible enough for users. (improve)

c The developers .... a number of bugs in their latest app. (deal with)

d In the latest version, a dragon .... overhead and .... when you .... it. (fly, explode, hit)

e The company .... an interface to allow users to personalise their documents. (develop)

f Back-up copies .... time to prepare, but they are essential. (take)

g Whenever you .... , the system .... you to enter your password and then it .... a random security question. (log on, require, generate)

h If a computer .... , you .... the file you .... on unless you .... it regularly. (crash, lose, work, save)

5 **Skim the extract from an article about 'googlewhacking' on the opposite page. Then fill each gap with a suitable present tense of one of the verbs in the box. Use each verb once only. There is one extra verb you do not need.**

> add become believe change create
> encourage find out google mean
> ~~refer~~ sound spend submit update

Compare your answers with another student.

In which gaps can both the present simple and the present continuous be used? Is there any change in meaning?

Which of the verbs that you used do not have a present continuous form? Verbs not normally used in the continuous tenses are called 'stative' verbs. Do you know any more verbs like this?

G → page 167

An experienced web user, Gary Stock, came up with the term 'googlewhack', which **(0)** _REFERS_ to a single entry on a Google search page. It **(1)** .... increasingly difficult for googlewhackers like Gary to achieve their aim: the appearance of the message "Results 1-1 of 1" on their computer screen. For one thing, people **(2)** .... new web pages and **(3)** .... existing ones all the time, which in turn **(4)** .... more and more entries on Google. Also, anyone who **(5)** .... their googlewhack to a website **(6)** .... another entry just by doing that.

Perhaps all of this **(7)** .... like a waste of time, but Gary Stock **(8)** .... that googlewhacking is a meaningful activity that **(9)** .... people to surf the web again, just like during the early days of the Internet. According to many, Google **(10)** .... our lives by broadening our knowledge of the world. People certainly **(11)** .... about new or unusual things by googlewhacking – from 'bartok nosepieces' to 'jillionaire incinerate'! But if you **(12)** .... these phrases on your computer today, will they still be googlewhacks?

Vocabulary

Word formation

Recognise words that are formed from a common base word and record them together to help you remember them. For example, at B2 you should know the noun *truth*, the adjective *true* and the adverb *truly*. Word formation using prefixes and suffixes is tested in the exam. You will also need to know some words with negative prefixes, as in this word family: *happiness, unhappiness; happy, unhappy; happily, unhappily*.

Many nouns have a related adjective formed with the suffix *-y*, as shown at the end of the dictionary example for *nerd* on page 16.

6 Make adjectives in this way from the nouns below. The first three are used in the reviews. What are the spelling rules in c and d?

a trick   **b** mess   **c** mud   **d** ice

7 Many of these adjectives came up on pages 16–17. Divide them into two meaning groups, positive and negative. Which adjectives contain a prefix or a suffix? Which one contains both?

accessible	colourful	dull
excellent	favourable	hopeless
impressive	mindless	sophisticated
tricky	unhelpful	

Three of these adjectives are tested in 8, and some may also be useful in the writing task on pages 20–21.

8 Use the word given in capitals to form a word that fits in the numbered gap. Look at the words on either side of the gap to decide whether an adjective, adverb or noun is needed.

Tablet computers are growing in **(0)** _POPULARITY_ . They generally weigh far less than laptops and are much more **(1)** .... for people on the move. Many **(2)** .... that are developed for tablets incorporate a pen-friendly user interface and/or the **(3)** .... to handwrite directly into a document. They are very **(4)** .... when it comes to viewing photo slideshows or movies, though reading books **(5)** .... on a tablet can be **(6)** .... , depending on the screen display.

0 POPULAR
1 ACCESS
2 APPLY
3 ABLE
4 IMPRESS
5 ELECTRONIC
6 TRICK

Writing folder 1

Paper 2 Part 2 Informal letters

1   Look at the extracts below. Which two would you describe as informal? How did you decide?

A This is to inform you of the decisions taken at last week's meeting. Please note that all members of this department are strictly required to be present at such meetings and action may be taken in future to ensure this.

B I want to let you all know about our staff get-together last week. It's a pity more of you weren't there as it was a terrific occasion. Why not come along next time? There's free coffee and biscuits!

C Anyway, let me tell you about the party Jack is having on Saturday. Well, just about everyone is coming – even that weird guy Sam from college! Jack says he wants us all to be there, so you'd better not miss it. Why not come down for a few days? You can stay at my place if you want.

Decide for each extract who could have written it, who it was probably written to and why.

Assessment focus

Think about the target reader and the purpose of the letter. This will help you decide on a suitable style. Style is assessed as part of **communicative achievement**, which carries up to five marks.

2   Underline the informal language in this exam task.

> You have received a letter from your English friend Alex. Read Alex's letter and then write your letter to Alex.

> Hi! Guess what? My parents have given me some money for passing my exam, so I can splash out on something really cool. I can't choose between buying a new computer game or saving up a bit more and getting some clothes. Which do you think would be better?
> And can you suggest what exactly I should get?
> Thanks, Alex

Write your **letter**. (140–190 words)

3   The sample answer below would get a low mark, for several reasons. What are they?

> Dear Alex
>
> What brilliant news in your letter! I wish to offer you congratulations about the exam. Moreover, how nice to have some spare cash.
>
> You say you can't decide if to buy a computer game or some clothes. Don't you think that if you choose some new clothes you must save up a bit more money first? Clothes are not as cheap than computer games and I know you like expensive designer outfits. If you choose computer game, which one? There are so many available and to my mind they are all the same. In my opinion you should spend the money in something else. Why don't you get yourself a new dictionary, for example? Then it would be easier for you to study, wouldn't it?
>
> I hope you will consider my suggestion seriously and I look forward to receiving a reply from you in due course.
>
> Yours sincerely

Correct the errors in paragraph 2 and rewrite paragraphs 1 and 3 in an appropriate style.

4   Work in pairs. Plan how will you answer the task using the advice below and on the next page. Then write your answer.

Content ideas

Decide whether you think your friend should buy a game or clothes and note down some reasons to support your view. Then think about one specific game or item of clothing. What is special about it? Compare your ideas.

Game: topic, best points, price
Clothes: material, colour, style

Language input

You need to include these functions:

Congratulations   Opinion   Advice/Suggestion

Organisation

Clear paragraphing is important. In the sample answer, paragraph 2 is too long and the ideas in it are muddled. Make a plan before you start writing.

- Use this plan for your letter.
  - Opening formula
  - Paragraph 1 Initial greetings and congratulations
  - Paragraph 2 Opinion about which item the friend should buy
  - Paragraph 3 Description of one specific item
  - Paragraph 4 Final remarks
  - Closing formula
- Choose appropriate linkers from the list in 5 opposite to improve the flow of ideas in each paragraph.

Style

Writing in a consistent style will help to keep the reader's attention. Here are some typical informal features. There is at least one example of each in the sample.

Contracted forms, for example *I'm, don't*
Phrasal verbs
Phrases with *get, take, have*, etc., for example *take a look*
Simple linking words, for example *Then*
Direct questions, for example *What about …?*
Some exclamation marks (not too many!)

Editing your work

You must read through what you have written and correct any mistakes. Ask yourself questions a–d.

- **a** Is the grammar accurate?
- **b** Is the spelling correct?
- **c** Is there enough punctuation?
- **d** Is the style consistent?

The first letters of the five headings above spell out the word C-L-O-S-E. It is important to think about these five elements (Content, Language, Organisation, Style, Editing) for all Paper 2 tasks. And the word 'Close' will also remind you to finish a piece of writing, for example by signing off a letter.

Formal or informal?

5   Write Inf next to the expressions that are informal.

Initial greetings
It was great to hear from you. Inf
I am writing with reference to your letter.
Thanks for writing to me.

Congratulations
Well done!
I would like to offer congratulations on
Let me congratulate you on

Opinion
In my opinion
To my mind
I hold the view that
Personally, I have no doubt that
My own thoughts are

Advice/Suggestion
Why not try
What about trying
It is recommended that you
You could
I urge you to
I suggest that
If I were you

Linkers
Moreover
Also
Then again
Furthermore
Better still
As well as that
What's more
Additionally

Endings
Do drop me a line if you have time.
I look forward to hearing from you without delay.
Hope to hear from you soon.
Keep in touch.
I hope to hear from you at your earliest convenience.

Opening and closing an email or a letter
Match these opening and closing formulae and say when you should use each of them.
Hi Brad   *Yours faithfully*
Dear Jayne   *Cheers*
Dear Sir   *Yours sincerely*
Dear Ms Jones   *Love*

Going places

Speaking

Exam spot

In Paper 4 Part 2, each candidate is given a pair of photos to talk about on their own. The task will involve comparing the two photos, rather than just describing each one.

1 Work in pairs. Student A look at photos 1 and 2, and Student B at photos 3 and 4.

Student A Who would enjoy these types of holiday?

Student B What are the advantages and disadvantages of these types of holiday?

Now talk about the following questions in pairs.

a Which of the holidays in the photos would you choose? Why?

b If you had a lot of time and money, where in the world would you most like to go on holiday? Why?

Exam spot

In Paper 3 Part 2, you will be asked to complete some sentences. You will need to write a word or short phrase and you will hear the recording twice. The words you write down are in the order you hear them. There is no need to make any changes to these words.

Listening

2 🔘 1 04 You will hear a man called Steve Jackson talking about his trip to Antarctica. Read questions 1–10 and, in pairs, try to predict what word or words you might need to fill each gap. Then listen to the talk and complete the sentences with a word or short phrase.

Trip to Antarctica

Steve says that the temperature was usually around (1) .... degrees during the trip.

Steve found (2) .... to be the most useful thing he took with him.

In his cabin, Steve had a (3) .... under his bed.

Steve says the nationality of the expedition leader was (4) ....

While Steve was on the cruise, the seas were (5) ....

Steve enjoyed seeing the wide range of (6) .... most of all.

According to Steve, the only people, besides tourists, in the region were working at a (7) ....

Steve says that empty (8) .... are the only evidence of fishing in earlier times.

Cruise ships are forbidden to get rid of (9) .... in the Antarctic.

Steve says it's important that the (10) .... isn't disturbed by tourists.

3 Do you approve of tourists being allowed to go to unspoilt areas of the world? Would you go to Antarctica if you had the opportunity?

Vocabulary

Topic set – travel and holidays

4 If you write down new words in categories, it will help you remember them. With a partner, put the words in the box into the following categories:

Transport   Seaside   Accommodation
Movement   People

> airline   backpacker   bed and breakfast
> campsite   caravan   cliff   coach   coast
> crew   ferry   flight   harbour   holiday-makers
> hostel   journey   landing   shore   travel agent
> voyage   yacht

What other words could go in each category?

Phrasal verbs

5 The phrasal verbs *in italics* are to do with travel. Match each phrasal verb in sentences a–h with one of the meanings 1–8 below.

a When we got to the hotel we went to the reception to *check in*.

b Paolo decided he really needed to *get away* to somewhere hot where he could rest and relax.

c The plane is supposed to *get in* at about 10.00.

d Dr Lee *set off* from his house around 6.00 this morning in order to catch his flight.

e When we fly to Japan we usually *stop over* in Delhi.

f When the family went to the travel agency, the travel agent *booked* them *into* a hotel on the coast for two weeks.

g All hotel guests must *check out* by midday.

h Please go to Gate 14 as the plane to Lisbon is due to *take off* in about 30 minutes.

1 to arrive at a destination
2 to leave the ground
3 to pay and leave accommodation
4 to stay somewhere for a short time when you are going somewhere else
5 to arrange for someone to stay in (a hotel)
6 to go on holiday
7 to register at your accommodation
8 to begin a journey

Now, in pairs, talk about your last holiday using vocabulary from the exercises above.

EXAMPLE:
A: Where did you travel to?
B: I went to Australia. I caught a plane and had to set off very early in the morning.

Collocations

6 Link the verbs in box A with suitable nouns in box B. There is sometimes more than one answer. Do the same words go together in your language?

A

> take   book   catch   board   get   go

B

> skiing   trip   sightseeing   ship
> plane   tan   hotel   flight

7 The task below is similar to, but simpler than, the one you will have in the Reading and Use of English paper. Decide which answer, A or B, best fits each gap.

The history of airports

The earliest aircraft takeoff and landing (**1**) .... were in fields or on dirt tracks. When it came to landing, a plane could (**2**) .... at any angle, depending on wind direction. However, fields and tracks only functioned well in dry conditions. In order to (**3**) .... year-round landings, concrete surfaces would be necessary.

The word 'airport' (**4**) .... in a *New York Times* article in 1902, where it was (**5**) .... that New York was expected to be the main world 'airport' within twenty years. However, there was competition for this title as a number of other airports such as Bremen Airport in Germany and Rome Ciampino in Italy began to open in the 1920s.

Today, the world's busiest airport is Hartsfield-Jackson Atlanta International, which is (**6**) .... in the United States. The airport has 151 (**7**) .... and 28 international gates, and two terminals where passengers (**8**) .... for their flights.

	A	B
1	sites	spots
2	reach	approach
3	let	allow
4	arrived	appeared
5	stated	told
6	set	located
7	home	domestic
8	check in	take off

3.2

Modals 1: Obligation, necessity and permission

1 Look at the extracts (a–g) from the recording in 3.1 and then match them with phrases 1–6.

  a you should take warm clothes
  b you really need a windproof coat
  c you don't have to socialise if you don't want to
  d cruise ships are not allowed to go where they like
  e they have to take scientists to lead the excursions
  f only small parties are permitted to land
  g you've got to keep quiet

  1 There's no choice.
  2 It's necessary.
  3 It's forbidden.
  4 It's allowed.
  5 It's not necessary.
  6 It's a good idea.

2 In small groups, talk about the following sentences. Decide why some sentences use *must* and others use *have to*.

  a I must remember to buy a newspaper on my way home.
  b The doctor says I have to try to take more exercise.
  c All cars must be left in the car park, not on the road.

G → page 167

3 Imagine you are extremely rich. In pairs, discuss your holidays in the places shown, using *must*, *have to* and *don't have to*. Talk about transportation, accommodation, food, activities, entertainment and people.

> When I go to Los Angeles, I tell my secretary that I must stay at the Beverley Wiltshire hotel. My suite must have a private swimming pool and jacuzzi. Luckily I don't have to queue at the airport as I have a private jet, and a limousine to meet me. Even though I'm very rich, I still have to take a passport like everyone else.

Corpus spot

Be careful with modal verbs – the *Cambridge Learner Corpus* shows exam candidates often make mistakes with these.

I **must fill in** an application form for a visa.

NOT I ~~must to fill in~~ an application form for a visa.

I **don't have to show** my passport at the border any more.

NOT I ~~haven't to show~~ my passport at the border any more.

Correct the mistakes that candidates have made with obligation and necessity.

  a You needn't much space to park your car.
  b Another thing, should I to take my camera with me?
  c You needn't smoke in this part of the restaurant; it's a no smoking area.
  d It is better when you go by car because you must not get up early.
  e We have get to the exhibition early or we won't get a ticket.
  f You don't have to swim off the rocks because it's dangerous.
  g My doctor says I need give up smoking.
  h Lisa must to buy a ticket before getting on the bus.
  i I don't have to be late or I'll miss my plane.

4   With a partner, talk about the following situations.

EXAMPLE: *I'm going to travel abroad.*
  – I need a new passport.
  – I have to have an injection.
  – I must pack my bag.
  – I should buy a new pair of sunglasses but I don't think I have time.

a   It's the weekend tomorrow.
b   My brother is 18 next week.
c   My friend is getting married soon.
d   I started a new job last week.
e   I've got toothache.
f   I'm having a party on Saturday.

5   You can use *permit, allow, let* and *can* to express permission. Notice that both *permit* and *allow* are followed by *to*, and *let* and *can* aren't.

What did your parents let you do when you were younger? What are you allowed to do when you are 18 in your country?

Using *permit, allow, let* or *can* once only, complete these sentences. You may need to add other words.

a   I wasn't .... to go on holiday with my friends until I was sixteen.
b   You .... stay at this campsite without booking in advance.
c   Peter .... me borrow his large suitcase when I went shopping in New York.
d   They .... us to board the plane early because we only had hand luggage.

G → page 167

G rammar extra

Prepositions of location

Complete the following sentences with these prepositions of location.

| across   at   in   into   off   on |

a   The hotel had a swimming pool .... its roof.
b   I arrived .... the airport very early in the morning.
c   When I walked .... the hotel I was amazed by the decoration.
d   I arrived .... Spain last Tuesday.
e   We showed our passports as we went .... the frontier.
f   I found a bank .... the town centre.
g   We sat .... the terrace drinking coffee.
h   There was a notice .... the wall telling us about trips.
i   I jumped .... the pool to cool off.
j   Singapore is an island .... the coast of Malaysia.

Exam spot

In Paper 1 Part 4 remember that a contraction – *don't, isn't* – counts as two words. There are only six sentences in the exam. There are two extra here to give you more practice.

6   Complete the second sentence so that it has a similar meaning to the first sentence, using the word given. Do not change the word given. You must use between two and five words, including the word given.

1   The travel agent said, 'All passengers for Marseilles must change trains in Paris.'
    TO
    The travel agent said that all passengers for Marseilles .... trains in Paris.

2   Smoking in the hotel restaurant is not allowed.
    FORBIDDEN
    It .... in the hotel restaurant.

3   I wasn't allowed to go on holiday in June last year.
    LET
    My boss .... on holiday in June last year.

4   This is a 'no swimming' area.
    PERMITTED
    You .... in this area.

5   It's a good idea to have health insurance when you go on holiday.
    GET
    You .... before you go on holiday.

6   It is not necessary for men to wear a jacket and tie to enter the restaurant.
    HAVE
    Men .... a jacket and tie to enter the restaurant.

7   It's not necessary to wear heavy clothing in the summer months.
    NEED
    You .... on heavy clothing in the summer months.

8   You must telephone the hotel and book in advance if you want to be sure of a room.
    GOT
    You .... up the hotel and book in advance if you want to be sure of a room.

Exam folder 2

Paper 1 Part 3 Word formation

In this part of the Reading and Use of English paper you are given a short text with eight gaps and an example. At the end of some of the lines there is a word in CAPITALS which you will need to change so that it will make sense when it is put in the gap in the same line. In the example below, you are given the verb 'arrive' and it needs to be changed into the noun 'arrival' in order for the sentence to make sense.

EXAMPLE: Their plane's late ..... was due to a thunderstorm during the flight. **ARRIVE**
ANSWER: Their plane's late _ARRIVAL_ was due to a thunderstorm during the flight.

You need to read the sentence carefully to decide what kind of word is missing – is it a noun, a verb, an adjective or an adverb? In English we often use prefixes (letter(s) that go in front of a word) and suffixes (letter(s) that go at the end of a word) to change the type of word it is.

Prefixes

1 The following prefixes all give the meaning of NOT when they come before a word.

il-   ir-   in-   un-
dis-   im-   mis-

We often, but not always, put *il-* before words beginning with *l*, *ir-* before words beginning with *r*, and *im-* before words beginning with *m* and *p*.

Which prefix do we use to make these words negative?

a satisfied   h happy
b patient   i responsible
c expensive   j understand
d legal   k appear
e possible   l regular
f comfortable   m moral
g honest

2 What meaning do you think these prefixes give to the word that follows? Can you think of some more examples?

a *non*-stop   d *un*tie
b *re*train   e *under*line
c *sub*way

Suffixes

3 NOUNS – Typical noun suffixes are:

-ation -ion -ness -ship -ity
-ism -ence -ment -al

Make these words into nouns.

a happy   d recommend   g friend
b intelligent   e act   h pay
c approve   f popular   i tour

4 Not all nouns follow the above pattern. Make nouns from these words.

a true   c die
b succeed   d high

5 ADJECTIVES – Typical adjectival suffixes are:

-ible -able -y -al
-ive -ful -less -ous

Make these words into adjectives.

a wind   d danger   g value
b attract   e end   h access
c hope   f accident

6 ADVERBS – Adverbs are usually formed by adding the suffix *-ly* to the adjective. Be careful with spelling.

complete – completely   reasonable – reasonably
temporary – temporarily   lucky – luckily
real – really

And there are some exceptions:

true – truly (NOT ~~truely~~)
shy – shyly (NOT ~~shily~~)
Adjectives ending in *-ic* usually add *–ally*: *basic – basically*.

Make these words into adverbs.

a steady
b active
c necessary

d annual
e extraordinary
f automatic

7 VERBS – It is less common in Part 3 of Paper 1 to have to form a verb. However, you may be asked to make changes to a verb by using a prefix such as *un-*, *dis-* or *re-*, or to make a noun or an adjective into a verb by using the prefixes *dis-* or *re-*.

Change these words using un-, dis- or re-.

a new
b courage
c do
d build

e pay
f approve
g lock

It is more likely that you will need to change a verb into a noun or adjective. Change these verbs to nouns.

h communicate
i measure
j satisfy
k maintain

l identify
m introduce
n criticise

8 Read through the text on the right and think about what kind of words you need to make. For example, 0 is a noun (PUBLICATION). List the parts of speech for gaps 1–8 and then complete the task.

1 = VERB
2 =
3 =
4 =
5 =
6 =
7 =
8 =

A DISTINGUISHED MAP-MAKER

Example: | 0 | P | U | B | L | I | C | A | T | I | O | N | | | | |

In 1538, the **(0)** .... of a world map showed North and South America as separate continents for the first time. The man who **(1)** .... this important map was called Gerardus Mercator. Mercator spent his **(2)** .... in Flanders, where he became known as an **(3)** .... talented map-maker. Besides teaching mathematics to the students at the University of Louvain, he also earned extra money making **(4)** .... instruments.

PUBLISH

PRODUCT
YOUNG
EXTREME

SCIENCE

In 1544, he was briefly imprisoned for his religious beliefs and, fearing for his family's **(5)** .... , he went to live in the Rhineland, where he remained for the rest of his life. Mercator's youngest son Rumold became his father's **(6)** .... after his death in 1594, supervising the **(7)** .... of the first complete edition of the Mercator world atlas the following year.

SAFE

REPRESENT
APPEAR

Although Mercator constantly updated his maps with new information, some were wrong because the earth is round. As maps are flat, it is virtually **(8)** .... to show the right scale, area and direction on one map.

POSSIBLE

4.1 Endangered

Reading

1 Match the animal or bird with the correct photo.

tiger shark   snow leopard
orang-utan   thick-billed parrot
polar bear   koala

Which of the above are endangered? Do you know why?

If you could save *one* of the above, which would you choose? Why?

2 These sentences include words which are used in connection with animals today. Use an English–English dictionary to look up the meaning of the words in bold and then match a–e with 1–5.

a Arctic animals are now **in danger** because of
b **Cutting down** the trees where animals live is
c Many animals **suffer** when rivers and streams
d There are very few Bengal tigers left because of
e Some animals such as the white rhino are

1 called **habitat destruction**.
2 **rising sea levels** affecting coastal areas of Bangladesh.
3 ice melting due to **global warming**.
4 **are polluted** by factories.
5 **facing extinction** because people hunt them for their horns.

Exam spot

Paper 1 Part 7 consists of four to six short texts on the same subject. Read the 10 questions first, so that you know what you are looking for. Then scan the text for the information you need.

3 Skim texts A–E opposite. They all come from one source. Which do you think it is?

a an encyclopaedia   **c** an article
b a novel   **d** a brochure

4 You will find that some of the texts are quite similar. It is important that you find the information that actually answers the question. Read the texts opposite and answer the following for practice.

a Which person went to the zoo with a relative?

You will see that all the relatives mentioned are highlighted in the texts, but only text E has the answer to the question.

b Which person thought the zoo was value for money?

All mentions of money are underlined – which answers the question?

Now read questions 1–10 and find the answers in texts A–E. When you think you have found the words that give you the answer, underline them.

Which person

says visitors can decide on the animal they want to support?	**1**
was surprised at first by the absence of some animals?	**2**
says that the zoo was as good as people said it was?	**3**
says that one particular aim of the zoo has succeeded?	**4**
mentions a particular problem which is endangering animals?	**5**
complains about how long it takes to see everything within the zoo?	**6**
was initially unsure about going to a zoo?	**7**
complains about some people's attitude to less familiar species?	**8**
says that after visiting a particular zoo they changed their mind about zoos?	**9**
was unconcerned by the number of visitors at the zoo?	**10**

A Julia

I went to Marwell Zoo with two friends. It has over 200 species of rare animals, from Siberian tigers to white rhino and snow leopards. Personally, the red pandas were my favourites – they're like cuddly teddy bears. The zoo was only started in 1972, with breeding as its objective, and some species, such as the scimitar-horned oryx, which was once extinct in the wild, have been bred so well that they have been re-introduced into the wild. I was initially amazed by the fact that there are no traditional zoo animals like elephants and penguins there. This zoo specialises in keeping rare and endangered species and there is not room or <u>money</u> enough to keep anything just because it happens to be popular.

B Peter

I took the decision to visit San Diego Zoo. It has a huge reputation and I was interested in whether it would live up to it. I wasn't disappointed. The zoo was founded in 1916 and the founders couldn't have picked a better place – benefitting from breezes from the Pacific Ocean, being close to the city but also having wooded canyons. The zoo is home to a huge number of endangered species. However, one problem for the zoo was that the visitors seemed to be mainly interested in the well-known species such as the polar bear and just walked straight past other more endangered but less well-known species like the thick-billed parrot.

C Karin

I was working as a nanny for two sisters in New York last year and I decided to visit the Bronx Zoo. Animals are kept in large, natural enclosures and the zoo is very keen on conservation. You get to go into the largest African rainforest exhibit in the world – and it actually felt like a real rainforest – with lots of different animals like, for example, gorillas. When you come out you are allowed to select which rainforest animal you want your <u>entrance fee to fund</u>. There were crowds of tourists at the zoo when I visited, but the place is so big that it didn't really matter that much. There are a number of <u>inexpensive</u> cafés you can go to, or do as I did and take a picnic.

D Tom

Many species are now endangered because of what is happening to our planet – things like global warming – but some zoos are actually doing something to try to conserve these species. Whipsnade Zoo in England is one of them. I visited it about a month ago when I was backpacking with a friend of my brother's. He's studying zoology at university in Australia. We had a really good time and it was <u>worth every penny</u>. There's a free bus that can take you round all the main sights and I would really recommend you take it. The penguin pool is particularly beautiful as it is on top of a hill and has great views.

E Lara

Last summer, I was staying with my aunt in Toronto and she suggested I take my nine-year-old cousin to the zoo as it was her favourite place. I wasn't certain at first that I wanted to spend a day at a zoo. I guess I had always regarded them as <u>over-priced</u> places with cages and unhappy animals, but Toronto Zoo soon made me think differently! It's quite big – a bit too big if you try to go everywhere, and it's a 20-minute journey getting from one area to another, which is a pain. You absolutely must take a map as well, as it's easy to get lost. I particularly liked the Malayan Woods Pavilion – there is artificial rainfall there, which makes children laugh.

5 Do you think zoos are a good way of saving endangered species? Why? / Why not?

What do you think of the zoos mentioned in the article?

Have you ever been to a zoo? What was it like?

Vocabulary

Word formation

When you look up a word in a dictionary, look also to see what other related words you can find and make a note of them.

6 Which words related to a–j occur in texts A–E?

EXAMPLE: *expensive (C) – inexpensive*

a tradition (A)
b danger (A)
c decide (B)
d visit (B)
e conserve (C)
f enter (C)
g zoo (D)
h see (D)
i happy (E)
j rain (E)

4.2

as and like

1 Read the explanations below. Some of the examples are taken from the article you have read in 4.1.

- *As* is used to refer to a person's profession:
  I was working as a nanny for two sisters
- *Like* is only used for comparison or similarity:
  they're like cuddly teddy bears
- *Like* and *such as* can be used to mean *for example*:
  different animals, like gorillas
  things like global warming
  such as the scimitar-horned oryx
- Some verbs can be followed by *as*:
  I had always regarded them as over-priced
  Other verbs of this type are *refer to, use, be known, describe, class, accept* and *treat*.
- *As* is normally followed by a subject and verb, while *like* is followed by a noun or pronoun:
  or do as I did and take a picnic
  it actually felt like a real rainforest

G → page 167

Corpus spot

The *Cambridge Learner Corpus* shows that exam candidates often confuse the use of *like* and *as*.

I would like to work **as** a babysitter.
NOT I would like to work ~~like~~ a babysitter.

Sometimes students use *like* or *as* when it isn't necessary to do so.

It was a small flat that looked empty.
NOT It was a small flat that looked ~~like~~ empty.

I expected the water to be crystal clear.
NOT I expected the water to be ~~as~~ crystal clear.

---

2 Complete the following sentences using *as*, *like* or nothing, as appropriate.

a The large cat looked .... a cheetah.
b I know it sounds .... foolish, but I want to buy a tiger.
c You can work .... full-time in the zoo souvenir shop.
d The new penguin area is very big – it's .... an Olympic swimming pool.
e She could photograph the animals just .... a professional.
f He went to the fancy dress party dressed .... a gorilla.
g Pete regarded his cat .... a member of the family.

3 Complete the second sentence so that it has a similar meaning to the first sentence, using the word given. Do not change the word given. You must use between two and five words, including the word given.

1 According to the brochure, the zoo was 'a perfect place to spend the day'.
AS
The zoo was ....
'a perfect place to spend the day'.

2 In my house, we store our bikes in the garage.
STORAGE
In my house, we ....
for our bikes.

3 Sue taught small children in a school in Sydney before returning to the UK.
WORKING
Sue ....
of small children in a school in Sydney before returning to the UK.

4 My friend, whose name is Edmund, is usually called Fuz at college.
KNOWN
My friend Edmund ....
Fuz at college.

5 They heard what they thought was a dog barking.
SOUNDED
They heard ....
a dog barking.

6 My uncle would call my dog 'the wolf' when he used to visit.
REFER
My uncle would ....
'the wolf' when he used to visit.

Compound adjectives

4 A compound adjective is an adjective which has two parts and is usually written with a hyphen. Many have a present or past participle in the second part of the compound, as in this example from 4.1:

a thick-billed parrot – a parrot with a thick bill

Work through the questions in a–d with a partner.

a 1 Who do you think our 'four-legged friends' are?
 2 What is a man-eating tiger?
 3 How would you describe a cat which has blue eyes, long hair and a bad temper?

b Do you know anyone who is:
 1 left-handed?
 2 cross-eyed?
 3 bad-tempered?
 4 sharp-tongued?
 5 narrow-minded?

Compound adjectives are very useful for describing people, both for character and physical characteristics.

EXAMPLE: *My mother's a brown-eyed, curly-haired woman. She's left-handed. She's a broad-minded and self-confident person.*

c Some compound adjectives have a preposition in the second part of the compound.
 1 Where would you sit at a drive-in movie?
 2 How would you feel if you were hard-up?
 3 How much money do you need to have to be well-off?
 Can you think of some more examples?

d The article in 4.1 talked about a '20-minute journey'. Notice that *minute* is singular not plural.

 How would you describe:
 1 a road which was fifty kilometres long?
 2 a girl who is twelve years old?
 3 a film which lasts 75 minutes?
 4 a car which costs £35,000?
 5 a pause which lasts ten seconds?

Vocabulary

Topic set – parts of animals

5 Decide which of the words below are used with each of these creatures. Some can be used more than once. Use an English–English dictionary to help you.

parrot bear tiger rhino

beak feathers fur horn paw tail wing

Expressions with *time*

When you learn expressions such as the ones below, try to write them in a sentence to help you remember them.

6 There are many common expressions with *time* in English, as in this example from the article about zoos.

… we had a really good time

kill time	ten times three
have a good time	one at a time
tell the time	from time to time
spend time	a time when
pass the time	time for breakfast/lunch
take time off	in time
waste time	at times
	(four) times as much

Complete sentences a–h with one of the expressions above.

a We all went into the aquarium .... through the automatic gate.

b I usually don't have enough .... , so I grab a sandwich on the way to work.

c He says he never puts on weight, but he eats three .... as I do.

d .... people will realise that not spending enough on education is very unwise.

e Although Peter decided not to come with us, he said he hoped we would ....

f I always take a book to the doctor's surgery to .... while I'm waiting.

g She was given a watch as soon as she learnt to ....

h I really hate .... doing stupid exercises.

7 Ask your partner these questions.

a Can you think of three ways of wasting time?
b What's the best way of having a good time?
c What do you do when you have to kill time?

Writing folder 2

Paper 2 Part 1 Essays

Question 1 on Paper 2 is compulsory – you must answer it. You are asked to write an essay outlining and discussing issues on a particular topic. The essay question and some relevant notes are presented on the question paper. You should use all the notes and include your own idea as well.

1 Look at the exam question below and read the sample answer. What has the writer forgotten to include?

In your English class you have been talking about animal welfare. Now your English teacher has asked you to write an essay.

Write an essay using **all** the notes and give reasons for your point of view.

Animals deserve to be treated better than they are by man.
Do you agree?

Notes
Write about:

1. animals kept in zoos
2. wildlife under threat
3. .... (your own idea)

The treatment of animals in our world today

This is a complex question. Many people depend on animals to live, whether they eat meat or just keep an animal for its milk. This essay will consider farming, § the role of zoos and endangered wildlife.

When zoos first opened, they had a real purpose – to educate people. There was no television and § people got to see animals from other places. Now we don't have the same need for zoos and it is cruel to lock animals up there. § I think all zoos should be closed.

§ I think some farmers look after animals well, but many don't care about the conditions that their animals live in. The best farmers give animals plenty of space and fresh grass to eat.

§ I think we could treat animals better.

2 The essay needs to be better linked. Replace the symbol § with the phrases a–e. You may need to add punctuation.

a for this reason
b to sum up
c as well as discussing
d in this way
e as for agriculture

3 With these phrases, the essay is 150 words long. Write a paragraph of 30–40 words to cover the missing content.

4 Apart from its use in the title, the word *animal(s)* is used eight times in the essay. Replace it with the words below.

cow   creatures   goat   them
they   wildlife

5 Now replace the words *I think* … with three of these phrases, changing the word order if necessary. Which one doesn't fit anywhere? Why not?

a *without a doubt*
b *personally speaking*
c *in my opinion*
d *it is true that*

6 Write a final sentence, to avoid a single sentence paragraph and improve the conclusion.

7 Read the exam question below and write an essay of 140–190 words, following the advice given. Look back at 4.1 for useful vocabulary and include the paragraph you wrote in 3.

In your English class you have been talking about wildlife conservation. Now your English teacher has asked you to write an essay.

Write an essay using all the notes and give reasons for your point of view.

Not enough is being done to protect endangered animals.
Do you agree?

Notes

Write about:

1. which animals are under threat
2. why we need to protect these animals
3. .... (your own idea)

In your essay, you must use grammatically correct sentences with accurate spelling and punctuation in a style appropriate for the situation.

5.1 Mixed emotions

1 Put these adjectives in two groups according to positive and negative meaning. Which two are used with *stiff* to describe a very strong emotion?

anxious	content	delighted	frightened
happy	petrified	pleased	satisfied
scared	tense	terrified	thrilled
uneasy	worried		

2 How do the things in the pictures make you feel? Use adjectives from 1 to describe your emotions.

Vocabulary

Collocations – adverbs of degree

> Be careful when using adverbs such as *absolutely* and *very* with adjectives. Think about the meaning of the adjective – is it 'gradable' or not? For example, *enormous* is ungradable, because it already contains the meaning of 'very, very big'.

3 Which sentence in a and b is correct? Why?

  a I'm very happy to see you. / I'm absolutely happy to see you.

  b Sam's very delighted with her present. / Sam's absolutely delighted with her present.

> When combining adverbs like these with adjectives, think whether the adjective already means 'a lot'.

4 Complete the sentences with a suitable adverb from the box. More than one answer is possible.

> absolutely   completely   extremely
> really   totally   very

  a Sally was .... astonished to hear that she had won the competition.

  b As he entered the dark, empty flat, Alex felt .... uneasy.

  c Simon's father sounded .... proud of his son's achievements.

  d I arrived late for the film and James was .... furious with me!

  e Martin gets .... irritated by people asking him the same questions time after time.

  f I was .... relieved to find out I didn't have to pay the bill after all.

Corpus spot

Exam candidates often make mistakes in the spelling of these adverbs:

absolutely NOT ~~absolutly~~
completely NOT ~~complitely~~
extremely NOT ~~extreamly~~
totally NOT ~~totaly~~

Listening

5 **1·05** Listen to this recording, where a man is talking about something frightening that happened to him. Say where the man was and how long he spent there.

Now listen again and describe in detail what happened to the man. Use these questions to help you.

1 Why was he in the building?
2 What time of day was it?
3 Which two things did he try to do?
4 Why was he there for so long?

6 Here is the question for the extract you have just heard.

1 You hear a man talking about something frightening that happened to him. What was his first reaction?
  A He sat down and cried.
  B He decided to call for help.
  C He tried to keep calm.

All three options are mentioned in the extract. Listening out for sequence words – that is, words which tell you what happened when – will help you to decide what his first reaction was.

Listen again and note down any sequence words and phrases. Which one signals the answer?

7 **1·06** Before you listen to extracts 2–8, read these questions. Think about the words in bold and what to listen out for. Then listen and answer the questions.

2 You hear a man talking about how to deal with fear. **Who** is he?
  A an ex-teacher
  B an ex-pilot
  C an ex-actor

3 You hear a woman talking to her son on the phone. **How** does she **feel**?
  A furious
  B anxious
  C relieved

4 You hear a woman talking about something that happened in her home. The woman was **most** scared
  A when she heard a burglar upstairs.
  B while she was watching a horror film.
  C when she suddenly saw a frog.

5 You hear a man leaving a phone message. **Why** is he **proud of his daughter**?
  A because she is going to have a book published
  B because she has won a writing competition
  C because she is doing so well at university

6 You hear a woman describing what happened to her on a journey. **Where** did she **end up** that night?
  A on a country road
  B in hospital
  C at her house

7 You hear a man being interviewed about a sailing accident. The **worst** part of his experience was
  A being cold.
  B feeling hungry.
  C avoiding sharks.

8 You hear a woman talking on the radio about an incident abroad. **Why** was she able to **escape**?
  A She was by the door.
  B She wasn't noticed.
  C She had a radio.

8 How much can you remember about the last account? Discuss with a partner what happened and note down everything in the order it happened. Then listen to extract 8 to check your notes.

Grammar extra

This unit revises past tenses. Before the next lesson, copy and complete the table of irregular forms. All the verbs below have occurred in the listening extracts. An example is given.

Infinitive	Past tense	Past participle
become	became	(has/had) become

burst buy creep drive find get hear hold keep
know run see shake sink spend take think weep

Which verb has the same form throughout? Do you know any other verbs which are like that?

G → page 168

Review of past tenses

1 Look at examples a–j, which come from the listening in 5.1. Decide which tenses they contain. Where there are two different tenses in the same sentence, list both.

past simple	(PS)
past continuous	(PC)
present perfect tense	(P)
past perfect tense	(PP)

a I'd had this interview for a job.
b I got in the lift and pressed the button.
c I've never been in one since.
d I was watching a horror movie.
e It was the next door neighbour's cat I had heard.
f While I was putting away the books, I found something else.
g The others were looking at a map on the table, but I was standing by the back window.
h I knew they hadn't seen me.
i When I realised that they had gone, I ran inside.
j You have recently sailed around the world.

Look again at the examples containing two different tenses. Can you explain why each tense is used? Think about when each action happened.

Past simple / Past continuous

The most important difference between these two tenses is the duration of an action. For example, in example f above, the past continuous describes an action that happened over a longer time period than the second action, which happened at a specific moment and may have interrupted the longer continuous activity:

————X————

While I was putting away the books … I found something else.
Like the present continuous tense, the past continuous is used to describe temporary situations, as in example d.

————————X

I was watching a movie. … I turned off the TV.
Note that this use can be an effective way of setting the scene at the beginning of a story, as in example g.

————————X

The others were looking at a map … About six of them burst in.

2 Complete this text using the verbs in brackets in either the past simple or past continuous tense.

Quite late one evening I (1) .... (walk) home alone from college. The wind (2) .... (blow) hard and it (3) .... (pour) with rain, so there (4) .... (be) no one around. Anyway, this big black van (5) .... (drive) past me and (6) .... (stop), just where the road (7) .... (curve) round. I (8) .... (decide) to go on, though I (9) .... (feel) increasingly uneasy. However, as soon as I (10) .... (get) close to the van, it (11) .... (drive) off. This (12) .... (happen) twice more further down the same road. Each time, the van (13) .... (pull up) about fifty metres ahead of me and then (14) .... (wait) until I almost (15) .... (draw) level with it, then (16) .... (pull away) again. By this stage I (17) .... (be) absolutely petrified. So I (18) .... (stand) for a moment under a tree. The rain (19) .... (come down) in torrents now. I (20) .... (shake) and (21) .... (wonder) what to do next, when a policeman (22) .... (come) past. He (23) .... (push) his bike because of the heavy rain. I (24) .... (grab) him by the arm and (25) .... (make) him stop. Then I completely (26) .... (go) to pieces. While he (27) .... (try) to calm me down, I (28) .... (hear) the van drive off, thankfully for the last time. I've never walked home on my own since.

Past simple / Past perfect
The past perfect is used for actions in the past that occur earlier than the time period that is being described, as in example i:

When I realised they had gone, I ran inside.

3 Complete these sentences with the verbs in brackets in either the past simple or past perfect tense.

a We .... (spend) the last three nights shivering in a tent in the middle of nowhere, so we were really pleased when we .... (get) to the hotel.

b Jenny .... (tell) us in great detail what .... (happen) to her and .... (explain) why she .... (find) it so scary at the house.

c I .... (keep) still for over half an hour and I .... (think) it .... (be) safe at last to come out of my hiding place.

G → page 168

4 Look at this set of four pictures from an action story. Describe what happened in each scene, starting with the last one (4), and making reference back to what had happened earlier. Remember to use a range of past tenses.

5 Read this extract from the thriller *The Big Sleep*, ignoring the gaps for the moment. Why do you think the man telling the story wasn't frightened of the gun? Turn to page 47 to find out if you are right!

The gun pointed at my chest. Her hand seemed to **(0)** _BE_ quite steady. I laughed **(1)** .... her. I started to walk towards her. I saw her small finger tighten on **(2)** .... trigger and grow white at the tip.

I was about six feet away from her **(3)** .... she started to shoot. The sound **(4)** .... the gun made a sharp slap, a brittle crack in the sunlight. I didn't see any smoke. I stopped again **(5)** .... grinned at her.

She fired twice more, very quickly. I don't think **(6)** .... of the shots would have missed. There were five in the little gun. She **(7)** .... fired four. I rushed her.

I didn't want the last one in my face, **(8)** .... I swerved to one side. She gave it to me quite carefully, **(9)** .... worried at all.

I straightened up. 'My, but you're cute,' I said.

Her hand **(10)** .... holding the empty gun and began to shake violently. The gun fell out of **(11)** .... Her mouth began to shake. Then her whole face **(12)** .... to pieces.

6 Now fill each gap, choosing a suitable word from the box below. There are three words you do not need.

and	any	at	~~be~~	because	it	had	has
not	of	so	some	the	was	went	when

Can you put these words into grammatical categories? For example, *and* is a conjunction. These words are typical of the kinds of words that are tested in Paper 1 Part 2.

Exam folder 3

Paper 1 Part 2 Open cloze

In this part of the Reading and Use of English paper you are asked to complete a text containing eight gaps. You must write only one word in each gap. The missing word is usually a grammar word, but occasionally, vocabulary is tested. There is an example at the beginning. You must write your answers in CAPITAL letters.

1   Here are some examples of what is tested in Paper 1 Part 2. Complete each sentence with one word.

a Quantifiers – *many, every, each,* etc.
There were only a .... people at the zoo yesterday.

b Collocations – *set an example, change the subject, be in favour of,* etc.
I expect you to .... your promise to give me a lift.

c Determiners – *a, some, the,* etc.
I've lived in .... USA for some years now.

d Modals – *would, should,* etc.
You absolutely .... not use this path through the valley – it's dangerous.

e Verb forms – *done, taking, see,* etc.
He's .... working on his car for two hours now.

f Phrasal verbs – *give up, carry on, make out,* etc.
Susie has taken .... photography.

g Pronouns – *me, it, that,* etc.
Tom hurt .... while playing football – he had to go to hospital.

h Relative pronouns – *who, whose, which,* etc.
My wife, ... is Brazilian, works in the university.

i Comparison – *more than, one of the worst,* etc.
Suzanne has twice as .... clothes as I do.

j Linkers – *if, although, before,* etc.
You won't lose weight .... you go on a diet.

k Prepositions – *on, by, in,* etc.
According .... the website, all flights to Berlin are delayed this morning.

EXAM ADVICE

- Look at the title so you have some idea what the text is about. The title is there to help you.
- Read the whole text through carefully before you decide on an answer.
- Always write something down, even if you are not sure of the right answer.
- The word you write MUST be spelt correctly.
- Check whether the word you need should be singular or plural, past or present, etc.
- Make sure that the word you write makes sense in the sentence and text.
- You will need to transfer your answers to an answer sheet. Make sure you transfer each answer correctly.

2 Read this text through and then choose the best title from the three below.

   1 DON'T TAKE THE RISK!
   2 NOTHING TO WORRY ABOUT
   3 BALANCING THE RISKS

3 For questions 1–8, read the text below and think of the word which best fits each gap. Use only one word in each gap. There is an example at the beginning (0).

Write your answers **IN CAPITAL LETTERS on the separate answer sheet.**

Example: | **0** | O | N | | | | | | | | | |

What are the chances of slipping **(0)** .... a banana skin or being struck by a meteorite? These are not the sort of unlucky events that most people **(1)** .... their time thinking about, **(2)** .... one has already happened to them. **(3)** .... surprising number of people have imagined aliens kidnapping them. Some even have recurring nightmares about it, whereas relatively **(4)** .... are afraid of dying from flu, even **(5)** .... it is something that is more likely to happen. No doubt many people who go rock climbing will be among the people drinking bottled water on the grounds that it is safer **(6)** .... drinking tap water. Amazingly, our fear of flying outweighs our fear of driving, but going by plane is so much safer. People worry more about the possibility of dropping out of the air than of crashing on land. **(7)** .... an attempt to educate people about risks, scientists have constructed a scale they can use to compare any new and unfamiliar risks, **(8)** .... as those involved in taking new medicines.

Reading

1 If you suddenly became famous, how would you feel? What would be the advantages of achieving instant success? Would there be any drawbacks?

2 Read the headline and the first paragraph of the article. Why has this girl become famous?

3 Now read the whole text, paying attention to the highlighted parts around gaps 1–6. These give you content clues for the missing sentences.

British student, 19, becomes instant superstar in China

UNTIL RECENTLY, her greatest showbusiness moment had been winning £45 in the Undiscovered Youth Talent Contest in the small town of Stroud in Gloucestershire, close to her family home. But now, Mary-Jess Leaverland has found fame in China overnight, following her appearance in a regional TV talent show there.

1 ___ Indeed, thanks to YouTube, she is being talked about not just by her friends at home but the whole world over, and has appeared in TV interviews to discuss her story.

The 19-year-old exchange student won Jiangsu province's equivalent of *The X Factor* show by singing in Mandarin. And although there are no million-pound record deals on offer as yet, she is discovering what life is like as a superstar. **2** ___ She claims to be enjoying this new-found celebrity status. 'It is really strange, but nice,' she said. 'It was the most exciting thing I have ever done in my life. My friends think it is cool because they just know me as me.'

Mary-Jess, who is fluent in Mandarin and Italian, is studying for a degree in Chinese and Music. As part of her course, she has been spending a year in Jiangsu province. Shortly after she arrived in the country, she took part in a small singing competition for foreigners, which she won. It was through this event that she was talent-spotted for the show *Min Xing Chang Fan Tian* (the name translates as *I Want to Sing to the Stars*).

Min Xing Chang Fan Tian is a live competition on Chinese television, though it is broadcast only in Jiangsu province. **3** ___ The show follows a similar format to *The X Factor*, and has a judging panel of three experts. These are drawn from local record executives and songwriters.

Mary-Jess won first place on *Min Xing Chang Fan Tian*. To reach the finals, she had sung the Puccini aria *O Mio Babbino Caro* before performing Sarah Brightman's *Time To Say Goodbye*. **4** ___ Her winning performance in Mandarin was *Yue Guang Ai Ren* (*Moonlight Lovers*), the theme tune to the hit film *Crouching Tiger, Hidden Dragon*. 'I was the only foreign person in the finals and I still can't believe I won.'

She was rewarded with a cash prize of around £3,000, as well as gaining a trophy and a CD recording of herself. **5** ___ 'If I hadn't won, I wouldn't have been able to come home for Christmas because I wouldn't have been able to afford the flight,' said Mary-Jess, who has a 17-year-old sister, Chez.

According to Mary-Jess, her singing talent is part of a family tradition. **6** ___ 'She was a real inspiration but my mum is my main inspiration. We even sing together in a duo when I am home.' For obvious reasons, her mother Liz was unable to watch her daughter triumph. 'I would have loved to be there but I saw some of the videos and seeing Mary-Jess in the limousine and on the red carpet was amazing,' she said. 'I'm just so proud of her and hope she can continue in the industry.'

4 Now use the highlighted words in A–G to help you decide where each sentence fits. Remember that one sentence is not needed.

A This was the song that had won her that original 'best in show' title in Britain.

B Although it pales into insignificance beside the amounts involved in *The X Factor*, this sum was still very welcome.

C She has really missed her family and friends though.

D However, it is no small-scale event, as the region has a population of 70 million.

E Her grandmother was a semi-professional opera singer.

F People keep on stopping the singing sensation in the street to ask for her autograph.

G She has also made the headlines back in Britain.

5 Would you have taken part in the competition? Why? / Why not?

Vocabulary

Phrasal verbs with *keep*

6 The verb *keep* occurs in many phrasal verbs, as in this example from the article.

People keep on stopping her in the street.

Match definitions a–f to the correct phrasal verb. One is used twice with different meanings.

keep away   keep down   keep in
keep to   keep up with

a stop the number, level or size of something from increasing
b make someone stay in hospital
c understand something that is changing very fast
d stay with something such as a plan, subject, path
e move at the same speed as someone or something
f not go somewhere or near something

7 Use a phrasal verb with *keep* in the correct tense to complete a–h, adding a pronoun if necessary.

a Professor Grant's lectures would be much shorter if he .... the point!
b I rarely .... British news when I was living in Chile.

c We generally .... from the city centre during the day as it's so crowded.
d Sally swims so fast! I never manage to ....
e Mark had the operation on Saturday but they're .... for more tests.
f It's easy to get lost on the mountain, so make sure you .... the path.
g If Ben .... time at the meeting, we'll be finished by three.
h My weight .... increasing – I have to exercise to ....

Word formation

8 Use the word given in capitals to form a word that fits in the numbered gap.

Celebrity culture

Why do we find celebrities so (0) *FASCINATING* ?

These days, it seems to be almost (1) .... to open a newspaper or magazine without seeing an image of a celebrity in it. The (2) .... often made by members of the press is that they are only responding to public demand – it seems that people are far more interested in celebrity gossip and scandal than in the reality of our modern world.

Rightly or wrongly, the paparazzi make a very good (3) .... by keeping up with the rich and famous. However, some high-profile celebs are (4) .... hounded by the media. In these cases, does the press go too far? Don't these individuals have a right to some (5) .... privacy?

Then again, celebrities often do seem to lead such interesting lives that it is perhaps (6) .... that we want to find out more about them. In fact, some evolutionary (7) .... have said it is natural for humans to look up to the most successful individuals in a society. In prehistoric times, this would have meant respecting good (8) .... Today's equivalents are our celebrities, whose fame and fortune we are so envious of.

0 FASCINATE	5 PERSON
1 POSSIBLE	6 UNDERSTAND
2 ARGUE	7 SCIENCE
3 LIFE	8 HUNT
4 END	

6.2

Conditionals with *if*

1 🔊 **1 07** You are going to listen to four short extracts, where people talk about winning the lottery. How would their lives change if they won?

2 Explain what the contracted verb forms are in these examples of conditional sentences. How do the sentences differ in their use of tenses?

  a If I won the lottery, I'd buy a beautiful house in Spain.
  b If I hadn't won, I wouldn't have been able to afford the flight.

Which types of conditional sentences are a and b? Choose from 0–3.

  0 a situation that happens often
  1 a situation that may happen in the future
  2 a situation that is unlikely to happen
  3 a situation that could have happened in the past, but didn't

G → page 168

3 Match the two halves of each sentence.

  a If you did more revision, …
  b If it snows, …
  c If I have time, …
  d If Helen comes round, …
  e If there had been a vote, …
  f If they finish early, …
  g If you swam regularly, …
  h If I'd known about the risk, …

  1 we'll get our skis out.
  2 she'll be able to tell you.
  3 Sam and Bernie usually have a coffee.
  4 you'd pass the exam.
  5 I'd never have eaten seafood.
  6 they would have lost.
  7 I like to walk to work.
  8 your body would be in better shape.

Conditionals with *unless*

4 Read these examples and explain the meaning of *unless*.

  a We'll miss the start of the match unless Juan arrives soon.
  b Unless you've already got tickets, you won't be able to get in.

Corpus spot

Correct any mistakes with *unless* that exam candidates have made in these sentences. Tick the correct sentences.
  a There will be no improvement in my tennis unless I don't get some training.
  b I will not remain silent about the letter unless you give me my money back.
  c People hardly ever use candlelight today unless there isn't anything wrong with the power supply.
  d There isn't much to do in the city unless you haven't got friends.
  e You must stop working so hard unless you don't want to end up in hospital sooner or later.
  f If there were no televisions, we wouldn't know much about other countries unless we visited them.

---

5 There are eight mistakes with tenses in this story. Correct the mistakes and fill the gaps with *if* or *unless*. Examples have been done for you.

hadn't been
Yesterday was a very bad day. **(0)** ..*If*.. it ~~wasn't~~ raining, perhaps it wouldn't have been so difficult. The thing is, I never drive to work **(1)** .... it's raining. But it was pouring and I needed to get to an important meeting, so I took the car. It broke down on the way. **(2)** .... I had it serviced regularly, I know it won't be so unreliable, but garages charge so much these days that I don't bother. I decided to call the breakdown company on my mobile phone. Well, I would have done that **(3)** .... my mobile hasn't run out of battery! Never mind, I thought, **(4)** .... I'll find a public phone, I'll be able to call from there **(5)** .... it's out of order! It was, so I can't! By this time, I was in a panic. What will my boss say **(6)** .... I didn't get to the meeting? **(7)** .... people don't arrive on time, he will get really angry with them. Luckily, a taxi pulled up. 'Mason Square,' I shouted, 'and **(8)** .... you will do the journey in under ten minutes, I'll pay you double!' 'Forget it,' said the driver. 'The centre of town's gridlocked. You'd never get there in ten minutes **(9)** .... you went by helicopter.' So I ended up late for the meeting and the boss was furious with me.

6 Talk to a partner. Take it in turns to finish these sentences. Then tell the class what your friend said.

  a Unless I get up early tomorrow, …
  b If I had enough money, …
  c My life would be a lot easier if …
  d If I hadn't come to class today, …

G → page 168

Vocabulary

Word formation

> ### Exam spot
>
> Paper 1, Part 1 tests vocabulary. You have to fill eight gaps in a text, choosing from sets of four words. All four words will be the same part of speech and the eight questions will test a range of different parts of speech, such as nouns, verbs, adverbs, etc.

7 Look at the words in the box. They form four sets and all four words in a set have a similar meaning. Can you group them into the four categories in the table? Be careful: some words can be more than one part of speech. Think carefully about their meanings when you decide which category to put them into.

accepted	attempt	by	delicate	experiment
gathered	gentle	in	light	on	received
tiny	to	trial	try	welcomed

Nouns	Verbs	Prepositions	Adjectives

8 Now read the short newspaper article below. There are four gaps in it. Decide which part of speech is required in each gap. Then choose the correct option to fill each one from your four sets of words.

Speaking

9 Discuss these questions.

  a Should lottery winners receive so much publicity?
  b What are the pros and cons of winning the lottery?
  c If you won the jackpot, would you go public?

Useful language

As I see it …
To my mind …
For one thing …
For another (thing) …
On the one hand …
On the other (hand) …
The main advantage is …
One drawback is …

Could it possibly be YOU?

Camelot is to make a final **(1)** .... today to track down the winner of an unclaimed £2.1 million jackpot prize. A **(2)** .... aircraft will fly over Hull trailing the banner: '£2 million winner – is it you?' for two hours at lunchtime.

The city became the focus of attention after a local newspaper **(3)** .... an unsigned letter from an elderly local widow saying she did not want the prize. Her reason was that 'the fuss would finish me off'. If the money is not claimed **(4)** .... 11 pm it will go into the lottery's 'good causes' fund.

Writing folder 3

Paper 2 Part 2 Reports

In Part 2 of Paper 2 you may be asked to write a report. This will involve the presentation of mainly factual information, with suggestions or a recommendation. You should think carefully about who the target reader is and why they need this report.

1 Read this exam question and the sample answer. Does the report give the reader useful information? Why? / Why not?

> Your local tourist office has asked you to write a report on a museum because it is not very popular. You should briefly describe what is wrong with the museum and suggest how to make it more appealing to visitors.
>
> Write your **report**.

Wademouth Museum

1..........

The aim of this report is to outline what can be seen in this museum and to make some recommendations on how the museum could attract more visitors.

2..........

The museum mainly contains items connected with the pottery industry. Generally, objects are shown in glass cabinets with explanations on small bits of card. These are difficult to read and some are placed too high for small children. The lighting inside the building is also poor.

3..........

This permanent exhibition will remain unappealing to visitors unless it is updated. It is therefore recommended that video animation is developed to illustrate the process. In addition, the museum could run regular afternoon workshops, where experts demonstrate how the pots are produced.

4..........

Most visitors take it for granted nowadays that a museum will include a gift shop and a café. Wademouth has neither of these, which could partly explain the low attendance figures.

5..........

To sum up, Wademouth Museum would have a brighter future if its displays were improved. Furthermore, it needs to create a more welcoming atmosphere.

2 Reports are often easier to follow if they include headings. Choose headings from A–G for 1–5. There are two extra headings.

A Lack of facilities
B Conclusion
C Educational improvements
D Negative aspects of the display
E Temporary exhibitions
F Introduction
G Evening events

Assessment focus

In Part 2, choose the question you feel most confident about. For each piece of writing in the exam, there is a maximum of five marks available for **language**. To score 5, you need to show a wide range of structures and vocabulary, and produce an answer that is generally accurate.

3 Find the conditional structures in paragraphs 3 and 5. Then complete a–e with the right word. Which of the extra headings in 2 matches each of these sentences?

a People might visit more often … there were different objects for them to see each time.

b … the museum extends its opening hours and offers extra attractions, working adults won't come through its doors.

c A series of after-work talks would be more popular … visitors didn't have to pay for them.

d The museum could organise special exhibitions on a monthly basis … funding was available.

e It wouldn't be possible to hold concerts at the museum … it stayed open late.

4 Write a paragraph for each extra heading. Include two sentences from 3 in each one, making any changes necessary.

5 Now read this exam question. List recommendations to deal with the problems given. Then add a further problem and recommendation of your own.

> Your college is going to create a new student café. You have been asked to write a report for the principal, explaining why students don't use the existing facilities and making recommendations for the new café.
>
> Write your **report**.

Problems	Recommendations
closes too early	
not much choice	
uncomfortable	

6 To persuade the target reader to take action, recommendations need to be clear, reasonable and polite. Tick the four sentences in a–f that would have a positive effect on the principal. Then rewrite the remaining sentences to achieve the same effect.

a It would be a good idea to extend the opening hours of the new café.

b You must get some decent furniture in there instead of the old stuff.

c Perhaps the college could review the café's prices and consider some financial support?

d If the menu choices were more interesting, more students would use the café.

e There's no point even having a café unless it gives us what we want!

f If possible, vegetarians should be offered a different main dish each day.

EXAM ADVICE

Content
- Make a paragraph plan and organise your ideas.
- State facts clearly and give some examples.

Communicative achievement
- Write in a formal and impersonal style.
- Be polite and constructive in any criticism.

Organisation
- State the aim of the report in an introduction.
- Include headings to make your report clearer.
- Repeat your most important recommendation(s) in a conclusion, using different words.

Language
- Use passive forms and conditional structures.
- Include some longer, complex sentences.

Units 1–6 Revision

Topic review

1 Together with a partner, read these sentences and discuss which are true for you, giving more details. Try to use as much of the vocabulary and language as you can from the units you have just studied.

   a I always get out of bed early in the morning.
   b If I had some money, the first thing I would buy is a fast car.
   c I'm worse at English than I am at Maths.
   d I'm always getting into trouble for forgetting things.
   e I'm not afraid of anything!
   f I think I'm broad-minded.
   g I must try to work harder.
   h I like to follow fashion.
   i Books interest me more than computer games.
   j Beach holidays are not for me.

Grammar

2 Read the text below and think of the word which best fits each gap. Use only one word in each gap. There is an example at the beginning (0).

Most (0) ..OF.. us go a little crazy when we jet off (1) .... holiday, but some go completely mad. They see giant rats eating through their luggage and even lose their mother-in-law in (2) .... back of a stolen caravan. So says WorldCover Direct, the holiday insurer. These are just some of the claims the company (3) .... received in the past 12 months.

A director said, 'One of our policyholders skied into a tree (4) .... he was on holiday and made a claim for injuries. What he didn't mention was that he (5) .... blind and in the process of testing a new radar system for blind skiers.'

But what if you were in the Mediterranean in August and had had (6) .... much sun? Take a dip in the pool, sit in the shade for a while – or phone your holiday insurance company requesting repatriation (7) .... you were 'feeling a bit hot'? One holiday maker, (8) .... was in Spain, did just that.

Phrasal verbs

3 Complete the following sentences using the appropriate verb.

UP

   a If Elizabeth had been able to .... up just a little more money, she would have bought a faster computer.
   b Every time I go shopping for clothes, I find that prices have .... up yet again.
   c Come just as you are, there's really no need to .... up.
   d Sara was walking so fast that I couldn't .... up with her.
   e When you manage to find his address, ... me up and let me know what it is.

OUT

   f Tourist guides often carry umbrellas so that they .... out in a crowd.
   g Sheila decided to .... out of the hotel a bit early so she wouldn't miss her plane.
   h 'I don't know how you can .... out looking like that,' Sue's mother said.
   i I'm not sure I can .... out how to play this computer game.

Now look at these mixed examples and replace the verb or phrase in italics with a phrasal verb or compound noun.

   j If you want to look good in that outfit, you'll have to *reduce* the amount of chocolate you eat.
   k We *spent some time* in Singapore on our way to Sydney.
   l I really hate shops that make you feel guilty when you *return* clothes that shrink in the wash or fall to pieces.
   m We decided to *start the journey* to the castle at midnight, in the hope of seeing the ghost.
   n The police officer told them *not to go near* the edge of the cliff.
   o My friend had to spend about two hours waiting in the plane for it to *leave*.

Revision of present and past tenses

4 Read through this text and put the verbs in the correct tense.

The statistics on the safety of flying **(1)** .... (BE) immensely comforting. It **(2)** .... (SEEM) that the chances of being involved in an accident **(3)** .... (BE) a million to one – the equivalent of flying safely every day for 95 years. Try telling that to the white-faced, petrified aerophobic, who **(4)** .... (SEE) every frown on a stewardess's face as a portent of disaster. For some years now, psychologist Henry Jones **(5)** .... (TRY) to tell them, and he **(6)** .... (DO) a lot more besides. He **(7)** .... (DEVELOP) both a theory and practice for treating air travel anxiety. Apparently, it **(8)** .... (BE) a widespread phobia. One American survey **(9)** .... (PUT) it as the fourth most common fear, preceded only by snakes, heights and storms. Jones **(10)** .... (HAVE) nearly 500 clients during the last decade. Before they **(11)** .... (COME) to him, some of his clients **(12)** .... (never FLY), others **(13)** .... (HAVE) just one bad experience after years of flying. One man **(14)** .... (TAKE) over 200 flights a year for five years and **(15)** .... (never WORRY) up till then. Then, one day, on a flight to Chicago the pilot **(16)** .... (ANNOUNCE) that they were going to turn back because of an engine fault. The man then **(17)** .... (HAVE) a panic attack and **(18)** .... (TRY) to get off the plane in mid-air. After Jones's course, the man **(19)** .... (OVERCOME) his fears and **(20)** .... (MANAGE) to fly again.

5 Complete the second sentence so that it has a similar meaning to the first sentence, using the word given. Do not change the word given. You must use between two and five words, including the word given.

1 Andrea said she would only go dancing if her husband bought her a new outfit.
UNLESS
Andrea said she .... her husband bought her a new outfit.

2 I have never seen such a terrible film before.
WORST
This is the .... seen.

3 I'm sorry I didn't meet you at the airport – my car wasn't working.
MET
I .... at the airport if my car had been working.

4 This party is 'evening dress' only.
ALLOWED
You .... dress casually for this party.

5 I'm not as frightened of flying as I am of ghosts!
THAN
I'm .... I am of flying.

6 It was a mistake for me to buy you that computer game.
BOUGHT
I .... that computer game.

7 The play started before we could get there.
HAD
The play .... when we got there.

8 I need to wear glasses to drive.
SEE
I can't .... my glasses.

> **5.2 exercise 5**
> The man talks about the incident later in the story.
> He says:
> 'All five chambers are empty. She fired them all. She fired them all at me. From a distance of five or six feet. Cute little thing, isn't she? Too bad I had loaded the gun with blanks.'

Life's too short

Gerunds and infinitives 1

1 Identify the equipment in pictures a–o, and name each sport.

2 With a partner ask and answer these questions.

   a What sports do you really enjoy watching?

   b Is there a sportsperson or team who you particularly like watching?

   c Which sport can't you stand watching?

   d Which sports have you either taken up or given up recently?

   e Which do you prefer – watching a sport live or watching it on TV?

   f Are there any sports you like doing on holiday?

3 A gerund, which is a verb used as a noun, always ends in *-ing*, but not all *-ing* forms are gerunds. An *-ing* form might be a present participle or an adjective. What is the *-ing* form in these sentences?

   a I pulled on the climbing rope to show I was safe.

   b Anna was running along the track when she tripped and fell.

   c Snowboarding is a very popular sport.

4 Look at these sentences:

   1 I enjoy going swimming.

   2 After learning to ice skate, I'm going to learn to play ice hockey.

   3 I want to take up rowing.

   4 Climbing is a fairly safe sport nowadays.

   5 It's not worth going to watch our local football team because they always lose!

Find an example of a gerund above which:

   a follows a preposition.

   b is the subject of the sentence.

   c follows an expression.

   d follows a verb.

   e follows a phrasal verb.

5 When we put a verb after a preposition, we usually use a gerund. Complete the following sentences with a preposition and one of the verbs in the box.

do   drop   get   learn   play   swim   teach

   a She was doubtful .... to the training session on time.

   b Steve is very proud .... to scuba dive so quickly.

   c I've been very successful .... my cousins to ride their bikes.

   d Mark was in trouble .... his muddy sports clothes on the changing room floor.

   e I believe .... some exercise every day in order to keep healthy.

   f You don't have to be good .... to enjoy it.

   g I'm looking forward .... against her again in tomorrow's match.

G → page 169

6 Infinitives are forms like (*to*) *do*, (*to*) *say*. They are usually used with 'to', but not always.

Look at the following sentences, which show the most common uses of the infinitive.

1 I'm going to the pool *to have* my swimming lesson.
2 I want *to enrol* for netball practice next term.
3 They are unlikely *to hold* the Winter Olympics in Britain.
4 They let me *do* the judo classes even though I had never done judo before.
5 You must not *run* with the ball in some sports.
6 We encouraged them *to run* faster by cheering loudly.

Now say which of the infinitives above:

a follows an adjective.
b follows a modal auxiliary.
c follows a main verb.
d is used to express purpose.
e has an infinitive without 'to'.
f follows the object of a verb.

G → page 169

Corpus spot ◉

Be careful with gerunds and infinitives – the *Cambridge Learner Corpus* shows that exam candidates often make mistakes with these.

I look forward to **hearing** from you.

NOT I look forward to ~~hear~~ from you.

Correct the mistakes that candidates have made with gerund and infinitive forms in these sentences.

a I should give up to swim every morning.
b Do you want go out with me?
c I'm used to sleep in a tent.
d There's no point play today.
e I suggest you to go to the sports centre.
f I really enjoy to read about the old tennis stars.
g I recommend you going there.
h I hope hearing from you soon.
i I am interested to receive documentation about the courses.
j I agree with you to find a job.

7 Read through this email and put the verbs in brackets in the correct form. Give your reasons.

To: Jill Campbell
Cc:
Subject: Trip to Mont Blanc

Dear Jill,
I've just got back from (**1**) .... (climb) Mont Blanc in the Alps and I must (**2**) .... (tell) you what a great time I had. On (**3**) .... (arrive) in Chamonix we were introduced to our guides. We were then kitted out with ice-axes, crampons and climbing boots and were sent straight out into two days' (**4**) .... (train) in and around the Le Tour glacier. The guides used this time (**5**) .... (assess) our ability (**6**) .... (make) the ascent and (**7**) .... (teach) us the basics of (**8**) .... (mountaineer), such as how (**9**) .... (use) an ice-axe and how best (**10**) .... (work) in a team.
The first day consisted of (**11**) .... (climb) for five hours from the Nid d'Aigle to the Gouter Hut. I thought I'd be too cold (**12**) .... (sleep) but in fact that wasn't a problem at all! Day 2 started at 2 am with a four and a half hour walk to the summit. (**13**) .... (reach) the summit was only a third of the day's work. The descent route included (**14**) .... (jump) across gaps in the ice and took seven hours.
I'm really looking forward to (**15**) .... (see) you next weekend so I can (**16**) .... (tell) you all the details.
Love, Sue

8 Complete the second sentence so that it has a similar meaning to the first sentence, using the word given. Do not change the word given. You must use between two and five words, including the word given.

1 The newspapers said that Pete had pushed the other player.
ACCUSED
The newspapers .... the other player.

2 The pitch isn't dry enough to play on.
TOO
The pitch .... play on.

3 It wasn't easy for me to learn how to paraglide.
DIFFICULTY
I .... how to paraglide.

4 'I wouldn't go diving by yourself, if I were you,' the instructor said.
ADVISED
The instructor .... diving by myself.

5 I prefer to go on walking holidays than lie on a crowded beach.
RATHER
I .... walking holidays than lie on a crowded beach.

7.2

Speaking

1 **Discuss these questions with a partner.**

  a Which sports would you consider to be extreme or dangerous? Why?

  b Have you ever tried or watched a dangerous sport? What was it?

Exam spot

Paper 3 Part 3 consists of five questions and five short extracts linked by a theme. You need to match each extract to one of the eight options, A–H. There are three extra options that you do not need.

Listening

2 **1 08** **Listen to this extract, where a woman is talking about a sport she has recently taken up. As you listen, try to work out what the sport is. What clues did you hear?**

3 **1 09** **Now you're going to hear the first speaker again and also four other people talking about dangerous sports. For questions 1–5, choose from the list (A–H) what each speaker says. There are three extra letters which you do not need to use.**

Speaker 1	1
Speaker 2	2
Speaker 3	3
Speaker 4	4
Speaker 5	5

  A I like to set myself challenges.
  B I've always enjoyed taking risks.
  C It's not as dangerous as some ordinary sports.
  D Knowing I might be killed makes it more enjoyable.
  E I'm not sure I want to do it again.
  F It puts some excitement in my life.
  G I wanted to prove to everyone that I could do it.
  H I prefer to do it in the company of other people.

4 **What dangerous sports do the speakers mention? Are they popular in your country?**

Vocabulary

Collocations – sports

5 **Match the sports (A) with the correct verb (B) and the place where the sport takes place (C).**

A		B	C	
aerobics	snowboarding	do	pitch	course
martial arts	golf	play	court	track
swimming	running	go	stadium	studio
athletics	football		gym	pool
basketball	gymnastics		piste	

6 **Decide which is the correct word in each sentence and explain the meaning of the other word to your partner.**

  a Sally had only done three *marathons / laps* of the stadium before she fell.

  b The *spectators / defenders* all cheered when their team won.

  c The football *umpire / referee* sent two players off during the game.

  d In the French Open tennis final they had only completed two *sets / penalties* before rain stopped play.

  e A midfield player scored a *goal / shot* just before half-time.

Expressions with *do*

7 **Speaker 5 in the Listening said 'I did my best'. Here are some other expressions with *do*. Complete the sentences below, putting *do* into the correct tense.**

do damage	do business with someone
do a good job	do something for a living
do without	do someone a favour

  a I've always found that they are a very good company to ....

  b What does your father .... ?

  c The engineers .... on building the new stadium.

  d The fire .... a lot of .... to the sports hall.

  e I'd forgotten my wallet, so Tom .... and lent me some money.

  f The players always .... for the team and that's why they win.

  g One thing I can't .... is my bicycle – I use it all the time.

8 Ask and answer the following questions with a partner.

  a What couldn't you do without?

  b What do you do / would you like to do for a living?

  c When was the last time you did someone a favour?

  d Do you always do your best? Why? / Why not?

Word formation

9 Use the word in brackets to form a word that fits in the gap.

With some personal fitness trainers charging as much as £150 an hour, it's not surprising that only the rich and famous can afford the kind of one-to-one that will **(1)** .... (SURE) they work out enough to stay in shape. However, the idea that they are only for the elite is about to be shattered by *Get Motivated*, a new London-based company that charges just £25 for an hour with a fully qualified trainer. I decided to put this scheme to the test and asked *Get Motivated* to send a personal trainer to my home for a **(2)** .... (TRAIN) session. When 23-year-old Stephanie arrived, I was initially **(3)** .... (CERTAIN) about her as she seemed so young, but what followed was a very **(4)** .... (DEMAND) hour. Stephanie grew up in Australia and has a degree in Human **(5)** .... (MOVE) Studies and a diploma in **(6)** .... (EDUCATE) – the minimum **(7)** .... (QUALIFY) *Get Motivated* requires. Stephanie says that what appeals most to her about the GM scheme is that it gives her the **(8)** .... (FREE) to design her own sessions for clients.

Do you think it would be useful to have a personal trainer? Why? / Why not?

Speaking

10 Imagine that your town is going to build some sports facilities. Below are some facilities that could be built. Talk to each other about how popular/ useful these sports facilities would be. Then decide which two facilities would be best for your town.

Below are some useful phrases.

Being polite
OK, where shall we start?
What do you think?

Hesitating
Well, um, I'm not sure …
Well, let me see …

Asking for repetition
I'm sorry, could you say that again?
Could you repeat that, please?

Making things clear
What I mean is, …
What I'm trying to say is, …

Giving a different view
Well, it is true that …, but …
Of course, …

Concluding
So, let's come to a decision.
Right, what we've decided is that …

Exam folder 4

Paper 1 Part 1
Multiple-choice cloze

In this part of the Reading and Use of English paper you must choose one word or phrase from a set of four (A, B, C or D) to fill a gap in the text. There are eight gaps and an example. The text always has a title, which will give you some help in telling you what it is about before you start reading.

Below are some examples of the type of words that are tested in this part of Paper 1.

Expressions

1 I .... the conclusion, after failing to win any matches, that I would do better to give up playing tennis altogether.

A reached **B** got **C** did **D** came

A is the right answer. The expression is to reach a/the conclusion. You can come to a conclusion.

Verb/Adjective + preposition

2 The man was .... with burglary at the police station.

A accused **B** charged **C** investigated **D** arrested

B is the right answer. Investigated and arrested are followed by for; accused is followed by of.

Phrasal verbs

3 Susie fell .... with her best friend last week.

A for **B** out **C** apart **D** through

B is the right answer. To fall out means to no longer be friends. The other phrasal verbs here, fall for, fall apart and fall through, all exist but mean something different.

Linking words

4 I really like skiing, ... my friend prefers snowboarding.

A once **B** provided **C** whereas **D** or

C is the right answer. Whereas means but. Provided, or and once are used in a different type of clause.

Vocabulary

5 The .... of the party welcomed us at the door.

A guest **B** companion **C** household **D** host

D is the right answer. All the other words are connected with people, but are used differently.

For questions **1–8**, read the text below and decide which answer
(**A**, **B**, **C** or **D**) best fits each gap. There is an example at the beginning (**0**).

Example:

0 A dates   **B** calls   **C** looks   **D** stands

```
0 | A   B   C   D
    ▬   ▭   ▭   ▭
```

The History of Football

Football or soccer, which is so popular all over the world, **(0)** .... back to the Middle Ages. At that time it was very different from the game we play today. Any number of players could **(1)** .... part and the matches usually developed into a free-for-all. In its modern **(2)** .... , football is less than two hundred years old.

In 1846 the first rules to govern the game were drawn up at Cambridge University. The number of players was **(3)** .... to 11 per side, which made things much more orderly than before. Later, in 1863, the Football Association was **(4)** .... up to help promote the game in Britain.

The game is played on a grass or artificial pitch with a goal net at each end. The **(5)** .... is to move the ball around the field, with the feet or head, until a player is in a **(6)** .... to put the ball into the net and score a goal.

Professional football is not only the most popular **(7)** .... sport in the world, but also more people actually play football themselves than any other team sport. In 1904 FIFA, the world **(8)** .... for football, was founded. It promotes the World Cup tournament every four years.

1 A play	**B** make	**C** take	**D** do
2 A form	**B** shape	**C** fashion	**D** pattern
3 A limited	**B** checked	**C** counted	**D** defined
4 A put	**B** set	**C** born	**D** called
5 A objective	**B** reason	**C** focus	**D** purpose
6 A place	**B** point	**C** position	**D** spot
7 A witness	**B** audience	**C** spectator	**D** viewer
8 A group	**B** band	**C** collection	**D** organisation

8.1 Growing up

Speaking

1 Student A: Look at photos 1 and 2. They show children playing. Compare the photographs and say which of the activities the children would enjoy more. Student B: give your opinion.

2 Student B: Look at photos 3 and 4. They show teenagers at home. Compare the photographs and say what the photos tell you about modern teenagers. Student A: give your opinion.

Reading

3 Below is an extract from an autobiography. Read it quickly and then say whether you think the writer had a happy or unhappy childhood.

GROWING UP

I lived in the same house in Westpark Grove for my whole childhood. There was no major landmark to help you find your way around in my neighbourhood. Every street looked almost identical, like a soap opera set. Our two-storey house was set a few metres back from the road and was a perfectly hideous pink colour, which my parents seemed to like. The only feature we had that no-one else had was a huge garage, over the door of which my dad had painted the words GARAGE ENTRANCE in large black letters. Anyone silly enough to park in front of the driveway should beware. You didn't want to get on the wrong side of my dad, believe me!

We had three bedrooms and I used to share mine with my sister Lucy, who is two years older than me. We had a bunk bed – I slept on top – a wardrobe and a desk. Our brother Tom, who is a year younger than I am, had a room the size of a broom cupboard at the very back of the house, overlooking the garden. The three of us used to have terrible fights with each other in those days. We always worried that my mum would find out about the fights. We used to slip handwritten notes under the bedroom doors, asking, 'Are you going to tell Mum?' There were boxes to tick for 'yes' or 'no'.

We all had chores to do before and after school. It seems hard now but we were used to doing them. Meanwhile, the neighbourhood kids would be playing in the street outside. Sometimes we would go out and play with them, but we kept an eye open for Mum, who disapproved of us playing outside. There was a big supermarket just on the edge of town, but my mum and I would struggle the six kilometres into town by bus every Saturday to the weekly market in the centre of town. It was better and cheaper than a supermarket, she said. We would then come home laden down with what seemed like a mountain of plastic bags and sink gratefully onto the sofa in the living room when we got in. Dad thought that getting the car out for shopping was a waste of time.   line 30 / line 32

My first best friend was Sarah. We got on really well and she was good at keeping secrets. I can't remember a single occasion when we fell out. I used to sleep over at her house and we'd have midnight feasts of chocolate. We spent all our spare time together – like sisters. I used to hang around the local shops with her, if there was nothing decent showing at the local cinema. I wanted to be a pop star or be in films when I grew up and poor long-suffering Sarah was very good about listening to me singing all the latest pop songs and showing off my dancing to practise my stage technique. I think it helped having a critical audience as when I finally started at drama school, I felt quite confident and this showed.

In the summer, Sarah and I and the rest of our class went to school camp. It was on an island off the coast. It seemed so adventurous to spend the night sleeping in a tent miles from anywhere. Sarah was more sensible than I was and often kept me from getting into trouble with the narrow-minded Mrs Dodd, our teacher. Once I thought it'd be a good idea to go swimming in the sea just before sunrise. I'd forgotten that Mrs Dodd would be coming round to wake us up and would see immediately if anyone wasn't in bed. Sarah covered for me, though, and put a pillow under the sheets so Mrs Dodd would think I was there. We actually got away with it, too! Great times.

Part 5 of Paper 1 is a text with six multiple-choice questions, where you have to choose the answer to a question or finish a sentence from four given alternatives. You should read the text and the questions carefully, because this part of the exam tests detailed understanding. It is helpful to underline the words in the text which contain the answers to the questions.

4 Read the first paragraph more carefully and answer question 1. Then look at the explanation below – were you right?

1 What does the writer say about her father in the first paragraph?

   A He was very proud of his garage.
   B He could get angry if you annoyed him.
   C He disliked his neighbours.
   D He was quite a selfish person.

> The answer is B. – *Anyone silly enough to park in front of the driveway should beware. You didn't want to get on the wrong side of my dad, believe me.*
>
> A, C and D are all likely, but there is nothing in the text which says this.

Now read the notes and answer questions 2–4.

> There will often be a question which asks you what the writer is 'suggesting' or 'implying'. This is called an inference question and you have to decide from various clues in the text what the writer means to say.

2 In the second paragraph, what does the writer suggest about her family?

   A There was a large age difference between the girls and Tom.
   B They were afraid their mother would tell their father about the fights.
   C Some members of the family got on with each other better than others.
   D They had only limited living space while they were growing up.

> Sometimes a 'reference' question is included, which tests your understanding of words such as *it* and *this*. You must read the lines before and after the word carefully before deciding what it is referring to.

3 What does 'It' refer to in line 30?

   A the supermarket
   B the centre of town
   C the weekly market
   D the bus

> There is often an item of vocabulary such as a word or phrase which is unusual or idiomatic, or one that is used by the writer in a special way. You should work out the meaning by looking at the context around the word or phrase itself.

4 What does 'laden down with' mean in line 32?

   A carrying
   B having bought
   C having chosen
   D borrowing

Now do the next two questions, underlining the word or phrase in the text which gives you the answer.

5 What does the writer say about her friend Sarah in the fourth paragraph?

   A She lived in a nicer house than the writer did.
   B She was a very easy-going person.
   C She and the writer sometimes had arguments.
   D She had the same ambitions as the writer.

6 What happened when the writer went swimming in the sea one morning?

   A Sarah told the teacher what had happened.
   B The writer's absence went unnoticed.
   C Mrs Dodd didn't come into the tent that morning.
   D The writer managed to get back to bed in time.

5 In pairs, discuss the following questions.

   a What do you think about the writer's childhood? Was it similar to yours? Why? / Why not?
   b Do you think children should help their parents with housework? Why? / Why not?
   c How much time do you spend at home rather than doing activities outside the home?
   d Do you think that children grow up too quickly nowadays? Why? / Why not?

used to and *would*

1 **Read examples a–c and then match them with uses 1–3.**

   a The three of us used to have terrible fights. (*used to* + verb)

   b Sometimes we would go out and play. (*would* + verb)

   c We were used to doing them. (*be/get used to* + *-ing* verb)

   1 To talk about something in the past that doesn't happen now. This could be something permanent.

   2 To mean 'to be/get accustomed to'.

   3 To talk about a repeated action in the past which doesn't happen now. Note that the action must be repeated and this form is normally used for narrative.

   Look at the following sentences and decide what the difference is between them.

   I'm used to living away from home.
   I'm getting used to living away from home.

   > ### Corpus spot
   >
   > The *Cambridge Learner Corpus* shows that exam candidates often make mistakes with *used to* and *would*.
   >
   > I **used to** live in London.
   > NOT I ~~use~~ to live in London.

2 **Correct the following sentences, if necessary.**

   a Great Britain would have a large manufacturing industry.

   b People used to work very long hours in the past.

   c People are now used to working harder for less money.

   d It takes a long time to get used to do a new job.

   e My grandmother was used to work very long hours when she was a girl.

   f When I worked for the BBC, I would often have to travel abroad.

   g When I was a child, I use to go to the zoo with my parents.

G → page 169

3 **Discuss the following situations using *would*, *used to*, *get used to* or *be used to*.**

   a What did you used to do in the holidays when you were a child?

   b Have you ever had any problems getting used to doing something?

   c What did you used to do in the past that you don't do now?

   d What kind of food are you used to eating?

Vocabulary

Collocations

4 **Look at this example from 8.1.**

   *She was good at **keeping secrets**.*

   Choose the correct collocation in a–g.

   a My father's new car can *have / do* 200 kph.

   b I don't like people who *break / keep* their promises.

   c We're *doing / having* a holiday in South Africa this year.

   d Max *made / took* a fortune from computer software.

   e The music from the festival *made / kept* me awake for ages last night.

   f This ice cream *gets / tastes* really good.

   g Lily *spends / keeps* too much time at her friend's house.

Phrasal verbs with *get*

5 **In the text in 8.1 the writer says, 'We got away with it, too.' Complete the sentences using the phrases in the box.**

   > the flu   washing the floor   the tennis team   some work
   > the angry neighbour   not paying

   a The two boys got away from .... as quickly as they could.

   b Susie needs to get down to .... because she has exams soon.

   c Tom got out of .... , which put him in a good mood.

   d I'm just getting over .... after being in bed for a week.

   e He was delighted when he got into .... at the weekend.

   f You won't get away with .... taxes.

6 In pairs, look at a–f in 5 again and decide what each phrasal verb means. Then talk about the following questions.

   a What sort of things do you try to get away with not doing?
   b Do you need to get down to some work soon?
   c Have you ever had a bad dose of flu? How long did it take you to get over it?
   d Have you ever got into a sports team?

Word formation

7 For questions 1–8, read the text below. Use the word given in capitals at the end of some of the lines to form a word that fits in the gap in the same line.

HOW YOUR FRIENDS AND THEIR FRIENDS CAN AFFECT YOUR MOOD

Recent research shows that our moods are more **(0)** _STRONGLY_ influenced	**STRONG**
by friends than we tend to think. Not only that, but the moods of friends	
of friends affect us too – even up to three degrees of **(1)** .... Indeed, it is	**SEPARATE**
becoming clear that a whole range of things are transmitted through **(2)**	**SOCIETY**
networks of friends in ways that are not entirely understood, from **(3)**	**HAPPY**
to a **(4)** .... for certain types of music or to what you watch on TV.	**PREFER**

Your **(5)** .... to be happy increases with the number of happy friends you	**ABLE**
have and if a good friend who lives within a couple of kilometres of you suddenly	
becomes happy, that increases the chances of you becoming happy by more	
than 60 per cent.	

Psychologists have shown that people **(6)** .... copy the facial expressions,	**CONSCIOUS**
manner of speech, body language and general **(7)** .... of people around them,	**BEHAVE**
often with **(8)** .... speed and accuracy, despite being unaware they are doing	**REMARK**
it. This causes them to actually experience the emotions associated with what	
they are copying.	

Speaking

8 How important are your friends to you? Discuss the following questions with a partner.

   a Do you think you make friends easily? Why? / Why not?
   b How long have you known your best friend?
   c Have you ever fallen out with a friend?
   d What is the most important quality to you in a friend?
   e Do you sometimes get on with your friends better than with your family? Why? / Why not?
   f Do you usually do the same things as your friends? Why? / Why not?
   g Do you copy your friends' clothes or manner of speech?

Writing folder 4

Paper 2 Part 1 Essays

Look back at Writing folder 2 on pages 32–33, which focused mainly on content and language. This Writing folder looks at planning and organising your ideas.

1 Read the following exam question and then look at the essay plan which follows.

In your English class you have been talking about jobs and salaries. Now your teacher has asked you to write an essay.

Write an essay using all the notes and give reasons for your point of view.

> Compared to people in other jobs, sportspeople are paid too much for what they do.
> Do you agree?
>
> **Notes**
> Write about:
>
> 1. which jobs are important in society
> 2. why some sportspeople are paid a lot of money
> 3. .... (your own idea)

2 Put paragraphs A–E in order so they follow the essay plan.

A

On the other hand, a sportsperson's career does not last long, so the high salary is only for a limited period of time. Furthermore, injury can cut short a career. Therefore it is reasonable that sportspeople receive substantial earnings.

Essay plan

Paragraph 1
– a general introduction

Paragraph 2
– jobs that are important

Paragraph 3
– sportspeople's salaries

Paragraph 4
– sport's importance today

Paragraph 5
– a conclusion

B

First of all, it is true that playing sport for a living is not essential to society. Nurses do an essential job but they earn very little compared to many sportspeople. Also, a football player, for example, will only be playing for a few hours a day while a nurse could work at least twelve hours a day.

C

To sum up, sportspeople are highly paid but they often deserve the money. The real issue is that people in more important jobs are paid too little.

D

The topic of sportspeople's earnings often causes a great deal of discussion, especially in the media. Many people have strong feelings on the subject, and so do I.

E

In addition, sport has a central place in modern society, giving pleasure to many people. The fact that it is such a popular form of entertainment means that high salaries can perhaps be justified.

3 Look at these examples from the essay. The adjectives used show good language range and would impress an examiner. Suggest an alternative adjective for each phrase.

substantial earnings	an essential job
the real issue	strong feelings
a central place	

4 Sort the linkers in the box into these three types. The examples given come from the essay in 2.

Addition	Contrast	Result
In addition	On the other hand	Therefore

as a result	as well as	at the same time
consequently	furthermore	in contrast
nevertheless		

Assessment focus

A well-organised answer to Part 1 will score a high mark for **organisation**, where up to five marks are available. The essay should contain an introduction and a conclusion, and be suitably paragraphed and linked.

5 Read this exam question and add your ideas to the diagram opposite.

In your English class you have been talking about the benefits of regular exercise. Now your teacher has asked you to write an essay.

Write an essay using all the notes and give reasons for your point of view.

Should people who are studying or working hard take regular exercise?

Notes
Write about:

1. lifestyle
2. health benefits
3. .... (your own idea)

6 Using some of these ideas, write your essay in 140–190 words. Make sure you use appropriate linkers (see 4).

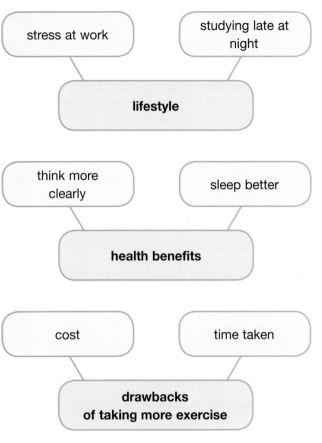

EXAM ADVICE

Content
- Focus on the three main ideas.
- Give examples from your personal experience.

Communicative achievement
- Make sure your argument is easy to follow.
- Write in a fairly formal style.

Organisation
- Make a plan before you start writing.
- Outline the main ideas in an introduction.
- Organise your essay in paragraphs.

Language
- Rephrase key language in your own words where possible.
- Use adjective–noun collocations to show your range of vocabulary.
- Include complex clauses and a variety of other structures.

The hard sell

Modals 2: Speculation and deduction

1 Look at the advert opposite. What do you think it is selling? Discuss your ideas with a partner, using some of these openers.

Well, it could be advertising …
Or perhaps it might be for …

I think it must be a …
It can't be for … because …

Look at page 85 to find out if you guessed correctly.

2 The modal verbs in the first pair of examples above indicate that the speaker is unsure about something. It is also possible to use *may*, though less common. However, *can* is not used in this way.

Is the speaker unsure in the second pair of examples? Which words tell you?

Now look at this example. Is the speaker unsure?

It couldn't possibly be an advert for chocolate.

Does the meaning change if the full stop is replaced by a question mark? Say the sentence and the question aloud to your partner. The question would sound better with extra words at the end. Which words?

G → page 170

3 Now read the text about a TV advert and underline examples of the modals used in 1.

4 Explain the meaning of these words from the text.

   a voice-over
   b jingle
   c celebrity
   d verdict
   e brand
   f cunning

Why is the title of Bob's article appropriate?

The best ad missed the boat at Cannes

This is the title of an article by Bob Garfield, an American expert on advertising. He was writing about the International Advertising Film Festival, which takes place some time after the main film festival in Cannes.

For Bob, the best ad of the year was from Delvico Bates, Barcelona, for *Esencial* hand cream. The ad shows a woman riding her bike, which has a very squeaky chain. The woman gets off the bike, opens her jar of *Esencial* and rubs some of the cream onto the chain. Then she rides away – but the squeak remains. Why? Because, as the voice-over says, '*Esencial* moisturises, but it has no grease.'

Why is this ad so good? It can't be for its special effects, because there aren't any. Might it be the music? No, there isn't even a jingle. Could it be that the woman is a celebrity? No. Bob's verdict: 'It's a vivid demonstration of brand non-attributes. Inspired. Cunning. Brilliant.' In other words, by showing failure in a different context, the quality of the product is reinforced – grease is good for bike chains, but not for the skin.

So surely this ad must have won at Cannes? No. The simple truth is that it couldn't win, because the agency failed to enter it in time for the festival deadline!

5 In the final paragraph, it says *So surely this ad must have won at Cannes?* Here, the modal is referring to a past action. Say whether the speaker is sure or unsure in sentences a–c below.

a Their latest TV commercial must have cost a fortune to produce.

b There's one commercial showing a man sitting in an armchair on a mountain peak. That couldn't have actually happened – it must be done by special effects.

c Advertising has come a long way in the last forty years. Audiences of the 1960s might have been totally overwhelmed by an action-packed commercial of today!

G → page 170

6 Read this text and think of the word which best fits each gap. Use only one word in each gap. There is an example at the beginning (0).

DAVID OGILVY
THE KING OF MADISON AVENUE

David Ogilvy, originally from Scotland, has often **(0)** _BEEN_ called 'The Father of Advertising'. He believed that you should see **(1)** .... single aim or idea through with passion and 'Go the whole hog!' A larger **(2)** .... life figure, he showed endless enthusiasm for the things that really interested him.

The role he played best, and indeed defined, was that **(3)** .... the British gentleman in New York. When he set **(4)** .... the advertising agency Ogilvy and Mather there in 1948, he drove a Rolls-Royce, wore a full-length cape and used to attend parties in a Scottish kilt, **(5)** .... sure to pause at the top of the stairs to give fellow guests 'the full effect'.

Starting from a two-room office, Ogilvy hired bright young staff and developed the advertising agency into a huge empire, transforming **(6)** .... into the most famous ad man in the world in the process. He was a complete workaholic and a rather moral individual, who walked away from cigarette advertising long before his competitors. He campaigned **(7)** .... billboards, which in his view made the world look ugly, and **(8)** .... never accept any marketing strategy that deceived the public. He told copywriters to just 'tell the truth, and make the truth interesting'.

Vocabulary
Collocations

7 Look at the adjectives below. Which ones collocate with each of the nouns on the right? List the phrases that are possible, for example *huge variety*. Use some in the role play in 8.

huge	variety
high	message
low	idea
deep	budget
shallow	market
narrow	character
wide	picture
	view
	voice

8 Role play: XK trainers. Get into small groups and read your instructions (A or B). Then spend a few minutes listing useful vocabulary, using a dictionary if necessary. When groups A and B are both ready, have a face-to-face discussion.

Metallic mesh upper for strength and breathability.

Inflatable cushioning to fit perfectly around foot.

Self tying, no need for laces.

Shock absorbing gel pumped into undersole to absorb impact.

Group A: Advertising agency
A leading manufacturer of sports shoes, XK, is about to launch their new trainer. Your agency hopes to get the contract for the TV commercial and you need to prepare your ideas. As there is a big budget for this, you should use famous people and exotic locations! Prepare to meet XK.

Group B turn to page 85.

9.2

Listening

1 Briefly describe a TV commercial to your partner, using some of the expressions below. Explain your feelings about it.

There's one commercial that is for …
The thing I really like about it is …
What I can't stand is …

2 **1 10** You are going to hear two people talking about some TV commercials. In Part 1, which of these aspects are mentioned by the speakers? Tick the ones you hear.

a a puzzling beginning
b a storyline with flashbacks
c a dramatic ending
d a setting that is out of the ordinary
e a surprising location
f a well-known personality
g a powerful slogan
h an extravagant production

3 **1 11** Listen to Part 2, where one particular advert is discussed. Answer the questions below by writing W for woman or M for man in the boxes.

1 Who didn't like the advert?	**1**
2 Who was surprised by part of the advert?	**2**
3 Who agrees that Ray was an effective character?	**3**
4 Who liked the music in the advert?	**4**

Exam spot

In Paper 3 Part 4, you have to answer seven multiple-choice questions about an interview or conversation between two speakers. The questions may focus on people's feelings or opinions.

4 Answer this practice question as you listen to Part 2 again.

What do the speakers agree is important in a successful advert?
A a strong storyline that people will find entertaining
B attractive characters that people will identify with
C an unpredictable element that will be memorable

5 **1 12** You will hear part of an interview with a man called Don Cooper, who makes TV commercials. For questions 1–4, choose the best answer (A, B or C).

1 According to Don, what is the key factor when making a TV commercial?
  A the type of location
  B the choice of actors
  C the depth of storyline

2 When developing the script, Don believes it is vital to
  A time the overall message.
  B feature the product by name.
  C use a lot of beautiful language.

3 According to Don, if the same advertising company produces several commercials for a product,
  A it could create a sense of boredom with the brand.
  B it may attract new clients with similar advertising needs.
  C it can be beneficial to include a familiar element in the series.

4 Before booking air time for a TV commercial, Don recommends
  A targeting a product to a suitable channel.
  B finding out accurate viewing figures.
  C giving priority to cost over timing.

G rammar extra

Order of adjectives

The woman talks about a *graceful silver vehicle*. Which of the two adjectives is used to give an opinion? Can the order of these adjectives be changed?

Underline the adjectives used in slogans a–d and then identify them according to the types below. What is the rule for opinion adjectives?

a The classic British motorbike
b The sensational new album from Jack Johnson
c Our popular full-length navy cotton nightshirt
d Bite-sized biscuits with a delicious creamy filling

OPINION
DESCRIPTION: SIZE SHAPE AGE COLOUR NATIONALITY MATERIAL

Descriptive adjectives are usually in the order above. It is quite unusual to have four adjectives in a row (as in example c). More commonly, any additional descriptive information is given in a separate phrase (as in example d).

Decide whether the following adjectives are in the correct order. Reorder them where necessary.

a a black huge dog
b an awful old woollen coat
c the Italian famous singer
d a red large apple
e an elaborate wooden square box
f a sophisticated new novel by a Scottish tremendous author

Vocabulary

Expressions for discussing ideas

6 There are a number of verbs in English that may signal an opinion or idea. Look at this example from the recording.

*I **reckon** I know pretty much what the magic ingredients are.*

In British English, *I reckon* is informal in register and would not be used in formal speech or writing. Which of these verbs are also informal?

admit   bet   doubt   expect   guess
suggest   suppose   stress

7 Put the phrases below into these groups. You heard some of them in the recordings. Use them in the next Speaking section.

Introducing an idea or opinion
Giving a different point of view
Adding to an idea

I suppose	Not only that, but
On the other hand	True enough, though
It seems to me that	What's more

Speaking

8 Look at the four photographs. Identify what product each billboard is advertising and discuss how effective it is at selling the product.

- Spend some time looking at the photographs and note down useful vocabulary for each one.
- Think about how to structure the discussion so that you and your partner have equal opportunities to take part. Use some of the phrases from Unit 7 on page 51 to achieve this.
- Try to speak together for about two minutes.

9 Now decide together which two adverts are the most effective and why. Be ready to justify your choice to the class.

10 Outline the possible advantages and disadvantages of outdoor advertising, using modal verbs from 9.1 and some of the words and phrases in exercises 6 and 7.

Well, I suppose it could be cheaper than advertising a product on TV. Though on the other hand …

Exam folder 5

Paper 3 Part 2 Sentence completion

In this part of the Listening paper you will hear a monologue, such as a talk or a lecture. The task is to complete a set of sentences. You have 45 seconds to read the questions for this part. Use the time before the recording starts to predict what you might hear, underlining key words and phrases.

1   Look at these examples of Part 2 sentences and find words and phrases in the recording script below that relate to the underlined words and phrases. Can you predict what the missing words are?

As an example of making a scientific claim, the speaker talks about an advertisement for **1** ....

The most important message in the advertisement for the car is to do with **2** ....

When targeting teenagers in advertisements, products are often linked to **3** .... which others would find unacceptable.

Advertisements aimed at parents may include young children or **4** .... and

.... , as they connect with their role as carers.

Recording script

1 To support the suggestion that one product is better than its competitors, the existence of actual proof is often mentioned. In one case, involving the promotion of .... , reference was made to an unnamed university research project, which analysed shades of white.

2 It must be true that there are more advertisements focusing on our love of driving than on anything else. While the messages of freedom and mobility are always important, it is above all the aspect of .... that is stressed in this particular one. We are supposed to believe that this car will take us to new places in society and change our role for ever.

3 Advertisers adopt different strategies as far as young people between the ages of 15 and 19 are concerned. For this population, it is not about conforming but about the complete opposite of that. Indeed, products for this age group are frequently connected with .... , the kind that older people such as parents might well disapprove of.

4 Turning to mothers and fathers as consumers, advertisements targeting these people often reinforce the experience of bringing up a family. An advert that links its product to young children or even, interestingly enough, to .... , will probably succeed because these images appeal directly to motherly or, perhaps less commonly, fatherly instincts!

2   **1 13** Now listen to the recording and write one or two words in gaps 1–4.

3   Transfer your answers to this sample answer sheet. Be careful with spelling.

Part 2 (Remember to write in CAPITAL LETTERS or numbers)		Do not write below here
9		9 1 0 u
10		10 1 0 u
11		11 1 0 u
12		12 1 0 u
13		13 1 0 u

4 Read this advice before you do the exam task in 5.

5 **1 14** You will hear part of a talk about advertising jingles. For questions 1–10, complete the sentences with a word or short phrase.

THE COMMERCIAL JINGLE

One example of the contents of a basic jingle is a (**1**) ....

The first modern jingle in 1926 advertised a (**2**) ....

The rules on radio advertising in the 1930s forbade the use of (**3**) .... of goods during peak listening periods.

The programme about a family began with a jingle for a (**4**) .... , which was the first of its kind in the USA.

In the 1950s, jingles were often created by (**5**) ....

When the jingle became less popular, advertisers started to use (**6**) ....

From the late 1980s, commercials have had to reflect a complete (**7**) ....

Payments from advertisers have covered earnings lost due to (**8**) .... of music.

According to some psychologists, music that has a (**9**) .... to the listener is easier to remember.

An 'ear worm' is up to (**10**) .... long.

We will we will rock you   We will we will rock you!!

I can't get this tune out of my head!

The final frontier

Speaking

1 The pictures show people in imaginary future situations away from the Earth. Compare the people and say whether you think these situations could happen in the future.

Reading

2 Skim the article on space travel for its general meaning, ignoring the missing sentences. Why do NASA and the SFF have different priorities?

CHEAP ACCESS TO SPACE

'Cheap' is an important word in space technology nowadays and re-usable rockets will be a key way of controlling costs. They will deliver things, bring stuff back to Earth and then go up again, perhaps with machinery for a space factory, or even carrying tourists. In the future, these space vehicles will be orbiting the Earth as efficiently as air freight carriers. There could be a billion-dollar market in taking packages from one side of the planet to the other in an hour.

NASA, the government-owned space program, once aimed to develop a re-usable rocket. **1** ⬚ It plans to launch a manned expedition to an asteroid by 2025 and since this will require different technology, it is more likely that people outside the NASA program will develop re-usable rocket design.

Rick Tumlinson, co-founder of the Space Frontier Foundation (SFF), has spent the past two decades pushing for human exploration and settlement of the solar system. *Space News* magazine described him as one of the 100 most influential people in the space industry. Tumlinson has always maintained that businesses should get involved, and views NASA as a bit of a dinosaur. **2** ⬚ '25 years after the Wright brothers flew a plane for the first time, people could buy a commercial plane ticket, but 25 years after landing on the Moon, we sat around watching old astronauts on TV talking about the good old days.'

Using his high profile, Tumlinson is going to try to prove a point. Space is our destiny, he says, so why not get on with it? He and his colleagues encourage any business that shares this aim. **3** ⬚ For example, in December 2010, SpaceX (Space Exploration Technologies) launched their re-usable space capsule *Dragon*. After circling the planet twice, it returned with parachutes, landing as planned in the Pacific Ocean. Tumlinson immediately congratulated the company on successfully completing the world's first commercial orbital space flight and recovery, saying, 'This flight will go down in history as a turning point for the opening of space to regular people.'

While it was a significant technical achievement for SpaceX as a company, the flight was also highly significant for the American taxpayer. With the retirement of the Space Shuttle, the United States has an urgent need for commercial manned space flight. Until that happens, NASA will be totally dependent on the Russian Soyuz to carry astronauts to and from the International Space Station, at a price of over $50 million per seat. **4** ⬚ They submitted their proposal to NASA just days after *Dragon* returned to Earth.

At one point, the SFF ran a survey on the internet called 'Cheap Access to Space', where it asked American taxpayers for their opinions on the US space program and future priorities for space transportation. Their own view has always been that it is impossible for NASA to offer an 'open frontier'. NASA is 'elitist and exclusive', whereas the SFF believes in opportunities for everyone: 'a future of endlessly expanding new choices'. The SFF wants to see 'irreversible human settlement' in space as soon as possible and maintains that this is only going to happen through free enterprise. It is inappropriate for government-sponsored astronauts to be constructing buildings and driving trucks. **5** ⬚ SpaceX's achievements to date demonstrate a willingness to make this happen.

Once space transportation becomes affordable, mass space travel will be possible. Many people believe that by 2025 space tourism will have become a viable industry. However, US government officials don't really see a future for space tourism. **6** ⬚ David Ashford, Managing Director of the British company Bristol Spaceplanes Limited, once said that space tourism would begin ten years after people stopped laughing at the concept. People have already stopped laughing.

3 Six sentences have been removed from the article. Choose from the sentences A–G the one which fits each gap. There is one extra sentence, which you do not need to use.

Work through the text, using the underlined phrases in sentence A to help you decide whether it fits in any of the gaps. Discuss your ideas with a partner.

Then underline the words and phrases in sentences B–G that link to the text and decide on your answers.

A   At the same time, the SFF accepts that NASA's missions could bring other scientific benefits.

B   More than one such firm has developed impressive solutions for getting into space and back cheaply.

C   Commercial activity such as this is what the private sector should be doing.

D   However, the USA's priorities have changed in the 21st century.

E   Here again, private companies may well prove them wrong in the very near future.

F   SpaceX is prepared to meet this need – and at less than half the cost.

G   In an early article he wrote about the government-owned space program, he made the following observation.

Vocabulary

Word formation

4 Go through the text again to find words related to a–j (i and j are in sentences A–G). An example is given. Which word contains both a prefix and a suffix?

a use   *re-usable*   f appropriate
b settle   g willing
c commerce   h afford
d achieve   i science
e end   j impress

5 The use of the negative prefixes *il-*, *im-*, *in-* and *ir-* depends on the first letter of the word they join, as in *inappropriate*. Look back at Exam folder 2 for guidance. Add a prefix to form negative adjectives in a–f.

a legal   d moral
b experienced   e regular
c responsible   f patient

6 Use four of the negative adjectives to complete a–d.

a Someone who wants something to happen as soon as possible is ....

b A young adult who has no knowledge of working life is ....

c Driving a car without a licence is ....

d Friends who only see each other occasionally meet at .... intervals.

Speaking

7 Discuss these questions, using some of the words from this unit.

a Do you think you will ever take a holiday in space? Why? / Why not?

b What benefits and drawbacks might the commercial development of space bring?

c Should governments spend tax-payers' money on space travel?

d Why are there so many satellites orbiting the Earth? Will this technology become more important, in your view?

10.2

Review of future tenses

1 Look at sentences a–e from the article on space and identify the future forms listed 1–4 below. What other tense is used in sentences f and g to refer to the future?

1 *going to* future
2 future simple
3 future continuous
4 future perfect

a They will deliver things, bring stuff back to Earth and then go up again.
b This is only going to happen through free enterprise.
c In the future, these space vehicles will be orbiting the Earth as efficiently as air freight carriers.
d Many people believe that by 2025 space tourism will have become a viable industry.
e Tumlinson is going to try to prove a point.
f It plans to launch a manned expedition to an asteroid by 2025.
g However, this situation is due to change.

2 Which of the sentences a–g mention the following?

1 a prediction about the future
2 a planned event that is expected to happen soon
3 an event that has not yet happened but will happen within a certain period of time
4 an intention to do something

3 How are predictions about the future expressed in these two examples?

a Private companies may well prove them wrong.
b There could be a billion-dollar market in taking packages from one side of the planet to the other in an hour.

4 Why is *would* used in this example instead of *will*?

David Ashford once said that space tourism would begin ten years after people stopped laughing at the concept.

G → page 170

5 Choose the correct option in italics in these sentences and explain why it is correct.

a Within the next twenty years, the cost of space travel *will be falling / will fall* dramatically.
b In the near future, it's likely that adventure holidays *won't be / aren't going to be* limited to remote places on Earth.
c People *will / may* one day have the opportunity to go to distant planets, but first we need to discover a way of travelling faster than the speed of light.
d Our 7-day trip is due to depart on 1st December, 2025 and *will carry / will have carried* you 100 km into space.
e I've decided I *am going to book / will book* a trip into space as soon as I can afford it.
f The Americans always said they *would fly / will fly* to Mars.
g Sooner or later people *will live / will be living* in space.
h The International Space Station *will have been / will be* manned for 14 years in November.

6 What will we wear in the future? Read these exam candidates' ideas and complete the summary, using the future perfect of the verbs in the box. You may need to use the passive form. One verb isn't needed.

A new technology will change fabrics so they will change their colour during the day. People will be even more concerned with pollution and harmful UV rays, so their clothes will have built-in protective filters to help them keep healthy.

You may think that people will wear silver clothes like in science-fiction movies but I think everyone will wear very colourful balloons. They will use a special gas inside the balloons to make them fly.

| become fill include manage rise take |

One person predicts that pollution
(1) .... to a dangerous level, but optimistically suggests that manufacturers
(2) .... some form of protection against this in their clothes. The other writes about people flying in their clothes, explaining that these 'balloons' (3) .... with gas to lift them off the ground. Neither feels that clothes (4) .... a uniform colour such as the silver of so many futuristic films. In fact, one person believes that a development in technology (5) .... place to create materials that can change colour while they are being worn.

What are your own ideas about future clothes?

Listening

7 🔵**1 15** You are going to hear three people talking about the future. Decide whether each speaker has a positive or a negative view of what life for human beings might be like.

Speaker 1 ....
Speaker 2 ....
Speaker 3 ....

Which speaker is closest to your own ideas about the future? Why?

Vocabulary

Phrases with *at*

8 Speaker 2 used the preposition *at* in three different ways:

I'm reading one of his sci-fi ones at the moment.
They live for at least three hundred years.
There will always be some country at war with another.

Choose the correct phrase for each of these sentences and explain the meaning of the incorrect options.

1 Hurry up, we'll be locked inside the building unless we leave ....
A at first   **B** at once   **C** at last

2 Jordi is looking forward to the move but, ... , I know he'll miss his friends here.
A at least   **B** at present   **C** at the same time

3 For the first time in ten years, this war-torn country is now .... , thanks to the skills of the negotiators on both sides.
A at peace   **B** at war   **C** at rest

4 Journalists often get scientific facts slightly wrong, but this article is inaccurate reporting ....
A at his laziest   **B** at its worst   **C** at their best

Notice, as in the last example, that *at* is commonly used with a pronoun and a superlative.

Writing folder 5

Paper 2 Part 2 Articles

1 Look at these titles of articles about the future. Which article would you most like to read? Why?

2 Match the titles to the opening paragraphs A–D. Do all four paragraphs fit their titles well? Why? / Why not?

Aliens are coming ...

3 – 2 – 1 Lift off!

Is anybody there?

A lifelong ambition

A

Imagine being launched in a rocket towards that final frontier. Strapped into your seat in a shiny silver capsule, you feel the power of the engines as they carry you up and away. And soon you are orbiting the Earth, covering vast distances and looking down on the planet you call home.

C

Our planet is going to be invaded – not by little green men but by a revolutionary new form of transport! Next week sees the launch of a worldwide advertising campaign, for a vehicle that could completely change our life on Earth.

B

I want to go up into space. I think it may be possible for ordinary people to go up into space soon. I read something about space travel. I want to be one of the first to go. I hope I can go up into space.

D

On some nights, I open my window and watch the stars. It's a nice thing to do. Sometimes I stay there for ages, wondering what the universe holds. It makes me feel small. Space is a big place. There are a lot of galaxies apart from our own – so there must be other life?

3 Look again at paragraph D. How could it be improved? Choose words and phrases from the pairs below to replace the words underlined. In each pair, both a and b fit the text correctly, so the final choice is up to you!

> On some nights, I open my window and <u>watch</u> the stars. It's a <u>nice</u> thing to do. Sometimes I stay there for ages, wondering what the universe holds. It makes me feel <u>small</u>. Space is a <u>big</u> place. There are <u>a lot of</u> galaxies apart from our own – so there must be other life?

a	b
stare at	gaze at
wonderful	brilliant
unimportant	humble
vast	huge
so many	an enormous number of

What parts of speech are the words in a–d below? Insert all these words into paragraph D where they fit best.

a cloudless   beautiful   twinkling
b forms of
c very   such
d truly   surely

Read through the paragraph once more. Could any sentences be joined together? Write out a final version.

4 Paragraph B is a poor attempt at an opening paragraph. Why? Rewrite it, making the following improvements, along with any others of your own.

- Order the ideas more clearly.
- Join any short sentences together.
- Include a first sentence that links back to the title.
- Replace any repeated words, e.g. *want, wish, hope.*
- Use a variety of sentence openers.
- Add suitable words to describe and emphasise.

Assessment focus

An article is not an essay. It is written for a wider audience and will appear in a certain type of magazine or on a website. Making your article interesting to read will hold the reader's attention and you will score a higher mark in the exam for **communicative achievement**.

5 Now look at this exam question.

You see this notice in an in-flight magazine and decide to enter the competition.

> **GALAXY TRAVEL COMPETITION**
>
> **What forms of transport will we be using in 50 years' time?**
>
> **Where will we take our holidays?**
>
> Write us an article, giving us your views on both of these questions. Science fiction writer John T. Price will choose the most original article, which will receive a prize of $1,000 and be published in our magazine next year.

Write your article in 140–190 words.

6 Answer these questions about the writing task.

a Which **two** topics do you need to write about?
b What is meant by 'forms'?
c Should the style be serious or lively?
d How many paragraphs should you write?

7 Read the Exam advice below and look back over Units 9 and 10 for relevant vocabulary and grammar. Then write your article in 140–190 words. Don't be afraid to use your imagination!

EXAM ADVICE

Content
- Make sure the reader is fully informed.

Communicative achievement
- Make your writing interesting to read.
- Write in a consistent style throughout.

Organisation
- Include an eye-catching title.
- Link the opening paragraph to the title.

Language
- Start your sentences in different ways.
- Avoid repeating the same word or phrase.

Like mother, like daughter

Speaking

1 Look at these photos of famous people and their children. Do you think the children resemble their mother or father? What similarities or differences can you see?

> ### Exam spot
>
> In Paper 4 Part 1, the examiner will ask you to give some personal information about yourself. The questions could be about where you come from, your family, your studies or work, your hobbies or your future plans.

2 With a partner try to find out as much as you can about each other. When you ask about each other's family, also ask these questions:

Who do you most look like in your family? Do you sound like anyone in the family when you answer the telephone? Who do you take after in character?

For extra practice take it in turns to think of a famous person but don't tell your partner who it is. Your partner has to ask you personal questions to try to find out your identity. Try not to make it too easy!

> ### Exam spot
>
> Remember that an option often contains the same vocabulary you hear in the recording, and although it might be true, doesn't actually answer the question. Read through the questions very carefully before you listen. You will have one minute to do this.

Listening

3 **1 16** You will hear an interview with the daughter of a Hollywood film star. For questions 1–7, choose the best answer (A, B or C).

1 For her 14th birthday, Hannah
 A took some friends to see a Harrison Ford film at the cinema.
 B went to watch the making of a film.
 C was given whatever she wanted.

2 How did Hannah's mother feel when Hannah said she wanted to be an actress?
 A She wasn't keen on her doing it.
 B She wasn't discouraging.
 C She didn't think she was serious about it.

3 What does Hannah say about the comparison with her mother?
 A They have the same shaped eyes.
 B They are both tall.
 C Their noses are similar.

4 Hannah and her mother both think that
 A they look identical.
 B they look a bit alike.
 C people are completely wrong.

5 How did Hannah feel about her mother's attitude to acting?
   A She was a bit upset.
   B She was angry.
   C She understood.

6 Why was Hannah encouraged to train to be an accountant?
   A Her mother had had a bad experience with money.
   B Hannah needed to learn the importance of saving.
   C Her mother considered it a useful profession.

7 What does Hannah say about her mother's voice?
   A She sounds very demanding.
   B She sounds slightly foreign.
   C She sounds like her daughter.

4 **Now listen to the interview again. What adjective or adjectives does Hannah use to describe:**

   a her childhood in Hollywood?
   b how her mother had felt when she first arrived in Hollywood?
   c part of her nose?
   d her mother talking about acting?
   e the quality they both possess?
   f her mother's attitude to money?
   g her mother's voice?

Speaking

5 **Find out who in your class has the same number of brothers and sisters as you, then form the following groups, where each person in the group is:**

- an only child
- the youngest of two or more children
- the oldest of two or more children
- the middle child
- part of large family (five or more children)

Talk to the others in your group about what your family is like, how you feel about the size of your family and what effect, if any, it has had on you. Talk about your place in the family, and whether it's best to be the eldest, youngest, only one, middle child and so on.

6 **Are there any special characteristics that run in your family? Is there anything you all like/dislike? Think about things such as: hair colour, height, occupation, the possibility of having twins, the need for glasses, etc.**

G rammar extra

You've heard already the expression *to look like* + a noun phrase, which means *to resemble* or *to take after physically*.
EXAMPLE: *She looks like her mother.*
Now look at these two questions.
A What's he/she like?   **B** What does he/she like?
Decide which of the words below can be used to answer the questions.

tall   swimming   friendly   hamburgers   watching TV
photography   amusing

11.2

Vocabulary

Adjectives describing personality

1 Use one of the adjectives in the box to answer questions a–n.

> aggressive bad-tempered bossy
> cheerful competitive impatient
> jealous lazy loyal optimistic
> stubborn unpopular
> unreliable witty

How do you describe a person who:
a uses words in a clever and funny way?
b is usually happy?
c always believes good things will happen?
d always wants what you have?
e always tells you what to do?
f is not liked by other people?
g never turns up on time?
h refuses to change their plans or ideas?
i is always in a hurry to get things done?
j becomes angry or annoyed easily?
k behaves in an angry and violent way towards others?
l wants to be more successful than others?
m will always support you even when others don't?
n never wants to do any work?

2 Which of the adjectives above are positive, and which are negative? What are their opposites? Remember you can extend your vocabulary by thinking of adjectives with opposite meanings. Use a negative prefix if necessary.

In pairs, say which of the adjectives in 1 you would use to describe:

a yourself
b your colleagues
c your brothers/sisters
d your neighbours
e your best friend
f your worst enemy

Phrasal verbs and expressions with *take*

3 In the interview Hannah talks about her grandparents not wanting her mother to 'take up acting'. Complete these sentences using one of the words or phrases in the box.

> account of after charge for granted
> off out seriously turns

a I took .... $300 from the bank yesterday.
b No one ever seems to take me .... – they always think I'm joking.
c My husband and I always take .... loading the dishwasher.
d I hate the way my sister always takes me .... and thinks I'm always available.
e I take .... my uncle Fred when it comes to height and weight.
f My grandmother always takes .... of what happens in her kitchen.
g Our business really took .... after we had a new website designed.
h Lisa took .... her sister's untidiness when she decided not to move into a flat with her.

Collocations – adverb or adjective?

> Normally adverbs are used with verbs.
> EXAMPLE: *Hannah acts beautifully.*
> This tells you how she acted.
>
> However, with certain verbs it is sometimes necessary to use adjectives. These verbs are usually connected with our senses – *look, sound, taste, feel* and *smell*. Other verbs include *be, appear* and *seem*, and *become*.
> EXAMPLES: *Hannah is **beautiful**.   Hannah looks **beautiful**.*

4 With a partner discuss what you would say in these situations.

EXAMPLE: You're eating a lemon.
It tastes sour.

a You're listening to a love song. It sounds …
b You're walking by the sea. It smells …
c You're walking home late at night. It feels …
d You're eating spaghetti. It tastes …
e You're looking through a travel brochure. It looks …
f You're wearing a designer suit. It feels …

5 Some of these verbs can have two meanings. Look at the underlined verbs and explain the differences.

   A The actor <u>looked</u> angry when she read the bad review.
   B The actor <u>looked</u> at her co-star angrily at one point in the film.

   A I <u>feel</u> fine.
   B I <u>felt</u> the water carefully to see if it was hot enough.

> In A examples, *looked* and *feel* are states, meaning 'seemed' and 'am'. In the B examples, *looked* and *felt* are both actions. If the verb means 'be' or 'seem', then an adjective is used after it. If the verb is used for an action, it can be followed by an object and/or an adverb.

Complete these sentences using an adverb or an adjective.

   a The food tasted ....
   b I felt the soft fur on the rabbit very ....
   c I didn't feel very .... when the bus was late again.
   d Ann looked .... to see if there was any traffic, before crossing the road.
   e Noises can sound quite .... at night.
   f Your coat looks ....
   g He looked at her .... when she entered the room.
   h The rabbit appeared .... out of the hat.

Past and present participles

Corpus spot

Be careful with *-ed* and *-ing* adjectives – the *Cambridge Learner Corpus* shows that exam candidates often make mistakes with these.

My friend was very **excited** about going to Hollywood on holiday.
NOT My friend was very ~~exciting~~ about going to Hollywood on holiday.

In our home we want to do many things otherwise we feel very **bored**.
NOT In our home we want to do many things otherwise we feel very ~~boring~~.

6 When Hannah is talking about her mother and her attitude to acting, she says her mother became quite embarrassed. Hannah means that her mother became a bit red or maybe blushed and wasn't sure what to say. What would it mean if Hannah had said 'my mother became quite embarrassing'?

Can you finish these sentences, which explain what the grammatical rule is?

   1 To talk about how we feel about something, we use

   ....

   2 To talk about the person or thing that is causing the feeling, we use ....

G → page 170

Speaking

7 In pairs, talk about how you feel when the situations in a–g happen.

Use some of these adjectives.

bored/boring
fascinated/fascinating
depressed/depressing
amused/amusing
pleased/pleasing
moved/moving
irritated/irritating
shocked/shocking
gripped/gripping

EXAMPLE:
There are only soap operas to watch when you and your family sit down to watch TV. *I'm bored by soap operas. They're not very amusing but my mother is fascinated by them.*

   a Your brother/sister keeps borrowing your stuff without asking.
   b You see a sad film with your mother.
   c People keep telling you that you look like your mother/father.
   d Your father has decided to move the family to another city.
   e People think your mother/father is actually your sister/brother.
   f A long lost relative has left your family a huge sum of money.
   g You find out that your cousin is coming to live with you.

y

w

LIKE MOTHER, LIKE DAUGHTER   75

Exam folder 6

Paper 3 Part 1 Short extracts

In this part of the Listening paper you will hear eight unconnected short recordings of about 30 seconds each. There will be either one or two speakers. For each question, you have to decide which is the correct answer from three possible options. The sentence which tells you what each recording will be about is recorded, which gives you time to think about what you will hear next. Each recording is repeated.

You should make the best use of the time available. During the pause before each recording starts, read through each question and think about what to listen out for. Underline any key words. After you have listened once, choose the option that you think is correct. As you listen for the second time, check that the other two options are definitely wrong.

If you do not know the answer to a question, keep calm and move on to the next one. At the end of the Listening test, you will have time to transfer your answers to an answer sheet. For any questions you haven't been able to answer, make a guess – there is a one in three chance of your being right!

1 Look through the questions on the opposite page and underline the key words.

2 **1 17** Now listen and answer the eight questions. Remember that each recording is repeated. When you have finished, check your answers.

3 Fill in this extract from the answer sheet for Part 1 with your answers.

Part 1			
1	A	B	C
2	A	B	C
3	A	B	C
4	A	B	C
5	A	B	C
6	A	B	C
7	A	B	C
8	A	B	C

EXAM ADVICE

- Think about what the recording may be about as you read through the questions before you hear the recording.
- Choose your answers at the first listening.
- Check your answers at the second listening.
- Keep calm and make a guess if necessary.
- Remember to transfer your answers to the answer sheet at the end of the Listening test.

You will hear people talking in eight different situations.
For questions 1–8, choose the best answer (A, B or C).

1 You hear a woman calling a friend.
   What is she doing?
   A confirming an arrangement
   B complaining about a delay
   C apologising for her behaviour

2 You hear a man and a woman talking about a film they have just seen.
   What is the man's opinion of the film?
   A It is longer than necessary.
   B It has a weak storyline.
   C Its actors are disappointing.

3 You hear a woman describing a music festival.
   What did she like best about it apart from the music?
   A the wide selection of food stalls
   B the amount of space at the location
   C the various free activities on offer

4 You hear a man and a woman discussing a skiing holiday they have just been on.
   What did they both dislike?
   A the amount of snow
   B the times of the flights
   C the facilities of the hotel

5 You hear this conversation in a hotel.
   The woman has come down to reception
   A to ask for another room.
   B to order some food.
   C to complain about the service.

6 You hear this radio report about a football match.
   What happened at the match?
   A Some fans ran onto the pitch.
   B A player was badly injured.
   C The referee stopped the match.

7 You hear part of an interview on the radio.
   Why did the man give up his job?
   A to recover from stress
   B to reduce his expenses
   C to move somewhere quiet

8 You hear a woman talking about an evening course.
   What does she enjoy most?
   A doing maths
   B watching films
   C having coffee

12.1 A great idea

Speaking

1   **Student A:** Look at photos 1 and 2. Compare the photos and say why electricity is important in modern life. Which electrical appliance couldn't you live without?

Student B: Look at photos 3 and 4. Compare the photos and say what the advantages and disadvantages are of each method of transport. Which method of transport do you prefer and why?

Reading

Exam spot

In Paper 1 Part 7 you need to match the meanings of the questions to the meanings of sections of the text.

2   You are going to read a magazine article about items that were invented or discovered by accident. You will have to decide which question is mentioned in each section. First of all, skim the text for general meaning. Then look at the first question below. The key words which you will need to find a paraphrase for in the text are underlined.

| Which section mentions the need to change people's attitude when <u>buying goods</u>? | **1** | |

The answer is in section E and the part that contains the answer is underlined. The key words are *purchase* and *groceries*.

Now answer questions 2–10 in the same way. Underline the part of the text in which you find the answer to the question.

Which section mentions		
the need to find a cheaper way of doing something?	**2**	
someone who didn't believe their discovery was important?	**3**	
an idea which resulted from someone not being able to find what they wanted easily?	**4**	
a misunderstanding of how to use something?	**5**	
a decision to keep on trying to make an idea better?	**6**	
the need for a new method of storage?	**7**	
the need to manufacture something in large amounts for it to be worthwhile?	**8**	
an idea which was a copy of something found in nature?	**9**	
an idea which arose from an attempt to improve on an already well-known item?	**10**	

Invented or discovered by accident?

A The teabag

The teabag is over 100 years old but not everyone is celebrating. A time-consuming ritual has been transformed by the little paper packet into a five-minute break, and it has saved the tea industry by fulfilling the modern need for convenience and speed. Like many inventions, the teabag came about by accident. Struggling to cut costs, Thomas Sullivan, a New York coffee merchant who turned to tea, sent out samples of poor quality tea in small silk sachets rather than as good quality loose tea. His customers failed to realise that they were supposed to cut open the sachet and empty its contents into a pot. The result was an immediate hit with American tea drinkers. It was viewed with suspicion by British drinkers at first and only took off in the 1960s.

B Potato crisps

George Crum reportedly created the potato crisp in 1853 near Saratoga Springs, New York. Fed up with a customer who continuously sent his fried potatoes back, saying that they were soggy and not crunchy enough, Crum sliced the potatoes as thinly as possible, fried them in hot grease, then sprinkled them with salt. Eventually, the crisps were mass-produced, but since they were kept in barrels or tins, they quickly went stale. Then, in the 1920s, Laura Scudder invented the airtight bag by ironing together two pieces of waxed paper, thus keeping the crisps fresh longer. Today, potato crisps are packaged in plastic or foil bags.

C Post-it Notes

In 1968, Spencer Silver from the company 3M attempted to make ordinary sticky tape, which was in use all over the world, even stickier. During an experiment, the researcher made a thick substance which did not sink into surfaces and could be removed with ease. However, no one at 3M was interested in the substance because it didn't stick. Sometime later, Spencer's colleague remembered the not-so-sticky substance. This man sang in a choir in his spare time. He had a problem knowing where in the book the various songs were. He managed to solve this problem with the help of the sticky substance invented by his colleague: the substance helped stick bookmarks in the song book without spoiling the pages. Post-it Notes were first sold in 1980.

D Velcro

The Velcro fastener was invented in 1941 by George de Mestral, a Swiss engineer. He noticed that flower seed heads (burrs) kept sticking to his clothes when he was walking in the Alps. He decided to devise a unique fastener that duplicated the burrs' tiny hooks. Although de Mestral first met with resistance and even laughter, he stuck to his idea. After many experiments, he realised that nylon, when sewn under infra red light, formed tiny but tough hooks, which easily attached themselves to softer, velvety nylon fabric. Velcro became a revolutionary fastening system which never goes wrong and is both simple and strong. It is still being used with great success today.

E The shopping cart

Silvan Goldman invented the first shopping cart in 1936 <u>when he saw his customers were reluctant to purchase a large number of groceries at any one time</u> at his store because they were too heavy to carry. Once, Goldman saw a customer putting her bag with groceries on a toy machine that her son was pulling with a string. He came to the conclusion that he needed to fix small wheels to an ordinary shopping basket. Later, Goldman created the first modern shopping cart with the help of mechanical engineers. They were first manufactured in 1947.

F Penicillin

Sir Alexander Fleming, a British biologist, was researching a strain of bacteria in 1928, and noticed that one of the glass culture dishes that had accidentally been left near an open window had become contaminated with a fungus. He noticed that the fungus was destroying the bacteria. When he first published his findings, Fleming didn't think anyone would be very interested because the fungus (penicillin) was difficult to cultivate and slow-acting. It wasn't until 1945 that penicillin was able to be produced on an industrial scale, changing the way doctors treated bacterial infections forever.

Vocabulary

Word formation

3 The following words are from the reading text above. In pairs, talk about what part of speech they are and then change them into nouns.

a celebrating   c hot   e various   g destroying

b failed   d fresh   f strong   h industrial

The passive

1 Which of the verbs in bold in these sentences from the text in 12.1 are in the passive?

a ... **has saved** the tea industry ...
b It **was viewed** with suspicion ...
c ... they **were** soggy ...
d ... potato crisps **are packaged** in plastic ...
e A time-consuming ritual **has been transformed** ...
f ... and **could be removed** with ease.
g ... **had** accidentally **been left** ...
h ... the substance **helped** stick bookmarks ...
i ... **is** still **being used** ...
j ... was able **to be produced** ...

2 How is the passive formed and why is it used?

G → page 171

3 Fill the gaps in the newspaper article with the passive form of one of the verbs or phrasal verbs in the box.

ask	disperse	dissolve	encourage	fill	hope	issue
make up	persuade	store	supply	talk into	use	

Shops with the sweet smell of success

It began with the smell of freshly baked bread. A supermarket with a sharp nose for business believed people (1) .... to spend more money if they smelled something pleasant. The idea was so successful that hundreds of other shops (2) .... to do the same. The smells of engine oil, leather and burning rubber (3) .... to launch and sell a new car, while banks and hotels (4) .... often .... with pleasant fragrances such as apple and lavender. Sports shops believe that customers (5) .... spending more money if they can smell the scent of freshly mown grass.

These kinds of business scents (6) .... by two companies, BOC Gases and Atmospherics. The fragrances (7) .... in carbon dioxide and (8) .... via air conditioning, or (9) .... in discreet cylinders and released when needed. BOC Gases is working with British firms to see how well the fragrances are doing. Soon customers (10) .... with questionnaires, and it (11) .... their answers will provide a clearer idea of the relationship between scents and increased sales. A spokesman for the company said: 'Any smell you want (12) .... for you. We (13) .... constantly .... for the same smells, like coffee and bread, but we want people to think of other things too.'

4 It isn't always necessary to use *by*. Which sentences are correct and which need *by* ... to complete them?

a Jurassic Park was directed
b A new road is now being built round the town
c She was given a job
d He was murdered
e She is being operated on
f The fire is said to have been started

G → page 171

5 Where would you see the following notices?

A
All crockery and cutlery to be returned after use.

B
You are requested not to smoke.

C
RESERVED FOR MEMBERS

D
Packet should be opened at the other end.

E
Lost treasure found in garden

6 In pairs, ask and answer these questions.

a Have you ever been photographed with someone famous or for a newspaper?
b It is said that in the future most people will work from home. Do you agree?
c Can you explain how paper is produced?
d Where was your watch made?
e What were you given for your last birthday?

7 Link the following pieces of information using a passive.

EXAMPLE: *social networking sites – millions of people*
Social networking sites are used by millions of people.

a watches – Switzerland
b gunpowder – China
c Tutankhamen's tomb – Lord Carnarvon
d satellites – 1957
e 2020 Olympic Games – not London
f togas – the Romans

Exam spot

When you have a key word transformation from active to passive or passive to active, it is important to keep in the same tense as the original sentence.

8 Complete the second sentence so that it has a similar meaning to the first sentence, using the word given. Do not change the word given. You must use between two and five words, including the word given.

1 Inventors don't like people copying their ideas.
OBJECT
Inventors ....
being copied.

2 Why were the students mixing up those chemicals in the lab yesterday?
BEING
Why ....
up in the lab yesterday?

3 They made her hand over her notebooks.
WAS
She ....
her notebooks.

4 People say that the local camera shop is very good.
SUPPOSED
The local camera shop .... very good.

5 My boss told me of his decision yesterday.
INFORMED
I ....
decision yesterday.

6 Our mother always used to hide our presents in the attic.
WOULD
Our presents ....
in the attic by our mother.

Corpus spot

Take care when using the passive – the *Cambridge Learner Corpus* shows that exam candidates often make mistakes with this.

The hotel **was opened** by a famous film star.

NOT The hotel ~~opened~~ by a famous film star.

Correct the mistakes that candidates have made with the passive in these sentences.

a I was give a leaflet, which contains some interesting questions.
b First of all you could go to the museum, which has been builded many years ago.
c My laptop has bought for me two months ago.
d This brand established in 1980.
e The meeting has cancelled.
f It located in a beautiful area.
g My friend called Cecile and she is very pretty.
h In your advertisement was written that there would be more than this.

Vocabulary

Collocations with *come*, *tell* and *fall*

9 In the article in 12.1, the collocation *come to a conclusion* is used. Match the sentences beginnings a–g with the endings 1–7.

a I was so tired that I fell
b I find it hard to tell the twins
c Dan found it hard to come
d She's so unlucky – she often falls
e Every night their grandmother would tell
f Paul told his boss
g There's no pill to make someone fall

1 to a decision about his future.
2 in love with you, unfortunately.
3 a lie so that he could avoid the company training weekend.
4 apart, they are so similar.
5 asleep in front of the TV.
6 ill on holiday.
7 them a story about her childhood.

In pairs, use the collocations to make some sentences that are true for you.

EXAMPLE: *I fell ill last winter.*

Writing folder 6

Paper 2 Part 2 Reviews

In Part 2 of Paper 2 you may be asked to write a review, for example of a concert, film, play or TV programme you have seen. A review is a type of article which is generally published in a magazine or posted on a website. It can be either serious or light-hearted, and should contain both information and opinion.

1 Think of the best and worst films you have seen recently. List their good and bad points. Then tell your partner about each film.

2 Look at the notes about two films below. Which film did the writer prefer, A or B?

A	B
fascinating storyline	boring love scenes
historical events	appalling dialogue
shocking violence	complicated plot
tremendous soundtrack	terrible costumes
excellent acting skills	dull characters
interesting locations	unrealistic ending
frighteningly realistic	disappointing special effects

3 Read the film review opposite and complete gaps 1–7 with one of the sets of phrases in 2.

4 A positive review usually ends with a recommendation, as in the review opposite. Which of the recommendations below are grammatically correct? Tick them and correct the other sentences.

a I suggest you to see this film without delay.
b This film is highly recommended.
c The movie has much to recommend it.
d I will advise you not to miss this film.
e I strongly advise you to go and see the film.
f I could recommend this film to you.

One of the best films I have ever seen is *The Last King of Scotland*, starring Forest Whitaker. His performance as Idi Amin is (1) .... and cleverly illustrates how strange Amin's behaviour was at times. Alongside Whitaker, newcomer James McAvoy displays some (2) .... as the young Scottish doctor Nicholas Garrigan, who arrives in Uganda just as Amin takes power and who eventually becomes his personal doctor.

Uganda has some amazing landscapes and the film's (3) .... show us the real beauty of the country. The (4) .... , based on a novel by journalist Giles Foden, blends fact and fiction in a very clever way, sweeping us along with the (5) .... that were such a tragedy for Uganda in the 1970s. There are a number of scenes of (6) .... and the film is frequently disturbing because of this, but at the same time it is totally gripping.

Last but not least, there is a (7) .... , with a wide range of African music that will have you dancing in your seat at times. I thoroughly recommend this film to you.

5 Complete these sentences with information of your own, using passive forms of the verbs in brackets. Try to vary the tenses you use.

   a The film .... (direct)
   b This wonderful story .... (set)
   c All of the costumes .... (design)
   d The main character .... (play)
   e The supporting cast .... (choose)
   f Most of the music .... (compose)
   g A subtitled version .... (show)
   h The screenplay .... (nominate)

6 Now read this exam question.

> You have seen this announcement on your college noticeboard.
>
> ### We want your reviews
> # NOW!
>
> Have you enjoyed a particular programme on TV recently? Or is there one that you just can't stand? Either way, why not write a review for the college website? Include plenty of information about the programme and give us your opinions on it, good or bad.
>
> Email your review to Sam at the Student Office: sam@unitel.ac
>
> Write your **review**.

7 Which programme will you write about? List as many nouns as you can related to each type of programme below.

   comedy: *jokes,*
   documentary: *photography,*
   game show: *quiz,*
   reality show: *celebrities,*
   soap opera: *drama,*

8 Make a paragraph plan before you start writing. Follow the exam advice opposite and use some of the language in 2. Write your review in 140–190 words.

EXAM ADVICE

Content
- Remember to mention what you are reviewing by name.
- Include both factual information and opinion.
- Add a recommendation unless the review is negative.

Communicative achievement
- Write in a consistently serious or light-hearted style, depending on the target reader.
- Communicate your ideas effectively.

Organisation
- Organise your review in paragraphs.
- State some basic facts in an introduction.
- Finish with a recommendation or reasons to avoid.

Language
- Use a range of tenses and passive forms.
- Include a variety of adjectives and adverbs.

Grammar

1 For questions 1–8, read the film review below and think of the word which best fits each gap. Use only one word in each gap.

The best film I have seen is *LA Confidential*, starring Kim Basinger and Kevin Spacey. It was set (1) .... 1950s Los Angeles, and (2) .... the budget wasn't particularly extravagant, the film had very powerful images and seemed totally authentic. For example, the costumes looked just like what people (3) .... have worn; the cars seemed to (4) .... exactly what people used to drive around in. (5) .... of the actors played their parts extremely well, and Kim Basinger in particular gave (6) .... truly outstanding performance. The film was absolutely gripping, largely (7) .... the storyline was so carefully put together. There were several ingredients: not only the obvious ones like murder and blackmail, but also corruption, Hollywood lifestyles and some moving family histories. (8) .... is an impressive film. Not to be missed!

Topic review

2 Read these sentences and say which are true for you, giving more details. Don't be afraid to use your imagination!

a I used to be different from how I am now.
b Next weekend I'm going to do something dangerous!
c I look like a famous film star.
d It must have been difficult looking after me when I was younger.
e I can't stand losing when I play sport.
f I'd like to invent something useful, like the Post-it Note.
g As a child, I was always made to finish my food.
h By this time next year I'll have passed *Cambridge English: First*.
i I really enjoy watching adverts on TV.
j I find it hard to believe that the Earth has been visited by aliens.

Vocabulary

3 Two common verbs are used in these sentences. Decide what they are and fill the gaps, using a suitable verb form.

a We're .... used to living in a village now.
b Luisa .... after her grandmother when it comes to looks.
c Don't try and .... out of doing the chores!
d Stefan is still at home .... over a cold.
e You should .... turns to borrow the car to go into town.
f I finally .... a letter from the company last week, offering me a refund.
g Susie gets really annoyed when Jack doesn't .... her suggestions seriously.
h I should really .... account of other people's feelings more.

4 Decide which is the odd one out in these sets and say why.

a disturbing, terrifying, cunning, appalling
b voice-over, jingle, slogan, campaign
c martial arts, snowboarding, aerobics, gymnastics
d fancy, detest, loathe, hate
e deep, wide, huge, shallow
f pitch, sports centre, court, track
g intend, pretend, expect, hope
h extravagant, economical, affordable, cheap

Phrasal verbs

5 Complete sentences a–h with phrasal verbs formed from the verbs given. There is one extra verb in each set.

ON | get keep look pass switch |

a The property market is .... on favourably by investors.
b It must be really hard to .... on in advertising – it's such a competitive business.
c Sally never gave up hope and .... on trying to get her novel published.
d How about .... on the lights for this court – it's too dark to see the ball!

OFF | break make put take work |

e Sales of electric cars could really .... off given the current price of petrol.
f I'm going to use the exercise bike in the gym later, to .... off that huge lunch!
g Jenny .... me off seeing that film; she said it was very shocking.
h He .... off a piece of the freshly baked bread and chewed it with great pleasure.

Writing

6 Read paragraphs A–C and decide what type of writing each one is:

1 letter
2 review
3 article
4 essay

A
To sum up, people should work fewer hours in the future, in my opinion. By doing this, unemployment could be reduced and working parents would be able to spend more time with their children. Moreover, life would be less stressful, which must be a benefit to society in the end.

B
The action takes place on the northwestern coast of the USA and the scenery is terrific – huge cliffs and crashing waves, not to mention giant mountain peaks and amazing forests. Although the pace seems a little slow at the beginning, things pick up quite quickly when the hero eventually appears. From then on, you'll be on the edge of your seat.

C
Have you ever thought of joining a gym? I recently did and it changed my life. I used to come home from my job and just sit watching TV, but now I work out every evening. My friends say my personality has changed. Before, I would be rather aggressive whenever my day had been bad, but now they say I'm much better tempered.

Which paragraph is an opening and which is a conclusion?

9.1 exercise 1

Here is the complete advertisement. It is for Samsung's 3D LED television, advertised in 2010.

Introducing the world's first 3D LED TV.
A new dimension in television.
Featuring Samsung's LED backlighting technology.
SAMSUNG
TURN ON TOMORROW
www.samsung.com/3D

9.1 exercise 8
Group B: XK Trainers
You are suspicious of advertising agencies, because two recent advertising campaigns failed. One used a famous basketball player, who was accused of taking bribes the same week the adverts appeared. Another, filmed at great cost in Antarctica, did not attract the public. Decide on the style you are now looking for.

Education for life

Speaking

1   Look at this pair of photographs, which show two different classrooms in Britain. Talk to a partner about the differences and say which school is closer to your own learning experience.

2   Now talk to each other about your early schooldays. You should each describe:

   a   a school you attended (size, location, atmosphere)
   b   a teacher you remember well
   c   something at school that you particularly enjoyed
   d   someone at school that you found really annoying

   Report your partner's answers to the class.

   X told me / said that he/she …
   X spoke about / talked about his/her …
   X thinks/feels/remembers that he/she …
   X claims / believes strongly / is convinced that …

   Which tenses did you use to report what you heard?

3   Write David's confession below as reported speech, being careful to use suitable past tenses.

   EXAMPLE: *David said that it wasn't Simon's fault. …*

   It isn't Simon's fault! I want to describe what really happened. I was inside the classroom during break and I saw a group of my friends outside. I went over to the window and tried to get their attention. I waved at them but they didn't see me, so I hammered on the window. I know glass is breakable but I just didn't think. When my hand went through, I panicked. I wasn't badly hurt and I wanted to avoid getting into trouble, so I put Simon's bag over the hole and left the room. I'm sorry I haven't told anyone the truth until now.

Listening

4   You are going to hear a radio interview with two work colleagues, Sandra Wilson and Mike Tripp, who also used to attend the same school.

   First, read the reported statements a–h below.

   a   Sandra explained that she had disliked Mike because of his attitude to school.
   b   Sandra accused Mike of deliberately forgetting certain things he had done at school.
   c   Mike explained that he had known at the time how irritating he was.
   d   Mike wished he had worked harder at school.
   e   Mike said that he had left the science exam because he couldn't answer the questions.
   f   Mike felt that his father had expected him to do well when he left school.
   g   Mike admitted that the school careers teachers had been quite helpful.
   h   Mike mentioned that his father had helped him financially in starting his business.

   2 02 Now listen to the recording and tick the statements that are true. Compare your answers and listen again to check.

Vocabulary

Word formation

5   What words in the same word family as the noun *education* do you know? Use a dictionary if necessary to complete the definitions below. Two are adjectives.

   a   .... : [*often passive*] to teach someone at a school, college or university
   b   Someone who is .... has learned a lot at school or in college and has a good level of knowledge.
   c   .... : providing education or relating to education

Collocations

6 Match the two adjectives from 5 to their noun collocates a–d. Which adjective is the more useful to learn, in your opinion? Why?

- **a** qualifications
- **b** person
- **c** opportunities
- **d** standards

7 Read these sentences written by past exam candidates and compare their experience of school and learning with your own.

- **a** There is no motivation in studying something you are not interested in.
- **b** Dad let me go to the cinema with my friends, as a reward for getting such good results in maths.
- **c** Although discipline is essential, I think the methods being used today are as awful as the old ones.
- **d** The school rules in my country are more strict than in other countries.

8 Opposite are some short descriptions of the first jobs some famous people had. Work out which job was done by each person.

9 In the descriptions there are several words commonly found in letters or emails of application, which will be dealt with in the next Writing folder. Underline any words you think may be useful. Check their meaning in an English–English dictionary and look for further examples of their use.

A · His parents divorced when he was 12 and his mother was left to bring up four children single-handed. All four kids had jobs – his three sisters worked for different local restaurants, while he cut grass and did a paper round. It probably took him a year to earn what he can now make in a single day.

Agatha Christie

B · He became an apprentice on a cargo ship at the age of 17 and his very first experience was gained on a voyage to Rio de Janeiro. Altogether he spent five years at sea. He devoted his spare time to his hobby, which was ultimately to become a full-time career, but only once he was 35.

Socrates

C · On leaving school at 17, the only jobs available were in the local fish factory. The smell was appalling and working on the filleting machine made her constantly want to throw up. She escaped to London in the end and found employment as a waitress.

Madonna

D · He inherited the family sculpting business but showed little interest in it. He had no talent for stonework whatsoever and so, not surprisingly, the business went downhill fast. Instead, it was his determination to solve the twin mysteries of life and death that led him to be considered the wisest man alive.

Paul Gauguin

E · She worked long hours at a hamburger restaurant and was so poor that she had to search through the dustbins after work for any thrown-out food. She also sold ice cream and was a coat-check girl at the Russian Tea Rooms in New York.

Annie Lennox

F · Initially, she took a position as an unpaid assistant in a chemist's shop, and later qualified in pharmacy. Her duties gave her a sound knowledge of poisons, that would subsequently be extremely relevant.

Tom Cruise

Reporting

1 Look at quotes a–c and explain why the tenses underlined have been used in reporting them.

  a 'I can't remember much about my first school; my mother will, though.'
    Greg claimed that he <u>couldn't</u> remember much about his first school, but thought that his mother <u>would</u>.

  b 'When Jack moved to secondary school he became less motivated.'
    His mother said that Jack <u>had become</u> less motivated when he had moved to secondary school.

  c 'Girls are now doing better than boys at school.'
    The expert said girls <u>are</u> now doing better than boys at school.

G → page 171

2 Match the quotes a–d with the reported statements 1–4.

  a 'I visited my old school recently and it was much smaller than I remembered.'
  b 'Perhaps we should educate parents about how they can help their children.'
  c 'We belong to an anti-learning culture.'
  d 'I'll make more of an effort.'

  1 She complained that society doesn't encourage education.
  2 He promised to work harder.
  3 She explained that she had been back and had found it very different.
  4 He suggested showing parents what to do.

Corpus spot

Be careful when using reporting verbs – the *Cambridge Learner Corpus* shows that exam candidates often make mistakes in the structures that follow them. Here are two of the most common mistakes.

My father suggested **that I should read** this wonderful story.
NOT My father ~~suggested me to read~~ this wonderful story.

We explained **the situation** to her, so she let us in.
NOT We ~~explained her the situation~~, so she let us in.

3 Decide which structures can be used after the following reporting verbs, giving examples. Two are done for you.

accuse *She accused him of cheating.*
admit *He admitted (to) being wrong. He admitted (that) he was wrong.*

apologise	deny	promise	suggest
argue	explain	refuse	urge
claim	insist	say	warn

Listening

Exam spot

In Paper 3 Part 3 the eight options A–H may be presented as sentences that summarise what each speaker says. Identify key words in the sentences to help you predict content.

4 You will hear five different callers to a radio phone-in giving their views about educational performance in Britain. First, read A–H and underline the key words.

  A Changes in society explain why boys and girls have different career ambitions.
  B The recently improved academic performance of girls should be recognised.
  C Young children often see older brothers and sisters as role models.
  D Limited educational opportunities are affecting some children's development.
  E Parents tend to raise boys and girls differently from a young age.
  F Boys can miss out on the influence of men while they are growing up.
  G Government figures show that there are fewer male infant teachers nowadays.
  H A different approach is needed to the early stages of learning.

5 **2 03** Listen to Speaker 1. Complete this summary using present tenses. Then match the content to one of the options A–H.

The first speaker claimed that there (**1**) .... too many women teachers in British schools and argued that boys (**2**) .... men as role models. He also suggested boys (**3**) .... more by broken marriages than girls.

6 **2 04** Now listen to Speakers 2–5 and note down the main points each person makes. Then report their views by writing summaries similar to the one in 5. Match your summaries to A–H and write your choices below.

Speaker **2**   Speaker **3**

Speaker **4**   Speaker **5**

7 As you listen again, listen out for words or phrases that mean the same as a–h. The number of the extract is given in brackets.

   a are usually (1)
   b make good progress (2)
   c misbehaving (2)
   d earners (3)
   e accepted (3)
   f referring to (4)
   g make longer (4)
   h be pleased about (5)

Grammar extra

Reported questions usually involve changes in word order. Look at the questions below and how they have been reported. Then report questions a–e.

What's the answer to number 14?
He asked what the answer to number 14 was.
Where are the scissors?
He asked where the scissors were.
When did this term start?
She asked when this term had started.
Are there enough books to go round?
He asked if there were enough books to go round.
Should I repeat the question?
She asked whether she should repeat the question.

   a Why are girls gaining more university places?
      He asked …
   b In what ways was the situation different twenty years ago?
      He asked …
   c Will things get better in the future?
      He asked …
   d Should British children spend more time at nursery school?
      He asked …
   e Why haven't we faced up to this problem?
      He asked …

Speaking

8 Look at the task and talk together for about two minutes.

parents

teachers

the media

How could these different groups help to raise educational standards in schools?

the government

local companies

9 Now decide which two groups have the most responsibility for a child's education.

10 Complete the second sentence so that it has a similar meaning to the first sentence, using the word given. Do not change the word given. You must use between two and five words, including the word given.

   1 'You put that frog on my chair, didn't you, Charlie?' said Sally.
     OF
     Sally ....
     a frog on her chair.

   2 'Stop misbehaving or you'll be sent to the head for punishment,' the teacher said to Johnny.
     WARNED
     The teacher ....
     or he would be sent to the head for punishment.

   3 'Please try to stay awake during the lesson,' the teacher told them.
     URGED
     The teacher ....
     asleep during the lesson.

   4 Susan denied wasting her time at school when she was younger.
     NOT
     Susan said ....
     her time at school when she was younger.

   5 'Have you tidied up in the science lab?' the chemistry teacher asked them.
     TIDIED
     The chemistry teacher wanted to know
     ....
     in the science lab.

   6 'I'm sorry, I've forgotten my homework,' Nicholas said.
     APOLOGISED
     Nicholas ....
     his homework.

Exam folder 7

Paper 3 Part 3 Multiple matching

In this part of the Listening paper you hear five short extracts which are all related to each other in some way. It may be that the speakers are all talking about the same subject or experiences. Another possible link may be feeling or job. You need to match each of the five extracts to one of eight options. You hear the extracts twice, and it is very important that you take the opportunity to check your answers carefully during the second listening. One mistake could affect two answers.

1　**2 05** **You will hear the first speaker talking about his experience of education. Look at the statements A–H and decide which one is true for the first speaker.**

  A I really enjoyed meeting new people.
  B My attitude to studying had been wrong.
  C I had great teachers while I was studying.
  D It taught me how to cope with money.
  E I'm not sure what I want to do now.
  F I realised I worked better in a freer environment.
  G I needed more support with my studies.
  H I had to work harder than I expected.

EXAM ADVICE

- Don't sit looking out of the window while you're waiting for the recording to start. Read the questions carefully.
- Try to predict what each person might say.

The answer for Speaker 1 is B. Now look at the recording script. The part containing the answer is underlined.

Recording script

Speaker 1:　When I started my last year at school, <u>I didn't take it seriously enough. I should've chosen subjects which were useful rather than ones I liked or that sounded easy</u>. By the time the exams came, I'd given up and I did very badly. I knew I'd have to work hard but I wasn't able to catch up with my friends. Because I failed at science, I can't be a teacher, which is what I really want to do. I'm doing a part-time job in order to make ends meet and next year I'll be starting evening classes to get better qualifications.

Look carefully at the options.

A I really enjoyed meeting new people.
  – *He doesn't mention new friends.*
B My attitude to studying was wrong. – *Right answer.*
C I had great teachers while I was studying.
  – *Although 'a teacher' is mentioned, it is not the speaker's own teacher.*
D It taught me how to cope with money.
  – *Money is mentioned (to make ends meet) but nothing is said about learning what to do with money.*
E I'm not sure what I want to do now.
  – *He's going to study, so this isn't the answer.*
F I realised I worked better in a freer environment.
  – *This isn't mentioned at all.*
G I needed more support with my studies.
  – *This isn't the answer as it is his own attitude rather than anyone not helping him that is the problem.*
H I had to work harder than I expected. – *This isn't the answer, as he knew he had to work hard.*

King's College, Cambridge

2 **2 06** Listen to the other speakers and for questions 2–5, choose from the list A–H in 1, what each speaker states. (Remember that B has already been used.) Use the letters only once. There are three extra letters which you do not need to use.

Speaker 2   [   ]   **2**
Speaker 3   [   ]   **3**
Speaker 4   [   ]   **4**
Speaker 5   [   ]   **5**

3 Now look at the recording script for Speakers 2–5 and underline the parts which give you the answers.

Recording script

Speaker 2: I left school and moved to a college to take my final exams. It was the best decision I could have made. At the college nobody seemed to care about homework and this really motivated me. I had to plan my work myself – there was no one to make you do it and no one to check up on what you'd done. I was still dependent on my parents for money – but that was OK. I learned a lot about real life there – things like getting on with people and organising your time – which has been really useful now I'm working.

Speaker 3: When I left school I didn't have a particular career in mind so I decided to do Environmental Studies at university, mainly because I'd enjoyed geography at school. I didn't really like the course at university and I did think about leaving, but instead I changed courses, which was easier than I expected. I think university was useful in that I learnt how to live alone and how to budget, and as I'm an underpaid teacher now, that really helps.

Speaker 4: I had no difficulty choosing what I was going to do – my parents are both doctors and ever since I was small I also wanted to do that. They really encouraged me and I did well at school and got into a good medical school fairly easily. It was surprisingly tough at medical school, but I had some good friends and we pulled through together. I think the doubts only began to set in when I graduated and got my first job in a hospital. I began to wonder if I'd missed out because I'd been so focused on becoming a doctor. So now I'm doing some voluntary work in Africa, which I'm really enjoying.

Speaker 5: I decided to take a year off after doing my last year at school. I'd had enough of revising and sitting in a library, so I decided to go off to Australia for nine months and earn a bit of money. I've got relatives there who put me up when I first arrived and found me a job. It wasn't doing anything particularly interesting, but the great part was that I was getting to know people who were completely different to the ones I'd known back home. I really recommend taking a year out, but you need to have a firm plan or it could end up a waste of time.

Career moves

Speaking

1 Identify the jobs in the photos and say what skills are important in each one. Which job would you prefer and why?

2 Check you know the meaning of these words and then choose four to complete the quotes below.

> adventurous   concerned   flexible
> redundant   secure   self-confident

a
> A career used to be for life. Once you had left school, you found a job and worked your way up the career ladder. Today, the job market is far less .... , and no one knows what tomorrow may bring.

b
> You have to be ready to accept change, in short be totally .... , if you are going to stay in the job market. There's a positive side to this – instead of feeling that you have to stay in the job you've been trained to do, you can be more .... and try different things.

c
> Women are more willing to take career risks, partly because they are less .... with status, but also because they like to experiment. It's just a question of saying: I think I can do this. And then giving it a go.

Reading

Exam spot

In Paper 1 Part 7, you don't need to read the texts word by word. Read the questions first, to know what to look for. Then scan the texts for the information you need. Always allow time to check your answers.

3 You are going to read a magazine article about five women who have recently changed careers. For questions 1–10, choose from the women (A–E). The women may be chosen more than once.

Which woman

reduced her working hours in order to study?	**1**
spends a lot of time outdoors?	**2**
felt grateful that her employers trusted her?	**3**
would like to start her own business?	**4**
began her studies in a new location?	**5**
travelled in her previous job?	**6**
chose to be made redundant?	**7**
is satisfied with her new lack of routine?	**8**
took a long time to get on top of the job?	**9**
had financial support from her parents?	**10**

4 Now answer these questions about the women.

a Why do you think Amanda felt increasingly *dissatisfied* with her life at the age of 29?

b What sort of things would Dani have been *inexperienced* at doing on the farm?

c How might Rachel's new life seem *uncertain* to some people?

Meet five women who have changed careers

A Amanda, 33

I had been working in sales for six years when I suffered an ankle injury that was to change my whole life. It didn't heal and someone suggested acupuncture, a traditional Chinese treatment for pain. I was so impressed by the treatment that I found out about classes. I had reached a point in my life where things had to change. In many ways I had it all: a company car, foreign business trips, my own house, a secure job. But at 29, I felt increasingly dissatisfied and wanted to be more adventurous. So I persuaded my boss to let me work a four-day week and did classes on the remaining day. It took four difficult years to qualify, as I was studying 25 hours a week on top of my job. It's been worth it though, and I get on well with the people I work for now. As for the BMW, I don't miss it at all!

B Dani, 30

I trained as a doctor but I knew all along it wasn't right for me. My parents had run their dairy farm for thirty years and needed a long holiday, so we decided that I'd look after things for six months while they visited my brother in Australia. It gave me the career break I'd been looking for, except that I never went back. Mum and Dad have emigrated, so now I'm in charge for good, which is fine by me. At the beginning, I was quite inexperienced, though it felt natural to be back on the farm and didn't take me long to master everything. I've learned to be flexible – to fit in with the weather! Being in the open air is the best thing of all. I've just started selling my own cheese and by this time next year, I'll have launched my own ice cream.

C Sue, 34

I'd never seen myself as academic. Hairdressing seemed glamorous and I wanted a car, so I went to work in a salon as an apprentice. I wasn't concerned about the poor pay – I had fun! Then, all of a sudden, my husband's job moved to London. This forced me to reconsider my own life and I decided to take English and Law at night school there. I was spending 45 hours a week cutting hair and working for exams as well. I lost ten kilos in weight, but for all the stress of studying, I knew I was doing the right thing. After leaving college I went into market research. My confidence has always been low and it was three years before I felt I could cope effectively in the role. But it was worth the wait.

D Rachel, 28

I worked for three investment banks in London, earning £60,000 a year in my last job. If I'd added up the hours I spent at my desk, it would have been huge – sometimes I was there until midnight. To begin with, I got a real buzz from the work, helped by the fact that everyone was willing to give me so much responsibility. But eventually, it got to me. At the time, the bank needed to reduce its staff and was offering a good leaving package, so I jumped at it. Now I'm working freelance, editing articles for financial magazines. I've set up the spare room as an office and I hope to pick up enough work. People who need certainty and structure would find my new life difficult, but all in all, I feel I've made the right decision.

E Eleanor, 25

I'd always loved skating and what I wanted above all was to be an ice dancer. Mum and Dad spent a lot of time driving me to classes and I'm so grateful to them for that, not to mention the huge sums they've invested in my training. I started competing at 14 and turned professional at 16. I've done a lot of great shows, but I chose to hang up my skates long before most ice dancers do. For the last six months, I've been working for a sportswear firm to gain experience in business and my dream is to set up a company before long, producing costumes for ice dancers.

Vocabulary

Word formation

5 **Choose suitable negative prefixes for these words. Then match them to the short definitions a–e.**

> honest   organised   patient
> responsible   successful

a not planned well
b easily annoyed
c not achieving what was intended
d likely to lie or do something illegal
e not thinking about the possible bad results of your action

G rammar extra

There are a number of expressions with *all* in the article. Say how *all* is used in a–h.

a I *had it all* (A)   **e** *all of a sudden* (C)
b I don't miss it *at all*! (A)   **f** *for all* the stress (C)
c *all along* (B)   **g** *all in all* (D)
d *the best thing of all* (B)   **h** *above all* (E)

Sometimes, *all* is confused with *whole*. In this example, it is not possible to use *all*.

… an ankle injury that was to change my whole life.

Now complete these sentences using *all* or *whole*. Where it is possible to use either, write both alternatives. Add any words necessary.

1 The firm acknowledged .... 279 applications the same day.
2 The recession had affected .... car industry, causing many redundancies.
3 .... world depends on electronic communications nowadays.
4 Accountants have a powerful voice in .... companies.
5 We had been staring at figures on screen .... day and .... us were fed up.
6 There are disadvantages to .... these jobs.

What rules can you make about the use of *all* and *whole* on the basis of these examples?

G → page 172

Perfect tenses

1 Explain the differences in meaning in these sentences and identify the tenses used.

a I have never sent an email.
b I never sent an email in my last job.
c I had never sent an email until I started working here.
d I will have sent over 500 emails by the end of this week!

2 Read these examples of perfect tenses from 14.1.

a I had been working in sales for six years.
b I've set up the spare room as an office.
c I'd always loved skating.
d By this time next year, I'll have launched my own ice cream.
e It gave me the career break I'd been looking for.
f My confidence has always been low.
g If I'd added up the hours …
h I've been working for a sportswear firm to gain experience …

Now look at the different uses of perfect tenses, 1–7, and find examples of them in sentences a–h. Some uses have more than one example.

1 talking about a recent event or situation which has been completed
2 talking about an event or situation which started in the past but is still true
3 emphasising the duration of a recent event or situation
4 talking about an event or situation that happened earlier than the past time being described in the sentence or paragraph
5 emphasising the duration of an event or situation which took place earlier than the past time being described
6 used in a conditional structure
7 talking about an event that will happen within a specified future time

Which perfect tense has not been exemplified in a–h? Give an example of this tense.

G → page 172

3 Choose the correct tense.

a What I *have been showing / had been showing* you today is only part of our huge range of products.
b Last week, the company *was voted / has been voted* top supplier for the third time.
c Since she started college, Sara *was studying / has been studying* every night, including weekends.
d On Friday, I *have been working / will have been working* in the department for exactly a year.
e The end of year results were not as bad as the directors *had feared / have feared*.
f By May, eight new designs *have been launched / will have been launched*, increasing our sales potential.
g Our sales director *has made / made* some appalling decisions recently and frankly, we'd be better off without him!
h They *have been waiting / had been waiting* for the report all day but when it came through the final page was missing.

Corpus spot

Correct any mistakes with tenses in these sentences written by exam candidates. Two sentences are correct.
a I felt very sorry after I've seen your report.
b Some months ago he has directed a movie.
c Their fans want to know what has been happening to them.
d For thousands of years our civilisation is making progress.
e When I left your house in Ljubljana, I've decided to visit the lakes.
f Some friends of mine have been working there last summer.
g If I hadn't met you, I wouldn't have been able to find my way home.
h The Astrid Hotel is closed since last year.

Listening

4 **2 07** You are going to hear five people talking about their skills and work experience which make them suitable for the following jobs. Note down the skills, qualities and experience mentioned by each person.

Speaker 1: office administrator
Speaker 2: interpreter
Speaker 3: shop assistant
Speaker 4: first-aid worker
Speaker 5: cook

What other skills and qualifications would be useful in each job?

5 Now read the role play instructions for Student A or B.

Student A

You are about to attend an interview for a job at an international sports event in Canada, next summer. The job will be one of the five listed in exercise 4. You don't know exactly which one it will be yet, but you really want to get a job. Spend a few minutes thinking about relevant experience and qualifications.

Remember to be enthusiastic at the interview and explain why you think you would be suitable.

Student B

You are going to interview someone for a job at a major international sports event in Canada. Tell the interviewee what the job involves (choose one of the five listed in exercise 4). Then ask the interviewee about relevant experience (including knowledge of English), qualifications, general commitment and suitability for the job you have in mind.

Then decide on a scale of 0–5 (5 being the most positive) how your interviewee has performed, according to these criteria:

Experience Qualifications Commitment
Inter-personal skills   Enthusiasm

6 Skim the article below to decide who it is aimed at. Then put the verbs in brackets into the correct perfect tense.

How to survive in business today

The current stripping away of management layers and large-scale staff redundancies (1) .... (shrink) companies radically. In some ways, this harsh new reality (2) .... (bring) bosses and workers closer together. At the same time, many new small businesses (3) .... (set up) in the last few years and a staggering 60 per cent of the population now work in small groups of five or less. Alongside these trends, the need to apply psychology in the workplace (4) .... (grow) constantly. 'Jobs for life' (5) .... (cease) to exist, and in contrast, survival skills at work (6) .... (become) absolutely essential. Here are some top tips on how to survive in the office.

- Email people at night – it will look as though you (7) .... (put in) extra hours.
- Try to remember people's names – recent studies (8) .... (show) that this simple gesture makes people think more highly of you.
- Spend money on smart clothes – a survey by Hays Personnel Services (9) .... (find) that 42% of men and 52% of women think well-dressed people have a career advantage.
- Become known as a safe pair of hands rather than a high-flying genius – in ten years' time, you (10) .... (give) the top job while your flashy colleagues (11) .... (claim) unemployment benefit for at least five years.
- Be concise in meetings – if you (12) .... (ramble on) at length, the chances are that you won't have got your message across.

Writing folder 7

Paper 2 Part 2
Letters of application

1 Give the adjectives related to these nouns, using your dictionary if necessary.

motivation ....
commitment ....
determination ....
cheerfulness ....
enthusiasm ....
energy ....
organisation ....
talent ....
skill ....
confidence ....

2 Read this advertisement. Decide which skills would be essential for the job, choosing from the nouns above and adding your own ideas.

WANTED

Friendly, English-speaking people to work as restaurant and bar staff on our Mediterranean cruise ships

Tell us about

• why you would like to work for us
• any relevant experience you may have
• personal qualities that would be useful on board.

Email your letter of application to info@coolblue, quoting reference PM44.
Cool Blue Cruises, Southampton

---

3 Now read these two letters of application. Has each applicant covered all the necessary points? Who would stand a better chance of getting the job?

Dear Sir or Madam

I have just seen your advertisement for jobs on board your cruise ships (reference PM44) and I would like to apply. I am a 20-year-old Swede with determination and commitment. I have often thought of spending time at sea and your job seems the perfect opportunity.

Although I have no on-board experience, I have been working as a waitress in a local restaurant for the last 18 months and I have also had some experience of bar work. My knowledge of English is quite good, as I have been attending classes for the last six years. I would like to add that I have visited many parts of the Mediterranean myself and could talk to guests confidently during the voyage.

As for other personal qualities which might be useful on board a ship, I am an organised and easy-going person, so sharing a cabin with other crew members would not be a problem.

I am sure I would make a success of this job and I hope you will consider my application.

Yours faithfully

Pernilla Axelsson

Dear Mr or Mrs

I saw the job you advertised and I want to give it a go. I love the idea of going on a cruise and I'm just the person you need. I never thought of working on a ship but it sounds fine.

By the way, I've worked in a bar, though I didn't enjoy it that much. I wouldn't mind being a waiter on your ship though. Do the staff eat the same food as the guests? I've heard it's very good.

You ask about me. Well, I tell good jokes. I'm always cheerful and I think you would have to be, stuck on a ship for so long.

Write to me soon.

Harry

4 Make improvements to the second letter, rewriting it according to these guidelines.

a Change the opening and closing formulae. Make sure the style is formal throughout.

b Rewrite the first sentence to make it clear which job is being applied for.

c Edit the first and second paragraphs to make them sound more positive. Build up the information about previous experience, including some reference to learning English.

d Write a new third paragraph on personal qualities, using some of the adjectives and nouns in exercise 1.

e Try to write around 190 words in all.

EXAM ADVICE

Content
- Remember to cover all the points in the question.
- Include relevant information that would support your application.
- Try to sound positive about yourself!

Communicative achievement
- Use a formal style, with suitable opening and closing formulae.
- Communicate your ideas effectively, to persuade the reader to select you.
- Don't include any postal addresses.

Organisation
- Start by explaining who you are and why you are writing.
- Organise your letter in clear paragraphs.

Language
- Describe your qualities and skills using a range of adjectives.
- Use the present perfect when talking about your experience.
- Check that your punctuation, spelling and grammar are accurate.

5 Now look at this exam question. Underline the parts of the task that you need to cover. Remember to plan your answer before you start writing.

You see the following advertisement in an international magazine.

Can you answer YES to these questions?

★ *Do you speak English confidently?*

★ *Do you enjoy visiting new places?*

★ *Do you get on well with people?*

If so, we would be interested in hearing from you! We are looking for energetic and cheerful guides to lead our 15-day coach tours round Europe. Tell us why you would be suitable.

Apply to: Europewide Coach Tours, PO Box 23, London W1X 6TY, stating where you saw our advertisement.

Write your **letter of application** in 140–190 words. Do not include any postal addresses.

Too many people?

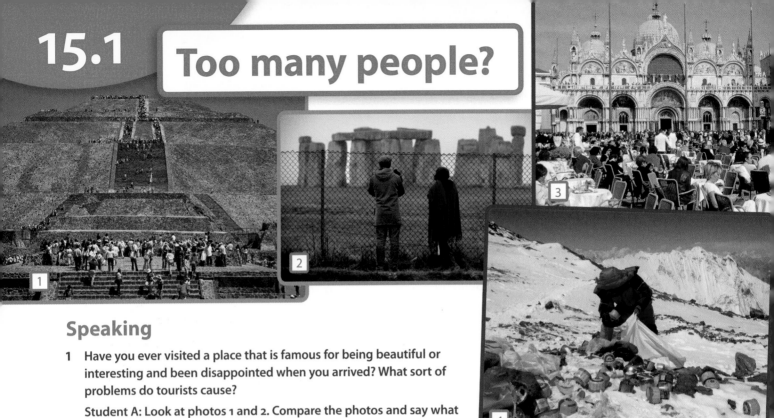

Speaking

1 Have you ever visited a place that is famous for being beautiful or interesting and been disappointed when you arrived? What sort of problems do tourists cause?

Student A: Look at photos 1 and 2. Compare the photos and say what you think tourists will feel when they visit these places.

Student B: Look at photos 3 and 4. Compare the photos and say what you think the local people feel about the tourists who visit these places.

Listening

2 **2 08** You will hear a woman talking about problems faced by the Grand Canyon National Park Service. Complete the sentences with a word or short phrase.

The Grand Canyon is located in the (1) .... part of Arizona.
The canyon is (2) .... deep from top to bottom.
The Grand Canyon National Park was opened in (3) ....
(4) ....people a year visit the Grand Canyon National Park.
The park provides visitors with (5) .... to help solve the problem of parking.
In the summer the park is affected by (6) .... , brought by southwesterly winds.
The park also suffers from a lack of (7) .... and this sometimes has to be brought in by truck.
The temperature of the Colorado river is now (8) ....all year round.
Some types of (9) ....have now totally disappeared.
The Grand Canyon is often said to be one of the (10) ....in the world.

Vocabulary

Topic set – the natural world

3 It is a good idea to learn words in meaning categories and check you know the differences in meaning. In the recording, you heard the following words that are all connected with water. Do you know what they mean?

> dam   floods   rapids
> reservoir   river

In pairs, write a sentence which explains the difference between each of the two words below.

a pond / lake
b stream / river
c canal / river
d waterfall / rapids

Word formation

4 Make nouns, adverbs and verbs from these adjectives.

> long   weak   deep   strong
> wide   short   warm

5 For questions 1–8, read the text below. Use the word given in capitals below to form a word that fits in the gap. There is an example at the beginning (0).

POLLUTING THE ENVIRONMENT

Vehicle exhaust fumes, litter and many other waste **(0)** ...*PRODUCTS*... are called pollutants. Pollutants can affect our health and harm animals and plants. Releasing **(1)** .... waste from factories and power stations is one of the main ways in which we pollute our **(2)** .... These waste substances are the **(3)** .... results of modern living.

Pollution itself is not new – a hundred years ago factories sent out great clouds of **(4)** .... smoke, and pollution has now spread to every corner on Earth. Our **(5)** .... have much to learn, but we do know more about how to control pollution. The use of solar energy will help in the fight as it is much cleaner than fossil fuels. We can also achieve some **(6)** .... in pollution by recycling waste.

The use of cars which run on **(7)** .... instead of petrol is also a key feature in the fight against pollution. It is up to everyone to be as **(8)** .... as they can with the Earth's limited resources.

0 PRODUCE	**5** SCIENCE
1 CHEMIST	**6** REDUCE
2 SURROUND	**7** ELECTRIC
3 WANT	**8** ECONOMY
4 POISON	

Speaking

6 How environmentally friendly are you?

a How can people recycle household rubbish?

b What could your town do to reduce pollution?

c What do you think about wearing second-hand clothes?

d What can be done to stop people dropping litter on the streets of your town?

e Are you economical about using water and electricity? Why? / Why not?

f How would you feel if you had to walk or cycle everywhere?

g What's your opinion of food that has been imported from thousands of miles away?

7 **2 09** You need to be able to say numbers correctly. Practise saying the following numbers and then listen to the recording to check your pronunciation.

Measurement	'0'
13 km	'0' can be pronounced
30 cm	in different ways in
0.5 km	English.
2.5 m	Telephone number:
153 kilos	012-323-66778
1m 53 cm	Football score: 3–0
½	Tennis score: 40–0
¼	Science and
⅔	temperature: 0 degrees
	Celsius

Dates
1st May 1899
3rd August 2000
12th February 2004
6th September 2016
25th December 1990
the 15th century
4/5/11

Telephone numbers
01256-311399
00-44-324-667012

Maths
$2 + 6 = 8$
$3 - 2 = 1$
$4 \times 4 = 16$
$10 \div 2 = 5$
20%
$3°$
$\sqrt{16}$

Money
10p
£1.45
$50
€20.30

8 Now ask and answer the following questions.

a What's your date of birth?

b What's your telephone number?

c What's your address?

d How tall are you?

e How much did you weigh when you were born?

f When did man first walk on the moon?

g What's the average temperature in summer where you live? In winter?

h What's the population of your country?

i How many people are there in a football team?

j In which century was your house or flat built?

k What was the score of the last sports match you saw?

Countable and uncountable nouns

Many English nouns can be countable and uncountable according to their different meanings. For example:

You really should take more exercise. (uncountable)
I do my exercises every morning. (countable)

1   Decide which words in the following pairs are countable.

Which words can be both countable and uncountable? What is the difference in meaning?

a information	note
b spaghetti	meal
c recommendation	advice
d travel	journey
e job	work
f money	coin
g lightning	storm
h weather	temperature
i English	verb
j vehicle	traffic
k seat	furniture
l hair	hairstyle
m luggage	suitcase
n mountain	scenery
o land	country

Corpus spot

Be careful with uncountable nouns – the *Cambridge Learner Corpus* shows that exam candidates often make mistakes with these.
I need to find alternative **accommodation**.
NOT I need to find alternative ~~accommodations~~.

These uncountable nouns are the ones which candidates make most mistakes with.

information
advice
transport
homework
knowledge
furniture
work
equipment
research
damage

Using determiners with countable and uncountable nouns
With **plural countables or uncountables**, e.g. *coins* or *money*, we use
plenty of, a lot of, lots of
With **uncountables**, e.g. *money*, we use
much, little
a great/good deal of, a large/small amount of
With **plural countables**, e.g. *coins*, we use
many, (a) few, several
a great/good/small number of
All verbs, determiners and pronouns referring to **uncountable** nouns are singular:
*A **great deal** of research **has been done** into the pollution produced by cars in cities. Unfortunately, very **little** of **it is taken** seriously by politicians.*

2   Use the information above to correct the following sentences where necessary.

a   How much of the tourists actually realises the problems they cause?

b   Little of the soils can be used for cultivation now the trees have been cut down.

c   A large number of equipment are needed to camp at the bottom of the Canyon.

d   Only few luggages can be carried on the back of a donkey down the dirt tracks.

e   A large amount of rainforest are being cut down every year.

f   The amount of traffic are causing too many congestions in major cities.

g   Much governments believes that nuclear power are the key to future energy problems.

h   The Park Ranger gave me several good advices about camping in the national park.

i   Little people nowadays wear fur coats.

3   Both these pairs of sentences are correct, but there is a difference in meaning. What is it?

I make few mistakes with English grammar.
I make a few mistakes with English grammar.

I have little time to watch the TV at the weekend.
I have a little time to watch the TV at the weekend.

Ⓖ → page 172

G → page 172

Grammar extra

some and any and no

Look at the following sentences and decide what the rule is for using *some* and *any* and *no*.

a At lunchtime the Prime Minister announced some of the government's plans for reducing congestion in cities.

b I haven't been able to see any stars in the sky recently because of light pollution.

c Would you like me to give you some information on ways you can cut down on using water?

d Have you any idea of the amount of food that is wasted each day in the developed world?

e No amount of persuasion will make some people use public transport rather than private cars.

f Have you got any/some change for the parking meter?

g Any of the students could have answered the question.

Vocabulary

Expressions of quantity

4 Expressions like *a piece of* or *a bit of* are often used to limit an uncountable noun. However, these words aren't very precise and it is better to use the right expression.

EXAMPLE: *In a shop you ask for **a loaf of** bread; at home you ask for **a slice of** bread.*

Which of the words on the left are used with the uncountable nouns on the right?

shower	clothing
slice	lightning
item	rain
glass	cake
clap	string
pane	people
ball	glass
flash	chocolate
crowd	water
bar	thunder

5 Using the information in this unit, complete the following sentences.

a Would you like .... chocolate to take on your trip?
– Yes, could you put in a couple of .... ?

b Did you have .... bad weather over the weekend?
– Yes, heavy rain and enormous .... of lightning.

c .... of the football hooligans spent Saturday night smashing all the .... of glass in the local school.

d I used to have short .... , but I've decided to grow it.

e Could you give me .... about travelling in India?

f My bank always refuses to change .... that I bring back from abroad.

g You can only take one small .... on board the flight and all other items of .... must be checked in.

6 For questions 1–8, read the text below and think of the word which best fits each gap. Use only one word in each gap. There is an example at the beginning (0).

The Pyramids

On (0) ...*THE*... great rocky plain of Giza in Egypt, stand some of the world's most remarkable buildings – three pyramids. There are quite a (1) .... other pyramids in Egypt, but these three are the largest and most famous. They were erected more than 4,000 years (2) .... and still stand today.

As the Egyptians believed (3) .... life after death, each ruler had a great (4) .... of his treasure buried with him. (5) .... the pyramids are enormous, the rooms inside are very small, because the pyramids themselves consist chiefly of solid stone. The largest, the Great Pyramid at Giza, was built by King Khufu in about 2500 BC.

The pyramids were made out (6) .... huge blocks of stone (7) .... were quarried, transported to the construction site and then piled on top of (8) .... another with astonishing precision. It is believed that over 10,000 men were needed to build the pyramids.

Exam folder 8

Paper 3 Part 4 Multiple choice

In this part of the Listening paper you will usually hear an interview. There are seven questions. Each question has three options (A, B or C). You must choose the correct option. The questions follow the order of the information in the interview. You will hear the recording twice and you have one minute to read through the questions before you listen.

EXAM ADVICE

- Read the questions carefully in the time you are given before the recording begins and try to predict what you might hear. It is very important to use this time well.
- The questions will repeat the ideas and some of the words you will hear in the recording.
- You might hear each option A, B or C referred to in some way but only one of them will correctly answer the question.
- You can write notes on the question paper as you listen for the first time.
- Remember to put your answers on your answer sheet. At the end of the test there will be a pause of 5 minutes on the recording for you to copy all your answers onto your answer sheet.
- Always choose an answer, even if you are unsure about it.

1 You will hear a radio interview with a girl called Lisa Greene, who is talking about her stay at an ecolodge, an environmentally friendly hotel in Costa Rica, Central America. For questions 1–7, choose the best answer (A, B or C).

Look at question 1.

1 How did Lisa feel about her journey to Costa Rica?
  A She was relieved when she eventually arrived.
  B She was worried about missing her flight connections.
  C She was surprised that it took so long to get there.

Here are some things to think about before you listen to the recording:

- Read the question carefully. It's asking about how she *felt*.
- You need to ask yourself the following questions:

A How did she feel when she arrived – had the journey been a bad one?

B Did she feel anxious about missing her flight connections?

C Does she make any comment about the length of the journey being surprising?

2 10 Now listen to the first part of the recording. The recording will be stopped when you hear the following words:

... travelling by myself for the first time.

2 Decide on the correct answer for question 1. Which sentence in the interview tells you?

Remember that incorrect options often repeat the vocabulary you hear in the recording, and might be true but don't actually answer the question.

Here is the part of the recording script for question 1. Underline the sentence with the right answer.

Interviewer:	I'd like to welcome Lisa Greene to the studio today. Lisa, you won a competition in a magazine to stay at an ecolodge, an environmentally friendly hotel, in Costa Rica, didn't you?
Lisa:	That's right. I had to write an article about recycling and why it is a good thing for the planet.
Interviewer:	You hadn't travelled outside of Europe before – how did you feel about the journey?
Lisa:	Well, I flew to Costa Rica from London and then had to take a small plane to an airport very near the ecolodge. I was then picked up at the local airport by the ecolodge manager in an electric car. It all took a bit longer than I was expecting but then I was only used to short journeys within Europe. Anyway, I was so excited I didn't care about having to change planes or travelling by myself for the first time.

Now, look at the other two possible answers in question 1. Why are they not correct?

3 **2 11** Read through questions 2–7 and try to predict what you might hear. Then continue listening to the rest of the interview and answer questions 2–7.

> **2** What does Lisa say about the animals and birds she saw from the observation gallery?
>   **A** It was great to see some of the larger animals.
>   **B** Some of the birds were very friendly.
>   **C** She enjoyed feeding the monkeys fruit.
>
> **3** What did Lisa fail to understand at first about her accommodation?
>   **A** the lack of hot water
>   **B** the lights switching off automatically
>   **C** the air conditioning being out of order
>
> **4** What does Lisa say about walking in the forest?
>   **A** The noises you hear can be quite frightening.
>   **B** You need a guide as it's easy to get lost.
>   **C** It's important you have a good level of fitness.
>
> **5** Lisa says that one of the best parts of her trip was swimming
>   **A** in the sea.
>   **B** in a natural pool.
>   **C** in the ecolodge swimming pool.
>
> **6** Lisa says that the main purpose of the conservation centre is to
>   **A** train local people in building methods.
>   **B** inform tourists about the area.
>   **C** provide food for the ecolodge.
>
> **7** People will be able to buy a copy of the magazine
>   **A** in November.
>   **B** in January.
>   **C** in February.

Listening

1   Make a list of what you normally eat in a day for breakfast, lunch and dinner. Compare your list with a partner.

2   What do you think people eat in Japan, Alaska and California?

Kunu (Alaska)

Akiko (Japan)

Gayle (California)

3   **2** **12** Now you are going to hear these three women talking about the food they normally have for breakfast, lunch and dinner. Listen and make brief notes.

Whose diet would you like to try?

4   Would you eat any of the following? Why? / Why not?
   - a very red apple?
   - a green banana?
   - a soft biscuit?
   - blue bread?
   - flat lemonade?
   - very red meat?

Reading

5   You are going to read an article about the taste of food. Six sentences have been removed from the article. Choose from the sentences A–G the one which fits each gap (1–6). There is one extra sentence which you do not need to use.

How sound and colour influence the taste of food

The sound diners hear while they are eating food can change the way they think it tastes, scientists have discovered. In fact, researchers have also found that changing the colour of a food can influence the flavour experienced by consumers. Food manufacturers are now hoping to exploit the findings in an attempt to make their foods more appealing.

Previously it was thought that the sense of taste and smell were the only human senses that played a role in experiencing flavour. Professor Charles Spence, a sensory psychologist at Oxford University, is a leading expert in his field. **1** ☐ For example, listening to waves hitting the sea shore can make diners detect seafood flavours, while the sound of chickens clucking brings out the taste of eggs.

Professor Spence has also discovered that simply changing the colour of a food can influence the way it tastes. **2** ☐ He said: 'This colour has strong associations with very ripe fruit. Another example is the colour orange, which has such strong flavour associations that just changing the amount of orange on the packaging can make the flavour seem more acidic.'

For some foods sound is incredibly important, particularly if the food makes a sound itself when it is consumed. With carbonated drinks, for example, a lot of the fizzy flavour comes from the sound of bubbles popping. Scientists have found that boosting certain high frequency sounds when volunteers bite into crisps and biscuits could make them appear to taste crunchier. **3** ☐ Another study has used

A   He found that by changing a drink from yellow to a deep red, it is possible to make it taste up to 12 per cent sweeter than it really is.

B   Indeed, much research has been done on all four of these.

C   In that setting, everything appeared to be a normal colour.

D   They seemed to become softer once the sounds were lowered.

E   By melting, it changes its physical characteristics and creates contrasts that continually keep your senses interested.

F   He believes that it is possible to change the flavour of food simply by exciting people's sense of hearing.

G   If they are too green, that is also undesirable as people think they don't taste ripe even though they are.

brain scanning equipment to identify the parts of the brain that are stimulated by frozen foods. It found that the change in texture that, for example, ice cream undergoes in the mouth as it melts, is part of what makes it so enjoyable.

Flavour is not just as simple as the way something tastes, as all the other senses come into play and some can dominate the way the brain interprets a food. Ice cream activates a part of the brain which is just behind the eyes and is where emotions are processed. | 4 |

Another study has found that the colour of food has a significant effect on people's appetites. Test subjects were placed in a room with special coloured lighting installed, and then given a steak and French fries to eat. | 5 | However, when it was revealed that the steak was blue and the fries were green, some participants became ill.

Recently, one firm held a special taste conference in Brussels to demonstrate how the colour of tomatoes can effect how consumers enjoy them. Ian Puddephat, a leading scientist, said: 'Amazingly, we have found that there is such a thing as tomatoes that are too red. | 6 | How they feel is also particularly important for consumers. Some prefer a firm skin, while others want something that is softer and more associated with ripe juiciness.'

So next time you are in a restaurant or a supermarket, or just sitting down at home to eat something, think about whether your choices have been influenced by sound or colour. You may be surprised!

6   In groups, discuss these questions.

   a What do you think about the scientists' findings?
   b Do you trust the food industry to provide you with safe, healthy food?
   c Do you think you have a healthy diet?
   d Are you, or could you become, a vegetarian?
   e Is there anything you can't stand or aren't allowed to eat?

Vocabulary

Collocations – food

7   Choose the correct adjective or adverb to complete each sentence.

   EXAMPLE: *This tastes like canned / dairy soup – I much prefer soup that is freshly made.*

   a Silvio's on a diet – he has to give up all *bitter / rich* foods for a month.
   b When I opened the fridge, I realised the milk had gone *rotten / off.*
   c The meat that the local supermarket sells is often *tough / rich.*
   d I always buy yellow lemons because I know they are *strong / ripe.*
   e I like curry, as long as it tastes quite *mild / weak.*
   f The last apple in the bowl had to be thrown away because it was *juicy / rotten.*
   g The coffee in the café was a bit *bad / weak* for my taste, with too much milk in it.
   h When I opened the pack of meat, I realised from the smell that it had gone *bitter / bad.*

Speaking

8   Your college is thinking of opening a new relaxation area for students. There is only a certain amount of money available for the project. In pairs, decide which two things would be the most popular to include. Then change partners and explain your previous choices.

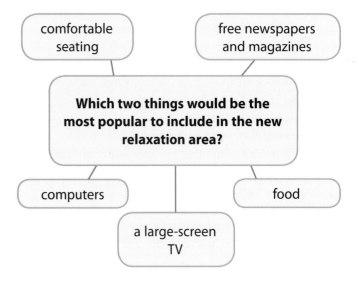

comfortable seating

free newspapers and magazines

Which two things would be the most popular to include in the new relaxation area?

computers

food

a large-screen TV

16.2

The article

1 Look at these nouns from the listening in 16.1:

waiter   noodles   fish   cheese   lunch

Which of these nouns are

- singular countable?
- plural?
- uncountable?

Which of them take

- *a/an* (the indefinite article)?
- *the* (the definite article)?
- nothing?

2 Match sentences a–j with rules 1–11. Some sentences match more than one rule. The rules can be used more than once.

a He's a waiter.
b The Earth is egg-shaped.
c The United States exports wheat.
d The British love curry.
e He's the best chef in Bangkok.
f I usually go to a restaurant that overlooks the River Thames.
g The Rocky Mountains are great for skiing.
h I hate fast food.
i There's a restaurant next to our house – it's the restaurant with a red sign.
j Football always makes me hungry.

    1 *the* is used with rivers, oceans, seas, mountain ranges
    2 no article is used with most streets, villages, towns, cities, countries, lakes, single mountains
    3 *the* is used with national groups
    4 *a/an* is used with jobs
    5 no article is used with sports
    6 *the* is used when there is only one of something
    7 *the* is used for countries in the plural, e.g. The Netherlands
    8 *the* is used with superlatives
    9 no article is used when a noun is used generally
    10 *a/an* is used when something is mentioned for the first time
    11 *the* is used when a noun has already been mentioned

3 Read through this article and decide whether to use *a/an*, *the* or nothing in the gaps. Some gaps can have more than one answer.

'I'll have what he's having.' That's what
(**1**) .... diners sometimes tell (**2**) ....
waiters when another customer is served
(**3**) .... meal that looks delicious. Wouldn't it be
simpler if you could see every dish on (**4**) ....
menu before making up your mind? In (**5**) ....
Japan, that's exactly what diners can do. There,
(**6**) .... restaurant displays of real-looking fake
food, called *sanpuru*, serve as (**7**) .... three-
dimensional menu.

At one time, restaurants in Japan used to display
real food to advertise (**8**) .... restaurant's
specialities, and to allow customers to 'preview' their
meal. (**9**) .... displays also meant that
(**10**) .... foreigners unable to read (**11**) ....
Japanese menu could figure out (**12**) .... best
thing to order. In the 1930s (**13**) .... first fake
foods were made from (**14**) .... wax. Eventually
such fake foods replaced (**15**) .... real foods.
Today *sanpuru* are made from vinyl, (**16**) ....
kind of plastic.

4 Decide whether you need to use an article or not in these sentences.

a I went to .... hospital to see a friend who was ill.

b I went to .... hospital when I was knocked off my bike.

c I go to .... library once a week.

d She always goes to .... bed early.

e I often get hay fever in .... summer.

f The shops in my town always close for .... lunch.

g My father used to go to work by .... bike.

h When are you going on .... holiday?

i Tom never gets to .... work on time.

j He earns £800 .... week.

k I'll visit you in .... October.

l I can't play .... football very well.

m George Washington once held .... office of US President.

n My uncle goes to .... prison to teach the prisoners computer skills.

o I've played .... flute ever since I was a child.

G → page 172

Possession

1 When we are talking about people we use *'s* or *s'*:
my sister's boyfriend, the visitors' cars
In the first example there is only one sister, so the apostrophe is before the *s*. In the second example, the apostrophe is after the *s* because there is more than one visitor.

2 *'s* is also used when we are talking about time or distance:
a month's holiday, a day's drive

3 We usually use *of* when we are talking about objects or position:
the back of the room, the film of the book
also for when a container has something in it:
a bottle of milk, a box of chocolates

4 Quite often we use a noun to describe another noun when it describes either the kind, use or place:
a pear tree, a coffee cup, a shop window

5 Correct the following sentences where necessary.

a The father of my husband works in an Italian restaurant.

b I looked through the restaurant's window but couldn't see anyone.

c He was sitting at the front of the terrace.

d I bought a magazine of cookery.

e I'm sure we all always look forward to pay day.

f Most waiters get tips to help supplement their day's pay.

g The boss of my company is having a big party to celebrate his birthday.

h Can I have a coffee cup and a piece of that delicious cake, please?

Corpus spot

The *Cambridge Learner Corpus* shows that exam candidates often have problems with expressions of time. A common problem is whether or not to use an article or preposition.

I received your letter **last week**.
NOT I received your letter ~~the~~ last week.

In the afternoon we're going to have tea in the Plaka.
NOT ~~At~~ the afternoon we're going to have tea in the Plaka.

Correct the mistakes candidates have made in the following sentences.

a I am coming at 24th June.

b So cycling at the rush hour is nearly as fast as driving a car.

c Young people have a nice time in the weekend.

d We had to wait long time for lunch.

e During evening she made a cake.

f At the first day of my holidays, I was afraid because I was alone.

g In afternoon we could go for a burger.

h I played tennis during seven years.

i The man is coming in Tuesday morning.

j I should arrive on 3 am in London.

Writing folder 8

Paper 2 Part 1 Essays

Look back at Writing folders 2 and 4, which focused on content and organisation. This Writing folder looks at communicative achievement and using appropriate language.

1 **Read this exam question and then look at the answer. Underline any language that is too informal for an essay.**

In your English class you have been talking about cycling to work. Now your English teacher has asked you to write an essay.

Write an essay using **all** the notes and give reasons for your point of view.

Is it better for people who live in towns and cities to travel to work by bicycle rather than using their cars?

Notes
Write about:

1. traffic
2. safety
3. .... (your own idea)

This essay discusses the advantages and disadvantages of cycling to work in an urban environment. It considers traffic congestion, the dangers to cyclists and the savings that can be made by using two wheels instead of four.

Nowadays there are loads of cars and trucks on the roads, causing long queues of traffic, especially during the rush hour. For drivers, the stress of waiting in a traffic jam must be unbelievable. So why don't they leave their vehicles at home and cycle instead?

Well, perhaps. Some people argue that it is healthier but I don't agree! You end up breathing in car fumes and risking your life every single day – cycling in cities can be incredibly dangerous and you can get seriously hurt.

On the other hand, it is much cheaper to use a bike. You don't have to buy petrol or pay for many repairs. I guess for this reason it is preferable to cycle to work, but only if you can avoid the busy main roads and follow more pleasant routes.

In conclusion, yes, we should cycle wherever possible. However, not enough is being done to encourage people to leave their cars at home and this needs to be addressed urgently.

2 **In pairs, look at the parts you have underlined and decide how they could be rewritten in an impersonal style. Which informal phrase should just be omitted?**

3 Think about the final sentence of the essay. Tick the ideas that could be solutions in a–h. Expand these ideas into full sentences, starting in one of the ways shown.

   a tax motorists more
   b give cyclists free helmets
   c restrict parking in cities
   d build more motorways
   e set lower speed limits
   f put up petrol prices
   g develop solar-powered cars
   h issue driving permits for use on certain days

The key to solving/reducing/dealing with … is …
One of the biggest questions/challenges/problems in the short term will be …
It is essential/vital/important that …
EXAMPLE: *It is essential that motorists be taxed more, so that their cars seem a less attractive option.*

4 The answer argues that *this needs to be addressed urgently.*

Some of the phrases below are used in jumbled sentences a–c. Reorder these sentences, adding commas where necessary.

in the short/medium/long term
within the next five years / our lifetime
urgent/immediate/instant action
of major importance / high priority / the utmost urgency

EXAMPLE: which cannot be justified / take urgent action / the government should / to cancel new road building
The government should take urgent action to cancel new road building, which cannot be justified.

   a whose exhaust fumes / is the introduction of tighter laws / cause greater pollution / on older vehicles / what is of high priority
   b to consult the public / in the short term / whose concerns have never been fully aired / it is essential
   c is needed / while in the medium term / to reduce the volume of cars / instant action / in our cities / on alternative forms of transport / further research should be carried out

5 Read this exam question and then make a paragraph plan. You can use some of the sentences from 3 and 4 in your final answer.

In your English class you have been talking about urban transport. Now your teacher has asked you to write an essay.

Write an essay using **all** the notes and give reasons for your point of view.

The only way to solve traffic problems in cities is to improve public transport.
Do you agree?

Notes
Write about:

   1. problems with public transport
   2. limiting the use of private cars
   3. .... (your own idea)

6 Write your essay in 140–190 words, following the Exam advice.

EXAM ADVICE

Content
● Include all three main ideas.

Communicative achievement
● Make your writing impersonal.
● Write in a fairly formal style.

Organisation
● Outline the main ideas in an introduction.
● Organise your essay in paragraphs.
● Summarise your main argument in the conclusion.

Language
● Rephrase key language in your own words where possible.
● Include passive forms and modal verbs.
● Introduce complex clauses with *while, which, whose,* etc.
● Use a range of vocabulary that is relevant to the topic.

Collectors and creators

Speaking

1 Here are two pairs of photographs showing various hobbies. Look at the first pair with another student. Decide who will be Student A and who Student B. Then read your instructions. Student A can also refer to the notes below.

> **Student A**
> Compare the pictures, describing the possible benefits and problems of collecting the things shown.
>
> *Shells – beautiful, many different kinds. Free! Need access to good beaches.*
>
> *Football badges – lots available. You can wear them. Don't take up a lot of space. Old ones may be expensive.*
>
> **Student B**
> When Student A has finished, say which hobby you would find more interesting, and why.

Now carry out the speaking task. Student A should try to keep talking for about a minute and then Student B should talk for a maximum of 20 seconds. Time yourselves.

2 Look at the second pair of photographs and change roles. Student A should listen carefully to what Student B says. Remember to keep talking for up to a minute.

> **Student B**
> Compare the pictures, describing the main differences between these two hobbies.
> (about 1 minute)
>
> **Student A**
> Say which hobby appeals to you more, and why.
> (20 seconds)

Did Student B manage to talk for a full minute? Suggest other ideas if necessary.

3 How many hobbies can you think of which involve collecting or making something? Work in two teams: the collectors and the creators. See who can produce the longer list! Then, in pairs, decide on the four most interesting hobbies from the two lists, giving your reasons why. You can agree to disagree!

Listening

4   **2 13** You will hear people talking in eight different situations. For questions 1–8 choose the best answer (A, B or C). You will hear each extract twice. Compare your answers with another student.

1 You hear a woman talking about making jewellery. What metal does she normally use?
   A gold
   B silver
   C copper

2 You hear two friends talking about postcards. The woman is keen to collect postcards which
   A are in good condition.
   B are from the 1930s.
   C have with a printed message.

3 You hear a radio talk about wooden objects. What is unusual about the objects the woman describes?
   A They were painted with beautiful designs.
   B They were made from different types of wood.
   C They were carved from a single piece.

4 You hear a man talking about his hobby. How does he spend his weekends?
   A pretending to be a soldier
   B doing a history course
   C producing different plays

5 You hear a girl talking about collecting beads. Which kind of beads does she have most of?
   A glass
   B wooden
   C plastic

6 You hear part of a conversation in a radio play. What is the man doing?
   A complaining about some goods
   B arranging to meet a journalist
   C describing what kind of model kits he buys

7 You hear an interview with a girl who collects pebbles. She paints them
   A to remind her of her holidays.
   B to improve her art technique.
   C to make some pocket money.

8 You hear an interview with a boy whose hobby is slot-car racing. Who introduced him to it?
   A his father
   B his friend
   C his cousin

5   In pairs, decide which of these hobbies would interest you least, explaining why. Report your views to the class.

Vocabulary

Phrasal verbs and expressions with *look*

6   In listening extracts 2 and 3, *look* was used as in a-c below. Seven more uses are given in d-j. Check their meanings before answering questions 1–10 below.

   a look for   f look at
   b be on the lookout   g look into
   c the look of   h Look out!
   d Now look here!   i look up to
   e look after   j look forward to

1 Who might you ask to **look at**
   A your wrist?   B a broken pipe?
   C faulty brakes?

2 What might you be planning to do if you are **looking for**
   A a needle?   B a saucepan?   C a dictionary?

3 Who might **be on the lookout** for
   A a missing yacht?   B murder clues?
   C tax savings?

4 Describe **the look of**
   A leather.   B thick mud.   C concrete.

5 Who **looks after**
   A patients?   B rose bushes?   C local residents?

6 Continue the statement **Now look here** …, as if you are arguing with
   A a bank manager.   B a young child.
   C a journalist.

7 What might someone discover if they **looked into**
   A a rejected proposal?   B an old murder case?
   C the possibility of working abroad?

8 Why might someone shout *Look out!* at you, if you were
   A driving?   B swimming in the sea?
   C walking under a ladder?

9 Who might these people **look up to**?
   A a six-year-old boy   B a first-year student
   C a trainee cook

10 What might these people be **looking forward to** doing?
   A someone who is running a marathon
   B someone who has been at sea for two months
   C someone who rarely has any time off

Relative clauses

1 Look at the pair of sentences a and b, then answer questions 1 and 2 for each of them.

a The children who were tired went straight to bed.

b The children, who were tired, went straight to bed.

1 Were all the children tired?

2 Did all the children go to bed?

Which sentence contains a defining relative clause? Which has a non-defining clause in it?

G → page 173

Explain the difference in meaning between c and d.

c It was getting late, so we decided to stay at the first hotel which had a pool.

d It was getting late, so we decided to stay at the first hotel, which had a pool.

2 Here are two examples of relative clauses from the listening extracts. Which sentence has a defining relative clause and which has a non-defining one?

a Jamie Eagle, who is the outright winner of today's slot-car racing, is with me now.

b I'm on the lookout for older ones that have text on the picture.

Identify the relative clause in each of these examples, underline the relative pronoun used, and decide whether the clause is defining (D) or non-defining (N).

c Looking at the stamps, they're older than you say, which is brilliant.

d I knew someone once who had an absolute passion for making things out of wood.

e It was my cousin who's to blame.

f Jenny Braintree, whose bedroom I'm sitting in right now, has a rather unusual hobby.

g I'm trying to paint a scene from every country in the world, most of which I haven't been to.

h The group that puts on these events was only formed about four months ago.

3 What relative pronoun has been left out in this example? Insert it in the correct place.

Here are those cards I bought for you in Oxford.

> Omission of the relative pronoun is quite common in spoken English, but can only be done when it is the object of a defining relative clause. So, for example, you could not leave out the word *that* in example *h*.

Decide what relative pronouns have been left out of these sentences and underline the defining clause in each.

a The picture I wanted to buy had already been sold.

b She was the teacher I really looked up to.

c The thing I can't stand about Harry is his odd socks!

d That boy you met at John's party plays tennis.

e The hotel we stayed at had luxurious bathrooms.

4 The last example could be rewritten like this:

The hotel where we stayed had luxurious bathrooms.

> You can use *where*, *when* and *why* in defining relative clauses after nouns to do with place, time and reason. Again, in spoken English, *when* and *why* are sometimes omitted. Here are two examples from 17.1.
>
> *2003 was the year my passion for jewellery making began.*
>
> *That's not the reason she's mad at me though.*
>
> In non-defining relative clauses, these words cannot be omitted.

Insert *where*, *when* or another *wh-* word into these non-defining relative clauses.

a The cycle race starts at the Hatchet Inn, ... many riders will be staying overnight.

b The earthquake happened shortly before dawn, ... most people were asleep.

c Aidan, ... lives in our road, plays the double bass.

d They sent an information booklet, ... was really helpful.

Relative pronouns

who or whom?

5 In informal English, it is always safe to use *who* as both subject and object. However, in formal written English, *whom* is the object form, often used with a preposition.

Rewrite sentences a–c using *whom*, adding commas where necessary and making any other changes.

EXAMPLE: *The man they had given all their money to took a one-way flight to Rio.*
The man to whom they had given all their money took a one-way flight to Rio.

a The collector I have bought many rare film posters from lives in Paris.
The collector ....

b The weird millionaire that my sister worked for expected her to clean his collection of antiques every day.
The weird millionaire ....

c I went riding with Wetherby and he was always the perfect gentleman.
Wetherby ....

whose

6 You use *whose* to add information about a person or thing just mentioned. Join the two sentences in a–d, using *whose*.

EXAMPLE: Johnson is going to sail around the world alone. His yacht is sponsored by a leading British firm.
Johnson, whose yacht is sponsored by a leading British firm, is going to sail around the world alone.

a The singer has always been a fan of modern British painters. His art collection is now worth millions.

b Maria works in a bank in central London. Her hobbies include skydiving and collecting antiques.

c The hot air balloon was designed by the Montgolfier brothers. Its first flight was made in 1783.

d The number of collectors has doubled over the last decade. Collectors form an increasingly large part of the buyers at local auctions.

G → page 173

Vocabulary

Word formation

7 What nouns are related to these adjectives?

a delightful	**c** exceptional	**e** remarkable
b elegant	**d** massive	**f** substantial

8 Confident and effective use of a range of adjectives in Papers 2 and 4 will impress the examiners. Put the adjectives in 7 into the groups below.

emphasising attractiveness
emphasising extent
emphasising rarity

9 For questions 1–8, read the text and think of the word which best fits each gap. Use only one word in each gap. There is an example at the beginning (0).

A PASSION FOR BOTTLES

Hobbies (0) *can* so easily take over your life, can't they? They make substantial demands on your time and, even (1) .... seriously, they sometimes invade your living space. One crazy friend of mine is haunted by the desire to collect bottles. This passion, (2) .... started quite by chance, has now reached an absurd stage. For my friend, (3) .... massive collection currently stands at 3,429 bottles, has had to rebuild his house to accommodate his obsession. Admittedly, there are some remarkable items, such (4) .... two elegant examples in Murano glass, an exceptional hand-painted wine bottle (5) .... the 1920s, and about fifty delightful perfume bottles in every colour, shape and size you could imagine. However, the vast majority of his bottles are very ordinary and (6) .... to have been taken away for recycling long ago. The reason he has hung on to them for all of this time is (7) .... at all clear. Just think, if only my friend had chosen bottle tops, his collection (8) .... only fill three drawers at most!

10 Underline the six adjectives from 7 in the text. Choose another noun from the box that collocates with each adjective (some nouns can be used with more than one adjective). Write sentences using your adjective–noun combinations.

> amount   challenge   memory
> painting   scale   woman

EXAMPLE: *My brother has a massive amount of information about model trains.*

Exam folder 9

Paper 1 Part 6 Gapped text

This part of the Reading and Use of English paper requires you to read a text from which six sentences have been removed, and then choose the correct sentences to fill the gaps. There is always one extra sentence which you don't need.

There are fewer questions in this part than in Part 7 but, as in Part 5, each question is 'double-weighted', that is, it is worth two marks instead of one. Part 6 is a difficult task and you must allow enough time for it.

Complete the exam task below using the steps in the Advice box. Try to keep to the suggested timings.

EXAM ADVICE

- Read the text quickly, in order to get an idea of what it is about. (2 minutes)
- Underline key words in the text to predict what each gap might contain. Look for linking and reference words too. (4 minutes)
- Scan the missing sentences for matching information and note down likely answers. (4 minutes)
- Read through the whole text with your answers in place to check that it all makes sense. (3 minutes)
- Make sure that the extra sentence does not fit anywhere. (2 minutes)

You are going to read a magazine article about building an unusual bridge. Six sentences have been removed from the article. Choose from the sentences A–G the one which fits each gap (1–6). There is one extra sentence which you do not need to use.

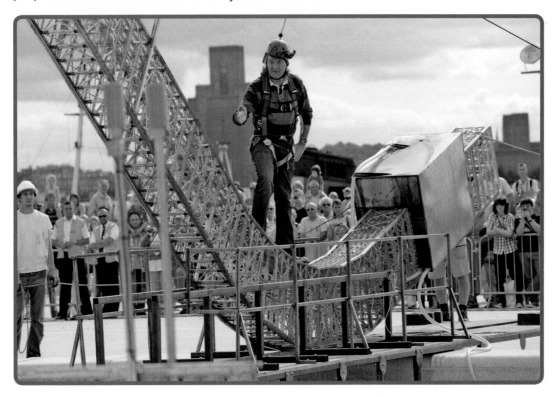

Building the Meccano bridge in Liverpool

Meccano is an educational toy that encourages children to construct models out of metal. Anything from a robot to a bridge or a plane can be made using this toy, whose basic parts consist of long strips and flat plates of metal, together with the nuts and bolts that are needed to put them together.

The idea for Meccano began in a small shop in Liverpool in 1898, when Franck Hornby invented a construction game for his children using screws and nuts. This gave rise to the Meccano system at the very beginning of the 20th century. **1** [ ] Some 66 years later, the factory here closed and production was moved to France, and later, also to China.

It was no accident therefore that Liverpool was chosen as the place where a lifesize bridge made solely from pieces of Meccano would be built. The project formed part of a TV series called 'James May's Toy Stories', which featured ambitious constructions out of some of Britain's best-loved toys. **2** [ ]

If the total length of Meccano used in the bridge was laid end to end, it would stretch over 5 kilometres. Around 100,000 individual pieces were needed and it took 11 weeks to build the bridge. **3** [ ]

For the earlier stage, Liverpool University was approached by the television company and asked to run a bridge design competition. **4** [ ] The winning proposal was drawn up by three of their most talented students, whose ideas were then taken forward by a structural engineering consultant and turned into professional drawings.

Engineering students at Liverpool University were largely responsible for the bridge's construction, assisted by members of the North East Meccano Guild. **5** [ ] They also organise regular museum visits and were eager to participate in the bridge-building project.

The Meccano bridge spans a canal and is in two sections. These are connected by a series of pulleys and work together. **6** [ ] The other rolls out vertically and both sections meet over the middle of the canal to form a level platform. At the public opening, TV presenter James May had to walk the whole way across the bridge. He admitted to feeling nervous as a big crowd encouraged him to take his first steps. However, there was no need for concern, as the bridge supported his weight without problems.

A Five teams from the School of Architecture took part in this and some excellent work was produced.

B One of the first places where it was made was the British city of Liverpool.

C This is a club where fans of the product get together to share ideas.

D That was the amount of time needed once the preliminary planning and design work had been done.

E One of the pair looks a bit like a canal lock gate and swings out horizontally.

F This canal extension runs from Liverpool to Leeds and the new bridge sits five metres above it.

G Other programmes included the building of a real house from Lego and a lifesize 'model' plane.

What's in a book?

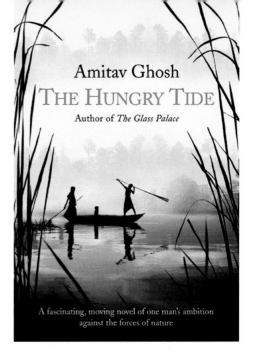

Amitav Ghosh
THE HUNGRY TIDE
Author of *The Glass Palace*

A fascinating, moving novel of one man's ambition against the forces of nature

Reading

1 Look at the illustration and decide what it shows. Which part of the world might this be?

2 The text is from *The Hungry Tide* by Amitav Ghosh. What do you learn about the novel from these reviews?

This is a story of adventure and unlikely love, of identity and history, set in a group of tiny islands known as the Sundarbans.

The author has a great talent for developing compelling plots out of apparently unpromising circumstances and characters.

3 Skim the first paragraph of the text. Where is the action taking place? Which character is mentioned? Continue reading the text quickly.

The train was at a standstill, some twenty minutes outside Kolkata, when an unexpected stroke of luck presented Piya with an opportunity to go for a seat beside a window. She had been sitting in the stuffiest part of the train compartment, on the edge of a bench, with her backpacks arrayed around her: now, moving to the open window, she saw that the train had stopped at a station called Champahati.

Looking over her shoulder, Piya spotted a tea-seller patrolling the platform. Reaching through the bars of the window, she summoned him with a wave. She had never cared for the kind of chai, Indian tea, sold in Seattle, her hometown in the USA, but somehow, in the ten days she had spent in India she had developed an unexpected taste for milky, overboiled tea served in earthenware cups. There were no spices in it for one thing, and this was more to her taste than the chai at home.

She paid for her tea and was trying to manoeuvre the cup through the bars when the man in the seat opposite her own suddenly flipped over a page, jolting her hand. She turned her wrist quickly enough to make sure that most of the tea spilled out of the window, but she could not prevent a small trickle from spilling over his papers.

'Oh, I'm so sorry!' Piya was very embarrassed: of everyone in the compartment, this was the last person she would have chosen to scald with her tea. She had noticed him while waiting on the platform in Kolkata and she had been struck by the self-satisfied tilt of his head and the way in which he stared at everyone around him, taking them in, sizing them up, sorting them all into their places.

'Here,' said Piya, producing a handful of tissues. 'Let me help you clean up.'

'There's nothing to be done,' he said testily. 'These pages are ruined anyway.'

For a moment she considered pointing out that it was he who had knocked her hand. But all she could bring herself to say was,

'I'm very sorry. I hope you'll excuse me.'

'Do I really have a choice?' he said in a tone more challenging than ironic. 'Does anyone have a choice when they're dealing with Americans these days?'

Piya had no wish to get into an argument so she let this pass. Instead she opened her eyes wide and, in an attempt to restore peace, came out with, 'But how did you guess?'

'About what?'

'About my being American? You're very observant.'

This seemed to do the trick. His shoulders relaxed as he leaned back in his seat. 'I didn't guess,' he said. 'I knew.'

'Was it my accent?' she said.

'Yes,' he said with a nod. 'I'm very rarely wrong about accents. I'm a translator you see, and an interpreter as well, by profession. I like to think that my ears are tuned to the nuances of spoken language.'

'I'm afraid English is my only language. And I wouldn't claim to be much good at it either.'

A frown of puzzlement appeared on his forehead. 'And you're on your way to Canning?'

'Yes.'

'But tell me this,' he said. 'If you don't know any Bengali or Hindi, how are you planning to find your way around over there?'

'I'll do what I usually do,' she said with a laugh. 'I'll try to wing it. Anyway, in my line of work there's not much talk needed.'

'And what is your line of work, if I may ask?'

'I'm a cetologist,' she said. 'That means –' She was beginning, almost apologetically, to expand on this when he interrupted her.

'I know what it means,' he said sharply. 'You don't need to explain. It means you study marine mammals. Right?'

'Yes,' she said, nodding. 'Dolphins, whales and so on. I'm hoping to wangle a permit to do a survey of the marine mammals of the Sundarbans.'

4 Read the text carefully to identify the parts that relate to each question. When choosing your answers, decide why the other options are wrong.

1 In the first paragraph, Piya is relieved when she gets a window seat because it means that
   A she doesn't have to stand up for the rest of the train journey.
   B there is less chance that she will miss her stop.
   C there is more room for her backpacks.
   D she no longer has to suffer from a lack of air.

2 Piya has found that the tea or *chai* she has bought while she has been in India
   A reminds her of her home in Seattle.
   B is disappointingly bland in taste.
   C is preferable to the *chai* she has had in the past.
   D would have tasted better if served fresh.

3 When Piya had first seen the man she had thought that
   A he seemed to think he was better than other people.
   B he had been looking for someone he knew on the station platform.
   C he had tried to keep his distance from his fellow passengers.
   D he was someone she should avoid if she could.

4 Piya asks 'But how did you guess?' in order to
   A find out what the man really thought about Americans.
   B try to calm the situation down by starting a conversation.
   C make sure the man knew he was being rude.
   D ensure the man realised that she had apologised.

5 What is Piya's attitude to the work ahead of her in Canning?
   A She is a little worried about what she might find there.
   B She is hoping to learn enough of the local languages to cope.
   C She knows that it will be a working environment she is familiar with.
   D She is doubtful whether there will be anyone there who speaks English.

6 How does the man react when Piya tells him her profession?
   A He is keen to point out that he knows quite a bit about it.
   B He is irritated that she thinks he doesn't understand.
   C He is relieved that she is not just an American backpacker.
   D He is pleased she is apologetic in her reply.

Vocabulary

Phrasal verbs with *come* and *go*

5 Read these examples from the text. What do the phrasal verbs in italics mean?

An unexpected stroke of luck presented Piya with an opportunity to *go for* a seat beside a window.

Instead she opened her eyes wide and, in an attempt to restore peace, *came out with*, 'But how did you guess?'

Make phrasal verbs with *come* and *go* to use in a suitable form in a–h.

	across
	ahead
	by
come	off
go	out
	through
	up
	up with

a The novelist has .... a remarkable plot for his latest book.

b It's risky to spend much time writing until a publisher has decided to .... with your proposal and issued a contract.

c Sales of all her titles .... after an extensive lecture tour.

d Time .... slowly while I was on my own and I managed to do a great deal of reading.

e When J. K. Rowling's last Harry Potter novel .... , there were large queues at bookshops around the world.

f I .... an exceptional detective novel the other day when I was browsing the library shelves.

g Towards the end of his life, the writer Ernest Hemingway .... a period of severe depression.

h I used to love science fiction but I've really .... it recently.

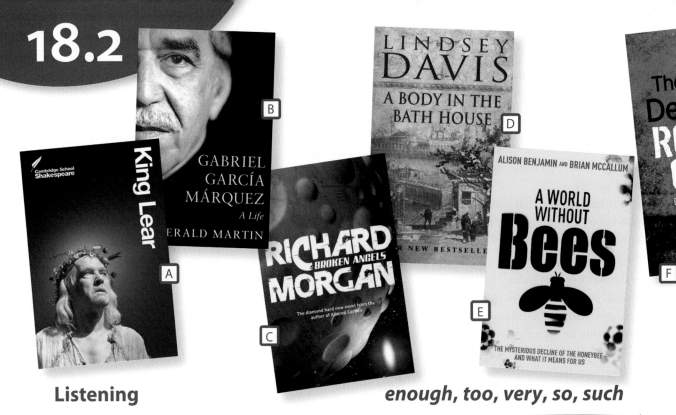

Listening

1 Identify the books shown, choosing from these types.

science fiction   biography   short stories
crime novel   non-fiction   historical novel   play

2 **2 14** You will hear five people talking about books they have read recently. Match the books shown above to the five speakers. There is one extra which you do not need.

Speaker 1   [**1**]
Speaker 2   [**2**]
Speaker 3   [**3**]
Speaker 4   [**4**]
Speaker 5   [**5**]

enough, too, very, so, such

> **Corpus spot**
>
> Be careful with word order when using *enough* – the *Cambridge Learner Corpus* shows that candidates often make mistakes with this.
>
> We were **lucky enough** to meet some famous writers.
> NOT We were ~~enough lucky~~ to meet some famous writers.

3 Read this article about the role of the book today, ignoring the missing words. Does the writer believe that the book has a future? Why? / Why not?

For questions 1–8, think of the word which best fits each gap. Use only one word in each group. There is an example at the beginning (0).

The book in the twenty-first century

How many times in (0) __THE__ last hundred years or so have people talked of the imminent death of the book? Films were an early threat, because they were so effective at telling stories in a visual way. Next there was radio, which swept into the mid-twentieth century and provided such alternatives to books (1) _____ drama, documentaries and discussions. When television arrived, many people believed that it (2) _____ finish the book off. Nowadays, (3) _____ the threat from TV, printed books are thought to be endangered by computers and the Internet, and by other technological attractions, too. If that is so, surely there are now enough reasons (4) _____ the book ought to be dead, or certainly very badly injured.

However, this is far from the case. Firstly, we have more leisure time than we (5) _____ to, and people are generally living longer. This means there is more time available to read and do other things we enjoy. Aside (6) _____ this, there is the strength of the book as a tradition. We are all too dismissive of traditions in our modern world, but they can have a very strong pull on us. Last but (7) _____ least, the book is such a practical tool: it doesn't cost too much, it is usually small enough to carry around, and it can easily (8) _____ revisited. We will never go without books, even if they are now read increasingly in e-book form rather than in print.

4 Find all the examples of the following words in the article in 3 and study the ways in which they are used. There are 12 examples in all. Then match the examples to the statements a–k. There is one extra statement which you do not need.

enough

a used before an uncountable noun or a countable noun in its plural form to say that there is as much of something as is needed

b used after an adjective or adverb to say that someone or something has as much of a quality as is needed

c used after an adverb in certain expressions

too

d used in front of an adjective or adverb to say that there is more of something than is acceptable or desirable

e used after a piece of information, to emphasise its importance

very

f used to give emphasis to an adjective or adverb

so

g used to emphasise an adjective or adverb

h used to indicate that an amount is approximate

i used to refer back to something that has already been mentioned

such

j used to give an example of something

k used to emphasise an adjective in a noun group

Now compare some of these examples. What are the differences in usage between the two words in brackets?

b and **d** (enough/too)
d and **f** (too/very)
f and **g** (very/so)
g and **k** (so/such)

G → page 173

5 Insert *enough* into each of these sentences in the correct place.

a Surely you've had time to finish the exercise?

b The room wasn't large to hold everyone.

c There weren't books to go round, so we had to share.

d I had had of other people's problems, so I left work early.

e The course was cancelled as not people had enrolled for it.

f – How much money do you have on you?
– I've got to pay for the cinema and buy us supper after.

g But that's quite about me! What about you?

h Funnily, I'm reading one of his books at the moment, too.

6 Complete the second sentence so that it has a similar meaning to the first sentence, using the word given. Do not change the word given. You must use between two and five words, including the word given.

1 The weather was too cold for us to go out.
SUCH
It was ....
didn't go out.

2 I'm sorry there's not enough time to explain.
TOO
I'm sorry there's ....
you an explanation.

3 Why not turn professional, as you are such a good swimmer?
SO
You swim ....
turn professional.

4 Barry really knows how to get other people involved.
VERY
Barry ....
other people involved.

5 I make all my clothes by hand, so it's very time-consuming.
SUCH
It ....
time because my clothes are all hand-made.

6 Provided this is the case, your money will be refunded.
SO
If ....
will be given.

Writing folder 9

Paper 2 Part 2 Reviews

Look back at Writing folder 6, which covered film and TV reviews. This Writing folder focuses on book reviews.

1 Read this review and correct the 20 spelling and punctuation errors.

The book 'Marcovaldo', by Italo Calvino is one of the jewels of 20th century fiction. It is actually a series of twenty short stories, all focusing on the same caracter – Marcovaldo – who lives with his large family in an unnamed city in the north of italy. Each story is set, in a diferent season: there are five about living in the city in summer, and so on.

Many aspects of modern life are described, such as advertiseing and pollution of the enviroment, though the book is not completly true to life. This is perhaps it's greatest strength. It has a unique mixture of realistic events and bizzare ones, which often take the reader by suprise.

One particluar story features the publicity campains of rival soap powder manufacturers. Marcovaldos' children and their frends collect hundreds of free cartons of washing powder, which they hope to sell to people in the neibourhood. In the end, they have to get rid of everything quickly and so throw the cartons into the River. The story closes with a memorable descripcion of soap bubbles being blown over the city their whiteness competing with the black factory smoke. Black wins.

2 Based on the content of these three paragraphs, choose the most suitable final paragraph for the review, A, B or C.

A

If you are looking for a thrilling novel with plenty of action, I strongly advise you to choose this book. You won't be able to put it down!

B

The adventures of this ordinary hero will move you at times and make you smile at others. This book is highly recommended.

C

Short story collections can be a disappointment and this one is no exception. Unfortunately, the episodes in Marcovaldo's life lack atmosphere and exist solely in black and white.

3 Paragraph C talks about episodes that lack atmosphere. Both words apply to events rather than to characters. Sort the nouns below into two basic categories. Which two words can apply to both characters and events?

action adventure ambition attitude
chaos determination enthusiasm
impact incident loyalty manner
mood reputation sympathy
temper theme

4 Use some of the nouns in 3 to complete sentences a–h.

a The bodyguard's .... is never in question and he remains at her side throughout the action.

b Great .... is shown by the writer in describing the man's miserable way of life.

c The passages on the utter .... of war are the most powerful in the book.

d This writer has earned a remarkable .... for creating suspense from the very first page.

e Although the event appears trivial at the time, it has a massive .... on both their lives.

f The author skilfully contrasts the quiet and polite .... of the servant with that of his unpleasant master.

g An important .... of the early chapters is the changing landscape and one event in particular illustrates this.

h One particularly shocking .... of cruelty proves to be the turning point of the story.

5 Read the exam questions and choose the one you would prefer to answer.

An online bookseller wants to post some positive reviews of novels on its website and you decide to take part. You should outline the writer's skill at creating characters and explain why you would recommend the novel to people of your own age.

Write your **review**.

Your college magazine has invited readers to submit book reviews for the next issue. In your review, you should mention a memorable event in the book and explain why you would recommend the book to other students at the college.

Write your **review**.

6 Plan your answer. Then write your review in 140–190 words, following the Exam advice below. You may be able to adapt some of the sentences in 4.

EXAM ADVICE

Content
- Remember to mention what you are reviewing by name.
- Add a recommendation for a positive review.

Communicative achievement
- Imagine your target reader and write in a suitable style for that person.
- Communicate your ideas clearly and effectively.

Organisation
- Organise your review in paragraphs.
- State some basic facts in an introduction.

Language
- Include a range of adjective–noun collocations.
- Use the language of opinion as well as description.

Units 13–18 Revision

Topic review

1 Together with a partner read these sentences and discuss which are true for you, giving more details. Try to use as much of the vocabulary and language from the units you have just studied as you can.

a Although I like to read at night, sometimes I'm just too tired to stay awake.

b I have never considered being a vegetarian.

c My cooking is so bad that no one will eat it.

d I'd rather have an interesting job than a large salary.

e There was one subject that I did at school that I just couldn't stand.

f My teachers told me that I would do well after I left school.

g I think that more men have hobbies than women.

h I don't have enough time to read books.

i I admit that I could have worked harder at school.

j I don't do enough to save the planet.

Vocabulary

2 For questions 1–8, read the text below and decide which answer (A, B, C or D) best fits each gap. There is an example at the beginning (0).

Example:

0 **A** made   **B** done   **C** got   **D** had

0	A	B	C	D

Kitchen Star

Peter White has (**0**) .... such a great success of his new restaurant Tastes that he has just received a second star. The fourteen-table restaurant is fully booked every evening this year, and two receptionists are on full-time duty to ensure the business (**1**) .... smoothly.

However, life hasn't always been so easy for Peter. He (**2**) .... in Northern Ireland, in a family which, although poor, always (**3**) .... on eating well and they never went without. After doing a (**4**) .... at catering college, and passing his exams with distinction, he moved to London to work in one of the city's (**5**) .... restaurants. On his first day, Peter remembers two things – the smell of baking bread and the chef throwing a pan of sauce at him because he hadn't stirred it enough! Peter (**6**) .... that he doesn't treat his own (**7**) .... in such a manner, (**8**) .... he does admit to shouting and regular outbursts of anger!

1 A runs	**B** happens	**C** flows	**D** moves
2 A brought up	**B** put up	**C** grew up	**D** showed up
3 A promised	**B** insisted	**C** accepted	**D** maintained
4 A training	**B** work	**C** course	**D** lecture
5 A head	**B** peak	**C** top	**D** lead
6 A tells	**B** claims	**C** denies	**D** speaks
7 A crew	**B** troop	**C** staff	**D** band
8 A despite	**B** because	**C** even	**D** although

Grammar

3 Correct the following sentences.

   a There are too much traffic in our town.

   b I have so a lot of the work to do, I don't know where to start.

   c The Netherlands and the Austria are both countries in the European Union.

   d Her house, which roof is thatched, is twelfth century.

   e John plays piano and he also plays the football, whereas his brother prefers playing the chess.

   f Let me give you an advice – don't go on a travel without checking whether you need any visa or not.

   g There's a man over there which has been watching us for about half an hour.

   h I lived in Las Vegas for ten years and I am still finding it exciting.

   i By this time next year I will taught since twenty years.

   j He asked me where was the police station.

   k I saw a bit of lightning when I was out in the garden.

   l Have you got information enough to object about the factory noise?

   m He's the one to whom I gave the book to.

   n My eldest son who lives in Paris is a physicist.

4 Complete the sentence beginnings a–g with their endings 1–7.

   EXAMPLE: **a** **5** *He apologised for overcooking the meat.*

   a He apologised
   b She denied
   c The chef claimed
   d The customer insisted
   e My neighbour warned
   f Next time you come, I promise
   g The waiter encouraged

   1 me that the restaurant was expensive.
   2 to make you a cake.
   3 overcharging them for the coffee.
   4 on seeing the kitchen.
   5 for overcooking the meat.
   6 them to try the chocolate ice cream.
   7 he hadn't forgotten to order the eggs.

Phrasal verbs revision quiz

5 The phrasal verbs here are from Units 1–18. Decide which answer (A, B or C) is correct. Then, if possible, write another correct answer of your own.

   1 What could you get over?
     A a bicycle
     B the flu
     C a difficult meeting

   2 What might take off?
     A a business
     B a walk
     C a coat

   3 What kind of thing might you come up with?
     A a talk
     B a suggestion
     C your foot

   4 What would you set off on?
     A a weekend
     B a party
     C a journey

   5 Where do you check in?
     A at a hotel
     B at a college
     C at a museum

   6 What can go by slowly?
     A food
     B time
     C weather

   7 If you come across someone or something, is it usually
     A by accident?
     B on purpose?
     C on time?

   8 What might you want to cut down?
     A your hair
     B your car
     C your expenses

   9 What might you want to get out of?
     A seeing relatives
     B a bus
     C a DVD

   10 What sort of things can go up?
     A prices
     B trees
     C windows

19.1 An apple a day ...

1 How often do you get a good eight hours' sleep?
- A Every night – and I prefer nine or ten hours.
- B Not often – I don't need much sleep.
- C I sometimes find it hard to get to sleep.

2 How often do you do any exercise?
- A Once a week.
- B Every day.
- C Hardly ever.

3 What do you usually have for lunch?
- A A large meal.
- B Salad or sandwiches.
- C Nothing.

4 When did you last have a cold?
- A I usually have one or two a year.
- B I can't remember.
- C I get them all the time.

5 How many cups of tea or coffee do you drink a day?
- A No more than three.
- B I don't drink anything with caffeine in it.
- C Between four and fourteen.

6 You have a headache. Do you
- A go straight to the doctor?
- B take an aspirin?
- C hope it will go away?

7 Do you think it's necessary to add salt to your food?
- A Sometimes.
- B Never.
- C Always.

8 Which is true for you?
- A I've given up smoking.
- B I've never smoked.
- C I smoke about five cigarettes or more a day.

9 Which is true for you?
- A I think I'm fit and healthy.
- B I think illness is all in the mind.
- C I sometimes worry about my health.

How did you score?

Mostly As

You are fairly healthy and have a good attitude to life. You <u>should try</u> to watch what you eat a little more, and if I were you, I'd try to do a little more exercise. Too much work and not enough play isn't good for you! I think it's about time you thought about your diet.

Mostly Bs

You are obviously in the peak of condition! I recommend you relax, as you ought to get some rest, even if you don't need much sleep. Overdoing things can lead to illness! Why don't you try doing more reading, or go on holiday – or have you ever thought of playing a musical instrument?

Mostly Cs

Oh dear! It's time you took a good look at your lifestyle. Missing meals and not getting enough sleep and exercise are very bad for you. My advice to you is to start right away – you'd better join a gym. I also suggest cutting down on coffee and drinking more water and fruit juice. Too much caffeine will keep you awake!

Speaking

1 Look at the photos above and say why you think the people have chosen these activities. Then discuss the following questions in pairs.

- Do you prefer to exercise alone or in a class? Why?
- Would you like to spend time in a gym like the one in the photo?
- What do you think of the exercise facilities in your town?
- What do you think is the best type of exercise? Why?

Modals 3: Advice and suggestion

2 How healthy are you? Complete the questionnaire. Do you agree with what is said about your results? Compare with a partner.

3 Underline the verbs and phrases which are used to give advice and make suggestions. One has been done for you in the 'Mostly As'. This is an example of advice. Make a note of what follows the verb or expression.

EXAMPLE: *should* + infinitive without *to*

Look at these problems and, with a partner, give advice and make suggestions. Try to vary the verbs and phrases you use.

EXAMPLE: *I can't stop sneezing.*
ADVICE: *If I were you, I'd take a cold shower.*

a I woke up covered in spots this morning.
b I've burnt my hand.
c I'm hoping to be picked for the local cycling team.
d I think I've broken my wrist.
e I'm going on holiday to a tropical country.
f I'm going to faint.
g I've been stung by a wasp.
h I never seem to have any energy.

4 The expressions *It's time …*, *It's about time …* and *It's high time …* are used to express strong feelings about something that hasn't been done or about something that should happen very soon.

*I think it's about time **you thought** about your diet a bit more.*
*It's time **you took** a good look at your lifestyle.*
*It's high time **you did** some exercise.*

Corpus spot

The *Cambridge Learner Corpus* shows that exam candidates often forget to use the past simple with these expressions.
It's about time I **joined** a serious riding club.
NOT It's about time I join a serious riding club.

When you are talking generally, it is possible to use the infinitive, but only after *It's time*, not after *It's high time* or *It's about time.*

It's time to go home now. (referring to everyone, including the speaker)
It's time I/you/he/she/we/they went home now. (referring to specific people)

What would you say to a friend in these situations?

EXAMPLE: Your friend's hair is too long.
It's time you had a haircut.

a He smokes 40 a day.
b She drives everywhere.
c She watches TV for six hours a day.
d He lost his job six months ago.
e He likes eating chips.
f He's been living with his parents for 30 years.
g Her coat has holes in it.
h She's always borrowing your books.
i He's always late for work.
j Her car is always breaking down.

G → page 174

Vocabulary

Topic set – parts of the body

5 Can you point to these body parts in the photo?

chest
elbow
knee
wrist
ankle
thigh
jaw
waist
eyebrow

6 If A happened to you, what in B would you do?

EXAMPLE: *If I broke my arm, I'd wear a sling.*

A If I …	B I'd …
broke my leg	take an aspirin
had a headache	have stitches
cut my knee badly	go to bed
grazed my elbow	take some cough medicine
sprained my ankle	put a bandage on it
had flu	get an elastoplast / a plaster
had a cough	have it put in plaster

Phrases with *on*

7 In the questionnaire on health, the phrase *on holiday* was used. Look at these expressions with *on* and then complete the sentences with a suitable expression.

on offer   on purpose   on duty   on average
on condition that   on behalf of   on balance

a I go to the gym .... two or three times a week.
b I had to accept the prize .... my brother because he was ill at the time.
c I didn't break the vase ....
d I'd hate a job as a nurse or police officer where I had to be .... at weekends.
e I'll do more exercise .... I can watch more TV in the evening.
f .... I prefer running to cycling.
g I always try to buy things which are .... in the shops.

Which of the above statements are true for you?

Listening

1 Do you know what these forms of alternative medicine are?

homeopathy   osteopathy   reflexology   herbal medicine

2 Acupuncture is a type of alternative medicine. It is used in Chinese medicine. It consists of steel needles being inserted into the skin. Have you ever tried it?

3 How do you think the patients in the photos feel at this moment? What differences do you think there are in the types of treatment being given?

4 ● 2 15 You will hear an interview with Dr Sylvia Carpenter, who is talking about acupuncture. For questions 1–7, choose the best answer (A, B or C).

1 What do we find out about Sylvia's time in Hong Kong?
  A She was there to study acupuncture.
  B She practised acupuncture while she was there.
  C She enjoyed seeing a different approach to medicine.

2 Patients who Sylvia recommends for acupuncture
  A should have a blood test done first.
  B are able to choose an acupuncturist themselves.
  C need to go on a waiting list.

3 What does Sylvia say happens if you have a problem with backache?
  A You spend some time answering questions.
  B You have a needle inserted into the area which hurts.
  C You are given advice about changing your lifestyle.

4 What does Sylvia say happens after the first treatment?
  A You usually feel better.
  B You might feel tired.
  C You have to go to bed.

5 Sylvia says people who have acupuncture complain of pain when the needle
  A is put in.
  B is in position.
  C is taken out.

6 What does Sylvia say about acupuncture?
  A It works whether you believe in it or not.
  B It's best to keep an open mind.
  C A negative attitude will stop it working.

7 Sylvia says that in 1971 acupuncture received a great deal of publicity because an American reporter
  A went to China to investigate its use there.
  B was given some acupuncture treatment in China.
  C talked to patients who'd had operations without anaesthetic.

G rammar extra

'to have their chests X-rayed'
'to have a blood test done'

Why do you think we say:

I went to the hospital to have my chest X-rayed and have a blood test done.
and not:
I X-rayed my chest and did a blood test.

You can also say *to **get** a blood test done.*

Why do you go to the following?
a a dry cleaner's
b a hairdresser's
c a garage
d a dressmaker
e a tailor
f a manicurist
g a dentist
h a furniture maker   **G** ➔ page 174

5 Look at the photo. Have you ever tried yoga? Why? / Why not? For questions 1–8, read the text and decide which answer (A, B, C or D) best fits each gap. There is an example at the beginning (0).

Example:

0 A taken **B** lasted **C** spent **D** passed

0	A	B	C	D
	<u> </u>	=	=	=

Yoga

Yoga is one of the most ancient forms of exercise, originating in India 5000 years ago. Yoga has (**0**) .... many years to become recognised world-wide, (**1**) .... recently much more attention has been (**2**) .... to it because of the ways in which it can benefit health. Yoga can be practised by anyone, at any age, (**3**) .... any physical condition, (**4**) .... on their physical need. For example, athletes and dancers can practise it to restore their energy and to improve stamina; executives to give a much needed (**5**) .... to their overworked minds; children to improve their memory and concentration.

Contrary to what many people believe, you do not need to practise an hour of yoga (**6**) .... day. Just taking ten to fifteen minutes out of your schedule can (**7**) .... to be extremely helpful. The best (**8**) .... to practise is either early in the morning or in the evening.

1	**A** although	**B** whereas	**C** if	**D** unless
2	**A** put	**B** paid	**C** allowed	**D** provided
3	**A** at	**B** in	**C** of	**D** on
4	**A** according	**B** matching	**C** fitting	**D** depending
5	**A** pause	**B** break	**C** interval	**D** interruption
6	**A** each	**B** all	**C** either	**D** several
7	**A** demonstrate	**B** prove	**C** show	**D** turn
8	**A** point	**B** instance	**C** time	**D** occasion

Vocabulary

Word formation

6 Look at the sentences, or parts of sentences, below. They are all from the interview on the recording. Change the word in capitals into the right part of speech. Make sure you spell the word correctly.

a You're a great .... (BELIEF) in Chinese medicine, aren't you?

b We referred patients to .... (SPECIALISE) at the local hospital for .... (TREAT).

c When I was a .... (MEDICINE) student, ...

d ... I saw how .... (EFFECT) acupuncture could be.

e He will insert needles in .... (VARY) parts of your body.

f Some areas are more .... (SENSE) than others.

g Acupuncture has been used .... (SUCCEED) on cats.

h He felt no pain during or after the .... (OPERATE).

Topic set – health

7 Complete the sentences below with one of the nouns in the box connected with health.

> bruise bug examination scar
> surgery sweat symptom ward

a I found I had .... pouring off me when I got back from my run.

b The doctor told Sally that she would have to have .... on her ankle as it was a bad break.

c 'Go upstairs and along the corridor,' said the nurse. 'Your sister is on .... 11.'

d You can still see the .... where I cut my knee badly three years ago.

e Can you see my .... ? It's beginning to go blue.

f The dentist gave Pete's teeth a thorough ....

g I couldn't go on holiday because I had a .... – it was one that was going round at the time.

h The doctor said he thought the muscle pain was a .... of flu.

Exam folder 10

Paper 1 Part 5
Multiple choice – fiction

In this part of the Reading and Use of English paper you are tested on a detailed understanding of either a fiction or non-fiction text. (See Exam folder 12 for non-fiction.) There might also be the following types of questions:

- a question which tests global understanding, for example: *What does the text as a whole tell us about the man's character?* (Exam folder 12 has an example of this type of question.)
- a question which tests the meaning of a word or phrase from context, for example: *What does the writer mean by x in line 00?*
- a question which tests reference, for example: *What does 'it' refer to in line 00?*

EXAM ADVICE

- Skim the text to get a general idea of what it is about.
- All the questions, except for the global one, are in order, so you can concentrate on one part of the text at a time. The global question will come at the end, but you need to make sure you take **the whole text** into account when you answer it.
- Some of the options may be true but do not answer the question. Other options may seem very plausible and even contain elements of the same vocabulary, but do not answer the question correctly.
- The reference question may refer either forwards or backwards, so check carefully on either side of the pronoun to see what it refers to.
- As you read, underline the part of the text which you think contains the answer.

You are going to read an extract from a novel. For questions 1–6, choose the answer (A, B, C or D) which you think fits best according to the text.

1 How did the writer feel when he first woke up?
   A certain that it must be a Sunday morning
   B sure about what his senses were telling him
   C worried that something unusual was happening
   D unclear as to what time it was

2 What do we learn about the writer in the second paragraph?
   A He was keen to have his bandages changed.
   B He was pleased he had not been put on a ward.
   C He liked the sense of routine he found in the hospital.
   D He felt he no longer needed to be in hospital.

3 What does 'it' refer to in line 16?
   A the bathroom
   B a guiding hand
   C a close forerunner
   D the washing process

4 What does the writer say about the location of the hospital?
   A It was next to a large office block.
   B It was at a busy road junction.
   C It was beside a motorway.
   D It was at the top of a steep hill.

5 What does the writer mean by 'I restrained it' in line 27?
   A He controlled his wish to take a look.
   B He held back his need to get out of bed.
   C He tried to fight his feeling of fear.
   D He checked his desire to cry.

6 What does the writer say about Tuesday, May 7?
   A The hospital had held a fireworks display.
   B A comet made its expected appearance.
   C What happened on that day is well documented.
   D He had no memory of the unusual happenings on that day.

When a day that you happen to know is Wednesday starts off by sounding more like Sunday, there is something seriously wrong. I felt that from the moment I woke. And yet, when I started functioning a little better, I became doubtful. I went on waiting. But presently I had my first bit of real evidence – a distant clock struck what sounded to me just like eight. Soon another clock began. In a leisurely fashion it gave an unquestionable eight. Then I knew things were wrong.

The way I came to miss the end of the world was sheer accident. I was in hospital. Chance played it not only that I should be there at that particular time, but that my eyes should be enclosed in bandages. This morning I was feeling annoyed because someone should begin to wash and tidy me up at exactly three minutes after 7 a.m. That was one of the best reasons I had for appreciating a private room. In a public ward the proceeding would have taken place a whole unnecessary hour earlier. But here, today, clocks of varying reliability were continuing to strike eight in all directions – and still nobody had shown up. Much as I disliked the washing process, and useless as it had been to suggest that the help of a guiding hand as far as the bathroom could
line 16   remove it, its failure to occur was very worrying. Besides, <u>it</u> was normally a close forerunner of breakfast, and I was feeling hungry.

The day outside, I realised now, was sounding even more wrong than I had thought. Why the founders of St Merryn's Hospital chose to build their institution at a main-road crossing upon a valuable office site, I never properly understood. The buses thundered along trying to beat the lights at the corner. Then the released cross traffic would roar as it started up the slight slope. But this morning was different. No wheels rumbled, no buses roared, no sound of a car of any kind, in fact, was to be heard.

I had to fight down the same feeling of fear that I had had when I was a kid crying in the dark and when I had been too scared to put even a foot out of bed. The temptation to lift the bandages – just enough to get some idea of what on earth could
line 27   be happening – was immense. But I restrained it. For one thing, it was a far less simple matter than it sounded. It wasn't just a case of lifting a blindfold: there were a lot of pads and bandages.

Some little while must have passed, but after a bit I found myself looking once more for a possible explanation for the silence. I became absolutely convinced that it was Wednesday. For the previous day had been notable. You'll find it in the records that on Tuesday, May 7, the Earth's orbit passed through a cloud of comet debris. I was in no state to see what happened myself. All that I actually know is that I had to listen to eyewitness accounts of what was considered to be the greatest free fireworks display ever. And yet, until the thing actually began, nobody had ever heard a word about this comet. It was reported in the news bulletins during the day that mysterious bright green flashes had been seen in the Californian skies the previous night. Accounts arrived from all over the Pacific of a night made brilliant by green meteors said to be 'sometimes in such numerous showers that the whole sky appeared to be wheeling about us'.

Extract from *The Day of the Triffids* by John Wyndham.
John Wyndham is the pen name of British writer John Harris (1903–1969). He wrote *The Day of the Triffids* in 1951.

No place to hide

Speaking

1 Look at the five photographs of clues in a police case. Discuss which two clues are the most reliable, giving reasons for your choice.

2 Now discuss the following questions together.

a What do you think are the causes of crime? (e.g. unemployment)

b Do films and TV programmes about violent crime help to cause more crime? Why? / Why not?

c Should life imprisonment mean 'life'?

d Is prison really the answer to crime?

Reading

3 Look at the vocabulary related to crime below. These are all words and phrases that you will see in the article you are going to read. Fill the gaps in the sentences with the word or phrase which fits best. (You may have to change the form of the verb.) Remember to use your English–English dictionary to help you.

to cover your tracks	a forensic scientist
the suspect	genetic code
the proof	evidence
guilty	to take someone to court

a My sister studied to be a doctor but then decided she wanted to change careers and become .... , working alongside the police.

b It's up to the prosecution to find .... that someone committed a crime.

c Psychologists believe you can tell if someone is .... by their body language.

d Everyone has a completely different .... unless they are identical twins.

e When the police have enough .... they will arrest ....

f It is virtually impossible nowadays .... completely when you've committed a crime – there is always something that will give you away.

g If you are caught drinking and driving you will be .... and fined.

4   You are going to read an article about detecting crime. Six sentences have been
     removed from the article. Choose from the sentences A–G the one which fits
     each gap (1–6). There is one extra sentence which you do not need to use.

The professionals

When it comes to fighting crime, it is science which is king. Sherlock Holmes was right to spend his time examining every footprint and strand of hair in his search for the criminal. Today, though, things have moved on and scientists have a wider range of techniques they can use.

Modern scientists believe that it is impossible for someone to commit a crime without leaving something behind or taking something away with them. **1** [ ] They may take the form of fingerprints, hairs, fibres from clothing, tiny traces of chemicals, documents, bullets or fragments of glass. This evidence is collected and studied by forensic scientists.

line 10

Science is applied to crime-fighting now more than ever before. **2** [ ] In addition, old techniques are constantly being improved so that they can be applied to smaller and smaller traces of materials.

line 17

Not all evidence is equal in law. A fingerprint offers definite identification of a person's presence at the scene of a crime. **3** [ ] But even if an item does not offer enough proof to be used in a court of law, it can still assist the police in focusing their enquiries in a certain direction.

line 23

Fingerprints have been used to help identify criminals for almost 100 years. **4** [ ] In most cases it works very well, but sometimes different methods are needed.

line 27

Forensic scientists can now use a small portable laser, a kind of light beam, to look for fingerprints. The scientist 'paints' the scene of the crime with the laser beam. **5** [ ]

An even more recent technique is called DNA profiling. **6** [ ] Each contains a unique code, the genetic code that determines what we look like and how we develop. The code takes the form of long strings of molecules called DNA, and no two people have identical DNA unless they are identical twins. A technique for reading genetic codes was developed in the 1980s. DNA profiling, or genetic fingerprinting, was seen by the police and forensic scientists as an excellent way of linking suspected criminals with their crimes.

The process of making a DNA profile may begin with a piece of stained clothing found at the scene of the crime. A tuft of hair or spots of blood or saliva can be used too. With a good sample that is rich in DNA, the chance of two people producing the same genetic fingerprint is only one in 2.7 million, which is good enough for a court of law.

A   In that time, many new scientific research methods have been developed, although the traditional way of dusting surfaces for fingerprints is still used most of the time.
B   The human body is composed of millions of microscopic cells.
C   However, a footprint may only suggest that someone was there.
D   On the other hand, certain scientists specialise in gathering evidence from the scene of the crime.
E   As it sweeps across doors, walls and furniture, any fingerprints present glow because they are fluorescent.
F   As people find new ways to cover their tracks, scientists develop new techniques for linking suspects with their crimes and proving if they are guilty or innocent.
G   If these traces of evidence can be found, they may provide the proof needed to bring the criminal to justice – that is, to take them to court.

5   What do you think about DNA profiling?

     Do you think there should be an international database with everyone's DNA on it? Why? / Why not?

6   The following pronouns are underlined in the article. What do they refer to?
     a line 10 – They   c line 23 – it
     b line 17 – they   d line 27 – it

20.2

Listening

1 🔊 **2** **16** Before you listen to the recording, read through the questions and make sure you understand them. You are going to hear a radio news item about the arrest of a robber in the USA. Take notes while you are listening and then in pairs discuss the answers to the questions.

a How long will Curcio have to stay in prison?
b Where was Curcio arrested?
c Why did Curcio steal the money?
d When did Curcio get the idea of the robbery?
e Why did he put an advert on the internet?
f What did Curcio pretend to do immediately before the robbery?
g How did Curcio escape?
h Why were the police confused?
i What happened three weeks before the robbery?
j What evidence did the police have for arresting Curcio?

What do you think about Curcio and the robbery?

2 Look at these extracts from the story.

a … it stopped outside the bank to unload the money …
b Curcio stopped working and …
c Curcio remembered to remove his wig …
d … a police sergeant remembered getting the report.

What's the difference in meaning between *stop* and *remember* + gerund, and *stop* and *remember* + infinitive?

Corpus spot

The *Cambridge Learner Corpus* shows that exam candidates often make mistakes with the use of *stop* + infinitive and *stop* + gerund.

My advice to you is to stop **working** too hard.
NOT My advice to you is to stop ~~work~~ too hard.

Gerunds and infinitives 2

3 In Unit 7 you looked at which verb or expression took a gerund and which took an infinitive. However, there are some verbs that can take both.

> **No change in meaning**: start, begin, continue
>
> **A very slight change in meaning**: like, prefer, hate, love
>
> With these verbs, the gerund is used to talk about enjoyment – *I like having a mobile phone.*
>
> The infinitive is used to talk about habits and choices – *I like to have the latest mobile phone.*
>
> **A change in meaning**: try, stop, regret, remember, forget, mean, go on

In pairs, talk about the difference in meaning in these pairs of sentences.

1a I tried to stop the thief taking the woman's bag but I failed.
1b The burglar tried climbing through the kitchen window when he couldn't break the door lock.
2a The detective stopped at the top of the hill to look at the footprint.
2b Tom stopped working for the police last year.
3a Pete regrets leaving his car unlocked.
3b We regret to inform you that your stolen bicycle has been found in the river.
4a I remember our house being broken into when I was six.
4b You must remember to get travel insurance tomorrow.
5a Cycling without lights will mean getting a fine.
5b Sally means to write her first detective novel this autumn.
6a The police officer, after discussing personal safety, went on to talk about car crime in the town.
6b Lucy went on talking about having her suitcase stolen all evening.

G→ page 174

4 Complete these sentences with the right form of the verb.

a The householder tried .... (fit) a burglar alarm to the house to deter thieves.

b I remember .... (read) about that kidnapping case in the papers some years ago.

c I regret .... (inform) you that your car tax has expired.

d Selling my car will mean .... (walk) home in the dark every night.

e I'm sure Peter didn't mean .... (hurt) the little girl – he only pushed her.

f I wasn't shoplifting – I just forgot .... (pay) for the scarf.

g I regret not .... (tell) the police about my suspicions.

h Although he'd been arrested for drunk driving he continued .... (drink and drive) just the same.

i I like .... (keep) an eye on my neighbours' houses when they are away.

j The policeman talked about robbery in general and then he went on .... (talk) about sentencing.

k I was mugged as I stopped .... (do up) my shoelace.

l Susan tried .... (run) after the pickpocket but although she's a good runner she couldn't catch him.

5 This exercise revises the work done on gerunds and infinitives in this unit and Unit 7. Complete the leaflet with the correct form of the verb in brackets.

Personal Possessions

A thief only needs a moment (**1**) .... (make off) with your valuables. So try (**2**) .... (be) careful at all times. Carry your wallet in an inside pocket, preferably one it is possible (**3**) .... (fasten), not your back pocket. If someone bumps into you in a crowd, it's worth (**4**) .... (check) (**5**) .... (see) that you still have your purse. Try (**6**) .... (avoid) (**7**) .... (carry) large amounts of cash. When on holiday, try (**8**) .... (put) valuables in the hotel safe. If your credit card is stolen, tell the card company immediately. If you delay (**9**) .... (report) the loss, it could (**10**) .... (lead) to a crime being committed in your name. Never let anyone (**11**) .... (know) your PIN number and remember (**12**) .... (sign) any new plastic cards you receive.

G → page 172

Vocabulary

Topic set – crime

6 Look at the vocabulary below about crime. In pairs, decide which is the odd word out in each set and give your reasons.

a get away with	release	hang	let someone off
b illegal	guilty	innocent	suspicious
c robbery	theft	terrorism	arrest
d burglar	criminal	jury	gang
e trial	cell	court	prison
f punishment	offence	penalty	fine
g arrest	accuse	commit	charge

Writing folder 10

Paper 2 Part 2 Emails

Writing folder 1 dealt with informal letters and the importance of writing in a consistently informal style. This Writing folder looks at ways in which you can demonstrate your full range of language in an email.

1 **Read this exam task and the information on assessment. Then tick the grammatical areas you would expect to see in the reply to Jo.**

> You have just received this email from Jo, a friend in Canada.
>
> From: Jo
> Subject: Help me!
>
> I really want to be selected for the college ice hockey team but I know I'm not fit enough. There are only four weeks until the trials take place. What should I do between now and then? Please give me some advice!
>
> Write your **email**.

modal verbs for advice and suggestion ☐
passive forms ☐
conditional structures ☐
relative clauses ☐
perfect tenses ☐
future continuous tense ☐
gerunds ☐

2 **Read the sample answer and find examples of the things you ticked. Are there examples of the other grammatical areas?**

Assessment focus

In order to score a 5 on **language**, you need to include some impressive grammar and vocabulary, and also have the confidence to produce complex sentences that are generally accurate. Occasional errors won't stop you getting the highest mark.

Hi Jo

Wow, you're faced with a difficult challenge – but I know you'll make it! If I were you, I'd draw up a fitness programme without delay and stick to it 100%. Between you and me, it's high time I started eating more healthily again, like I used to when I lived at home, so why don't we do this together?

Anyway, the first thing you should do is alter your diet radically, which means cutting out junk food and sweet stuff. Just think, if you hadn't eaten all those burgers over the last year, you'd be in great shape now! So that's what needs to happen from today, my friend. I'll be checking out some website links on high-protein diets for you too.

Giving up unhealthy snacks is one thing, but you'll also have to work out more regularly – unless you are only going for the third team. I know you won't be happy with that because you've always aimed incredibly high, so get moving! In fact, you ought to be out running NOW rather than reading this!

The best of luck and let's keep in touch!

3 The answer would get a high mark for language, not only for its grammar range and accuracy, but for the choice of vocabulary. Look at the examples below and find more of each type in the answer.

Phrasal verbs	Prepositional phrases	Adverbs
draw up	without delay	more healthily

4 Remember to include words with prefixes and suffixes, like *unhealthy*. Complete sentences a–h with a word in the same word family as the word in bold.

a If you decide to follow a diet **temporarily**, you will be doing it on a .... basis.

b If you receive an email **unexpectedly**, you did not .... to receive it.

c If there is a **misunderstanding** between two friends, one of them has failed to .... the other.

d If someone suddenly **disappears**, the police will eventually be asked to investigate their ....

e If you don't **believe** a word of something you hear, you find it totally ....

f If a friend **recommends** a club to you and you go there, you have taken up their ....

g If you have a **passion** for football, you are .... about it.

h If you haven't been **careful** to protect your friend's feelings, you have acted ....

5 Now read this exam task. Make a plan and list useful vocabulary. Write your email, following the Exam advice given.

> You have just received this email from Nicky, an Australian friend.
>
> I need your advice! Two people I met on holiday last year have been staying in my apartment for the past week. I agreed to put them up because they didn't know anyone else in Sydney but the thing is, my place is too small and they never tidy up or cook – plus they seem to think they can stay indefinitely! What should I do?
>
> Write your **email**.

EXAM ADVICE

Content
- Read the question carefully and think about what the target reader needs to know.
- Include relevant information.

Communicative achievement
- Use an informal style and friendly tone.
- Try to get your message across effectively.

Organisation
- Refer to what your friend has told you.
- Start a new paragraph for each new idea.

Language
- Don't just use simple structures – think of ways to show variety.
- Include some informal phrases and phrasal verbs.
- Use more adverbs, especially ones with negative prefixes – they impress examiners!

Vocabulary

Collocations

1 Add these nouns to their partner nouns in the categories below. An example is given. Try to use them in the Speaking task in 2.

> art   community
> congestion   construction
> ~~high-rise~~   property
> residents   road
> rubbish   shopping
> street   traffic

Buildings
~~high-rise~~ blocks
.... value
.... work

Leisure facilities
.... gallery
.... mall
.... centre

Services
.... collection
.... maintenance
.... lighting

Transport
.... jam
.... charge
.... parking

Speaking

2 Follow the instructions below, working in pairs. Time yourselves.

Student A
Compare the photographs, and talk about the advantages and disadvantages of living in each neighbourhood. (1 minute)

Student B
Say which neighbourhood you would prefer to live in. (20 seconds)

Listening

3 🔊 2 17 You will hear an extract from a talk on high-rise buildings by a woman called Julia Banks. Listen to the introduction to the talk to decide what her profession is.

4 🔊 2 18 Before you listen to Part 2, read the sentences below to predict what you might hear. Then listen and complete the sentences with a word or short phrase.

High-rise buildings

Julia explains that some 1960s architecture came about because of
(1) .... policy.
Today, (2) .... regulations are stricter than they were in the past.
Julia used to live in a (3) .... as a child, in a poor part of Bristol.
The (4) .... used for new buildings have improved since the 1960s.
Julia mentions (5) .... as an example of an environmental requirement for new buildings in Britain.
When explaining what she sees as a problem today, Julia refers to the (6) .... as 'urban sprawl'.
Some city centre shops have shut because of
(7) .... facilities.
Julia believes that architects should design
(8) .... for city centres.
In a multi-use building, there might be
(9) .... downstairs.
People are unhappy about damage to their health caused by
(10) .... in cities.

Compare your answers with another student. Then listen again to check. Finally, check that your spelling is accurate.

5 **Say whether these sentences about the recording are true or false, explaining why.**

   a Julia believes that the public are generally given adequate opportunities to comment on planning proposals.

   b Julia's personal experience of below-average living conditions influenced her career choice.

   c Julia argues that urban sprawl has affected both city centres and the countryside.

   d Julia is pessimistic about the future of city centres.

   e Julia suggests that the majority of London residents would be willing to do without a car.

6 **These words with *up* all occurred in the recording. Match them to meanings 1–5. Do you know any other words with *up*-?**

   a uprooted   1 maintenance
   b upheld   2 expensive
   c upkeep   3 made to leave
   d upmarket   4 advantage
   e upside   5 supported

Speaking

7 **Say whether the purpose of these expressions is**

   1 to involve someone in the discussion
   2 to encourage someone to be quiet
   3 to support what someone is saying

   a You clearly know a lot about this, but let's move on.
   b Would you say that this is true in your case?
   c I believe your own view is slightly different?
   d Come on, you're talking rubbish!
   e Well, I have to admit you have a point.
   f I'm going to say something here.
   g What do you think?
   h Absolutely, I couldn't agree more.

   Do you consider any of these rude or offensive? In what other ways can a speaker or listener direct a conversation?

8 **Now practise these turn-taking skills. Get into groups of four to discuss the following statements. For each statement, one person in the group should stay silent and time how long each of the others speaks for.**

   a There are both good and bad examples of modern architecture.
   b Living conditions in our cities have got worse.
   c City centres should be traffic-free.
   d Urban sprawl is a serious threat to nature.

Mixed conditionals

1 Look at these two quotes from the recording in 21.1, which are examples of mixed conditionals. Explain what tenses are used and why.

If we were meant to live up in the sky, we would have been born with wings!
If 60s architecture hadn't happened, we would be making similar mistakes today.

In both examples, the second and third conditional forms are mixed.

2 You can use a mixed conditional to talk about a past action affecting a present situation, as in the second example above. Finish these mixed conditional sentences in a suitable way.

EXAMPLE: If we had bought that house, we *would be short of money now.*

a If people hadn't objected to the plans, the building …
b If Tom had remembered to book a table at the restaurant, we …
c If I hadn't seen that programme, I …
d If we had set off earlier, we …
e If she hadn't answered the advert, she …

3 You can also use mixed conditionals to talk about how a different present situation would have affected a past situation, as in this example:

If the city centre was traffic-free, the council wouldn't have needed to build all these car parks.

Finish these sentences in a similar way, using the ideas in brackets.

a If high-rise buildings were of better quality, more people (choose to live in them in the first place)
b If there weren't so many distractions, you (finish your essay by now)
c If the suburbs were smaller, local taxes (be so high for the last 20 years)
d If the supermarket was open 24 hours, I (go out at 3 am this morning to buy you some paracetamol)

G → page 175

4 Match the sentence beginnings a–f with their endings 1–6. Which sentence contains a mixed conditional? Notice the different ways of expressing a negative condition in a–c.

a **In the absence of** any shops,
b **Without** a police force,
c **Given a lack of** public transport,
d Unless public services were maintained,
e Should all schools be closed,
f If public hospitals hadn't been created,

1 rubbish would pile up on the streets.
2 education could no longer be taken for granted.
3 crime rates would increase dramatically.
4 people would be paying huge sums for healthcare.
5 consumers would have to adopt a different lifestyle.
6 bicycle shops might do substantially more business.

5 Discuss the impact of these problems on a city and its inhabitants. Try to use the sentence openers from 4 and different conditional structures.

a food shortages
b dangerous levels of pollution
c power cuts
d collapse of the banking system due to cybercrime

Vocabulary

Topic set – buildings

6 **Read the article about the architect Sir Norman Foster. For questions 1–8, decide which answer, A, B, C or D, best fits each gap. There is an example at the beginning (0).**

Example:

0 **A** chose **B** fixed **C** dealt **D** wished

0	A	B	C	D

The grand designer

When asked to select his favourite building, Sir Norman Foster **(0)** .... a Jumbo jet. His own structures frequently **(1)** .... materials and technology developed by the aerospace industry. Perhaps his most famous building is the Hong Kong and Shanghai Bank, a massive construction of three linked towers 41 **(2)** .... high. His most ambitious European **(3)** .... has been the reconstruction of the Reichstag, the new German parliament building, where he **(4)** .... the central roof area with a huge glass dome. He has also built a metro **(5)** .... in Bilbao, and two space-age communications towers in Barcelona and Santiago de Compostela.

Foster **(6)** .... in the vertical city, an architect's dream that began a hundred years ago and is still **(7)** .... to be fully realised. He says that the city is in a continuous process of renewal; if buildings cannot **(8)** .... to social or technological change, then unless they are outstanding, they should be replaced. It's all about balancing the past and the future.

1	**A** lend	**B** fetch	**C** borrow	**D** bring
2	**A** flights	**B** levels	**C** storeys	**D** stages
3	**A** activity	**B** project	**C** occupation	**D** post
4	**A** extended	**B** enabled	**C** experimented	**D** emerged
5	**A** method	**B** plan	**C** routine	**D** system
6	**A** believes	**B** hopes	**C** relies	**D** depends
7	**A** standing	**B** expecting	**C** waiting	**D** resting
8	**A** alter	**B** adapt	**C** fit	**D** match

7 **Widen your knowledge of vocabulary for this topic, starting from the article. List:**

- two nouns that mean the same as *building*.
- three verbs beginning with 'e' that mean *make bigger*.
- four adjectives like *massive* that describe very large buildings.

Now use some of these words to describe the biggest building you know of.

Word formation

8 **There are a number of words containing the prefix *re-* in the article, such as *reconstruction* and *renewal*. Make new words from the ones below, using the same prefix. Sometimes words with different parts of speech can be made. Use some of the words to complete sentences a–d.**

build	consider	generate
open	pay	possess	write

a The old industrial city of Duisburg has been .... and now has new, cleaner industries right in its centre, alongside schools and housing.

b Following extensive fire damage, the timber-framed buildings have now been fully .... in their original style.

c The city council's .... of the enquiry into noise pollution has been supported by local residents.

d Anyone who has left the city for the suburbs should .... their move, particularly in the light of how far rents have fallen in the centre.

Exam folder 11

Paper 1 Part 7 Multiple matching

This part of the Reading and Use of English paper focuses on your ability to find specific information in a set of texts, or in one text that has been divided into sections. There are 10 questions in all.

For this task, you will often need to locate words and phrases in the text(s) that reflect the meaning of the wording used in the questions. Sometimes more than one text will cover the same subject, so you need to decide which one matches the question wording.

EXAM ADVICE

- Look at the title and any information you are given about the text or texts.
- Skim the texts for their general meaning.
- Read through the questions carefully, underlining any key words and phrases.
- Scan the texts for the specific information you need, rather than reading them in detail.
- Don't be tempted to choose a text simply because it has the same wording as in the question. This may lead you to an incorrect answer.
- When you find an answer in a text, underline that part of the text and write the question number next to it.
- Don't spend too much time looking for an answer. Leave any challenging questions until the end and go on to the next ones.
- When you've finished, go back and look again at any questions you left unanswered. If you still don't know, guess. Never leave an answer blank on your answer sheet.
- Aim to spend around 15 minutes on this task – even though Part 7 questions are only 'single weighted', whereas the questions in Parts 5 and 6 count double.

You are going to read a magazine article in which four people talk about driving. For questions 1–10, choose from the people (A–D). The people may be chosen more than once.

Which person

chose a car that disappointed a family member?	**1**
couldn't really afford their chosen car?	**2**
used to imagine driving somewhere fast at night?	**3**
had to consider the size of the car before buying it?	**4**
qualified as a car driver in order to compete?	**5**
complains about their car?	**6**
had an accident in their car?	**7**
gives someone close to them a regular lift?	**8**
knows a lot of information about certain cars?	**9**
intends to keep their car despite some disagreement?	**10**

Me and my wheels

Four people talked to us about their favourite vehicles.

A Brett

I dreamt about having the car I drive now when I was at school and almost ruined myself financially to buy it! When I first got it, it had a really loud sound system, and I reversed into a brand-new car because I couldn't hear the horn beeping at me to stop. My best moment was when I was at the Glastonbury Festival and drove it up the hill there after dark. The whole of the site below was blinking with lights and it was fantastic. My wife isn't a big fan and used to complain about how uncomfortable it was on long journeys. Now that we've got a kid, pressure has been put on me to get rid of it, but I refuse to go that far. We are getting another family car though.

B Simon

As a child, I used to love memorising facts and few delighted me as much as those about cars. I can still produce all sorts of trivia about 0–60 acceleration times, top speeds, and the engine sizes of all the fastest and most exciting cars. I'm very fond of car magazines because of that, and I go through as many as I can get my hands on! Whenever I visit Britain, I pick some up and enjoy the deliciously technical writing and wonderful shots of car interiors – all those dials! If I couldn't get to sleep as a teenager, I'd pretend to be doing a long journey in the dark in an open-top sports car. But do you know what I currently drive? A VW estate with a small engine. It won't do; I must change my life.

C Marie

I haven't always had four wheels and, in fact, I only learned to drive a car three years ago. I passed my test quite quickly after that and was lucky enough to be given my car – a Mazda sports – as a present. It's very quick off the mark. I really switched to cars instead of bikes in order to join Formula Women, an organisation that's been set up to encourage more women to go into racing. I love the challenge of it all and I know my biking days have helped me to find the best racing line on the track. Dad comes to all my races and likes to get the crowd behind me! Mum used to worry about the danger involved but she's OK about it now, and she thinks I'm a good road user. Once a week I come and collect her in the Mazda and we go off to do the out-of-town shopping bit together.

D Sonja

My mum was almost in tears when I said I was going to buy the Mini. I'd previously owned an open-top Audi, which she loved being driven around in, but I felt it was time to downsize. I must admit I felt some sadness, knowing I wouldn't be able to drive with the wind whipping through my hair. But I soon got attached to the Mini. When I went for a test drive in one to see if it was really suitable, I realised that they are actually very roomy. Even my husband can fit in it and he's incredibly tall. It's faster than you'd think and I've already received three points on my licence for speeding, unfortunately. My favourite journey is driving home each evening during spring and autumn just as the light starts to fade.

A world of music

Speaking

1 Look at these two photos and discuss their similarities and differences.

2 **2 19** Now listen to the recording, which is an example of Paper 4 Part 2. One student will talk about the pictures for about a minute. Then another student will talk briefly at the end. How do their views differ?

3 What types of music do you enjoy? What do you dislike? Why?

Vocabulary

Topic set – music

4 **2 19** Listen to the recording again and tick any vocabulary you hear in the sets below.

Perform	Performers	Performance
play	musician	concert
take part	orchestra	gig
participate	cellist	festival
join in	conductor	rehearsal
sing a solo	choir	show

Explain the differences in meaning of the words in the 'Performance' column.

5 If a *cellist* plays a cello, who plays these instruments? Be careful with spelling.

a violin
b piano
c drums
d saxophone
e trumpet
f flute

Reading

6 Read the title and the first paragraph of the article. What is a *tribute band*?

7 Skim the main text for general meaning. Then underline content clues, as well as linkers and reference words. Time yourself as you do this.

Glastonbudget – the main event on the musical calendar for tribute bands

The Glastonbury Festival, which takes place in Britain in late June, offers an impressive line-up of famous bands over four days, but tickets aren't cheap at around £200. Glastonbudget, as the name suggests, is a low-priced music festival that specialises in booking tribute bands. A tribute band performs the songs, or 'cover versions', of the particular group they admire, usually copying the group's appearance closely and sometimes playing their music rather well. The tribute band's name is often deliberately similar to the original one, so Dread Zeppelin is a reggae version of Led Zeppelin. There are tribute bands everywhere: Umma Gumma in Brazil, Mun Floyd in Italy, Pink Division in Norway and The Pink Tones in Spain are just four of the many Pink Floyd sound-alikes.

Glastonbudget was dreamed up back in 2003 by Nick Tanner, who runs a village pub in Leicestershire, and his sister. **1** [ ] Nick loved holding it, as it earned double the money of a normal opening. As the pub wasn't big enough to fit in many more people, Nick suggested looking for another venue.

A year later they found themselves standing in a field, having spent £160,000 in setting up the first Glastonbudget festival. **2** [ ] Due to a combination of hard work, donations and goodwill from the local community, ticket sales have increased steadily. Nowadays, it is a sell-out event, not to mention being the biggest tribute and new music festival in Europe.

Like the budget airlines, there is a system of selling a limited number of low-price tickets: depending on when you book, it's possible to buy a weekend ticket for as little as 99 pence. **3** [ ] Even if they are not big-name acts, this makes it an extremely attractive alternative to Glastonbury.

People who attend Glastonbudget often comment not only on how well it is organised, but on how much of a community atmosphere there is at the event. **4** [ ] Not many festivals can boast a line-up that includes Coldplay, Guns N' Roses, The Foo Fighters and The Killers. Neither can Glastonbudget, although it comes quite close: Coldplace, Guns 2 Roses, The Four Fighters and The Fillers all rocked the main stage this year.

Another popular act at Glastonbudget this year was Iziggy, formed by lorry driver Brian Spiers after workmates kept pointing out his amazing likeness to Iggy Pop. Brian – who was mobbed at a recent Iggy And The Stooges show in London – explained that he had had to drop three jeans sizes and get some singing lessons before starting the band. **5** [ ] He's planning to get them removed by laser eventually.

6 [ ] Since the festival's second year, the organisers have featured more and more young, up-and-coming local bands. Closely associated with the Soar Valley Music Centre, the festival also provides training for young people in different aspects of the music industry.

8 Look for the missing information in sentences A–G and decide on your answers. Check that the extra sentence doesn't fit anywhere.

- **A** Glastonbudget isn't just about tribute bands though.
- **B** Despite losing money on that occasion, the festival has gone from strength to strength ever since.
- **C** Having chosen such diverse bands, the organisers were confident of success from the start.
- **D** Near or total strangers become part of a genuinely music-loving festival and enjoy some entertaining bands.
- **E** He also has to spend £50 per gig buying make-up to cover his tattoos because his hero doesn't have any.
- **F** The two were discussing ways to expand the monthly tribute band night.
- **G** This rises to a maximum of just over £50, which includes camping and parking.

9 Discuss these questions in pairs.

- **a** Why are there so many tribute bands performing today?
- **b** Can a cover version ever be better than the original song?
- **c** Would you pay to see a tribute band? Why? / Why not?
- **d** Have music festivals become too commercial?

Concessive clauses

1 Look at these sentences and explain the function of the underlined words and the clauses they introduce.

a <u>Despite</u> losing money on that occasion, the festival has gone from strength to strength ever since.

b <u>Even though</u> they are not big-name acts, this makes it an extremely attractive alternative to Glastonbury.

c I love listening to the 12-string guitar, <u>although</u> I can't play one myself.

d My brother and I listen to each other's albums, <u>even if</u> the bands are sometimes very different.

e <u>While</u> not at a professional level, I enjoy singing in a local choir.

Match statements 1–6 to sentences a–e. Some apply to more than one sentence.

1 The same subject is mentioned in both clauses.

2 In this sentence, it is not possible to re-arrange the order of the clauses.

3 The subjects of each clause are different.

4 The first clause has no verb or subject, but the subject is understood.

5 The main clause has a subject and a verb, but the other clause does not.

6 The underlined word is a different part of speech from the other examples.

> **Corpus spot**
>
> Be careful when using the preposition *despite* – the *Cambridge Learner Corpus* shows that exam candidates often make mistakes with this word. Compare *in spite of* in this example.
>
> The singer was excellent **despite** the poor sound system. OR
>
> The singer was excellent **in spite of** the poor sound system.
>
> NOT The singer was excellent ~~despite of~~ the poor sound system.

2 Join these sentences together using the conjunction or preposition in brackets and making any grammatical or stylistic changes necessary. An example is given.

EXAMPLE: James has injured his hand. He will play in tonight's concert. (in spite of)
In spite of injuring his hand, James will play in tonight's concert.

a The concert was supposed to start at 8.00. The concert actually started at 9.30. (although)

b The stage was very small. The group did a lot of dancing on the stage. (though)

c Damon Albarn is in the band Gorillaz. He is still a member of Blur. (despite)

d I manage to keep up to date by watching YouTube. I can't get to many gigs. (even though)

e You are allowed to use the school instruments in the music room. No school instruments should be taken away from the music room. (while)

f We might miss the first band. We'll still get to the festival in time for Arctic Monkeys. (even if)

 → page 175

Complex sentences

3 Both of these examples from 22.1 begin with a reason, to explain the underlined information. What is the effect of putting the reason first? You may want to look back at the whole text.

a As the pub wasn't big enough to fit in many more people, <u>Nick suggested looking for another venue</u>.

b Due to a combination of hard work, donations and goodwill from the local community, <u>ticket sales have increased steadily</u>.

Which sentence starts with a conjunction? What other conjunctions are used in this way?

 → page 175

4 Example b and examples c and d below illustrate sentence 'fronting', where a phrase containing information relevant to the main clause is put first.

c Having chosen such diverse bands, the organisers were confident of success from the start.

d Closely associated with the Soar Valley Music Centre, the festival also provides training for young people in different aspects of the music industry.

> **Exam spot**
>
> Using complex sentences in Papers 2 and 4 may impress the examiners!

5 Read part of an exam answer on the topic of live music. Varying how the sentences begin makes the writing more effective.

> I really enjoy going to places in which you can see a good concert. When I listen to live music, I always have a special feeling of having fun and relaxing at the same time. Sometimes, when I really like the music I am listening to, I forget the real world and start dreaming. Although I like almost everything about music, if I can choose between a classical concert and a blues concert I am going to choose the second one. Seeing blues or soul bands in concert is one of the things that I really enjoy.

Which sentence starts with a concessive clause? Which sentence uses an extended noun phrase as a fronting technique?

The writing could still be improved. Which adverb is used three times? What other adverbs could be used instead?

6 Rewrite the sentences in a–e to produce a single complex sentence. The first word of the new sentence is given in brackets.

EXAMPLE: The Squier guitar sounds very similar to a proper Stratocaster. It is a low-priced guitar. This is good. (What)
What is good about the Squier is that although it is a low-priced guitar, it sounds very similar to a proper Stratocaster.

a It was late. We decided not to stay for the final band. (Since)
b The cello, which has been beautifully made by hand and is reddish brown in colour, has an excellent sound. (Beautifully)
c Ellen learnt the recorder for three years. Then she went on to the flute. (Having)
d The trumpeter is technically brilliant. However, his playing has neither energy nor emotion. (Despite)
e The conductor made a mistake. The soloist had to miss out a whole verse. (Due to)

7 For questions 1–8, read the text and decide which answer (A, B, C or D) best fits each gap. There is an example at the beginning (0).

Example:

0 A remains **B** keeps **C** stays **D** continues

0	A	B	C	D

GEORGE GERSHWIN

George Gershwin, who was born in Brooklyn in 1898, **(0)** ...... one of the world's most popular composers today. He lived and worked in the perfect era for his unique talent to **(1)** .... It was at a time when the Jazz Age coincided with composers like Berg, and the first Broadway musicals. Although a gifted pianist, he had only basic reading skills in music, but due to his regular attendance at concerts, he was able to **(2)** ..... up his own repertoire. In 1924, Gershwin worked with his brother Ira on a musical comedy called *Lady Be Good*. This proved to be a successful **(3)** ...... that continued for the rest of his life.

George Gershwin was determined to **(4)** ..... an impression as a serious composer, which he also achieved in 1924. At its New York premiere, one of his most famous **(5)** ....., *Rhapsody in Blue*, received wild applause from an audience that included musical celebrities such as the Russian composers Rachmaninov and Stravinsky. Gershwin **(6)** ..... this success with innovative orchestral works such as *An American in Paris* and, in 1935, the memorable opera *Porgy and Bess*.

No one has been able to match Gershwin's ability to write original works that **(7)** ..... the boundaries of jazz, opera and classical music and his **(8)** ..... on modern music has been enormous. Sadly, Gershwin died at the early age of 38.

1	**A** become	**B** develop	**C** result	**D** invent
2	**A** grow	**B** pull	**C** move	**D** build
3	**A** company	**B** teamwork	**C** pair	**D** partnership
4	**A** make	**B** get	**C** put	**D** take
5	**A** writings	**B** exercises	**C** designs	**D** compositions
6	**A** brought	**B** followed	**C** adopted	**D** led
7	**A** enter	**B** split	**C** cross	**D** carry
8	**A** power	**B** direction	**C** control	**D** influence

DO YOU NEED MORE PRACTICE?
CD-ROM UNITS 21–22

Writing folder 11

Paper 2 Part 2 Reports

Look back at Writing folder 3 on pages 44–45. Remember that a report needs to be clearly organised, with an introduction and a conclusion. Reports are often written in an impersonal style, using passive forms to achieve this.

1 Read the following exam question and its answer. Then rewrite the answer, making the improvements suggested in a–d.

   a What would you add at the beginning and end of the report?

   b How could the highlighted headings be improved?

   c Why are the underlined parts of the answer inappropriate to a report? How could the passive be used to address this?

   d Where you see the symbol §, use a conjunction to join the two sentences together, making any other changes necessary.

> Every year, you help at a local music festival, which takes place outdoors over one weekend. The organisers want to improve the festival and have asked you to write a short report. You should comment on the facilities that were available at this year's festival and make recommendations for next year.
>
> Write your **report**.

Dear Organisers

Here is my report.

_____

The place in town where you hold the festival

The site this year was disappointing, mainly because it wasn't large enough. There was some car parking. § Many people had to park over two kilometres away.

Eating

There was some choice of catering at the site. § Very little vegetarian food was offered. Also, my friends and I had to go to one end of the field for food and then we ran over to the opposite end for a drink. This drove us nuts!

The programme

People seemed to enjoy the performances. § Each band should be allowed more time on stage.

The cost

Several members of the audience thought the tickets were unusually cheap. § The price could be raised next year. This would help us, wouldn't it?

Recommendations

You need a bigger site and better-organised catering – some changes to the timing of the event too.

_____

151 words

2 It is better to avoid short paragraphs. What else could you say under the heading about the festival programme? Finish this sentence with your own idea.

Furthermore, it might be preferable for next year's programme to …

3 You could be asked to write a report about shopping facilities in your town or city. If so, you should think carefully about the group of 'shoppers' you are writing the report for. This is different from the target reader of the report, who will be specified – for example, the festival organisers in the last question, or your boss at the tourist office.

For each target group on the next page, decide which types of shopping it would be suitable to focus on, choosing from a–j. Some will be used more than once. Remember to consider the advantages or disadvantages given in brackets and to recommend things that are realistic in the time allowed.

Target group

1 American exchange students on a limited budget
2 Elderly tourists visiting as a group one weekend
3 Business people spending a free hour after their appointments
4 Families camping outside the town for a week

Types of shopping

a an exclusive gift shop (in the main square)
b a large toyshop (limited parking)
c a central stationery shop (open late)
d the Saturday crafts market (very colourful)
e a discount computer warehouse (plenty of parking)
f a sports equipment store (good value)
g a supermarket on the edge of town (massive)
h a music store (very noisy)
i the university bookshop (discounts available)
j an art gallery (includes a coffee shop)

4 **Now read this exam question.**

> Some British students are on an exchange programme at your college for a month. The college has asked you to write a report on local shopping facilities for the teacher who is in charge of the group. You should give advice on best value for money, including areas such as food, study materials and souvenirs.
>
> Write your **report**.

5 **Match definitions a–j to these words about money and shopping. Which two are adjectives?**

bargain brand budget competitive economical expense fortune purchase savings stock

a as good as or better than other prices, services, etc.
b something that is on sale for less than its real value
c a lot of money
d something that you buy or the act of buying something

e not using a lot of money
f the money that you keep in an account
g not expensive
h the money that you spend on something
i a type of product made by a particular company
j all the goods that are available in a shop

6 **Now add some of the words from 5 in phrases a–f, making the nouns plural where necessary. You can use these phrases in your report in 7.**

Food
a luxury/ low-cost .... of
b .... prices

Study materials
c in / out of ....
d on a tight ....

Souvenirs
e (not) cost a ....
f hunt for ....

7 **Write your report in 140–190 words, following the Exam advice.**

EXAM ADVICE

Content
● Plan what you are going to say.
● Make sure you have enough ideas for every paragraph.

Communicative achievement
● Write in a consistently formal and impersonal style.
● Communicate your ideas effectively so that the reader can act upon them.

Organisation
● Include headings and/or bullet points to make your report clearer.
● Repeat your most important recommendation(s) in a conclusion.

Language
● Use passive forms and conditional structures.
● Try to show your full range of vocabulary.

Unexpected events

Speaking

1 In pairs, look at the photographs. What is each photo of?
Decide which set of words goes with each photograph.

  a a storm, thunder, a flash, lightning
  b to be stranded, torrential rain
  c a peak, ash, an eruption, gases
  d cracks, to tremble, to shake

2 Ask and answer the following questions.

  a Have you ever experienced a natural disaster? If so, what was it like?
  b Have you ever seen a natural disaster reported on the television?
     If so, which?
  c Do you think there is anything you can do to avoid a natural disaster?

Listening

3 **2 20** You are going to hear a woman called Liz, talking about a frightening experience she had when she was camping with her brother, Dave.
For questions 1–10, complete the sentences with a word or short phrase.

> Dave thought at first that the cloud was the result of a (**1**) ....
> Liz says that what she saw was different from a (**2**) ....
> Liz thought it was odd because it was completely (**3**) ....
> The heat melted the (**4**) .... of the coffee pot.
> Dave and Liz tried at first to reach (**5**) ....
> Dave and Liz had been protected in the hole by (**6**) ....
> Dave and Liz put their (**7**) .... round their heads to help them to breathe.
> It was hard to walk because of the depth of the (**8**) ....
> There was an awful smell similar to (**9**) ....
> Liz now regrets not having a (**10**) .... with them.

Vocabulary

Phrasal verbs with *off*

4 Match these phrasal verbs you heard in the interview with their meaning.

removed   began the journey
exploding

1 It was like a bomb *going off*.
2 We *took off* our shirts.
3 When we *set off* it was difficult to breathe.

Now complete the following sentences, choosing a phrasal verb that means the same as the word or words in brackets. Make sure you use the correct tense.

tell off	call off
let off	cut off
show off	wear off
send off	log off
break off	

a Tom (spoke angrily to) the boys for throwing stones at the windows.
b The Prime Minister's visit to Australia has been (cancelled) because of the floods at home.
c Anne (put in the post) fifty job applications before she got an interview.
d The excitement of living in New York soon (disappeared) and then I felt homesick.
e The village was (isolated) because of the flooding.
f My sister (ended) her engagement to Pete yesterday.
g The thief was (not punished) by the magistrate as it was his first offence.
h I (broke the connection with) my laptop and went to bed at about midnight.

Words often confused

5 In the following sentences there are two words or phrases which are often confused by students. Decide which one is correct, then write another sentence to show how the other word or phrase is used.

a We waited for the emergency services but *at the end / in the end* our neighbour rescued us from the floods.
b Our two-way radio was *invaluable / priceless* during the storm.
c You don't see many people taking risks outdoors *nowadays / actually*.
d Questions about another eruption were *raised / risen* at the meeting.
e *Lie / Lay* down and try to rest until the weather improves.
f *Tell / Say* me the story about how you coped after the earthquake.
g I'm an excellent outdoor *cook / cooker*.
h My camping gear was *stolen / robbed* yesterday.
i I *damaged / injured* my leg when I was running for shelter.
j My friend was very *sympathetic / friendly* when I broke my arm.
k Jean is so *sensible / sensitive* that she cries whenever she watches a disaster movie.

6 For questions 1–8, read the text below and think of the word which best fits each gap. Use only one word in each gap. There is an example at the beginning (0).

An Unchanging Planet?

If you think of Earth (0) __AS__ a stable and unchanging planet, think again. Nearly five billion years after it was first formed, the Earth is still developing – (1) .... alarming ways. Unlike earthquakes, which strike (2) .... warning, volcanoes build up (3) .... months and are usually easier to predict.

A volcano can erupt in many different ways and it can spill out a variety of materials. Mild eruptions spurt gas, steam and hot water and are (4) .... geysers. Larger volcanoes shoot out ash and large chunks of hot rock into (5) .... atmosphere, and enormous fountains of glowing red hot lava that flow down the sides of the volcano. This liquid lava quickly thickens into a steaming sticky carpet (6) .... can travel 150 km before it stops and turns solid. Famously, in AD 79, the Roman city of Pompeii (7) .... covered in lava and ash, preserving buildings and some of their contents to (8) .... day.

I wish / If only

1 In the recording, Liz says that she wished she'd taken a radio with her.

You can use *wish / if only* + past perfect tense to talk about a wish or regret in the past.

What other things do you think Liz wished after the eruption? Suggest five other things she might have said.

EXAMPLE: *I wish we had chosen a different place to camp.*

Now talk together about things that you personally regret doing or not doing in the past.

I wish I hadn't gone to that boring party.
If only I had worked harder for the test.

2 When Liz says, 'if only we could get in the tent, we'd be safe' she is saying what she felt at that particular moment.

You can use *wish / if only* + past simple or *would/could* to talk about a wish or a regret in the present.

Now write down ten things that you wish for right at this moment. Compare your sentences with a partner.

EXAMPLES: *I wish I was/were on a beach instead of in the library.*
I wish I could have something to eat.

Note: You can't say: *I wish I would / He wishes he would / They wish they would,* etc.

3 After *wish* and *if only*, *would* can be used to complain about or criticise a person or situation.

EXAMPLES: *I wish it would stop raining.* – It's raining at the moment and I want it to stop.
If only my neighbour would be quiet. – She's making a lot of noise at the moment.
I wish he would stop smoking. – I want him to stop smoking now (for example because the smoke is getting in my eyes).

Is there anything bothering you at the moment? Write down a few examples using *would*.

4 *Wish* is often confused with *hope*.

I hope I see you soon.
I wish I could see you soon.

Hope usually takes a present tense with a future meaning. When we use *hope* we usually don't know or can't tell the outcome, whereas with *wish* we do know the facts and they are the opposite of what we want.

Decide on the correct alternative in the following sentences.

a I *hope / wish* the rain stops soon.
b I *hope / wish* you can come to my party.
c I *hope / wish* I could speak Arabic.
d I *hope / wish* Peter would finish writing his book.
e I *hope / wish* I had remembered to bring the sleeping bags.

Corpus spot

Correct the errors that exam candidates have made with *wish* and *hope* in these sentences from the *Cambridge Learner Corpus*.
a I wish I had know it two days ago.
b I wish you were there with us.
c I hope you would be able to give me some more information.
d I wish you can come to Japan.
e I wish that you have a good time.
f So, I hope I could help you out a little bit.
g I wish I haven't said that.

5 Here are some other expressions followed by the past tense.

a *as if / as though*
It wasn't like a smoke cloud, it was as if it were alive. – It wasn't alive.

b *would rather*
This takes an infinitive without *to* or a past tense.
I'd rather not tell you what really happened.
I'd rather you didn't ask me about the experience.
(Don't confuse *I'd rather* and *I'd better* (= I had better) – they mean different things.)

Say what you *would rather do* in each situation.

EXAMPLE: *Would you like to go camping?*
– *I'd rather stay in a hotel.*
– *I'd rather we stayed in a hotel.*

a Would you like to come with us for a pizza?
b Would you like to study engineering?
c Would you like to travel to the Moon?
d Would you like me to teach you Latin?
e Would you like me to buy you an iPod?

6 For the following questions, complete the second sentence so that it has a similar meaning to the first sentence, using the word given. Do not change the word given. You must use between two and five words, including the word given.

1 I regret not taking the park ranger's advice.
TAKEN
I .... the park ranger's advice.

2 I think it's better for the children to stay inside in bad weather.
RATHER
I .... inside in bad weather.

3 What a pity we didn't see any wildlife on our trip.
ONLY
If .... wildlife on our trip.

4 I don't like living in an earthquake zone.
WISH
I .... somewhere else.

5 Don't walk so fast, I can't keep up with you!
WISH
I .... walk so fast, I can't keep up with you!

6 I'd prefer you not to repeat what I've just told you.
RATHER
I .... repeat what I've just told you.

G→page 175

Vocabulary

Word formation

7 Liz and Dave had to 'unroll' their trousers to empty out the ash that had collected in them.

What sort of things do you:

a untie?   **f** unearth?
b unbutton?   **g** unfasten?
c undo?   **h** unlock?
d unwrap?   **i** unwind?
e uncover?

Topic set – weather

8 Fill in the missing letters for these weather words.

a The Mid-West states of the USA suffer from TO_ _ _D_ _S.
b A typhoon is a type of T_ _P_ _ _ _ storm.
c It gets B_ _L_ _G hot inside the club when it's full of dancers.
d The weather F_ _ _C_ _ _ for tomorrow is quite good.
e My fingers were F_ _ _ _I_ _ cold after building the snowman.
f It P_ _ _ _D with rain all day, so we couldn't play tennis.
g H_ _ _ _C_ _ _S usually occur in the Caribbean.
h DR_ _ _ _T occurs when there isn't enough rain.
i Britain has a D_ _P climate, whereas parts of India are often H_M_D.

Exam folder 12

Paper 1 Part 5
Multiple choice – non-fiction

In this part of the Reading and Use of English paper you are tested on a detailed understanding of the text. For more information and advice on multiple-choice tasks, consult Exam folder 10 (multiple choice – fiction).

1 **You are going to read an extract from a newspaper article.**

   Skim through the text – what is it about?

2 **Now look at questions 1–6. Choose the answer (A, B, C or D) which you think fits best according to the text.**

   Underline the part of the text where you think the answer is.

1 What is the problem the writer has at the beginning of her holiday?
   A The weather is not good enough for painting.
   B She's brought the wrong materials with her.
   C There are no animals to paint.
   D She can't reproduce the exact colours.

2 The writer hid her work because
   A she believed Royale paints better.
   B it wasn't good enough to sell.
   C she thought it would disappoint Royale.
   D it was only a quick sketch.

3 What does the writer mean by the phrase 'what I am up to' in lines 38–39?
   A what I am painting
   B what I will give him
   C what I can teach him
   D what I might do

4 What does the writer say about her previous painting holiday?
   A She preferred the teacher she had had then.
   B The landscape was more familiar to her.
   C Her technique had improved much faster.
   D She had been able to complete a number of paintings.

5 The writer says that Susan Scott-Thomas
   A looks at things in a different way from her.
   B is a very capable person.
   C is not as good at cooking as her.
   D was a solicitor before going to Africa.

6 What is a suitable title for the article?
   A An unsuccessful holiday
   B Painting the natural world
   C Learning to work with others
   D Travelling in a different country

By the middle of the second day I know I'm in trouble. In front of me the land stretches up and away towards a distant hill, and into the space, between that summit and me, is crowded one of the most vivid concentrations of colour I have ever seen. It starts with the trees. The wet season is only a few weeks off and, almost as if they can smell the coming rains, they have put out their leaves. They are no ordinary green and the dry grasses beneath them are ablaze with golds, browns and reds. I want to recreate this scene with watercolours. Although I can make a try at it with words, trying to paint it in my sketch book is another matter altogether. I've already made one attempt: a series of zigzags in orange and red, with bluish trees placed across them, which now lies face down in the grass beside me.

I've put it there because the last thing I want right now is for someone else to come along and look at it. A young man called Royale walks up the hill. Royale is a sculptor, and, with several other local men, produces pieces of work in the local stone. Recently, and quite suddenly, this work, and that of several other local co-operatives, has acquired an international reputation. I certainly don't want a man capable of such things looking at my own awful brush-strokes. So I put my foot, as casually as I can, on the finished painting beside me and we resume the conversation started earlier in the day.

line 38　I want to talk to Royale about his life here.
line 39　He, however, is only interested in what I am up to. To begin with, it seems that he considers me a fellow artist, and for a moment I find myself staring into the depths of embarrassment. But when he asks me, 'What is painting like?' I realise that this professional artist has never painted anything in his life before. He just wants a go with my colours.

When I signed up for this holiday, I was hoping for an experience like the one I had had four years earlier in Wales. That was my first painting holiday, and I loved it. Two things made it great. First was the teacher, a man called Robin, who showed me that what is important about drawing and painting is not the finished article but the process of completing it. The second element of that week was the place. I grew up in places like that, and I connected with it immediately. But it was stupid of me to think that I could reproduce the experience down here, deep in the Southern Hemisphere. Zimbabwe is not a part of me, nor I of it. Trying to draw it for the first time, from a standing start, is like trying to start a conversation in Swahili.

There were compensations. The holiday was wonderfully organised by a friend of mine – Susan Scott-Thomas. Admittedly, there are some rather large differences between us – she's extremely wealthy and she inherited a farm in Africa when she was in her mid-twenties, and instead of taking the easy option of becoming a solicitor and staying in London, she came out to reclaim the land and rebuild the decaying farmhouse. In the process, she learnt how to lay foundations and make clay bricks. All of which she did while I was just about mastering making sauce for pasta.

Even my disastrous painting didn't detract from enjoying the holiday. Painting really forces you to look at things, to consider their shape and colour. And even if it is a disaster, that process of looking and thinking and transferring those thoughts into movements of your hand leaves an imprint of what you have seen.

Anything for a laugh

Speaking

1   Work in pairs. Stop your partner after one minute and answer the short question.

First long turn (photos 1 and 2):

Student A
Compare the photographs and say what makes something funny on film.

Student B
Which type of film do you prefer to watch at the cinema?

Second long turn (photos 3 and 4):

Student B
Compare the photographs and say what is important when watching live performances.

Student A
What kind of live show would you like to attend?

Reading

2   You are going to read four 'urban myths' – modern-day stories, usually humorous, which people enjoy telling each other at parties or at the pub. First, read questions 1–10.

In which urban myth does someone

need to withdraw money?	1
have an injured pet?	2
appear unconcerned?	3
mistake a person for a criminal?	4
have urgent treatment?	5
disobey a request?	6
have to make a hard decision?	7
break the rules?	8
try to hide something?	9
receive an apology?	10

3   Now scan the four texts for the answers, ignoring the highlighted words. Compare your answers with another student.

A   A woman was looking forward to an important dinner party, where her guests would include her husband's new boss. She wanted to serve a really special meal, so she bought a whole salmon, which she cooked and prepared beautifully. The dinner party started well, and the woman received many compliments about the starters she served. At a suitable moment, she went out to get the fish from the kitchen, where she found a rather horrifying sight: her cat was sitting on the work surface, tucking into the fish. She shooed the cat away and, in a state of total panic, hastily disguised the damage with some carefully placed slices of lemon and cucumber. Then she took the salmon through, to gasps of admiration. However, when the woman went to the kitchen to make the coffee, she found her cat writhing around on the floor in obvious pain. Convinced that the salmon was to blame, the poor woman went back in to tell her guests the truth. They all rushed off to hospital to have their stomachs pumped. The woman had only just returned home when the doorbell rang. It was the milkman, who explained that he was just calling to see if the cat was all right. It turned out that he'd dropped a metal milk crate on its head that morning.

B   A young man had been out for the evening in central London and was making for Charing Cross station to catch his train home, but then decided he would rather have something to eat first. Checking his pocket, he found he only had about £5. It was a difficult choice: go home or get a quarterpounder with all the trimmings. Then he remembered he had his cash card, so all was well. He bought himself the burger, which he had already started to eat when he reached the cashpoint machine. He put in his card, put the snack down next to the keypad, punched in his numbers and waited for the cash to come out. Instead, the screen flashed up: 'Sorry, you have used the wrong number. Do you wish to try again?' A bit nervous, he keyed in another number. Again the message appeared. He was convinced that the first number was right, so he keyed it in carefully. No sooner had he finished than a message came up, saying his card had been retained. This was not the only thing he lost either, for then the glass shield came down, locking away his delicious burger.

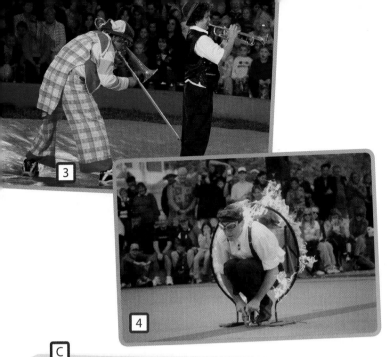

3

4

4 Which do you think is the funniest of the four urban myths? Are any of them not funny at all, in your view? Explain your reasons to another student.

5 Work out the meaning of the highlighted words in the text from the surrounding context. Then use some of them in a–j.

  a The walkers sensed movement and suddenly a huge bear .... out of the trees just ahead of them.

  b The hotel .... their passports for the duration of their stay.

  c Take that .... look off your face – it's me in disguise!

  d Murray .... the ball in the air badly and decided not to play the serve.

  e The baby's birth had been difficult and Jane looked exhausted, so her father .... everyone .... to allow her to get some rest.

  f Rob cooked an amazing Sunday lunch of roast beef and ....

  g We .... the bill between the three of us, as it was Gregor's birthday.

  h You can't go to a job interview dressed like that – you look so .... !

  i Thousands of villagers are thought to be .... their homes, fearing the worst after the second earthquake.

  j When we moved out of the apartment, we packed everything into large wooden .... , which we stored at my parents' place.

C

An English couple who were driving around the USA were spending a few days in New York. They'd had some great evenings out on the town, including a show on Broadway and an Italian meal on the Lower East Side. They'd been a bit anxious at first, having seen all those violent shoot-'em-up cop shows on TV, but by the final evening, they were really enjoying themselves. They drove back to the hotel, parked in the basement car park, and waited for the lift up to reception. It was quite dark and rather scary. Suddenly, a huge man with a Rottweiler loomed out of the shadows. The lift came and the couple hurried in, followed by the man and his dog. As the doors closed, the man shouted, 'Get down, lady!' Rather than put up a fight, the petrified couple tossed all their money at him and threw themselves on the floor. When the lift arrived, they scrambled to their feet and ran out in a panic. To their surprise, when they checked out the next day, the receptionist explained that a man had already settled their account, and she handed them an envelope. Inside was all the money they'd given the 'mugger' and a note saying: 'I'm real sorry about scaring you yesterday, and I hope paying your bill has made up for your ordeal. By the way, Lady is the name of my dog.'

D

Back in the 1980s, when businessman Robert Maxwell owned the *Daily Mirror* newspaper, he lived above their offices in London. One day, Maxwell, who was in the luxurious penthouse flat at the top, was coming down in the lift. At the next floor he was joined by a young lad in a rather scruffy suit, who happened to be smoking. Maxwell was furious to find one of his employees ignoring the company's no-smoking policy. The lad was promptly told to extinguish his cigarette, but rather than doing so he started blowing smoke in Maxwell's face. Maxwell angrily insisted that he put it out immediately. 'No way,' said the lad, and carried on puffing. At this, Maxwell demanded to know how much the lad earned a week. On being told £200, he took £400 in cash from his pocket and handed it to the lad, who looked totally bewildered. Maxwell said 'I'm giving you two weeks' notice. You're fired! Get out of my offices now.' 'Don't worry, mate,' said the lad, fleeing through the lift doors with his wad of cash, 'I'm going – I work for Telecom anyway!'

Grammar extra

rather

Look at these examples from the four urban myths and then answer questions a–c below.

1 But rather than doing so, he started blowing smoke in Maxwell's face.

2 At the next floor he was joined by a young man in a rather scruffy suit.

3 … but then decided he would rather have something to eat first.

4 It was quite dark and rather scary.

a In which example could you use *instead of*? Which word apart from *rather* would you also have to omit?

b In which example is *rather* used to mean *prefer*? Which word has to be used as well? What word could be added to these words to give the opposite meaning?

c In which two examples is *rather* used in the same way? What similar word is also used in one of these examples?

G → page 176

The grammar of phrasal verbs

A phrasal verb consists of a main verb and a *particle* – an adverb or a preposition. You have met many phrasal verbs throughout this course (pages 164–165 have a list of these). Now it is time to understand their grammar, which affects word order.

1 **Look at these examples from 24.1. Which two contain intransitive phrasal verbs (verbs which have no object)?**

   a A woman was looking forward to an important dinner party.

   b Her cat was tucking into the fish.

   c She shooed the cat away.

   d It turned out that he'd dropped a metal milk crate on its head.

   e He put the snack down next to the keypad.

   f He keyed it in carefully.

   g No sooner had he finished than a message came up.

   h Rather than put up a fight, the petrified couple …

   i I hope paying your bill has made up for your ordeal.

   j Maxwell insisted that he put it out immediately.

2 **Examine the word order for the transitive phrasal verbs in 1. Can the position of the object be changed in any of the examples? If so, give the alternative word order.**

EXAMPLES: a A woman was looking forward to an important dinner party.
   no change possible
   c She shooed the cat away. ✓
   She shooed away the cat.

3 **Check your ideas by matching examples a–j to these statements.**

   1 When a two-part phrasal verb is intransitive (has no object), the verb and the particle cannot be separated by other words.

   2 When a pronoun is used as the object of a two-part phrasal verb, it always comes before the particle.

   3 When a noun is used as the object of a two-part phrasal verb containing a preposition, the object has to come after the preposition.

   4 When a noun is used as the object of a two-part phrasal verb containing an adverb, it can generally come before or after the adverb. There are one or two exceptions, one of which is example … .

   5 In a three-part phrasal verb, the object cannot come between the two particles.

4 **Complete the sentences using the phrasal verb in brackets and a suitable noun or pronoun.**

   EXAMPLE: *My friend* has talked me into doing a 15-km run *at the weekend.* (talk into)

   a Please .... – you've watched far too much already. (turn off)

   b Sooner or later you'll have to tell me the truth, so let's .... , shall we? (get over with)

   c It was getting foggy, but they .... in the distance, which had its lights on. (make out)

   d That story .... driving in an open car for life! (put off)

   e While we were living in Sweden, we .... quite well. (pick up)

   f If there are any words you don't understand, ... in a dictionary. (look up)

   g I've just .... to that question! (work out)

   h You know you really should have .... before now – it's not good owing so much money. (face up to)

G→ page 176

Corpus spot

These three-part phrasal verbs with *up* are frequently used by exam candidates. Match them with the noun phrases to check your understanding of them.

catch up on	his expectations
come up with	your bad moods
keep up with	some sleep
live up to	the international news
put up with	some good ideas

G→ page 164

5 Match the first lines (a–o) and second lines (1–15) of these jokes. Then take a vote to decide on the three funniest ones, giving reasons for your choices.

a What do you call someone who hangs around with musicians?

b Every time I drink coffee I get a stabbing pain in my left eye.

c When a man has a birthday, he takes the day off.

d What's the definition of a modern artist?

e I ended up as the teacher's pet.

f What's the best way to make the landlord paint your apartment?

g Did you start out as an actor?

h What's the best way to stay out of the army?

i Why did you wake me up? It's still dark.

j My brother and I are inseparable.

k What are you doing in my tree, young lad?

l A Hollywood couple have finally worked out their divorce settlement.

m Would you please open up the piano?

n Old pickpockets never die.

o What would you do if you were in my shoes?

1 One of your apples fell down and I'm putting it back.

2 No, as a little boy.

3 Clean them up.

4 She couldn't afford a dog.

5 In fact, it takes six people to pull us apart.

6 I can't – the keys are inside.

7 Well, take the spoon out of the cup.

8 Join the navy.

9 Someone who tosses paint on a canvas, wipes it off with a cloth and sells the cloth.

10 A drummer.

11 Well, open your eyes!

12 Now they can get married.

13 Move out.

14 They just steal away.

15 When a woman has one, she takes a year off.

6 Read this biography of Jim Carrey. For questions 1–8, think of the word which best fits each gap. Use only one word in each gap. There is an example at the beginning (0).

Example: 0 MUCH

A funny man with a funny face

Jim Carrey's humour is very (**0**) .... his own brand. It is often slapstick, sometimes a bit tasteless, but always extremely funny. Carrey, who was born in Canada in 1962, believes that his sense of humour developed (**1**) .... his teenage years. This was his way of dealing with a difficult period in his life, when his father had lost his job and Carrey junior had to earn money and study (**2**) .... the same time.

Carrey first performed live when he was 15, at Yuk Yuks, a famous club in Toronto. Even (**3**) .... he failed to make his audience laugh on this occasion, he kept working on his material and within four years became the club's top comedy act. He moved to Los Angeles to tour the clubs there and later starred regularly in an American TV show. One of the many characters he played was Fire Marshall Bill, who always went (**4**) .... in smoke! Sadly, this character finally had to (**5**) .... dropped because of complaints that his fire act might have a bad influence on children.

Carrey's first feature film was *Ace Ventura: Pet Detective*, one of his (**6**) .... popular films ever. Another early film, *The Mask*, was the perfect vehicle (**7**) .... his weird humour. Other films (**8**) .... then have included *Batman Forever*, *The Truman Show* and *Yes Man*. His earnings are estimated at around $20 million per film.

Writing folder 12

Paper 2 Part 2 Articles

Look back at Writing folder 5 on pages 70–71, which focused mainly on communicative achievement. This Writing folder looks at accuracy and range of language.

1 Read this exam question and the facts about Eddie Izzard.

> You have seen this announcement in an international magazine.
>
> ### Which live entertainer do you really admire? Why?
>
> Describe what this person does and explain why you are so impressed by him or her.
>
> ### We will publish some of the best articles next month.
>
> Write your **article**.

2 Read the sample answer, underlining any mistakes you notice. There are ten in all.

Eddie Izzard – a man of many talents

Eddie Izzard has been a stand-up comedian for over 30 years and regularly sells out the biggest venues, included the Hollywood Bowl. I've seen one of his live show and they are hilarious. He loves experimenting with language and delivers also whole performances in French. The touring show *Force Majeure* has taken him to 25 countries around the world.

Not only that, but he has acted in much films and plays, and often appears in TV. The most impressive thing about him is the way he raises money for the charity. For example, for Sports Relief he spent seven weeks running marathons, covering more then 1100 miles across the UK with only one day off each week! Even though he had very few training beforehand, he somehow managed to keep going, in spite of be in pain at times.

That's why I respect him so much. Nothing is too challenging for him, from facing a huge live audience to the physical strain of marathon running. He received an Outstanding Lifetime Achievement Award from Harvard University, there he was described as an outstanding member of global society.

Eddie Izzard FACTFILE

1980s Worked as a street performer in Europe and then did stand-up comedy around Britain.

1991 Gets his first TV break.

1996 His first film part in the USA leads to the *Definite Article* show being transferred to New York.

1999 Plays the comedian Lenny Bruce in the play *Lenny*, in a London theatre.

2004 Plays Roman Nagel in the film *Ocean's Twelve*, starring George Clooney.

2009 Completes seven weeks of back-to-back marathon runs to raise money for Sport Relief, covering more than 1,100 miles across the UK.

2011 Three-month residency at a theatre in Paris doing a comedy show all in French

2013 Receives Outstanding Lifetime Achievement Award in Cultural Humanism from Harvard University

2013–14 *Force Majeure* comedy tour, covering 25 countries worldwide.

Eddie IZ Finishing
sportrelief.com

3 Did any of these mistakes stop you understanding the answer? Read the Corpus spot and then correct the mistakes.

Corpus spot

The mistakes shown are typical of B2 level. In the exam, apart from looking at spelling, check your answers for:
- word order, especially with adverbs *also, always*, etc.
- agreement with verbs and nouns
- choice of preposition
- use of articles *the, a/an*
- quantifiers, especially *few/little* and *much/many*

4 Now look at this exam question.

You see this announcement on a theatre website.

THE FUNNIEST PERFORMANCE EVER

Write us an article describing the funniest performance you have ever seen and explaining why it made you laugh. The performance could be a live comedy act, a TV programme, a video clip posted online, or something else – it is your choice!

The writer of the best article will win two free tickets to our next production.

Write your **article** in 140–190 words.

Assessment focus

Don't be afraid to take risks, even if it means you make a few mistakes. To score a high mark for **language**, you need to show a wide range of vocabulary and grammar, as the sample answer does.

5 Once you have decided on content, look at the synonyms given in a–d. Many of these words and phrases are used in the sample answer in 2.

a Adjectives that mean the same as *funny – amusing, entertaining, hilarious*

b Other verbs with a similar meaning to *perform – appear, deliver, present, produce*

c Linking phrases to emphasise or highlight something – *besides that, not only that, what's more*

d Linking phrases to explain why – *for this reason, that's why*

6 Write your article in 140–190 words, following the Exam advice.

EXAM ADVICE

Content
- Make sure the reader is fully informed.

Communicative achievement
- Make your writing interesting to read.
- Write in a consistent style throughout.

Organisation
- Include a title.
- Organise your ideas in paragraphs.
- Use suitable linking phrases to emphasise your ideas.

Language
- Use synonyms to show your language range.
- Check word order with adverbs.

Topic review

1 Answer these questions, giving your own opinions. If you are working in pairs or groups, remember to use turn-taking skills.

   a What should someone do to lose weight?

   b When should you tell someone it's time for them to leave a party?

   c Even if someone has committed a crime, is prison the best form of punishment?

   d What are the advantages and disadvantages of living in a city?

   e If you were woken up by an earthquake, what would you try to do?

   f Do you think the internet has increased or decreased crime? Why?

   g Which would you rather watch, a comedy programme or the news?

   h What do you hope to do after you have passed Cambridge First?

Vocabulary

2 Read the statements or questions and choose the best option, A, B or C.

   1 Someone has given you a present. Should you
   A uncover it?   B unfasten it?   C unwrap it?

   2 If you caught flu, would you have
   A a bug?   B a bruise?   C a sweat?

   3 Which performer would you not see at a classical recital?
   A a violinist   B a cellist   C a bass guitarist

   4 You are driving in torrential rain and a tree falls across the road 200 metres in front of you. Are you in danger of being
   A cut down?   B cut off?   C cut out?

   5 You see someone take another person's bicycle. Do you
   A arrest them?   B charge them?   C accuse them?

   6 If you don't see eye to eye with someone, do you
   A hate them?   B disagree with them?
   C find out about them?

   7 What would you do if your little brother broke your mobile?
   A tell him off?   B send him off?   C show him off?

   8 You need a plaster. Do you have
   A flu?   B a cut?   C a cough?

3 The twenty words below have all appeared in Units 19–24. Decide what they are with the help of the information given and then use one from each set to complete the sentences a–e.

   • two verbs to do with illness or injury:
      1 S P _ A _ _
      2 C _ _ _ H
   • three words to do with volcanoes:
      3 E _ U _ _ _ _ _
      4 _ _ H
      5 L _ _ _
   • four musical instruments:
      6 O _ _ _
      7 _ I _ _ O
      8 _ U I _ _ _
      9 _ L _ _ E
   • five nouns to do with crime and punishment:
      10 R _ _ _ _ _ Y
      11 _ O U _ _
      12 _ _ R G _ _ R
      13 T _ _ _ L
      14 F _ _ _
   • six words for parts of the body:
      15 E _ _ B _ _ W
      16 _ A _ S _
      17 _ _ W
      18 _ N _ E
      19 _ L B _ _
      20 T _ _ _ H

   a She picked up the shiny silver .... and began to play her favourite piece.

   b This belt is a bit tight around my .... – I must have put on weight!

   c The city of Pompeii was destroyed by the .... of Vesuvius in 79 AD.

   d It is very easy to .... your ankle when running to the back of the court for a difficult ball.

   e You will get a .... if you cycle without lights in our town.

4 Complete the story with a phrasal verb from the box in the correct form.

bring in	call up	end up	miss out on
put off	take aback	take on	work out

If the Royal Marines had drummed one thing into Sergeant Ken Murgatroyd during his twenty-two years of service, it was the importance of seizing opportunities. After he left the Royal Marines, his new job in telesales involved **(1)** .... computer companies. However, one morning he rang the direct line of Neil Corbould, a senior assistant to the film director Steven Spielberg, by mistake. Within minutes Mr Murgatroyd had been **(2)** .... for a leading role in the war film *Saving Private Ryan*.

No one was more **(3)** .... than Mr Murgatroyd. Mr Spielberg needed to **(4)** .... someone who could **(5)** .... how to make the scenes as realistic as possible. Mr Murgatroyd, who was one of the navy's foremost authorities on landing manoeuvres, was perfect.

'I hadn't even heard of the film when they gave me the job. I was trying to sell an internet database, when I pressed a wrong button and **(6)** .... talking to Spielberg's assistant. I told him I had made a mistake, but out of curiosity asked him what kind of work he did. When he told me, I thought, I can help with that.'

Working with celebrities didn't **(7)** .... Mr Murgatroyd at all. 'In fact, I found all the Hollywood types very pleasant. I don't think they had ever worked with someone like me before. I wouldn't have wanted to **(8)** .... an opportunity like that.'

Grammar

5 Read the text below and think of the word which best fits each gap. Use only one word in each gap. There is an example at the beginning (0).

How to make a small fortune

Have you ever wished you had some savings to fall back **(0)** _ON_ ? Perhaps you already have something put aside for a rainy day, but if **(1)** .... , here are some unusual ways to make a pile of cash. Look critically at your old toys. Very **(2)** .... remain in a condition that is good **(3)** .... for them to be sold, but a pre-1950, well-looked-after teddy bear could be worth **(4)** .... to £2,000. Musical instruments can also raise a large sum, sometimes unexpectedly. Hazel Morgan hadn't played her violin for more **(5)** .... forty years, so she decided to sell it. To her surprise, the violin itself was valued **(6)** .... £2,500 and the bow, despite **(7)** .... in bad condition, was expected to fetch even more. Old stamps can also be highly profitable, and even **(8)** .... your investment doesn't prove as big an earner as you hoped, you can still enjoy looking at them!

Speaking folder

Paper 4 Speaking

The Speaking test is an opportunity to demonstrate your level of English. Don't be too worried about making mistakes – you are not only assessed on your accuracy, but also on your range of grammar and vocabulary, your pronunciation, and your ability to communicate with other people in discussion.

EXAM ADVICE

- Try to be relaxed and cheerful – it will only take 14 minutes!
- Ask the examiner if you are unclear about an instruction.
- Don't be afraid to spend a few seconds thinking, in order to plan what you are going to say.
- Give detailed answers in Part 1, rather than answering the examiner's questions in a single word.
- Listen carefully to the other candidate's long turn in Part 2 so that you can make a short comment when asked.
- Keep going during your own long turn, remembering to compare the pictures, rather than describe an individual picture.
- Be sensitive to the other candidate in Part 3 and use turn-taking skills to ensure you both work towards completion of the task.
- Interact both with the other candidate and the examiner in Part 4.

Now put all the advice into practice in this complete Speaking Test.

Part 1: Answer these questions.

How do you like to spend your free time?

Do you go shopping because you have to, or because you enjoy it?

What kind of music do you prefer to listen to?

Can you describe a work of art that is special for you?

Part 2: Look at these pictures, which show two celebrities.

Student A is asked: Compare the photographs and say what would be the advantages and disadvantages of being famous.

Student B is asked: What do you think would be the best thing about being a celebrity?

Now look at these pictures, which show two different parts of the world.

> **Student B** is asked: I'd like you to compare these photographs and say which place you think would be the more difficult to live in, and why.
> **Student A** is asked: Which place would you prefer to live in?

Part 3: Imagine that you have to give advice to someone about health and fitness. Talk to a partner about what people should do to keep fit and healthy. Then decide which two ways of keeping healthy would be the most effective.

(join a gym)   (cycle to college or work)   (get ten hours sleep a night)

What should people do to keep fit and healthy?

(go running every day)   (become a vegetarian)

Part 4: Now discuss these questions.

Do you think people do enough to keep themselves fit and healthy? Why? / Why not?

Are there things that the government could do to help people stay healthy? What should they do?

Do you think that children get enough physical exercise nowadays? Why? / Why not?

What are the most important things to think about when deciding on a new fitness programme?

Is there one single thing that would improve the level of fitness of a working adult? If so, what is it?

Some people say that swimming is the best form of exercise. What do you think?

Phrasal verb list

This list covers the phrasal verbs practised in *Objective First Student's Book*, with definitions taken from the *English Vocabulary Profile*. (The Unit and page numbers are given in brackets.) Where the position of the object can be moved, you will see both options given, for example **call off sth** or **call sth off**. Note that some phrasal verbs occur both with and without an object, for example **break (sth) off**. Remember that phrasal verbs without an object cannot be separated, for example **fall apart**. Several phrasal verbs have more than one meaning and the words in capital letters show you which meanings are covered in the course, for example **take off** AIRCRAFT, SUCCESSFUL.

add to sth PUT WITH to put something with something else (U1, 11)

book (sb) into to arrange for someone to stay at a hotel (U3, 23)

break down If a machine or vehicle breaks down, it stops working. (U19, 125)

break off (sth) or **break (sth) off** to end (something) suddenly (U23, 149)

call off sth or **call sth off** to decide that a planned event, especially a sports event, will not happen, or to end an activity because it is no longer useful or possible (U23, 149)

call sb up to telephone someone (U18–24, 161)

calm down to stop feeling upset, angry, or excited, or to make someone stop feeling this way (U5, 36)

catch up on sth to do something that you did not have time to do earlier (U24, 156)

check in HOTEL to go to the desk at a hotel in order to say that you have arrived, and to get the key to your room (U3, 23)

check out to leave a hotel after paying your bill (U3, 23)

come across sth SEEM to find something by chance (U18, 117)

come down FALL to fall and land on the ground (U5, 36)

come out BECOME AVAILABLE If a book, record, film, etc comes out, it becomes available for people to buy or see. (U18, 117)

come up MOVE TOWARDS to move towards someone (U24, 156)

come up with sth to suggest or think of an idea or plan (U18, 117)

consist of sth to be formed or made from two or more things (U15, 101)

cut down sth or **cut sth down** REDUCE to eat or drink less of something, or to reduce the amount or number of something (U1, 11)

cut down sth or **cut sth down** REMOVE to make a tree or other plant fall to the ground by cutting it near the bottom (U4, 28)

cut off sb/sth or **cut sb/sth off** to cause a person or place to become separate, or cause someone to be or feel alone (U23, 149)

do without (sb/sth) to manage without having someone or something (U7, 50)

dress up FORMAL to put on formal clothes for a special occasion (U1, 11)

end up to finally be in a particular place or situation (U5, 35)

face up to sth to accept that a difficult situation exists (U24, 156)

fall out (with sb) to argue with someone and stop being friendly with them (EF 4, 52)

fill in sth to write the necessary information on an official document (U3, 24)

find out (sth) or **find (sth) out** to get information about something, or to learn a fact for the first time (U2, 18)

fit in with sth If one thing fits in with another thing, they look pleasant together or are suitable for each other. (U1, 11)

get away HOLIDAY to go somewhere to have a holiday, especially because you need to rest (U3, 23)

get away with sth to succeed in not being criticized or punished for something (U8, 56)

get down to sth to start doing something seriously and with a lot of attention and effort (U8, 56)

get in VEHICLE ARRIVING If a train or other vehicle gets in at a particular time, that is when it arrives. (U3, 23)

get into sth BE CHOSEN to succeed in being chosen or elected (U8, 56)

get on (with sb) (UK) If two or more people get on, they like each other and are friendly to each other. (U8, 57)

get out of sth/doing sth to avoid doing something that you do not want to do, especially by giving an excuse (U8, 56)

get over sth/sb GET BETTER to get better after an illness, or feel better after something or someone has made you unhappy (U8, 56)

get sth over with to do or finish an unpleasant but necessary piece of work or duty so that you do not have to worry about it in the future (U24, 156)

get through sth FINISH to use up or finish something (U2, 17)

go ahead ALLOW something that you say to someone to allow them to do something (U1, 11)

go ahead START to start to do something (U18, 117)

go back to return to a place where you were or where you have been before (U1, 11)

go by TIME If time goes by, it passes. (U18, 117)

go for sth CHOOSE to choose something (U1, 11)

go off EXPLODE If a bomb or a gun goes off, it explodes or fires.(U23, 149)

go off sth/sb to stop liking or being interested in someone or something (U18, 117)

go on HAPPEN to happen (U1, 11)

go out LEAVE to leave a room or building, especially in order to do something for entertainment (U1, 11)

go over sth to talk or think about something in order to explain it or make certain that it is correct (U1, 11)

go through sth to experience a difficult or unpleasant situation (U18, 117)

go up INCREASE to become higher in level (U1, 11)

hang around (with sb) to spend time with someone (U24, 157)

keep (sb/sth) away to not go somewhere or near something, or to prevent someone from going somewhere or near something (U6, 41)

keep on doing sth to continue to do something, or to do something again and again (U6, 41)

keep sb in to make a child stay inside as a punishment, or to make someone stay in hospital (U6, 41)

keep sth down NO INCREASE to stop the number, level, or size of something from increasing (U6, 41)

keep to sth NOT CHANGE PLANS to do what you have promised or planned to do (U6, 41)

keep up (with sb/sth) UNDERSTAND to be able to understand or deal with something that is happening or changing very fast (U1, 11)

keep up (with sb/sth) SAME SPEED to move at the same speed as someone or something that is moving forward so that you stay level with them (U6, 41)

key sth in to put information into a computer or a machine using a keyboard (U24, 154)

let off sb or **let sb off** to not punish someone who has committed a crime or done something wrong, or to not punish them severely (U23, 149)

live up to sth to be as good as someone hopes (U4, 29)

log off to stop a computer being connected to a computer system, usually when you want to stop working (U23, 149)

look after sb/sth to take care of or be in charge of someone or something (U17, 111)

look at sth EXAMINE If someone, usually an expert, looks at something, they examine it. (U17, 111)

look for sth/sb to try to find someone or something (U17, 111)

look forward to sth/doing sth to feel happy and excited about something that is going to happen (WF2, U17, 109)

look into sth to examine the facts about a problem or situation (U17, 111)

look up sth or **look sth up** to try to find a piece of information by looking in a book or on a computer (U24, 156)

look up to sb to respect and admire someone (U17, 111)

make for swh to move towards a place (U24, 154)

make up for sth to reduce the bad effect of something, or make something bad become something good (U24, 156)

make out sth/sb or **make sth/sb out** to see, hear or understand something or someone with difficulty (U24, 156)

miss out on sth to fail to use an opportunity to enjoy or get an advantage from something (U19–24, 161)

pick up sth or **pick sth up** to learn a new skill or language by practising it rather than being taught it (U24, 156)

pull away START MOVING If a vehicle pulls away, it starts moving. (U5, 36)

pull on sth CLOTHES to put on clothes quickly (U1, 11)

pull up If a vehicle pulls up, it stops, often for a short time. (U5, 36)

put down sth or **put sth down** to put someone or something that you are holding onto the floor or onto another surface (U24, 154)

put off sb or **put sb off** to make someone dislike something or someone, or to discourage someone from doing something (U24, 156)

put out sth or **put sth out STOP BURNING** to make something that is burning, such as a fire or cigarette, stop burning (U24, 155)

put sth together or **put together sth JOIN PARTS** to create something by joining or combining different things (U1, 11)

put up sth to show or express a particular type of opposition to something (U24, 156)

put up with sb/sth to accept unpleasant behaviour or an unpleasant situation, although you do not like it (U24, 156)

save up (sth) or **save (sth) up MONEY** to keep money so that you can buy something with it in the future (U1, 11)

send off sth or **send sth off** to send a letter, document or parcel by post (U23, 149)

set off to start a journey (U3, 23)

slip on sth or **slip sth on** to quickly put on a piece of clothing (U1, 11)

slip out If a remark slips out, you say it without intending to. (U24, 154)

stand out NOTICE to be very easy to see or notice (U1, 11)

start out to begin your life or the part of your life when you work, in a particular way (U24, 157)

stop over to stay at a place for one night or a few nights on the way to somewhere else or before returning home (U3, 23)

take after sb to be similar to an older member of your family (U11, 74)

take back sth or **take sth back [THING]** to return something to the place you borrowed or bought it from (U1, 11)

take off AIRCRAFT If an aircraft takes off, it begins to fly. (U3, 23)

take off SUCCESSFUL to suddenly become successful (U11, 74)

take off sth or **take sth off** to spend time away from your work (U24, 157)

take out sth or **take sth out** to remove something from somewhere (U11, 74)

take sth off or **take off sth REMOVE** to remove something (U1, 11)

take sth on to accept a particular job or responsibility (U19–24, 161)

talk sb into (doing) sth to persuade someone to do something (U12, 80)

tell off sb or **tell sb off** to speak angrily to someone because they have done something wrong (U23, 149)

tell sb/sth apart to be able to see the difference between two very similar things or people (U12, 81)

turn on sth or **turn sth on** to move the switch on a machine, light, etc so that it starts working, or to start the supply of water, electricity, etc (U2, 16)

turn out BE DISCOVERED to be known or discovered finally and surprisingly (U24, 154)

turn up sth or **turn sth up** to increase the level of sound or heat that a machine produces (U2, 16)

wear off If a feeling or the effect of something wears off, it gradually disappears. (U23, 149)

work on sth to spend time repairing or improving something (U24, 157)

work out sth or **work sth out CALCULATE** to do a calculation to get an answer to a mathematical question (U24, 157)

work out sth or **work sth out PROBLEM** to understand something or to find the answer to something by thinking about it (U24, 156)

Grammar folder

Unit 1
Comparison
There are various ways of making comparisons in English.

1 Comparative and superlative adjectives

Regular adjectives of one syllable have forms like these:

Adjective	Comparative	Superlative
young	young**er**	(the) young**est**
large	larg**er**	(the) larg**est**
slim	slim**mer**	(the) slim**mest**

Note that if an adjective ends in a single vowel and consonant (not w), the final letter is doubled, as in *slim* above. Some common examples are:
sad, big, thin, fat, hot, wet.

Two-syllable adjectives ending in a consonant followed by the letter y are formed like this:

Adjective	Comparative	Superlative
dirty	dirt**ier**	(the) dirt**iest**

Some common examples are:
angry, busy, easy, funny, happy, heavy, silly, tiny.

Most other two-syllable adjectives and all longer adjectives form their comparative and superlative forms like this:

Adjective	Comparative	Superlative
careful	**more** careful	(the) **most** careful
casual	**more** casual	(the) **most** casual
outrageous	**more** outrageous	(the) **most** outrageous

Some common two-syllable adjectives have both forms:

Adjective	Comparative	Superlative
simple	simpl**er** OR **more** simple	(the) simpl**est** OR (the) **most** simple

Other examples are:
clever, common, cruel, gentle, likely, narrow, pleasant, polite.

Irregular adjectives have the following forms:

Adjective	Comparative	Superlative
good	better	(the) best
bad	worse	(the) worst
far	farther/ further	(the) farthest/ furthest
old	older/ elder	(the) oldest/ eldest

2 Adverbs of degree

These adverbs of degree can be used in front of comparative adjectives:
a bit, a good deal, a great deal, a little, a lot, much, rather, slightly.
This T-shirt is a bit cheaper than the others because it's last year's design.
Helen is much more intelligent than the rest of the group.

These adverbs of degree can be used in front of superlative adjectives:
by far, easily, much, quite.
You're easily the cleverest person I know!

3 not as … as

This structure is used to compare two things or people. A less common form is *not so … as*.
Sally is not as tall as her brother.

4 Comparative and superlative adverbs

Comparative adverbs are usually formed by adding *more* to the existing adverb:

commonly	→	more commonly
readily	→	more readily

Superlative adverbs are usually formed by adding *(the) most* to the existing adverb:

commonly	→	(the) most commonly
readily	→	(the) most readily

A few adverbs are not formed with *more / most* and consist of a single word for both the comparative and superlative forms. Here are some common examples:

badly	→	worse	→	worst
close	→	closer	→	closest
early	→	earlier	→	earliest
far	→	farther/further	→	farthest/furthest
fast	→	faster	→	fastest
hard	→	harder	→	hardest
near	→	nearer	→	nearest
well	→	better	→	best

Unit 2
Adverbs
Most regular adverbs are formed by adding *-ly* to a related adjective:
quick → quickly, endless → endlessly
Adjectives ending in double *ll* just add *y*:
full → fully
However, there are sometimes spelling changes when an adverb is formed in this way:
-le becomes -ly: gentle → gently, remarkable → remarkably
-y becomes -ily: easy → easily, cosy → cosily
-ic becomes -ically: tragic → tragically, automatic → automatically
-ue becomes -uly: true → truly

Some irregular adverbs do not end in *-ly*:
fast, hard, late, well.

The adverbs *hardly* and *lately* have different meanings from *hard* and *late*:
I worked hard on the project all day.
I hardly had time to stop for a coffee all day.

I finished the work late in the evening.
I've put in some long hours at work lately.

Review of present tenses

Uses of the present simple tense

- Permanent situations
  Most people access the Internet for information.
- Habitual situations
  I check my emails twice a day.
- In time clauses
  Once you finish your work, give me a ring.
  We usually play tennis until it gets dark.
- In zero conditionals
  If you use all seven letters in the board game Scrabble, you get fifty extra points.
  Steam forms when water boils.

Uses of the present continuous tense

- Temporary situations
  I'm living at home until I find my own flat.
- Developing situations
  Traffic is becoming heavier and heavier.
- Events happening now
  Sit still while I'm talking to you!
- Events in the near future
  Tim's leaving for Hanover next week.

See Unit 10, Review of future tenses (page 170), for further information about the present simple and present continuous tenses.

Stative verbs are not normally used in continuous tenses. The commonest of these are:

admire be believe belong consist dislike doubt fit forget guess hate hear imagine include keep know like love mean prefer realise recognise remember seem smell sound suppose taste understand want wish

*She **keeps** talking when I'm trying to watch TV.*
*We **wish** we could be with you right now.*

Unit 3
Modals 1: Obligation, necessity and permission

Strong obligation: *must* and *have to, have got to* (Informal)

Present and future	*must*	*have to*	*have got to*
Past	*had to*		

1 *must*
Must is used to talk about strong obligations in the present and future that are imposed by the speaker.
You must brush your teeth before you go to bed.
I must arrange to have my windows cleaned.
(It is also used to talk about laws: *Drivers must obey traffic signals.*)

2 *have to/have got to*
Have to/have got to are used to talk about strong obligations in the present and future that are not imposed by the speaker.
I've got to do some homework tonight. (My teacher says so.)
If in doubt whether to use *must* or *have to*, use *have to*. Do not use *I've to*, which is incorrect.

3 *had to*
Had to is used to talk about past and reported obligations:
I had to help on the farm when I was young.
We were told we had to get a visa before we left on holiday.
There are also other ways to express obligation:
to make someone do something
to be compulsory

Weak obligation: *should ought to*

Present and future	*should do* *ought to do*
Past	*should have done*
	ought to have done

There is no difference in meaning between *should* and *ought to*.
You ought to/should write home more frequently.
In the past *should have done* and *ought to have done* are often used for criticism or regret, because an action didn't happen:
We should have bought/ought to have bought your sister a card for her birthday.

Asking for and giving permission: *can could may*

Can is the more usual way of asking for and giving permission. *Could* is a bit more polite and *may* is quite formal:
Can/may/could I borrow your bike?
Yes, you can/may.

Other ways of asking for and giving permission are:
to allow someone to do
to permit someone to do
to let someone do

Prohibition: *mustn't can't*

Present and future	*mustn't* *can't*
Past	*was not to* *couldn't*

Mustn't and *can't* are used when something is forbidden:
You mustn't cross the road without looking.
Elizabeth can't go out this evening – her father says so.

Other verbs which can be used are:
to forbid someone to do something
to ban someone from doing something
to not allow someone to do something
to not permit someone to do something
to not let someone do something.

It is also possible to use an imperative:
Don't cycle on the pavement!

Unit 4
as and *like*

(See also grammar summary in Unit 4)

Like can be used as a preposition and is followed by a noun (*like a house*), a pronoun (*like it*), or a gerund (*like swimming*). It is used to give a comparison:
Your house is like our house/ours. (is similar to ours)
My bed is so hard it's like sleeping on the ground.

As can be used as a preposition to tell you what job or function a person or thing has:
As a chef, I have to cook one hundred meals a day.
I used the tin as a cup to drink out of.

Please note these other uses of *as* and *like*.
It's like living in a palace, living in your house. (It's not a palace.)
As a palace, Windsor is very impressive. (It is a palace.)

As is used in prepositional phrases:
At my school, as at most schools, pupils were expected to respect their teachers.

Some verbs can be followed by an object and *as*:
He is known as a generous person.
I don't regard learning a language as optional.

Like and *such as* can be used to mean 'for example':
I enjoy films like/such as thrillers.
I dislike sports such as/like skiing.

As can be a conjunction and is followed by a subject and verb:
She cut up the vegetables as I had taught her. (in the way I had taught her)

In British English it is becoming more common to hear *like* followed by a subject and verb. *Like* followed by a subject and verb is acceptable in American English:
I don't speak like he does.

Unit 5
Table of common irregular verbs

INFINITIVE	PAST TENSE	PAST PARTICIPLE
become	became	(has/had) become
bet	bet	bet
burst	burst	burst
buy	bought	bought
cut	cut	cut
draw	drew	drawn
drive	drove	driven
eat	ate	eaten
feel	felt	felt
find	found	found
get	got	got
hear	heard	heard
hit	hit	hit
hold	held	held
keep	kept	kept
know	knew	known
leave	left	left
lose	lost	lost
put	put	put
run	ran	run
say	said	said
see	saw	seen
send	sent	sent
set	set	set
shake	shook	shaken
shut	shut	shut
sink	sank	sunk
speak	spoke	spoken
spend	spent	spent
swim	swam	swum
take	took	taken
tell	told	told
think	thought	thought

Review of past tenses

Past simple
This is used to talk about events in the past which:
- occurred at a particular time
  The Titanic sank in 1912.
  I drove back from London last night.
  This indicates a completed action in the past with a fixed time phrase.
- happened regularly
  Matthew spent most weekends at tennis tournaments.
  She burst into tears every time she heard his name.
  Note that *would* and *used to* are also used to talk about the past in this way – this is dealt with in Unit 8 (page 169).

Past continuous
This is used to talk about events in the past which:
- had a longer duration than another action
  I was cutting up vegetables in the kitchen when I heard it on the six o'clock news.
- were temporary
  Norwich were losing two-nil, with only five minutes to go.

  It is also used to set the scene in a story: *The sun was shining when the old man set off from the cottage.*

Present perfect
This is used to talk about events or a period of time which:
- started in the past but are still true or are still continuing
  We've lived here for eight years.
  Ellen has eaten no meat since she was six.
- happened in the past but have an effect in the present
  They've cancelled tonight's concert so we'll have to do something else.
  I've heard from Iain again.

Past perfect
This is used to talk about events which:
- happened earlier than something else
  Ken sat in the dark miserably and thought about what he had said to his girlfriend.
  Once I had finished my exams, I started clubbing again.

  Note that the past perfect needs to be used when it is important to show a time difference.

  Unit 14 deals with the perfect tenses in more detail (page 172).

Unit 6
Conditionals with *if* and *unless*
These are normally used to talk about possible events and the effects of them. There are four main types:
- Zero conditional
  Not a true conditional, as the events described both happen.
  If I stay up late, I feel awful the next day.
  When the moon passes between the earth and the sun, there is an eclipse.
  If/When + present tense | present tense
- First conditional
  Used to talk about likely events in the future if something happens.
  If I pass Cambridge First, I'll have a big party!
  If you don't stop talking, I'll send you to the head teacher.
  If + present tense | future tense *will*

- Second conditional
  Used to talk about unlikely or impossible situations.
  If I won the lottery, I'd give all the money to Oxfam.
  People might behave differently if they had the chance to repeat their lives.
  If + past tense | would, could, might
- Third conditional
  Used to speculate about the past.
  If we'd had more money, we'd have gone to the States last year.
  If you'd told me the truth in the first place, I wouldn't have asked the teacher.
  If Tom had taken his guitar, he could have played with the band that night.
  If + past perfect | would have, could have, might have + past participle
  (Unit 21 deals with mixed conditionals.)

Unless is a conjunction meaning 'if not', so the clause following *unless* never contains a negative verb form:
I'll see you at the station at 7.00 unless I hear from you.
Unless we book train tickets in advance, we won't get a discount.

Unit 7
Gerunds and infinitives 1

The gerund

The gerund is a verb which is used as a noun. It can be the subject of a clause or sentence: *Climbing the hill took them all day*, or the object: *I consider learning to save to be an essential part of growing up.*

You use the gerund:

- after certain verbs and expressions, especially those expressing liking/disliking:
  I don't mind getting up early in the morning.

  Common examples:
  like   love   enjoy   adore   fancy   feel   don't mind
  detest   hate   loathe   can't stand   dislike
  finish   avoid   give up   keep   miss
  suggest   consider   imagine
  it's not worth   it's/there's no use   there's no point (in)

- after all prepositions except *to*
  (Some exceptions to this rule are: *to look forward to doing, to object to doing, to get used to doing.*)
  On hearing the news, she burst into tears.

- after adjective and preposition combinations
  Steven is fantastic at cooking Thai food.

  Common examples:
  good/wonderful/fantastic/bad/awful/ terrible at
  happy/pleased/glad/anxious/sad/worried about
  afraid/frightened/scared/terrified of
  interested in
  keen on
  capable of
  proud of

  Another common use is with the noun *difficulty* (*to have difficulty in*).

- after verb and preposition combinations
  I don't approve of people drinking and driving.

  Common examples:
  insist on   approve of   apologise for
  consist of   believe in   succeed in
  accuse someone of   congratulate someone on

- after phrasal verbs
  I gave up playing tennis when I hurt my knee.

The infinitive

The infinitive is used:

- after certain verbs
  I learnt to speak Spanish in Valencia.

  Common examples:
  afford   agree   ask   choose   help   hope   want
  intend   pretend   promise   expect   prefer   used

- after certain adjectives
  I was surprised to see him at the party.

  Common examples:
  difficult   possible   happy   certain   simple

- after verbs which follow the pattern verb + someone + *to do* + something
  I asked her to open the window.

  Common examples:
  encourage   permit   allow   persuade   teach   force

- to express purpose
  I went to the shops to get some bread.

The infinitive without *to*
This is also used after modal auxiliaries (*can, must*), after *let, had better* and *would rather.*
Make has no *to* in the active, but adds *to* in the passive:
I made him go to school /He was made to go to school.

Unit 8
used to and *would*

Used to and *would* express habitual actions in the past.
- *Used to* is followed by the infinitive and is used for actions which no longer happen. It is used for permanent situations as well as habitual actions.
  I used to have a tricycle when I was five years old.
  John used to have long hair before he joined the army.

  The negative is *didn't used to*, though sometimes *didn't use to* is used.
  I didn't used to go abroad for my holidays before I won the lottery.

- *Would* is used for past habitual actions which were repeated. *Would* takes an infinitive without *to*.
  I would get up for work at seven, then get the bus at seven-thirty.

- *Get/Be used to doing* means to get or to be accustomed to. It can be used with all tenses and is always followed by a gerund (an *-ing* word).

Unit 9
Modals 2: Speculation and deduction

- *could, might, may* are used to speculate about something the speaker or writer is unsure about:
  It could be a sea eagle, though the feathers look too dark.
  That star you're looking at might in fact be Jupiter.
  The answer may be to readvertise the job.

- *must* is used to indicate certainty:
  That car must be doing over 50 mph at least!
  It must be possible to make a booking on the Internet.

- *can't/cannot* and *couldn't/could not* are also used to indicate certainty, in relation to impossible ideas and situations:
  It can't be her birthday – she had a party in August.
  You cannot be serious!
  They couldn't possibly be here before lunchtime.

- *couldn't/could not* can also be used in questions, sometimes with *possibly*, to speculate about something:
  It couldn't possibly be a case of mistaken identity, could it?
  Couldn't it be a computer error?

- *could have, might have, may have* are used to express uncertainty about something in the past:
  It could have been Greg you saw on the bus – he often catches the 206.
  The dinosaurs might have survived without the meteor impact.
  I think I may have met you before.

- *couldn't have / can't have* are used to express certainty that something in the past was impossible or didn't happen:
  He couldn't have damaged your bike – he was with me all evening.
  It can't have been raining, as the path is completely dry.

- *must have* is used to express near-certainty about something in the past:
  It must have been cold that winter.
  Jan must have arrived home by now.

Order of adjectives

Opinion adjectives always come before descriptive adjectives:
the brilliant French film 'Le Bossu'
an appalling old brown tracksuit
Descriptive adjectives generally follow this order:
size shape age colour nationality material
a small oval brooch
the young American film star
It is unusual to have four or more adjectives together –
a separate phrase is more commonly used:
a slim-cut black leather jacket with a classic Italian look

Unit 10
Review of future tenses

There are many ways of talking about the future in English. Sometimes, more than one tense is possible, with no change of meaning.

The future simple tense *shall/will* can be used for:

- future plans
  I'll give you a ring sometime.
- definite future events
  Our representative will meet you at the airport.
- predictions based on general beliefs
  Mass space travel will soon become possible.

- offers or promises relating to the future
  I'll prepare some salads for the party.
  I'll do my homework after this episode of 'The Simpsons'.

  Remember that the future simple is also used in the first conditional.

The 'going to' future can be used for:

- future plans, particularly if they are likely to happen soon
  I'm going to clear out the kitchen cupboards at the weekend.
- intentions
  James says he's going to work harder.
- predictions based on facts or events in the present
  It's going to snow tonight.

The present continuous tense can be used for:

- imminent future events
  I'm having a meeting with Charlotte at two o'clock.
- definite future arrangements
  Johnny's starting school next September.

The present simple can be used for:

- events based on a timetable or known date
  The plane leaves at 09.45.
  'Twelfth Night' opens on Saturday at the Arts Theatre.
- future intentions
  NASA plans to send further rockets to Mars.
- definite planned events
  The new pool is due to open in April.

The future continuous tense is used:

- to indicate certainty, when we are thinking ahead to a certain point in the future.
  Tom will be sharing an office with Fran.

The future perfect simple is used:

- to refer to events that have not yet happened but will definitely do so at a given time. This tense also conveys the idea of completion at some point in the future.
  This time next year I'll have finished my course.
  Space tourism will have become a reality by 2030.

The future perfect continuous tense is used:

- to indicate duration.
  At the end of June, Henry will have been working here for sixteen years.

Unit 11
Past and present participles

The past participles *bored, interested, thrilled*, etc. are used when we want to talk about how people feel:
I was thrilled when I received her birthday invitation.

The present participles *boring, interesting, thrilling*, etc. are used to describe what causes the feeling:
The film was so boring that I fell asleep.

Unit 12

The passive

The passive is used:

- when the action is more important than the person doing it:
  The film is loaded into the camera automatically.
- when we don't know who did something:
  The camera was put together in a factory.
- frequently, in news reporting, scientific writing and other kinds of writing where we are more interested in events and processes than in the person doing the action:
  A factory was set alight during the weekend and two million pounds' worth of damage was caused.

Formation of the passive

The passive is formed with the verb *to be* and the past participle of a transitive verb. For modals it is formed with the modal + *be* + past participle.
Get can sometimes be used informally instead of *be*.
It is used with all tenses except for the present perfect continuous and the future continuous.
Compare these sentences:
A *George Eastman invented the Kodak camera.*
B *The Kodak camera was invented by George Eastman.*

Sentence A is active and follows the pattern of Subject (George Eastman), Verb (invented) and Object (the Kodak camera). Sentence B is passive and the pattern is Subject (the Kodak Camera), Verb (was invented) and Agent (by George Eastman).
Sometimes there are two objects:
My uncle gave me some money for my birthday.
It is more common to say:
I was given some money by my uncle.
than:
Some money was given to me by my uncle.

The agent *by*

It is sometimes unnecessary to include the agent – if for example we don't know who did something or it is obvious from the context of the sentence who did it:
She was arrested for speeding. (It's obviously going to be by a policeman so it's not necessary to include it.)

The infinitive

When the situation is in the present and the sentence needs to be impersonal, you can use the passive form of the verb plus the infinitive:
The President is believed to be in contact with the astronauts.
In the past we use the passive plus the past infinitive:
He is said to have poisoned his opponents in order to gain power.

Unit 13

Reporting

When direct speech is reported, it becomes indirect speech. There is usually a change of tense in the indirect speech, which is called 'backshift':
'I want to go home straightaway,' said Jennifer.
Jennifer said that she wanted to go home straightaway.

'Can I show you my stamp collection?' asked Billy.
Billy asked if he could show me his stamp collection.

'After Robert left primary school, he grew up very quickly,' said his mother.

Robert's mother said that after he had left primary school, he had grown up very quickly.

When something is reported that is a general truth, there is often no tense change:
'Girls' exam results are generally better than boys',' the head teacher admitted.
The head teacher admitted that girls' exam results are generally better than boys'.

There are a number of different reporting verbs in English. Here is a list of common ones, showing the structures they can take:

accuse + of + -ing
Mary accused Nick of deliberately forgetting to tell her.

admit + to (optional) + -ing; admit + that (optional)
The company admitted to selling banned products.
I admit that I was to blame.

apologise + for + -ing
James apologised for being late.

argue + for + -ing; argue that (optional)
The department argued convincingly for having extra staff.
Sally argued that it was unnecessary to delay the expedition.

claim + that (optional)
Newspapers are claiming that Mr Blair was told in advance.

deny + that (optional); deny + -ing
He denied his part in the crime.
Kirsty denied hiding the files.

explain + that (optional)
Geoff explained that there was no more money available.

insist + on + -ing; insit + that (optional)
The children insisted on staying up late.
Keith insisted that the project was too difficult.

promise + that (optional); promise + to + infinitive
Mum promised she would pick me up at 4 pm.
Jackie has promised to look after the cats while we're away.

refuse + to + infinitive
The MP has refused to comment on these rumours.

say + that (optional); in passive, 'is said' + to + infinitive
People said that the flames were visible ten miles away.
The CD is said to include many new songs.

suggest + that (optional); suggest + -ing
Vera suggested that they should seek sponsorship for the exhibition.
Hugh suggested contacting everyone by phone.

urge + to + infinitive
Owen urged them to keep calm.

warn + that (optional); warn + to + infinitive
His sister warned us that he might not come.
The police warned people not to use that part of the motorway.

Unit 14

all and *the whole*

All is used with plural nouns and cannot be used on its own with a singular noun. You cannot say *All company is moving*. Instead you say *The whole company is moving*.

The whole is not used with plurals. You cannot say *The whole businesses are affected by computerisation*. Instead you say *All businesses are affected by computerisation*.

Note that it is possible to say *Whole businesses are affected …* without the definite article, but this gives a change of meaning: you are now referring to each individual business.

Possessive pronouns are also used with *whole*:
Your whole career has been ruined.

You can use *of the* with both *all* and *the whole*:
All of us were sad to leave.
The whole of the world is watching the event.

Perfect tenses

See other units for information about:
- the present perfect tense, the past perfect simple tense (Unit 5)
- the future perfect simple and continuous tenses (Unit 10)

Present perfect continuous tense

This is used to emphasise the duration of a recent or ongoing event:
Lars has been talking about his own experience – does anyone share his views?
I've been learning Italian for six years.

Past perfect continuous tense

This is used to emphasise the duration of a past event:
I'd been working for the same company for twelve years and it was time to move on.

Unit 15

Countable and uncountable nouns

1   A noun can be either countable or uncountable. Uncountable nouns cannot be made plural, and they only have one form. They take a singular verb. Uncountable nouns are often the names of things or substances or abstract ideas which cannot be counted.
    Examples of common uncountable nouns:
    accommodation, traffic, news, bread, milk, wine, information, advice, electricity

2   Some nouns can be countable and uncountable and have a difference in meaning:
    a *Her hair is very long.* Uncountable noun meaning the hair on her head.
    b *There's a hair in this sandwich!* Countable noun.
    a *Coffee grows in Brazil.* Uncountable noun for the product.
    b *Would you like to come round for a coffee?* Countable noun meaning 'a cup of coffee'.
    a *I haven't got enough paper left to finish this composition.* Uncountable noun.
    b *Run out and buy me a paper will you?* Countable noun meaning a newspaper.

3   Uncountable nouns can be limited by using a countable expression. *A bit* or *a piece* are often used with uncountable

nouns, although it is usually better to use a more specific expression.
a piece/slice of cake
a clap of thunder
an item of news
a loaf of bread

4   Determiners can be used with countable and uncountable nouns.
    Singular countable nouns can use *a/an* and *the*.
    A new table was delivered this morning.
    The man next door is a chef.

with uncountable nouns	with countable plurals
how much	how many
a lot of	a lot of
lots of	lots of
little	few
a little	a few
some/any/no	several
the	some/any/no
plenty of	the
a large amount of	plenty of
a great deal of	a large number of

5   There is an important difference in meaning between *a few/few* and *a little/little*:
    a *I've seen little improvement in your work recently.*
    b *I've seen a little improvement in your work recently.*
    Sentence **a** is considerably more negative than **b** in tone. Compare:
    a *There were few people at the meeting.* (It was disappointing because not many people were there.)
    b *There were a few people at the meeting.* (There weren't many people there, but there is no suggestion that more were expected.)

some, any and no

In general we use *some* in positive sentences and *any* in negative sentences and questions:
I bought some new CDs this morning.
Did you get any bread at the supermarket?
I haven't had any breakfast this morning.

However, *some* is also used in questions when we offer something to someone:
Would you like some cake?

We also use *some* when we expect the answer to be 'yes':
(In a tourist office) *Do you have some information about the museum?*

Any is often used to show we don't have a preference:
You can take me to see any film at the cinema – I don't mind which.

With *no, nothing* or *nobody/no one* we use a positive verb:
I saw nobody when I went swimming this morning.

Unit 16

The article

1   We use the indefinite article *a/an* before a singular, countable noun. It is used when we are talking about something in general or when it is mentioned for the first time:
    I saw a man outside the bank selling watches.
    A pet can be a good companion for the elderly.

    The indefinite article is also used for jobs:
    My aunt is a doctor.

2 The definite article *the* is used in the following ways:
- when something has been referred to before or is common knowledge:
  I wouldn't buy a watch from the man standing outside the bank.
- when there is only one of something:
  the Earth, the Sydney Opera House.
- with rivers, seas, oceans, mountains, regions, national groups and countries which are groups of states:
  the United States, the Netherlands, the Atlantic, the Himalayas, the Irish
- with buildings:
  I'm going to the prison to visit a prisoner.
  He's in the office at the moment.
- with species:
  the cat, the polar bear
- with superlatives:
  the biggest tower in the world, the greatest sportsperson, the most important question
- with musical instruments:
  I play the piano.
- when talking specifically about something:
  The life of an airline pilot is hard.

3 There is no article:
- With most streets (except for *the High Street*), countries, single mountains, towns, cities (except for *The Hague*), lakes:
  Austria, Mont Blanc, Tokyo
- When talking about sports:
  I play football well.
- When a noun is used generally:
  Life is hard.
- With illnesses:
  She's off school with chickenpox.

4 Expressions
You go *to prison* if you have been found guilty of a crime. You go *to hospital* if you are ill.
You go *to the prison* or *to the hospital* to visit someone there or to work.
Other expressions which don't take an article include:
to go to bed, to have lunch/dinner/breakfast, to go on holiday, to go to work, in October, to hold office, etc.

Unit 17
Relative clauses

There are two types of relative clause: **defining** and **non-defining**. A defining relative clause gives essential information about the subject of the sentence. A non-defining relative clause gives additional but non-essential information. In other words, this information could be omitted without affecting the sense of the sentence:
The girl who is studying to become a vet is called Sarah.
Sarah, who is 20, is studying to become a vet.
As these examples show, punctuation is used in non-defining clauses but is absent from defining clauses. It is very important to use commas accurately in relative clauses, as inaccurate use may change the meaning of the sentence:
The sports facilities which are not in regular use will be sold.
The sports facilities, which are not in regular use, will be sold.
In the first example, only the sports facilities which are not being used will be sold, whereas in the second example, all the facilities will be sold, as none are being used.

Relative pronouns

In defining relative clauses, you can use:
- *who* or *that* when talking about people
  The boy who is playing is county champion.
  The teacher that I met is Head of Maths.
- *which* or *that* when talking about things
  Colours which can be worn are black, navy and grey.
  The book that I recommend costs £8.50.

The relative pronoun can be left out when it is the object of the verb in the relative clause, as in the second example of each pair above. It must be included when it is the subject of the relative clause.

In non-defining clauses, you use:
- *who* when talking about people
  Ned, who plays the violin, is living above a music shop.
- *which* when talking about things
  The new brand of shampoo, which is selling well, contains only natural ingredients.

That cannot be used, because there is no linking of the clauses, unlike in sentences containing a defining relative clause.

Instead of using a relative pronoun, *where, when* or *why* can be used after a noun. It is possible to omit *when* and *why* in defining relative clauses:
The hotel where we stayed had a beautiful garden.
Christmas is the time (when) many people start thinking about their next holiday.
That's the reason (why) she's so upset.
In non-defining relative clauses, *when* and *why* cannot be omitted:
I moved to London in 1975, when I started teaching.

Relative pronouns

who or *whom*?

Both pronouns are used in relative clauses. *Whom* is a formal word, which can only be used as the object of a verb or with a preposition:
Ruth Gresham, who cannot sell her house as a result of this new rail route, says she will seek compensation.
The people for whom this new housing development is planned are unhappy about the lack of public transport.

whose

This pronoun is used to refer to both people and things:
Professor Newton, whose latest book on urban sprawl has had excellent reviews, will open the conference.
This revolutionary new car, whose energy comes from solar panels, is expected to go into production shortly.

Unit 18
enough, too, very, so, such

enough can be used:
- after an adjective or adverb
  The room wasn't large enough to hold everyone.
  You haven't worked hard enough this term.
- before an uncountable or plural countable noun
  The car has enough space for five people and their luggage.
  There are not enough girls doing science subjects.
- as a pronoun
  Enough has been made of this in all the papers.

- with a modifying adverb
  There is hardly enough memory in the computer.
- with certain adverbs for emphasis
  Funnily enough, we heard from him only last week.

too and *very*

These words are often confused. Here are the main uses.

- each can be used in front of an adjective or adverb, but *too* indicates an excessive amount of something, whereas *very* is just an intensifier:
  It is too cold in winter for many plants to survive.
  It is very cold in winter but a few plants do manage to survive.
- *too* can be used to show that two things or people have something in common:
  Dictionaries are useful at school and in the home too.
  You're Swedish too, aren't you?
  Note that here *too* always comes at the end of a clause.
- *too* can be used for emphasis:
  Computers are much more powerful than they were, and less expensive too.
- *too* can be used with a quantifier:
  There are too many loose ends to this story.
  A lot of people earn too little money to pay tax.

so and *such*

These words are also confused sometimes.

- Both can be used for emphasis and to express the same idea, but in different grammatical structures:
  It rained so much that most of the area was flooded.
  There was such a lot of rain that most of the area was flooded.
- *such* is used with *as* in giving an example of something:
  Dairy ingredients such as cheese and milk are best avoided.

Unit 19
Modals 3: Advice and suggestion

Giving advice

You should	try to watch what you eat.
You ought	to get some rest.
You'd better	book a place in the gym.
If I were you,	I'd try to do more exercise.
My advice to you is	to go to the doctor's.

Making a suggestion

I suggest	(that) you (should) cut down on coffee.
	cutting down on coffee.
I recommend	(that) you (should) relax a little more.
	relaxing.
What about / How about	doing some reading?
Why don't you try	doing some reading?
Have you thought of	playing a musical instrument?

It's time …, It's about time …, It's high time …

After these phrases we use the past simple tense, even when we are talking about the present or the future:
It's time you went to bed. – You need to go to bed now.

It is also possible to use an infinitive with *to* after *It's time* if we are speaking in general terms rather than to particular people:
It's time to go. – Everybody needs to go now.

to have/get something done

Compare: *I cut my hair. – I did it myself.*
     I had my hair cut. – Someone else did it for me.

A *have* + object + past participle
B *get* + object + past participle
Both of these forms are used, but B is more informal than A.

Unit 20
Gerunds and infinitives 2

Some verbs can be followed by both a gerund and an infinitive. Depending on the verb, this can result in a change in meaning.

No change in meaning

Verbs such as *start, begin, continue, attempt, intend, be accustomed to, be committed to, can't bear.*
These can be used with either a gerund or an infinitive with no real change in meaning:
The audience started to clap when the performance finished.
The audience started clapping when the performance finished.

Slight change in meaning

Verbs such as *like, prefer, hate, love*
Compare:
I like swimming. – In general.
I like to swim in the morning. – Talking about a habit.

Note that in American English, the infinitive is used more often than the gerund for both meanings.

After *would like, would prefer, would hate* and *would love*, an infinitive is used for a particular occasion or event:
Would you like to dance?

A change in meaning

Verbs such as *try, stop, regret, remember, forget, mean, go on.*

try
I tried to open the window, but it was stuck. I couldn't do it as it was too difficult.
It was hot, so I tried opening the window. I did it as an experiment to see if some fresh air would help.

stop
I stopped the car to get some petrol. Purpose.
I stopped going to that garage when they put their prices up.
I didn't go there any more.

regret
I regret to tell you that we have no more rooms available. Giving bad news.
I regret not making more friends when I was at school. For past events.

remember and **forget**
I remember/never forget going to New York on Concorde when I was quite small. This happened in the past.
I must remember / mustn't forget to buy a newspaper while I'm out shopping. This still hasn't happened.

mean

I mean to work hard at university. Intention.

It will mean going to the library more often. This is what it involves. This is the result.

go on

When I've finished shopping, I think I'll go on to see a film. A change of activity.

Please don't stop, go on showing us your photos. Continue.

Unit 21
Mixed conditionals

- *If* + past tense (second form) with *would(n't)/might(n't)/could(n't)/should(n't)* (third form):
  If I weren't so busy all the time, I could have come along.
  This is used when a change in a present situation would have affected a past situation.

- *If* + past perfect tense (third form) with *would(n't)/might(n't)/could(n't)/should(n't)* + infinitive (second form):
  If you had told me about the skiing trip, I would be there with you now!
  This is used when a change in a past situation would have caused a different present situation.

Unit 22
Concessive clauses

These are used in English to give contrasting information to the information in the main part of the sentence.

James insisted on playing in the match, despite feeling ill.

A number of different conjunctions can be used in front of the concessive clause:

although	even if	even though
much as	though	whereas	while

Much as and *whereas* are less commonly used and occur mainly in formal written English.

I prefer to buy free-range eggs, even though they are more expensive.

Although we were very tired, we watched the whole of the play.

The prepositions *despite* and *in spite of* are also used to introduce contrasting information:

Robyn went ahead with the concert despite having a sore throat.

In spite of arriving at the festival early, we couldn't get near the stage.

Sometimes it is possible to reduce the concessive clause by leaving out the main verb.

Although very tired, we watched the whole of the play.

You should only do this when the concessive clause refers to the subject of the main clause. So, for example, you would not say:

Although very boring, we watched the whole of the play.

Remember that *despite* and *in spite of* cannot be followed by a main verb. You cannot say:

Despite he was late, John had another cup of coffee.

Both can be followed by a gerund or a noun:

In spite of being late, John had another cup of coffee.

Despite the time, John had another cup of coffee.

You can add *the fact that* and follow this by a verb clause:

Despite the fact that he was late, John had another cup of coffee.

Complex sentences

It is possible to draw attention to information by 'fronting' it in a sentence. Fronting often improves the cohesion and naturalness of a piece of writing. So, for example, a reason clause, which explains information in the main clause, can present information in a logical way by coming first:

As the organisers had paid attention to detail, the festival was a great success.

Since I had bought an extra ticket for the concert, I invited Mike to go with me.

Conjunctions commonly used in reason clauses are:
as, because, since

Unit 23
I wish / If only

Talking about the past – things you regret doing/not doing:
wish / if only + past perfect
I wish I hadn't been so rude to my mother last night.

Talking about the present – things that haven't come true now and things that might come true in the future:
wish / if only + past simple
I wish I were/was lying on a beach somewhere instead of being here.
I wish I could speak Japanese.
Both *were* and *was* are acceptable but *were* is more formal.

Talking about irritating habits – things which are annoying you:
wish / if only + would
He wishes his daughter would wear smarter clothes.

as if / as though

Both *as if* and *as though* mean the same.
To talk about 'unreal' situations you use the past tense after both *as if* and *as though*:
He looks as if he's tired. He is tired.
He looks as if he was/were exhausted. He isn't tired.

would rather

Would rather + past simple is used to talk about the present or future:
I'd rather you didn't go to the disco tonight.

Would rather + past perfect is used to talk about the past:
She'd rather they had gone to an Italian restaurant.

Would rather + infinitive without *to* is used to talk generally about the present and future:
The government would rather not give out too many benefits to young people.
Do not confuse this phrase with *had better*, which means 'should'.

Unit 24

Uses of *rather*

- Used as an adverb, in the same way as *quite*:
  Eddie Izzard's humour is rather surreal at times – elephants on skis, that sort of thing.
  Some comedians are quite direct and indeed rather rude to their audiences.

- Used with *would* to mean 'prefer':
  I'd rather go to a live show than watch a video.
  John says he'd rather not come with us, as he's very tired.

- Used as a prepositional phrase to contrast two things or situations:
  The jokes were about society in general rather than being purely political.
  Rather than stay at home watching TV, he got changed and went off to the party.

- *Rather* can also be used as an adverb immediately before a verb of thought or feeling, to express an opinion politely:
  I rather think his recent success has gone to his head.
  I rather like your hair cut short.

The grammar of phrasal verbs

Phrasal verbs consist of a main verb and a particle (which is an adverb or a preposition).

- When used intransitively (that is, without an object), the verb and particle of a phrasal verb cannot be separated:
  The engine cut out and they drifted on the waves.

- When the particle is an adverb, transitive phrasal verbs can usually either be separated or followed by a noun as object; they are always separated by a pronoun as object.
  He keyed the number in carefully.
  He keyed in the number carefully.
  He keyed it in carefully.

  Could you put the drinks down on that table?
  Could you put down the drinks on that table?
  Could you put them down on that table?

- When the particle is a preposition, no separation is possible:
  The lorry ploughed into a barrier.
  My older sister keeps getting at me!

- For three-part phrasal verbs, no separation is possible:
  The sparkling blue sea more than made up for their difficult journey.
  I was really looking forward to that concert – what a shame it's been cancelled.

Answers and recording scripts

The following pages contain the answers to the exercises, sample answers for the writing tasks, the recording scripts, and background information on some of the texts and topics. The *Map of Objective First Student's Book* on pages 4–6 gives full details of the language and exam skills covered in each unit. The *Content of the Cambridge English: First* on pages 7–8 provides information about the exam, with links to the relevant Exam folder or Writing folder.

Unit 1

1.1 pages 10–11

Speaking

1   Some useful sentence starters are:

Likes
I really like …
I prefer to wear …
What I absolutely love is …

Dislikes
I hate …
I wouldn't be seen dead in …

> **Possible answer**
> Generally, I prefer to wear casual clothes like jeans and T-shirts. If I have to attend a meeting, I'll put on a smart suit, but I don't feel very comfortable in it. I wouldn't be seen dead in a tie!

2

> **Further topic vocabulary**
> *Clothes:* jeans, jacket, T-shirt, polo shirt
> *Footwear:* trainers
> *Jewellery:* necklace, ring
> *Headgear:* hat, baseball cap
> *Materials:* cotton, silk, polyester, suede, fur
> *Appearance:* untidy, scruffy, fashionable

3

> **Possible answers**
> **1a** This guy is dressed in a striped jumper, a pair of faded jeans and casual shoes. He's wearing a baseball cap back to front.
> **1b** The man must be a biker, because he's wearing all the gear and he's carrying a bike helmet. Those clothes would protect him if he fell off his bike.
> **2a** This girl looks really cool! She's got outrageous hair and her eye make-up matches her bright blue and green outfit. I think she likes to stand out in a crowd.
> **2b** This girl is wearing jeans and sandals, and a T-shirt with an interesting design on it. She's got long, dark hair.

> **3a** The man is probably in his work clothes or maybe he has dressed up for a special event. He's wearing a dark suit and a white shirt with a striped tie. He's got a moustache and a bit of a beard – perhaps he's growing it?
> **3b** This guy is casually dressed in jeans, an open-necked shirt and a V-neck red jumper. He looks very friendly and laid-back.
> **4a** This woman has just been shopping for clothes, I think! She's wearing a short-sleeved black dress with a stylish silver necklace. She's got a big hat, perhaps to keep the hot sun off her head and shoulders? She's got high-heeled shoes.
> **4b** For me, this girl likes to experiment with her outfits. She's wearing an unusual combination of clothes, some of which might be second-hand, including what looks like a heavy red woollen shawl under her jacket. She's also wearing a knitted hat. Perhaps it's cold in the woods where she is standing.

Listening

6

> Speaker 2 – 2a   Speaker 3 – 1a   Speaker 4 – 4b
> Speaker 5 – 3a

Recording script 1 03

Speaker 2: I started working this year, so I'm able to get new clothes more regularly than before, when I had to save up for months. I buy a lot online. My mum thinks I should cut down the amount I spend on clothes, but my image is really important to me: if someone sees me in something once, I don't like to go out in it again – well, not for a while, in any case. I like to wear bright colours and my make-up's a bit outrageous. I always dress up when I go clubbing. I buy a big range of styles and I try to keep up with the latest fashions.

Speaker 3: Shopping for clothes isn't really my scene, if you know what I mean. I don't really mind what I wear, to tell you the truth. I'm the least fashion-conscious person I know! I suppose if anything I favour the casual look. I've got two pairs of jeans and I wear them mostly with a sweatshirt or something. I have got one favourite T-shirt, which a girlfriend gave me. It's red and it's got a sort of abstract design printed in navy blue on the back. She said she gave it to me so I would always stand out in a crowd!

Speaker 4: My clothes have to be comfortable, make me feel relaxed as soon as I slip them on. I often put together outfits from stuff I find in street markets – they're less expensive that way. Second-hand clothes can be real bargains, and usually they've hardly been worn! I'll change the look of my clothes quite frequently, you know, sew in a new piece of material, swap buttons, dye something a different colour, just for a change. I make a lot of my own jewellery, though having long hair, I don't wear earrings very often.

Speaker 5: My friends take far less trouble with clothes than I do – sometimes they wear the tattiest things ever! As my job involves dealing with people, I have to make an effort to look good all the time. I like to present a classy, sophisticated image. I go shopping for clothes about once a month, though if I see something by chance, I'm quite likely to go for it there and then. I think I've got good taste and I very rarely make a mistake when I buy clothes. I did take a jacket back last week, but that was because it was badly made.

Vocabulary

7

The phrasal verbs heard are: cut down   dress up   go out   keep up with   put together   save up   slip on   stand out   take back

The speaker is given in brackets in the answers.

a stand out (3)
b put together (4)
c take back (5)
d dress up (2)
e save up (2)
f cut down (2)
g slip on (4)
h go out (2)
i keep up with (2)

Corpus spot

The authors have referred extensively to the *Cambridge Learner Corpus*, an electronic collection of Cambridge ESOL candidates' scripts from all over the world. Currently containing more than 47 million words of data, around 3 million words of recent candidate writing are added to the *Cambridge Learner Corpus* each year. This unique resource has given the authors a more accurate and up-to-date picture of what B2 learners around the world can and can't do.

8

a gone up   **b** going on   **c** went for   **d** went back
e go over   **f** go ahead

9

1 went out   **2** slipped on   **3** dressed up
4 put together   **5** stood out   **6** keep up with

1.2 pages 12–13

Comparison

1 The text contains a number of superlative adjectives: *the youngest and skinniest, the most underweight, the least achievable.*

2 You have probably been taught all the basic structures by now. *Objective First* will review these structures using an 'inductive' approach, which means that you will be asked to work out grammar rules for yourself, by looking at examples. The Grammar folder on pages 166–176 gives important information about the grammar covered in each unit, with more examples.

a Single-syllable adjectives add *-er/-est*; longer adjectives use *more / the most*.
b With some two-syllable adjectives, e.g. *common, likely, narrow, pleasant, simple, stupid*, we can either add *-er/-est* or use *more / most*.
c Adjectives ending in a single vowel and consonant double the consonant (*slim → slimmer*); adjectives ending in *-y* change to *-ier/-iest*.

Corpus spot

a What are **the best** clothes to wear at the camp?
b He is **more famous** than all the others in the film.
c You look more tired and **thinner**.
d I would like to buy a **much better** one.
e It's now **easier** to get there.
f This is even **worse** than before.

3 You need to be careful with spelling when making some comparative and superlative forms: for example adjectives ending in *-y* become *-ier/-iest*; some adjectives double their final consonant.

bigger	the biggest
thinner	the thinnest
dirtier	the dirtiest
more/less casual	the most/least casual
more/less outrageous	the most/least outrageous
better	the best
worse	the worst

4

a brighter
b the most outrageous / the brightest
c more casual
d the dirtiest
e thinner
f the worst
g bigger
h better

Grammar extra

> **a** a bit; much
> **b** a bit / a great deal / much; much (*much* can be used with both comparative and superlative adjectives)

5 The structure *not so ... as* is less common in everyday English.

6

> more commonly   more readily   less exclusively
> less seriously

7

> **Possible answer**
> Often, knock-offs look as good as the real thing. If I saw a fake designer bag in a market and I liked it, I'd buy it. It isn't my place to judge the goods on display – that's for governments or lawyers to act on.

8 This exercise is an exam task (Paper 1 Part 4, key word transformations). The task is introduced in Exam folder 1, which follows Unit 1. Note that these transformations are below the level of the exam, as a first introduction to the task format.

> **1** were a bit cheaper / were a bit less expensive
> **2** the most talented designers
> **3** as straight as it
> **4** the least expensive of / less expensive than
> **5** more elegantly dressed than
> **6** is a lot quicker/faster than
> **7** less smartly when
> **8** as old as

Exam folder 1 pages 14–15

Paper 1 Part 4

Key word transformations

1 There are two marks available for each question, so even if you cannot produce the whole answer, you can still get a mark if one element is accurate.

3 Use the Exam advice when you do the transformations in the next exercise. Remember that you cannot change the key word.

4

> **1** told Sally about a new
> **2** took it back
> **3** make an effort
> **4** were not / weren't as fast as
> **5** much more easily if/when
> **6** far the most interesting

Unit 2

2.1 pages 16–17

Speaking

1

> **Possible answer**
> I disagree with this statement. I enjoy playing computer games with my friends, so it isn't anti-social, and we're quite normal people, not nerds!

2

> You can play your favourite games with friends in other places.
> On the other hand, you waste a lot of time playing when you could be studying!

3 The phrases appear in the games reviews in 4.

Reading

4

> **a** 4 Prices come at the end of 'The Verdict', at the foot of each review.
> **b** 3 Five stars in The Verdict indicates this is the best review.
> **c** 4 The Verdict says 'suitable for a very young audience'.
> **d** 1 At the end of the review, it says the background music is 'truly original and builds well in scary moments'.

5 The purpose of this exercise is firstly to get you to skim quickly for general meaning. The second aim of the exercise is to show you how opinions are signposted in reviews. If you scan for key words and phrases, such as *the great thing about* and *it's a shame that*, you will find answers in texts more efficiently.

	Good points	Bad points
1	*you need to adopt its unique way of thinking* *the absence of instructions (part of the game's charm)* *original background music*	*the absence of instructions (can also be a drawback)*
2	*impressive gameplay touches*	*It's a shame that the gun resets to weak*
3	*guarantees a game demanding enough* *super-slick bike racer*	*motorbike games never provide the same thrill*
4	*nice double- jump facility* *really nice background animation* *Graphically, the game looks good*	*only six levels* *a bit disappointing* *a slow rate* *extremely boring* *It's just too bad there isn't more content* *puzzles ... far too simple*

Vocabulary

6

a solve puzzles   *also* solve a crime, a problem
b spend time   *also* spend a fortune, money
c reach the point (of)   *also* reach a conclusion, a goal
d take control   *also* take advantage (of), an interest (in)

Grammar extra

easy: remove -*y*; add -*ily*
endless: (regular) add -*ly*
graphic: add -*ally* **NB** This applies to all adjectives ending in -*ic* apart from *public*, which becomes *publicly*.
remarkable: remove *e*; add -*y*
true: remove *e*; add -*ly*

a She didn't think much about work.
b He thought deeply/carefully.
c There have been a lot of good films recently.
d We arrived after the film had started.

Corpus spot

a **Unfortunately**, I'm quite busy at the moment.
b If I were you, I would **definitely** spend my evenings reading by the fireside.
c You just have to say your name and the computer opens the door **automatically**.
d Entering the restaurant, you **immediately** feel comfortable.
e We **really** started to work hard the morning before the show.
f You must adjust the laser **extremely** carefully to get it in the correct position.
g I would like more information, **especially** about accommodation.
h The computer **completely** takes hold of our lives.

2.2 pages 18–19
Review of present tenses

1

a present simple
b present continuous
c present simple
d present continuous

The present **simple** tense is used for permanent situations (example **a**) or to talk about actions which are habitual or repeated (example **c**). On the other hand, the present **continuous** tense is used for temporary situations (example **b**), or for situations that are changing or developing (example **d**).

2

a used for talking about an event in the near future (present continuous)
b used in the zero conditional (present simple)
c used for talking about something that is happening now (present continuous)
d used in a time clause (present simple)
e used for talking about something that is true (present simple)

3

a ✓
b is selling (present continuous for a temporary situation)
c ✓
d play (present simple in a time clause)
e is giving (present continuous for a temporary situation)
f get (zero conditional)
g bookmark (present simple for a habitual or repeated action)

4

a finish; get   **b** is improving   **c** are dealing with
d flies; explodes; hit   **e** is developing   **f** take
g log on; requires; generates
h crashes; lose; are working; save

5

1 is becoming   **2** are creating / create   **3** (are) updating / update   **4** means   **5** submits   **6** is adding / adds   **7** sounds   **8** believes   **9** is encouraging   **10** is changing   **11** find out   **12** google

The extra verb is *spend*. See the Grammar folder on page 167 for information about stative verbs.

Vocabulary

6

a tricky
b messy
c muddy (Rule: consonants *d, g, m, n, p, r, s, t* are doubled before adding -*y*)
d icy (Rule: *e* is removed before adding -*y*)

Additional nouns and adjectives:

blood – bloody
curl – curly
dust – dusty
fog – foggy
fun – funny

juice – juicy
noise – noisy
risk – risky
sun – sunny
wind – windy

7

Positive: accessible, colourful, excellent, favourable, impressive, sophisticated
Negative: dull, hopeless, mindless, tricky, unhelpful
Unhelpful has both a prefix and a suffix.

8

1 accessible (adjective)
2 applications (noun)
3 ability (noun)
4 impressive (adjective)
5 electronically (adverb)
6 tricky (adjective)

Writing folder 1 pages 20–21

Paper 2 Part 2 Informal letters

In Paper 2 Writing, it is important to write in a register that is suitable for the task set. Part 1 is a compulsory essay task requiring an unmarked or semi-formal register. In Part 2, where there is a choice of questions, there may be a letter or email task. If this is a letter of application, the register should be formal. If the task is a letter or email to a friend, it should be informal.

1 The informal words and phrases are given below.

> **B** – get-together, It's a pity …, terrific, Why not …?
> **C** – Anyway …, Well …, weird guy, you'd better not, why not …?, at my place

In the exam, it is important to understand who you are writing to and why.

> **A** – written by a department head to staff; a report on the last meeting and a reminder about the next one
> **B** – written by a departmental secretary to staff in the department; an invitation to the next get-together
> **C** – written by a friend to a friend; an invitation to stay for a party

2

> Hi!, Guess what?, splash out, cool, I can't (contraction), a bit more

3 In the exam you are assessed on *content* (how fully you cover the points given in the question), *communicative achievement* (appropriate use of register and format), *organisation* (including use of linking words) and *language* (range and accuracy of the vocabulary and structures you have used). The sample answer would score low marks for the reasons explained below.

> failure to answer the question set (the answer ends up talking about something different)
>
> inconsistent register (paragraphs 1 and 3)
>
> poor organisation: long middle paragraph with an absence of linkers
>
> language errors in middle paragraph

> **Corrected and improved answer**
>
> Dear Alex
>
> What brilliant news in your letter! Congratulations on passing the exam – and how nice to get some extra cash as a result.

You say you can't decide whether to buy a computer game or some clothes. As you say, if you choose clothes, you'll need to save up more first. Clothes are not as cheap as computer games and I know you like really expensive designer outfits.

The next question is, if you choose a computer game, which one? There are so many available – although, to my mind, they're all the same! Personally, I would spend the money on something else, but you've asked me for advice, so I'll try to help you. My brother says the new version of Sim City is very good, or you could get a sports game, perhaps one of the Madden ones? They've all got excellent graphics and they're not too expensive.

Well, I hope you find these suggestions useful. Let me know what you end up buying.

Love

4 Plan your letter, working through the ideas given under the C-L-O-S-E headings. This does not mean writing the whole piece in rough first. You don't have time to do this in the examination and it is not advisable – hurrying to copy out the final version leads to words and even sentences being missed out, and leaves no time to check for errors.

5

> *Informal expressions*:
> Initial greetings: 1, 3
> Congratulations: 1
> Opinion: 2, 5
> Advice/Suggestion: 1, 2, 4, 7
> Linkers: 2, 3, 5, 6, 7
> Endings: 1, 3, 4
>
> Opening and closing an email or a letter:
>
> *Hi Brad … Cheers* (informal)
> *Dear Jayne … Love* (informal)
> *Dear Sir … Yours faithfully* (formal; use when the reader's name is not known)
> *Dear Ms Jones … Yours sincerely* (formal)

> **Sample answer**
>
> Dear Jan
>
> Thanks for your letter and well done for passing that exam. Your parents sound much more generous than mine!
>
> I'm not sure that you need any more computer games, do you? If I were you, I'd save up for a bit longer and then buy some clothes. In fact, why not get something special, like a new pair of boots or a coat? There are some lovely winter coats in the shops, and many of them are quite a bargain. Also, you said you needed a new coat last year – well, now's your chance.
>
> I think a charcoal grey one would suit you really well, especially something stylish and well-cut. Make sure you choose wool, and find one with nice deep pockets, to stuff all your bits and pieces in. I'd go for a longish one, below the knee or even full-length. Then you'll be nice and warm when the snow comes!
>
> Let me know what you decide and have fun shopping.
>
> Lots of love

Unit 3

3.1 pages 22–23

Speaking

1

> *Photos 1 and 2*
> Younger people who like adventure would probably enjoy an activity holiday such as white-water rafting. It's fun to do a sport with other people, because you can make new friends. This type of holiday is never boring. Older people, who want to rest and relax on holiday, might prefer sunbathing on the beach. Some teenagers enjoy a beach holiday because they want to get a good sun tan.
>
> *Photos 3 and 4*
> A backpacking holiday can be fairly cheap and it's a good way of meeting people. Youth hostels are usually in interesting places, often in a central location, and you can move around an area or country as you please. On the other hand, carrying your rucksack is quite hard work, and youth hostels aren't as comfortable as luxury hotels. In a luxury hotel, everything is done for you, the food is delicious and the hotel has lots of facilities such as a beautiful pool, and this hotel is in a very exotic location. But perhaps it might become boring after a few days? And it will certainly cost a fortune!

Listening

2 **The answers are in the order in which they are heard.**

The underlined parts of the recording script confirm the answers.

> **1** plus seven/7 **2** sunglasses **3** cupboard **4** Australian
> **5** calm **6** birds **7** research station **8** buildings
> **9** rubbish **10** wildlife

Recording script 1 04

Good morning, everyone. My name is Steve Jackson, and I'm here today to tell you about my recent trip to the Antarctic. Now, the first question people generally ask me, is did I freeze? And my answer is that, amazingly, no, I didn't. The temperature can go as low as minus ten degrees even during the summer months, but while I was there it was about <u>plus seven</u> and I found it quite comfortable. However, you should take warm clothes with you and you really need a windproof coat. But what I found most useful were some <u>sunglasses</u>. The sun can get really strong with the reflection off the snow and ice.

On the ship, I had my own cabin and pretty small it was too. At first I wondered where I was going to put my things, as there was no wardrobe. However, whoever designed the ship thought of just about everything a passenger would need and under the bed there was a <u>cupboard</u>.

The atmosphere on board the ship was great. The crew were mainly American and they really did their best to get everyone to mix. But, of course, you don't have to socialise if you don't want to. The expedition leader was <u>Australian</u>, and he sat at a different table for dinner every night so he'd get to meet us all. He was really friendly and informative.

As to the weather, well, it can get stormy in the Antarctic but the ocean was <u>calm</u> while I was there. That was good, because I was worried about getting sea-sick before I went. Luckily, I was OK, and few of the other passengers had problems.

Do I have any special memories? Well, it's hard to say, really – there are so many. We saw a few whales, especially near a place called Cuverville Island, but I guess what I most treasure is the large variety of <u>birds</u> we saw. They were terrific.

Of course, the Antarctic doesn't have many people living there and the only people we saw, apart from tourists, were a few of the scientists at a <u>research station</u>. They gave us coffee and biscuits one morning! There's a landing strip there, but no harbour or anything like that. You have to get onto shore in a small rubber motorboat.

In the past there used to be a thriving fishing industry in the area, but all that's left are some deserted <u>buildings</u> now. No old boats or machinery or anything like that though.

I'm often asked if I felt guilty about disturbing such an untouched region as Antarctica. I guess, yes, and no. Cruise ships are not allowed to dump <u>rubbish</u> or to go where they like, and they have to take scientists to lead the excursions.

There are rules of course. Only small parties are permitted to land in one area at a time and you've got to keep quiet and not bother the <u>wildlife</u>. So, all in all, I felt that well-run trips, like this one, would do more good than harm. I also felt completely changed by the experience – it was like going to another world.

Now, if any of you have any questions ...

3

> **Possible answer**
> Yes, I would go to Antarctica if I had the chance. I think it's acceptable to visit unspoilt parts of the world as long as this is done responsibly – the number of tourists needs to be limited and people need to behave properly, not leaving any rubbish around or digging up rare plants.

Vocabulary

4

> *Transport*: yacht, coach, ferry, airline
> *Movement*: journey, landing, flight, voyage
> *Seaside*: shore, cliff, coast, harbour
> *People*: backpacker, holiday-makers, crew, travel agent
> *Accommodation*: caravan, campsite, hostel, bed and breakfast

5

a 7	**b** 6	**c** 1	**d** 8	**e** 4	**f** 5	**g** 3	**h** 2

6

take	a trip, a ship, a plane, a flight
book	a trip, a hotel, a flight
catch	a plane, a flight
board	a ship, a plane, a flight
get	a plane, a tan, a hotel, a flight
go	skiing, sightseeing

7

1 A	**2** B	**3** B	**4** B	**5** A	**6** B	**7** B	**8** A

3.2 pages 24–25

Modals 1

1

a 6	**b** 2	**c** 5	**d** 3 and 1	**e** 1	**f** 4	**g** 1

2

a The speaker is telling him/herself to do something. (The obligation comes from the speaker.)

b Someone else is telling the speaker what to do. (The obligation doesn't come from the speaker.)

c *Must* is used in laws, notices and rules, where there is no choice of action.

Must is often used in a friendly way in conversation, e.g. *You must come to dinner sometime.*

Corpus spot

a You **don't need** much space to park your car.

b Another thing, **should I take** my camera with me?

c You **mustn't** smoke in this part of the restaurant; it's a no smoking area.

d It is better when you go by car because you **don't have to** get up early.

e We have **to** get to the exhibition early or we won't get a ticket.

f You **mustn't** swim off the rocks because it's dangerous.

g My doctor says I need **to** give up smoking.

h Lisa **has to** buy a ticket before getting on the bus.

i I **mustn't** be late or I'll miss my plane.

4

Possible answers

a I must tidy up the flat and I should do some washing, but I don't really want to. I have to meet my uncle at the airport on Saturday afternoon.

b I must buy him a birthday present. I should organise a party for him.

c I must buy a new outfit and I should try to find out what she would like as a wedding present.

d I have to get an identity card from Security. I must introduce myself to some of the people in the other departments.

e I need some paracetamol, and I must make an appointment at the dentist's.

f I have to buy food and drinks, and I must organise some music. I should warn the neighbours and invite them.

5

a allowed/permitted	**b** can	**c** let	**d** permitted/allowed

Grammar extra

For this exercise it helps to visualise where exactly things are.

The following prepositions are used in these cases:

1 a line (e.g. a road): on, off, across, along, over

2 a point (e.g. a bus stop): to, from, at

3 an area (e.g. a neighbourhood or park): in, into, out of, across, within, around

4 a volume (e.g. a building): in, into, out of, around

5 a surface (e.g. a table): on, onto, off, over, under, across

a on	**b** at	**c** into	**d** in	**e** across	**f** in	**g** on	**h** on
i into	**j** off						

6 This is examination practice for Paper 1 Part 4.

1 had to change

2 is forbidden to smoke

3 did not / didn't let me go

4 are not / aren't permitted to swim

5 should get health insurance

6 do not / don't have to wear / do not / don't need to have

7 do not / don't need to put

8 have got to ring/phone

Exam folder 2 pages 26–27

Paper 1 Part 3 Word formation

The word formation task is the third part of the Reading and Use of English paper. The whole paper takes 1 hour and 15 minutes to do and you should aim to spend about 10 minutes on this part. This may seem too short a time at first, but you will become faster with practice. There are eight questions in this part of the paper. You should read through the whole passage before you start trying to do the answers.

1

a	dis-	dissatisfied
b	im-	impatient
c	in-	inexpensive
d	il-	illegal
e	im-	impossible
f	un-	uncomfortable
g	dis-	dishonest
h	un-	unhappy
i	ir-	irresponsible
j	mis-	misunderstand
k	dis-	disappear
l	ir-	irregular
m	im-	immoral

2 Remember that not all prefixes are negative.

a	without stopping:	*non-* = not, e.g. *non-smoker, non-stick*
b	to train again:	*re-* = again, e.g. *re-grow, replace, redo*
c	a path/passage under the road:	*sub-* = under, e.g. *submarine, subtotal, substandard*
d	undo an action:	*un-* = reverse an action, e.g. *unlock, unfasten*
e	put a line underneath / emphasise something:	*under-* = below e.g. *underwater, undervalue*

You can enlarge your vocabulary by learning how a word can be changed into a noun, adjective, verb or adverb. There are no easy rules to help you (the suffix often depends on the origin of the word – Latin, Anglo-Saxon, Greek, etc.) and therefore you just need to learn them.

3–7 These exercises summarise the different kinds of suffix.

3

a happiness b intelligence c approval
d recommendation e action f popularity g friendship
h payment i tourist/tourism

4

a truth b success c death d height

5

a windy b attractive c hopeful/hopeless d dangerous
e endless f accidental g valuable h accessible

6 Normally we change an adjective into an adverb by adding -*ly*.
Words ending in -*y* – the *y* usually changes to *i* + -*ly*.
Words ending in -*le* – change *le* to *ly* after a consonant.
Adjectives ending in -*ic* – add -*ally*.

a steadily b actively c necessarily d annually
e extraordinarily f automatically

7

a renew b discourage c undo, redo d rebuild
e repay f disapprove g unlock, relock
h communication i measurement
j satisfaction, dissatisfaction k maintenance
l identification m introduction n criticism

8 Always look carefully for prefixes, especially negative ones, and plurals.

1 verb – PRODUCED
2 noun – YOUTH
3 adverb – EXTREMELY
4 adjective – SCIENTIFIC
5 noun – SAFETY
6 noun – REPRESENTATIVE
7 noun – APPEARANCE
8 adjective – IMPOSSIBLE

Unit 4

4.1 pages 28–29

Reading

1

1 polar bear 2 thick-billed parrot 3 tiger shark
4 snow leopard 5 koala 6 orang-utan

All the animals are endangered except for the tiger shark. The snow leopard is endangered because of hunting; the polar bear from global warming; the orang-utan, thick-billed parrot and koala because of habitat destruction.

Possible answer
This is an impossible choice but I suppose I'd choose to save the polar bear because it is such a magnificent animal.

2

a 3 b 1 c 4 d 2 e 5

3

a an article

4 Questions **a** and **b** give practice in the type of scanning you need to do and raise your awareness of distractors in the texts (words that might at first seem to give the answers, but in fact do not).

b D
1 C   **2** A   **3** B   **4** A   **5** D   **6** E   **7** E   **8** B   **9** E   **10** C

5

Possible answer
I think zoos have a role to play in conservation but we should do more to protect species in the wild too. It is not enough to breed endangered animals in captivity.

It seems that they are doing good work and I'd be interested in visiting some of them – Toronto Zoo, for example.

I've been to London Zoo, which still has some areas in need of improvement! Some of the birds in cages look really sad there. There are some good modern buildings though, and a great café. You can see a lot of different animals there.

Vocabulary

6

a traditional   **b** endangered   **c** decision   **d** visitors
e conservation   **f** entrance   **g** zoology   **h** sights
i unhappy   **j** rainfall

4.2 pages 30–31

as and *like*

1 *As* and *like* are often confused. Read the examples and the Corpus spot carefully.

2

a like   **b** –   **c** –   **d** like   **e** like   **f** as   **g** as

3

1 described in the brochure as
2 use the garage as/for storage
3 was working as a teacher
4 is usually known as
5 what sounded like
6 refer to my dog as

Compound adjectives

4 Use compound adjectives in your writing to describe people and things, as this will show the examiner your range of language. It is also important that you learn to recognise them when you come across them in your reading.

a **1** animals in general
   2 a tiger which eats people (not just men!)
   3 a blue-eyed, long-haired, bad-tempered cat
c **1** You would sit in a car.
   2 If you are hard-up, you don't have much money, so you may not be very happy.
   3 You need to have a lot of money.
   More examples of this type are: *a phone-in programme, a pick-up truck, a standby flight, a takeaway meal*
d **1** a fifty-kilometre road
   2 a twelve-year-old girl
   3 a seventy-five-minute film
   4 a thirty-five-thousand-pound car
   5 a ten-second pause

Vocabulary

5 Look up any words you don't know in an English–English dictionary. By doing this, you will also learn about related forms and other meanings.

parrot – beak, feathers, wing, tail
bear – fur, paw, tail
tiger – fur, paw, tail
rhino – horn, tail

6

a one at a time   **b** time for breakfast   **c** times as much
d In time   **e** have a good time   **f** kill time / pass the time
g tell the time   **h** wasting time / spending time

7

Possible answers
a That's easy! Number one, playing computer games. Number two, watching television. Number three, chatting to friends online.
b For me, the best thing to do is to hang out with friends, whether that's at a great party or just being together somewhere, like in a café.
c If I have to kill time, I get out my mobile and send messages to my friends.

Writing folder 2 pages 32–33

Paper 2 Part 1 Essays

1 Although mentioned in the introduction, point 2 – wildlife under threat – is missing.

2 Phrases inserted are in **bold**:

> THE TREATMENT OF ANIMALS IN OUR WORLD TODAY
>
> This is a complex question. Many people depend on animals to live, whether they eat meat or just keep an animal for its milk. This essay will consider farming, a**s well as discussing** the role of zoos, and endangered wildlife.
>
> When zoos first opened, they had a real purpose – to educate people. There was no television and in **this way**, people got to see animals from other places. Now we don't have the same need for zoos and it is cruel to lock animals up there. **For this reason**, I think all zoos should be closed.
>
> **As for agriculture**, I think some farmers look after animals well, but many don't care about the conditions that their animals live in. The best farmers give animals plenty of space and fresh grass to eat.
>
> **To sum up**, I think we could treat animals better.

3

> **Sample paragraph**
>
> In terms of endangered wildlife, man is often to blame for the disappearance of species. Pollution from factories and cars causes severe problems. Some chemicals are being released into the environment, which are harmful to bees, for example.

4–6 See the reworked essay opposite, which includes the new paragraph in 3, replacement words for **animals** (exercise 4), the *phrases* from exercise 5 and a final sentence (exercise 6).

5 Phrase b doesn't fit grammatically.

> **Sample answer**
>
> THE TREATMENT OF ANIMALS IN OUR WORLD TODAY
>
> This is a complex question. Many people depend on animals to live, whether they eat meat or just keep **a cow or a goat** for its milk. This essay will consider farming, as well as discussing the role of zoos, and endangered wildlife.
>
> When zoos first opened, they had a real purpose – to educate people. There was no television and in this way, people got to see **wildlife** from other places. Now we don't have the same need for zoos and it is cruel to lock **creatures** up there. For this reason, all zoos should be closed ***in my opinion***.
>
> In terms of endangered wildlife, man is often to blame for the disappearance of species. Pollution from factories and cars causes severe problems. Some chemicals are being released into the environment, which are harmful to bees, for example.
>
> As for agriculture, ***it is true that*** some farmers look after animals well, but many don't care about the conditions that **they** live in. The best farmers give **them** plenty of space and fresh grass to eat.
>
> To sum up, we could treat animals better ***without a doubt***. **We need to respect all living creatures**.

7

> **Sample answer**
>
> WILDLIFE IN NEED OF PROTECTION
>
> As the statement suggests, there are many species at risk today. This essay will give some examples of endangered animals, argue for their better protection and explain what action could be taken now.
>
> Arctic animals, such as polar bears, are in danger of extinction due to global warming. Other species, such as the white rhino, are facing extinction because they are hunted.
>
> If we let these beautiful creatures disappear, our world will never be the same. Think of a forest without any birds singing or an ocean with no whales. Furthermore, when species die out, the whole balance of nature is threatened.
>
> So what is to be done? There are already several protection programmes but these often lack money. It is also necessary for governments to pass additional environmental laws, in my opinion, so that the pollution from factories can be better controlled.
>
> In conclusion, there is no doubt that more could be done to save endangered species. They are worth saving so that future generations can admire them.
>
> (174 words)

Unit 5

5.1 pages 34–35

1

> *positive*: content, delighted, happy, pleased, satisfied, thrilled
>
> *negative*: anxious, frightened, petrified, scared, tense, terrified, uneasy, worried
>
> (anxious = worried, frightened = scared, petrified = terrified, tense = uneasy)
>
> *Scared* and *worried* combine with *stiff* (as does *bored*). *Scared stiff* means extremely scared.

2

> **Possible answer**
>
> I'm absolutely petrified of bats and I generally feel a bit uneasy in dark places like caves. I'd get very tense if I had to cross that river on a rope bridge – it looks rather unsafe! I love watching the sky at sunrise and sunset and it makes me feel content with life. Fast motorbikes aren't my thing, but I can see that someone might be thrilled to be driving along at speed, watching the countryside go by. I'm always delighted when people give me flowers. Travelling in planes during a dramatic thunderstorm makes me worried, though such bad weather never lasts long, fortunately.

Vocabulary

3

> In **a**, the first sentence is correct. (*very* happy = a lot)
>
> In **b**, the second sentence is correct. (*absolutely* delighted = 100%)

> The adverbs in the box in exercise 4 are adverbs of degree, which are used to indicate the extent of something – in this case, the strength of an emotion. Adverbs like *absolutely, completely, totally* are examples of emphasising adverbs which are used with adjectives to strengthen or emphasise the meaning to the extent of 100% the adjective described. They are used with adjectives whose meaning already suggests extreme feeling or size, such as *terrified*. We cannot say 'very terrified' or 'a little terrified'. Adverbs of degree like *very, extremely, really* also strengthen the meaning, but only to the extent of 'a lot', rather than 100%. We can say 'very frightened' and also 'a little frightened'. Another adverb of this type at B2 level is *entirely*.

4

> *absolutely, completely* and *totally* can be used in **a** and **d**; *extremely, really* and *very* can be used in **b**, **c**, **e** and **f**.

Listening

5

> The man was in a lift.
> He spent over four hours there.
> **1** to attend an interview for a job
> **2** early evening
> **3** He tried to press the emergency button and use the phone.
> **4** Most people had already left and it was four hours before the night porter realised he was there.

Recording script 🔵1 05

1

I'd had this interview for a job, up on the twenty-seventh floor of a big office block. It was after six and a lot of people had already left. I got in the lift and pressed the button. At first, I noticed that it sort of shook but it started to go down. Then there was this horrible sound of twisting metal and it shuddered to a stop. I was stuck between the twelfth and thirteenth floors! To begin with, I was determined not to panic. There was an emergency button, which I pushed for ages. Next, I saw a phone, but when I lifted the receiver, it was dead. At this point, I completely went to pieces. I shouted and screamed, I hammered on the doors, but nobody helped. Eventually, I sank to the floor and wept like a child. In the end, it was a good four hours before the night porter realised what had happened and called the Fire Brigade. I've never been in one since.

6

> **1 C** The phrase *to begin with* signals the answer. Other sequence words and phrases are: *at first, then, next, at this point, eventually, in the end.*

7 Each extract will be heard twice. Remember to check your answers at the second listening.

> The underlined parts of the recording script confirm the answers.

> **2** B   **3** C   **4** C   **5** A   **6** B   **7** A   **8** B

Recording script 🔵1 06

2

Somehow I have to sort out their problem, this fear they have of flying. First, we talk as a group, and one by one they tell me about particular times when they've flown and what happened. Nine times out of ten they describe regular, <u>problem-free flights, just like the hundreds I flew myself</u>. You see, most of their worries are only in their imagination. I also use drama and role play to teach them how to deal with other people's fears, because through that they sometimes forget their own problem, or take it less seriously than before. Finally, but only if I think it's still necessary, we go up in a plane. My passenger is accompanied by an actor, who plays the part of the nervous first-time traveller. I sit a few rows behind and it's wonderful to watch my 'student' staying calm, offering advice to this stranger. I've never failed yet.

3

On the phone

Son: Mum, it's me. Look, I know you must be really angry and I'm very sorry, we didn't mean to get lost out on the hills, but …

Woman: <u>Oh Tom, it's so good to hear your voice!</u> We've been worried stiff since the police called round – we were sure this phone call would be bad news. I mean, it's been three days! Are you really OK?

Son: Yeah. Helen's got a few bruises from her fall, and we haven't eaten much in three days obviously, but other than that, yeah, we're doing fine.

Woman: Well, that's something. Your dad is still absolutely furious with you, of course. When do you think you'll be able to get home?

Son: The day after tomorrow, all being well. We …

4

It was late at night and I was in the living room watching television on my own. Funnily enough, I was watching a horror movie – it wasn't very scary though! Well, I thought I heard a noise upstairs. So I turned off the TV, held my breath and listened. And then, there was this horrific crash. My first thought was – it's a burglar. I was scared stiff but I knew I had to go up there. I remember I picked up an umbrella – goodness knows what I would have done with it! Anyway, I crept up the stairs and the first thing I saw was a bookcase on its side, with hundreds of books on the floor. Then I heard this whimpering sound, coming from underneath the pile of books. It was the next-door neighbour's cat I'd heard! While I was putting away the books, I found something else. <u>A live frog! That's when I was absolutely petrified!</u> It sort of jumped out at me.

5

Hi, Julie. If your phone's switched off, I guess you must be celebrating! Wow! This must feel as good as the day you graduated from university! No, even better than that! Anyway, just to say you've made me a very proud dad! I'm absolutely delighted for you. You've worked so hard to achieve your goal and you thoroughly deserve what they've offered you. <u>I can't wait to see your novel in the shops</u> – when will it be coming out, do you know? It's funny, isn't it, all those writing competitions you went in for as a child and you never won a thing, but you never gave up, did you? Well, as I said, I am really, really proud of you. Speak soon. Love you.

6

We were all living in a small house in the countryside at the time. The house was in the middle of nowhere and it was quite a long journey back from the university each evening, so I'd bought myself a small motorbike. Anyway,

on one particular evening I was on my way home when a really thick fog came down. I didn't know where I was and I became very uneasy. I went on – rather slowly – but couldn't see anything I recognised. At one point the road curved round, but because of the fog I didn't see this and carried straight on … and hit a wall. The impact threw me off the bike and I ended up underneath it, with my leg trapped. I screamed for help but of course there was no one about. I realised that I had to get up and carry on – or stay there all night. So I pulled myself out from under the bike, got back on and somehow arrived home, where my friends all took one look at me and <u>called an ambulance</u>. I needed seven stitches and they kept me in for observation.

7

Interviewer: Malcolm Jarvis, you have recently sailed single-handedly around the world. At one stage, you were shipwrecked all alone in the middle of the ocean, clinging on to your damaged yacht. Weren't you terrified?

MJ: Not at the time. I suppose I was too busy trying to survive.

Interviewer: You mean finding things to eat?

MJ: More basic than hunger! First, I had to get myself out of the sea. Sharks had been a problem there. I managed to pull myself back into the yacht but it had taken in a lot of water. So I spent a bit of time sorting that out.

Interviewer: And then were you able to keep yourself warm?

MJ: Only for a while. I wrapped myself in whatever I could find, including the sails, but by the second day I was in a really bad way because <u>I couldn't feel my fingers and toes, they were completely numb. That was the most dreadful time.</u> It was just as well they found me when they did.

8

We were all in the main room planning what to do that day. The others were looking at a map on the table, but I was standing by the back window. About six of them burst in, waving guns and shouting things in a dialect we didn't understand. <u>I knew they hadn't seen me</u> over by the open window. They grabbed John and Gary. Ruth rushed to the doorway but they got her too. In the meantime, <u>I had managed to throw myself safely outside</u> and had crawled underneath the house – because of the rainy season, all the houses there are raised above the ground on wooden stilts. I kept totally still. I remember watching a beetle on a leaf, staring at it and hoping that they wouldn't find me. Finally, when I realised that they'd gone, I ran inside and radioed for help. My friends weren't so lucky. They were held as hostages for over three months.

Grammar extra

The verb forms appear on page 168 of the Grammar folder. *Burst* has the same form. Other verbs like this are, for example, *cut, hit, set, put, bet*.

5.2 pages 36–37

Review of past tenses

1

> **a** PP **b** PS; PS **c** P **d** PC **e** PS; PP **f** PC; PS **g** PC; PC **h** PS; PP **i** PS; PP; PS **j** P
>
> In **e**, **h** and **i**, the past simple and the past perfect are both used (the past perfect for an action further back in the past).
>
> In **f**, the past continuous describes an action that happened over a longer time period than the second action, which happened at a specific moment.

2

> **1** was walking **2** was blowing **3** was pouring **4** was **5** drove **6** stopped **7** curved **8** decided **9** was feeling **10** got **11** drove **12** happened **13** pulled up **14** waited **15** drew **16** pulled away **17** was **18** stood **19** was coming down **20** was shaking **21** (was) wondering **22** came **23** was pushing **24** grabbed **25** made **26** went **27** was trying **28** heard

3 You must use the past perfect tense to make time differences clear.

> **a** had spent; got
> **b** told; had happened; explained; had found
> **c** had kept; thought; was

4

> **Useful vocabulary**
> Picture 1: hold up a bank, a hold-up/a bank raid, masked robbers, balaclava, pointing a gun at /at gunpoint, cashier
> Picture 2: make a getaway, drive off, bag/holdall
> Picture 3: car chase, police siren, catch up with
> Picture 4: force to stop, pull over, arrest, take off (the balaclavas)
>
> **Sample answer**
> Eventually, the police forced the robbers to stop and arrested them. They had chased them all over town at high speed with their sirens blaring and blue lights flashing. The thieves had made their getaway in a blue car, dressed in balaclavas and with the banknotes stuffed into a holdall. At the bank, the three robbers had worn masks to avoid being identified. They had held up the cashiers at gunpoint.

5

Background information

Raymond Chandler, author of *The Big Sleep*, was born in Chicago but went to school in London. For most of his life, he lived in Southern California, which is where most of his novels are set. His most famous character is the private detective Philip Marlowe, who has been played in films by Humphrey Bogart, Robert Mitchum and Elliot Gould.

6 This exercise is an introduction to the 'open cloze', Paper 1 Part 2, which tests mainly grammar. Exam folder 3, on the following pages (38–39), focuses on this task.

> **1** at **2** the **3** when **4** of **5** and **6** any **7** had **8** so **9** not **10** was **11** it **12** went

> Most words tested here fall into the grammatical categories given below. These areas are commonly tested in the open cloze task.

> *adverb*: not
> *conjunctions*: and, because, so, when
> *determiner*: the
> *prepositions*: at, of
> *pronoun*: it
> *quantifiers*: any, some
> *verbs*: be, had, has, was, went

Exam folder 3 pages 38–39

Paper 1 Part 2 Open cloze

The open cloze consists of eight gaps and an example at the beginning. Each gap can only be filled with one word – you can't use contractions. If you put in more than one word, you will be marked wrong. The word must be spelt correctly. The gaps are mainly grammatical in focus, but there are sometimes one or two vocabulary items in the form of a collocation or phrasal verb.

1

> **a** few **b** keep **c** the **d** must **e** been **f** up **g** himself **h** who **i** many **j** unless **k** to

2

> 'Balancing the risks' is the best title, as the text looks at both sides of the question.

3

> **1** SPEND **2** UNLESS **3** A **4** FEW **5** IF/THOUGH **6** THAN **7** IN **8** SUCH

Unit 6

6.1 pages 40–41

Reading

1

> **Possible answers**
> If I suddenly became famous, I'd be shocked and a bit surprised. But I'd be proud of myself too and pleased for my family. I'm not sure I'd like all the media attention though. The biggest drawback for me would be the lack of privacy.

2

> The girl, Mary-Jess Leaverland, appeared on a regional TV talent show in China.

3   Read the advice in the Exam spot carefully.

4

> 1 G   2 F   3 D   4 A   5 B   6 E
> The extra sentence is C.

5

> **Possible answer**
> No, I wouldn't have taken part because I get really nervous singing in public. I really admire what she did, especially as it was in another country.

Vocabulary

6   Think about the particles as you do this – for example, *down* might be to do with position, movement or direction.

> **a** keep down   **b** keep in   **c** keep up with   **d** keep to
> **e** keep up with   **f** keep away

7   The number of words indicated by the gaps will help you decide whether a pronoun is needed.

> **a** kept to   **b** kept up with   **c** keep away
> **d** keep up with her   **e** keeping him in   **f** keep to
> **g** keeps to   **h** keeps on; keep it down

8   Think about the words around each gap to work out what part of speech is needed.

> 1 impossible   2 argument   3 living   4 endlessly
> 5 personal   6 understandable   7 scientists   8 hunters

6.2 pages 42–43

Conditionals with *if*

1   Don't worry if you don't understand every word. Listen out for the second conditional form *I'd / I would,* which will give you the answers.

> Speaker 1 would buy a new car and a new house. He'd also buy a house in Spain and a flat in Manhattan. He'd employ a chef and a masseur.
>
> Speaker 2 would buy a yacht and hire a crew and chef and sail around the world.
>
> Speaker 3 would pay off her and her family's debts. Then she would buy a huge house in the country and invite friends and people who didn't usually have the opportunity to visit the countryside.
>
> Speaker 4 would also pay off his and his family's debts. Then he would invest the rest of the money and live off the interest. He'd move from Britain to a warmer country.
>
> Notice the speakers' use of phrasal verbs in extracts 2, 3 and 4:
>
> extract 2: *stand out* – here, the meaning is 'be better' (than other memories) (Students also met this phrasal verb in 1.1, meaning 'easy to see'.)
>
> extracts 3 and 4: *sort out* – here, the meaning is 'solve (a problem)'; another meaning of this phrasal verb is 'tidy'

Recording script 1 07

1

I'd buy a Seychelles blue Bentley convertible. I'd buy a nice fat house in Holland Park. I'd get a lovely big house in the countryside. I'd buy a beautiful house in Spain, with swimming pool, palm trees, that sort of thing. I'd get a flat in Manhattan probably. Um … I'd also have a permanent chef … top of the range chef who could cook all different types of food, so I could have whatever food I wanted whenever I wanted it. I'd have my own personal masseur …

2

I think I would just alter my life entirely. I love the sun, and a Caribbean holiday stands out in my memory … surrounded by clear turquoise sea … so I think I'd buy a yacht. And as I don't know anything about um … sailing, I'd have to buy a crew as well. So, um, I'd get … I'd get this luxurious yacht and a very skilled crew – and probably a skilled cook – who would just take me all around the world going from hot spot to hot spot, so I could have a really great time.

3

Well, I know I'd have a problem with having all that money. I'd … I think it is a problem really, in some ways, because you … you'd have a sort of social responsibility and there are all kinds of people who you need to help, which I would want to do very much. Um, so of course I'd sort out my debts, my family's, but in the end I think what I'd do is buy – depending on how much money I had – buy a huge house, a really massive house somewhere in the country and just surround myself by all the people I want to be with, um and people who perhaps never had a chance to get out into the country at all.

4

Again depending on how many millions I won, um it would change what I would or wouldn't do with it. Frankly, if it was a lot, I mean five million upwards ... sort out my own debts, which God knows are bad enough, sort out the family's debts and then invest as much as possible and just try and live off the interest, keep it there, nice little nest egg, growing and growing and growing, developing, flowering bountifully, and holiday, get away, move, anywhere but cold Britain.

2

> **a** I'd = I would (Type 2 conditional)
> **b** had not won ... would not have been able (Type 3 conditional)

3

> **a** 4 **b** 1 **c** 7 **d** 2 **e** 6 **f** 3 **g** 8 **h** 5

Conditionals with *unless*

4

> *Unless* means *if not*, e.g:
> **a** ... if Juan doesn't arrive soon
> **b** If you haven't already got tickets ...

> **Corpus spot**
> **a** There will be no improvement in my tennis unless I ~~don't~~ get some training.
> **b** *correct*
> **c** People hardly ever use candlelight today unless there ~~isn't anything~~ **is something** wrong with the power supply.
> **d** There isn't much to do in the city unless you **have** (got) friends.
> **e** You must stop working so hard **if** you don't want to end up in hospital sooner or later.
> **f** *correct*

5

> **Tense errors**
> won't → wouldn't (be so unreliable)
> hasn't → hadn't (run out of)
> I'll find → I find
> can't → couldn't (i.e. couldn't call)
> will say → would say OR didn't get → don't get
> will get → gets (really angry)
> will do → do (the journey)
>
> **0** If **1** unless **2** If **3** if **4** if **5** unless **6** if **7** If
> **8** if **9** unless

6

> **Possible answers**
> **a** Unless I get up early tomorrow, I won't finish my essay.
> **b** If I had enough money, I'd buy a Ferrari.
> **c** My life would be a lot easier, if I cut down on my work.
> **d** If I hadn't come to class today, I would have gone swimming.

Vocabulary

7

> *Nouns:* attempt, experiment, trial, try
> *Verbs:* accepted, gathered, received, welcomed
> *Prepositions:* by, in, on, to
> *Adjectives:* delicate, gentle, light, tiny

8

> **1** attempt (NOT try – we *make* an attempt, but *have* a try)
> **2** light
> **3** received
> **4** by

Speaking

9

> **Possible answers**
> **a** I think it cannot be avoided – the public are interested in people who win large amounts of money.
> **b** The advantages of winning the lottery are that you might not ever have to work again, and you would certainly be able to afford a nice big house and garden with a swimming pool. I think the main negative thing would be the publicity, and you might find that your friends start behaving strangely and asking you for money.
> **c** No, definitely not.

Writing folder 3 pages 44–45

Paper 2 Part 2 Reports

1

> Yes. It states what is wrong with the museum and makes recommendations.

2

> **1** F **2** D **3** C **4** A **5** B

3 Paragraph 3: This permanent exhibition will remain unappealing to visitors *unless* it is updated.

Paragraph 5: Wademouth Museum would have a brighter future *if* its displays were improved.

a	if	E
b	Unless	G
c	if	G
d	if	E
e	unless	G

4

Sample paragraphs

Temporary exhibitions
At present, the museum only has one permanent exhibition but people might visit more often if there were different objects for them to see each time. Obviously this would require financial suppport. The museum could organise special exhibitions on a monthly basis if funding was available.

Evening events
The museum opening hours are very limited and unless it extends these, working adults won't come through its doors. On certain evenings, the museum could hold a series of talks. These would be more popular if visitors didn't have to pay for them on top of the entrance charge.

5

Suggested answers

Problems	Recommendations
closes too early	*extend the opening times*
not much choice	*have a broader menu*
uncomfortable	*replace the furniture*
too expensive	*reduce the price*

6

Sentences a, c, d and f would have a positive effect.

Improvements to b and e:
b As the old furniture needs replacing, the college could opt for slightly more comfortable chairs.
e It is worth meeting students' needs, as the café will then be far more popular.

7

Sample answer
REPORT ON THE EXISTING AND PROPOSED COLLEGE CAFE
Introduction
This report outlines the issues raised in relation to the college café and makes recommendations on how these problems could be addressed.

Opening times
At present, the opening hours are too limited. Apart from Saturdays, the café closes at 18.30, just when many students are leaving the library and likely to want to purchase a meal or drinks.

Menu
The lack of choice puts many students off using the café. Vegetarians feel that they are not being catered for and would like to see a range of healthy options.

Furniture
The tables and chairs in the present café are old and basic. There is nowhere to sit comfortably with friends, as you would find in the cafés in town.

Pricing policy
A common complaint is that most dishes are overpriced and are not affordable on a student budget. If possible, this needs to be reviewed.

Recommendations
From all of the above points, it is clear that several improvements could be made, from replacing the furniture to widening the choice of meals. If the opening hours could be extended and the prices reduced slightly, the new café would undoubtedly be more popular with students.
(202 words)

Units 1–6 Revision

pages 46–47

2

1 on	**2** the	**3** has	**4** while/when	**5** was	**6** too
7 as/because	**8** who				

3

a save	**b** gone	**c** dress	**d** keep	**e** ring/call/phone
f stand	**g** check	**h** go	**i** work	**j** cut down
k stopped over	**l** take back	**m** set off		
n to keep away from	**o** take off			

4 Sometimes more than one answer is correct, as shown.

1 are	**2** seems **3** are **4** sees **5** has tried / has been trying
6 has done / has been doing	**7** has developed **8** is
9 puts / has put	**10** has had **11** came
12 had never flown	**13** had had **14** had taken / took
15 had never worried	**16** announced **17** had **18** tried
19 overcame / had overcome	**20** managed / had managed

5 This is practice for Paper 1 Part 4. Remember that you can't use more than five words, and that contractions count as two words.

1 wouldn't go dancing unless
2 worst film I've ever
3 would have met you
4 aren't allowed to
5 more frightened of ghosts than
6 shouldn't have bought you
7 had (already) started
8 see to drive without

Unit 7

7.1 pages 48–49

Gerunds and infinitives 1

1

a ice skates –ice skating
b swimming goggles and hat
c shuttlecock – badminton
d basket for basketball
e squash racket and ball
f rugby ball
g football
h table tennis bats and ball
i baseball bat
j oars – rowing
k tennis racket and ball
l volleyball
m snowboard – snowboarding
n golf clubs and ball
o ski poles and skis – skiing

2

Possible answers
a I really enjoy watching tennis and football.
b I'm keen on seeing Rafael Nadal play, because he's so talented.
c I can't stand watching wrestling.
d I've taken up volleyball recently.
e I much prefer watching sports live. It's exciting being part of the crowd.
f I feel more like relaxing on holiday, so I only do water sports then.

3 Gerunds are verb forms which are used as nouns.

a adjective (describing the kind of rope)
b participle (past continuous tense)
c gerund (gerund – subject of sentence)

4

a 2   b 4   c 5   d 1   e 3

5 Some verbs and adjectives are followed by a preposition and we usually use a gerund after them. Watch out for verbs followed by *to* as a preposition. Common ones are *to look forward to doing* and *to object to doing*. They are frequently tested in the exam. There is a list of common verbs which are followed by a gerund on page 169 of the Grammar folder.

a about getting   b of learning   c at teaching
d for dropping   e in doing   f at swimming   g to playing

6

a 3   b 5   c 2   d 1   e 4, 5   f 4, 6

Corpus spot
a I should give up **swimming** every morning.
b Do you want **to** go out with me?
c I'm used to **sleeping** in a tent.
d There's no point **(in) playing** today.
e I suggest (that) you **go** to the sports centre. / I suggest **going** to the sports centre.
f I really enjoy **reading** about the old tennis stars.
g I recommend (that) you **go** there.
h I hope **to hear** from you soon.
i I am interested **in receiving** documentation about the courses.
j I agree **that you should find** a job.

7

1 climbing   2 tell   3 arriving   4 training   5 to assess
6 to make   7 to teach   8 mountaineering   9 to use
10 to work   11 climbing   12 to sleep   13 Reaching
14 jumping   15 seeing   16 tell

8 Gerunds and infinitives are frequently tested in Paper 1 Part 4.

1 accused Pete of pushing
2 is too wet to
3 had difficulty (in) learning
4 advised me not to go / advised me against (going)
5 would rather go on

7.2 pages 50–51

Speaking

1 The photos show three examples of extreme or dangerous sports: heli-skiing, free-style mountain biking and sky diving.

Possible answers
a I think sky-diving is dangerous, because your parachute might not open. Heli-skiing is also dangerous because you might land badly and hurt yourself or even ski off the side of a mountain.
b I've tried horse riding – some people think that is dangerous, because riders can be badly injured if they fall.

Listening

2

The sport is bungee jumping.
Clues are: Dangerous Sports Club, ground seemed far away, jumps, attached to a rope

Recording script 1 08

Speaker 1: All of us in the office where I work love doing it, probably because we're all desperate to get out of that 9 to 5 routine. It's an expensive sport but we all joined a <u>Dangerous Sports Club</u> to help keep costs down. The first time I did it I really was frightened as <u>the ground</u>

seemed so far away, but I said to myself that nothing would happen and I wasn't going to die. I did my first two jumps in Canada and London. Apparently, in Germany they're doing it without being attached to a rope, but with just a net beneath. That could be pretty scary, couldn't it?

3 The underlined parts of the recording script confirm the answers.

1 F 2 A 3 D 4 C 5 G

Recording script 1 09

Speaker 1: All of us in the office where I work love doing it, probably because we're all desperate to get out of that 9 to 5 routine. It's an expensive sport but we all joined a Dangerous Sports Club to help keep costs down. The first time I did it I really was frightened as the ground seemed so far away, but I said to myself that nothing would happen and I wasn't going to die. I did my first two jumps in Canada and London. Apparently, in Germany they're doing it without being attached to a rope, but with just a net beneath. That could be pretty scary, couldn't it?

Speaker 2: About four years ago I was very ill and nearly died. Sometime later I was involved in a serious car crash. It made me realise how risky everyday life is, and it seemed to cure me of fear, so I said to myself, why not push things to the limit? So, I had a go at white-water rafting in the States and then moved on to other things. It's been brilliant. I've done all sorts of things, from abseiling down mountains to skydiving. Now I try to keep giving myself difficult and exciting things to do – not that I've got anything to prove, it's just a personal thing really. I'm thinking of doing river sledging next.

Speaker 3: I took part in a trek to ski across the Arctic last year. It was probably the most dangerous thing I've ever done, but I'd do it again tomorrow. I was conscious all the time that death was very near and in a strange way that made it seem more fun. I cried in absolute terror sometimes, especially when the ice began to melt and great holes would suddenly appear just in front of me. It was the ultimate challenge for a skier like myself and I guess I'm not afraid of anything any more. In fact, I'm looking forward to skiing in the Antarctic next year!

Speaker 4: I've always enjoyed diving as it's quite an exciting sport, but last winter I had the ultimate experience of going shark-feeding in the Caribbean. The sharks were about three metres in length and obviously they are quite aggressive and can bite you, but if you put on the right protective clothing and take precautions it's no more of a risk than driving fast motor cars. I must say I had more accidents when I went horse riding. I did feel a bit nervous as I went over the side of the boat – after all, I've seen stories about shark attacks on TV like everyone else! But I was never in any real danger.

Speaker 5: Some of my mates had started doing this free climbing – you know where you don't use ropes, only your hands and feet. I guess they needed to have a bit of excitement in their lives, didn't they? Me, I think I get enough from my job as a motorbike courier in London. Anyway, I went with them one weekend. It was terrifying and I was sure I'd end up lying in a hospital bed, but I felt I had to do it, especially with them looking on. There was no pressure from them, but you know how it is. Anyway, I did my best and I have to say it gave me a real 'buzz'. I can understand why people go in for this type of thing now.

4

1 bungee jumping
2 white-water rafting, abseiling, skydiving, river sledging (going down rapids on a small sledge)
3 skiing
4 diving, driving fast cars, horse riding
5 free climbing (without a rope or harness)

Vocabulary

5

do aerobics – gym, studio
do martial arts – gym, studio
go swimming – (swimming) pool
do athletics – track, stadium
play basketball – court
do gymnastics – gym, studio
go snowboarding – piste
play golf – course
go running – track
play football – pitch, stadium

6 Use an English–English dictionary to decide on the right word and also to check on the meaning and use of the other word.

a laps b spectators c referee d sets e goal

7

a do business with   b do for a living
c are doing / did a good job   d did (a lot of) damage
e did me a favour   f do their best   g do without

8

Possible answers
a One thing I absolutely couldn't do without is my phone because I need it to keep in touch with my friends.
b If I could, I'd really love to be a vet, looking after horses in particular.
c Actually, I helped my mother this morning by getting my little brother ready for school so that she could leave early for work.
d Generally I do, but sometimes when I feel very tired or upset about something, I don't try quite as hard.

9

Background information

A personal trainer is a person who comes to your house to encourage you to work out or who works with you individually at the gym. Many film stars employ a trainer so that they can exercise in private.

1 ensure   **2** training   **3** uncertain   **4** demanding
5 Movement   **6** Education   **7** qualification(s)   **8** freedom

Exam folder 4 pages 52–53

Paper 1 Part 1 Multiple choice cloze

Although this is the first part of Paper 1, you can do the seven parts of the paper in any order you want. Remember to read the passage from beginning to end before you start deciding on answers. You might easily get an answer wrong if you don't understand the meaning of the whole passage.

1 C   **2** A   **3** A   **4** B   **5** A   **6** C   **7** C   **8** D

Unit 8

8.1 pages 54–55

Speaking

1 and 2

Possible answers
Photos 1 and 2
In the first photo some children are playing together outdoors and in the second one a child is indoors playing a computer game. I think it's hard to decide which activity children would enjoy most as I think they would enjoy both. I prefer playing computer games myself.

Photos 3 and 4
In the first photo a girl is lying in her room with her laptop and music player and in the second photo the boy is helping out at home. I think the photos show you that nowadays, teenagers are dependent on technology and can't live without a laptop or music. Also it does show that modern teenagers are willing to help out in the home so they don't totally isolate themselves from the rest of the family and are keen to live in a clean, tidy environment.

Reading

3

The answer is probably that the writer had a happy childhood.

4

1 B   **2** D   **3** C   **4** A   **5** B   **6** B

5

Possible answers
a   I think the writer had quite a happy, though not an easy childhood. Her parents are a bit strict. My parents are very friendly and always let me see my friends.
b   Yes, children should help their parents because usually, both of them work outside the home and they need support.
c   I spend quite a lot of time at home, especially in the winter when it's too cold to stay out late.
d   Older people always say this about the generations below them. I'm not sure whether it's true, though there does seem to be a lot of commercial pressure on kids nowadays – to buy the right clothes, to listen to the latest songs, and so on.

8.2 pages 56–57

used to and *would*

1   It is important to understand the differences between *would* and *used to*. Read the section in the Grammar folder on page 169.

We can use *used to* when we use *would* but we can't always use *would* for *used to*:
We can say: *I used to have long hair.*
We can't say: *I would have long hair.*
We can say: *I used to go to town on the bus.*
We can also say: *I would go to town on the bus.*

This is because we don't use *would* for past states or situations – only for past actions. *Would* is more formal than *used to*. It is a common structure in narrative writing and it is often tested in the exam.

a 1   **b** 3   **c** 2
I'm used to living away from home. – The speaker has probably lived away from home for some time and is used to it.
I'm getting used to living away from home. – The speaker probably hasn't lived away from home for long and is **not** completely used to it yet.

2

a used to have   **b** *correct*   **c** *correct*   **d** get used to doing
e used to work / was used to working   **f** *correct*
g used to go

3

Possible answers

a I would often go to the park with my friends and play on the swings. We used to visit my grandparents and they would sometimes take us to the beach.

b One thing I've found it hard to get used to is using the functions on my new mobile phone. My old one was much simpler to use!

c I used to walk to school but now I don't, because my new one is too far away.

d I'm used to eating most types of food, even spicy curries, although it took me a while to get used to those.

Vocabulary

4

a do **b** break **c** having **d** made **e** kept **f** tastes
g spends

5

a the angry neighbour **b** some work **c** washing the floor
d the flu **e** the tennis team **f** not paying

6

get away from – escape from
get down to – start
get out of – avoid
get over – recover from
get into (a team) – be allowed to join
get away with – succeed in not being punished for

Possible answers

a I often try to get away with not tidying up my things.

b I definitely do as I have an exam in a couple of months.

c Yes, last year. I was in bed for nearly a week and felt really bad for about a month afterwards.

d Yes, I'm in the school football team. I'm the goalkeeper. I was really pleased to be picked for the team.

7

1 separation **2** social **3** happiness **4** preference
5 ability **6** unconsciously **7** behaviour/behavior
8 remarkable

8

Possible answers

a Yes, I think I do. I'm quite friendly, I think, and I'm always curious to know about people.

b For about six years – since we came to the same college.

c Yes, when I was twelve. I had an argument with my friend about going to see a film.

d I think I like friends who are loyal and can keep a secret.

e Sometimes. I think my friends think like I do and understand the problems we have, such as school, relationships, etc.

f I don't always do the same things – for example, I play tennis and none of my friends do.

g Not really. I like to look a bit different when I go out and choose clothes that suit me, rather than following fashion. Some of my friends use slang and I don't like to use it.

Writing folder 4 pages 58–59
Paper 2 Part 1 Essays

In the exam, essays are usually written for a teacher and generally ask you to give your opinions about a statement. Any essay requires careful organisation and you should make a plan before you start writing. Remember to include an introduction and conclusion, and use a suitable number of paragraphs.

2 Paragraphing is a very important part of the Writing paper. Work which isn't paragraphed has a very poor effect on the examiner. You should try to use a minimum of two and a maximum of five paragraphs in your essays. Avoid writing one-sentence paragraphs or lists of sentences.

1 D **2** B **3** A **4** E **5** C

3

substantial earnings	significant earnings
an essential job	a vital job
the real issue	the actual issue
strong feelings	deep feelings
a central place	a key place

4

Addition: as well as, furthermore
Contrast: at the same time, in contrast, nevertheless
Result: as a result, consequently

6

Sample answer

FITNESS WHEN WORKING HARD

Physical exercise is generally believed to be good for the mind as well as the body. This essay considers its place in a busy lifestyle, looking at the advantages to health but also considering possible drawbacks.

People in stressful jobs with a heavy workload can profit enormously from taking regular exercise. Similarly, students who work late at night to meet essay deadlines will function better if they leave their desk for a run or play tennis for an hour.

Aside from the obvious improvements to health and fitness, such as being in better shape and keeping weight under control, people who take exercise sleep more soundly. This is because they are physically exhausted.

At the same time, there are some drawbacks in committing to regular exercise, not least the expense. Joining a gym usually requires a monthly fee. As well as the cost, taking time out of a busy schedule is not always easy. Nevertheless, the benefits outweigh the disadvantages.

In conclusion, setting aside time each day for exercise brings rewards. For those who spend most of their waking hours at a computer, whether working or studying, physical activity seems especially important.

Unit 9

9.1 pages 60–61

Modals 2

1

> **Possible answer**
> I think it might be for a holiday, or it could be for insurance to cover you in dangerous situations. It can't be for food, because they always show the product. It could be advertising a TV programme perhaps.

2

> The speaker is certain – the words *must be* and *can't be* tell you this.

> In the final example, when the sentence is read as a statement (with a full stop), the speaker is certain. As a question, the same sentence becomes a speculation. The use of *possibly* changes: in the statement, it confirms the certainty, whereas in the question, it becomes a 'hedging' device – it shows uncertainty. The question would be improved by the addition of the question tag *could it*?
>
> These modal verbs may be useful when discussing the photos in Paper 4 Part 2.

3

> *3rd paragraph*: can't be; Might it be; Could it be
> *4th paragraph*: must have won; couldn't win

4

> **a** spoken commentary played over a film
> **b** a short, memorable tune, often with words, used to advertise a product
> **c** someone famous
> **d** decision
> **e** a type of product made by a particular company
> **f** clever
> The use of the idiom 'missed the boat' in the title is appropriate, as it refers to the failure of Delvico Bates to meet the festival deadline, and also to the fact that the advert should have won. It is also a play on words, as Cannes is a port, where there are a lot of boats.

5

> **a** sure   **b** sure   **c** unsure

6

> **1** every/each   **2** than   **3** of   **4** up   **5** making/being
> **6** himself   **7** against   **8** would

Vocabulary

7

huge:	variety, budget, market, picture
high:	budget, voice
low:	budget, voice
deep:	message, character, voice
shallow:	message, idea, character
narrow:	picture, view (+ narrow ideas)
wide:	variety, market, picture

9.2 pages 62–63

Listening

1

> **Possible answer**
> There's one advert that keeps coming back on TV – it must be very successful, I suppose. It's for a DIY product called Ronseal, which you paint onto wooden doors and fences to protect them. The actor looks like a normal person and he's dressed in casual clothes. At the end, he says to camera the now-famous words: 'does exactly what it says on the tin'. This is a no-nonsense advert, promoting an everyday product. I think it's really clever.

2 The underlined parts of the recording script confirm the answers.

a, **d**, **f** and **h** are mentioned

Recording script 1 10
Part 1
Man: There's one car advert that opens with part of a song by Bjork – it must have <u>cost a *fortune* to make</u>, and it looks tremendous …

Woman: I've seen that one. You're not sure what it's advertising to begin with, are you? A graceful silver vehicle <u>moving through an unusual landscape</u> … it could be a spacecraft of the future. All very stylish. The trouble is, it's a bit of a let-down when you realise it's just another *car* advert!

Man: Yes, <u>the beginning *is* a bit misleading</u> … It's funny, isn't it, sometimes the most effective ads are the really simple ones – you know, like a football manager sitting down at the breakfast table with his family, enjoying a particular cereal …

Woman: … he eats it, so it *must* be good. And <u>that actress from *Friends*</u> advertising shampoo – Jennifer Aniston, wasn't it? You know, seeing famous people on screen can be a huge influence on us. We see them as … well, as role models.

Man: Definitely. The ads they put on TV before the World Cup or the Olympics always use mega stars, don't they?

Woman: Yeah, remember the one that had a *whole team* of top footballers from around the world! The special effects were incredible – <u>the budget must have been *huge* … all for *one* advert!</u>

Man: But the company probably earned *millions* of dollars in increased sales, so for them it was worth it.

3 In Part 2, the same speakers talk about one specific advertisement, which is for Bacardi rum. The underlined parts of the recording script confirm the answers.

| 1 M | 2 W | 3 M | 4 W |

Recording script 1 11
Part 2

Woman: There's one advert I really like, partly because it's brilliantly put together …

Man: And it's for …?

Woman: Bacardi – it's set on a tropical island somewhere in the Caribbean. And there's this radio DJ who's broadcasting in a studio and …

Man: Oh no, not Ray on Reef Radio?

Woman: You've seen it too!

Man: Yep. <u>Detest it, actually</u>. All about some friend of Ray's who's leaving for the mainland and how he's going to miss his wonderful life on the island …

Woman: And you see what he's been up to – I adore the way the DJ, Ray, tells the storyline on air and you see flashbacks of the other guy like 'I know you're going to miss the way they serve Bacardi around here' – and you see a girl throw a glassful in the friend's face! Such a striking image and <u>totally unexpected</u>.

Man: Mmm, I suppose ads do work well when they contain something out of the ordinary – I guess they stick in your mind that way.

Woman: Right … and of course, the ending itself is unforgettable – quite spectacular, isn't it? Seeing the friend sailing away on the boat, listening to all this on his radio – and then, what does he do … ?

Man: He dives off the deck and swims back to the island.

Woman: For another night on the town and a glass of …

Man: Yes, yes … You know, I must admit that although I personally loathe the ad, it sells the product pretty well. It's got the right ingredients – you know, exotic location, powerful images …

Woman: So what *didn't* you like about it?

Man: The characters themselves, I think … especially Ray!

Woman: Oh but come on, <u>the very fact that you remember him now means he made an impact on you … which must mean that the ad has worked</u>.

Man: <u>True enough</u> … And what about you? You said it makes you laugh. Is that why you like it so much?

Woman: That … and the way it succeeds in telling a story in such a short time. I think that's quite clever, getting the message across like that. <u>The music's great, too</u>.

Man: But was it *truly* successful? I mean, did you dig into your pocket and buy a bottle?

Woman: Well, no … I don't drink spirits! I bet plenty of people were persuaded to rush out and buy some, though …

4 You will need to listen carefully, as all three options will be referred to in the recording in some way. Before you listen, read the question and options, and underline the key words. Notice the verb *agree* in the question itself: you must find an opinion that is shared by both speakers.

> The answer is C.

5 Before you listen, read the question and options, and underline the key words. The underlined parts of the recording script confirm the answers.

| 1 B | 2 B | 3 C | 4 A |

Recording script 1 12

Interviewer: In the studio with me today is Don Cooper, who has been very successful in producing commercials for television. Don, what is the most important thing to get right in this type of advertising?

Don: Well, I've made at least thirty commercials for television over the last few years, so I reckon I know pretty much what the magic ingredients are. I used to think that the setting was all-important, but I've come to realise that you can have the most exotic location in the world and a truly fantastic storyline, but <u>your commercial will not succeed if you ignore the people factor. It takes time and effort to select the perfect individuals to play your characters but by getting this right, you'll draw your target audience in</u>, make them relate to what's on the screen, and hopefully persuade them that they want a piece of what they're seeing. It's as simple as that.

Interviewer: Mmm, I see. And what advice would you give to anyone writing a script? What's crucial there?

Don: The average TV commercial runs for just 30 seconds so you haven't got long to get your message across. Don't opt for long, flowery sentences – keep it short and punchy. Not only that, but remember that some people might not actually be watching the screen while the commercial is on. <u>My golden rule is to mention the product itself in the audio</u>, so that anyone who has wandered off to make coffee or check the kids' homework will still pick up on it.

Interviewer: Right! Now, your work is very creative, but is it difficult to keep coming up with new ways of promoting the same product?

Don: That can become a challenge, yes. If a company likes what you're doing, as likely as not you'll be asked to make more than one commercial for a product over time, so it seems to me that consistency is an important issue. <u>If you use the same voice-over, or a jingle that echoes the last one in some way, you start to strengthen the company's image, and if the viewer begins to recognise the brand through links like these, you're halfway there already</u>. The drawback with all of this is that you may have to walk away from new business, in order to concentrate on a small number of favourite clients.

Interviewer: And when you're ready to broadcast a commercial, how do you decide on where to show it – and when?

Don: Selecting the most appropriate time and place for your finished commercial is absolutely crucial. Having it go out at three in the morning will save you money, but in actual fact, there's little point in doing this if your core audience, however large or small, is fast asleep! The same holds true for where you choose to broadcast your ad: <u>a bad match between product and station can only spell disaster, so avoid it at all costs</u>.

Interviewer: Well many thanks Don, we'll be back to you with listeners' questions a bit later in the programme. In the meantime …

Grammar extra

The order cannot be changed because an opinion adjective (*graceful*) always comes first.
Opinion adjectives: classic, sensational, popular, delicious
Size: full-length, bite-sized
Age: new
Colour: navy
Nationality: British
Material: cotton, creamy

a a huge black dog
b *correct*
c the famous Italian singer
d a large red apple
e an elaborate square wooden box
f a sophisticated new novel by a tremendous Scottish author

Vocabulary

6

The other informal verbs are *bet* and *guess*. For example:
I bet he's going to be late again!
I guess everyone has an ad that they can't stand.

7

Introducing an opinion: I suppose   It seems to me that
Giving a different point of view: On the other hand
True enough, though
Adding to an idea: Not only that, but   What's more

Speaking

8 If you are studying on your own, record your opinions on the billboards for practice, using the language you have learnt in this unit.

Here is some information about each billboard.

1 British Gas
This is a leading gas supplier in Britain, which also sells and services appliances like cookers and central heating boilers. The ad is emphasising the scale of the company's household support, with its 7000 engineers ready to come out in their vans in the middle of the night to attend to an emergency. The slogan 'Looking after your world' is short and effective, and the image of the vans against the night sky is interesting.

2 Swiftcover car insurance
This billboard features the well-known rock star Iggy Pop, who is being used to sell instant car insurance here (he also appears in TV commercials promoting the same company). The claim is that you can get a quote in 60 seconds and the number 60 is very prominently displayed. The stopwatch covering Iggy's right eye is quite a clever way of reinforcing the idea of limited time and the use of colour is quite strong.

3 Vodafone
This billboard uses balls of knitting wool to represent a family and includes a play on the idiomatic phrase 'Be closer-knit'. The colours are very bright and contrast with the shade of red associated with the company. The two 'children' are formed from two different colours of wool, which is quite a striking image. They must be grown-up and living away from home though, or they wouldn't need to call their 'parents' on the phone.

4 Vauxhall cars
Although this is one car advert among many, it uses the powerful image of a beach under different weather conditions. The idiomatic expression 'Come rain, come shine' implies that whatever the weather is like, this Vauxhall car will be perfect for you.

Exam folder 5 pages 64–65

Paper 3 Part 2 Sentence completion

1 The key words and phrases are underlined for you in these examples of Part 2 sentences.

2 You should never write more than three words in a gap. Here, you need to write only one or two words. You must complete the sentences with words that fit grammatically, including plurals where necessary.

1 washing powder   **2** lifestyle   **3** unusual behaviour
4 puppies (and) kittens

Recording script ①13

1 To support the suggestion that one product is better than its competitors, the existence of actual proof is often mentioned. In one case, involving the promotion of <u>washing powder</u>, reference was made to an unnamed university research project, which analysed shades of white.

2 It must be true that there are more advertisements focusing on our love of driving than on anything else. While the messages of freedom and mobility are always important, it is above all the aspect of <u>lifestyle</u> that is stressed in this particular one. We are supposed to believe that this car will take us to new places in society and change our role for ever.

3 Advertisers adopt different strategies as far as young people between the ages of 15 and 19 are concerned. For this population, it is not about conforming but about the complete opposite of that. Indeed, products for this age group are frequently connected with <u>unusual behaviour</u>, the kind that older people such as parents might well disapprove of.

4 Turning to mothers and fathers as consumers, advertisements targeting these people often reinforce the experience of bringing up a family. An advert that links its product to young children or even, interestingly enough, to <u>puppies</u> and <u>kittens</u>, will probably succeed because these images appeal directly to motherly or, perhaps less commonly, fatherly instincts.

3 **The actual answer sheet starts at question 9 as this is the first question in Part 2. Before you transfer your answers, check your spelling.**

5 **Give yourself 45 seconds to read through the questions and try to predict what you might hear. Then listen to the recording twice, as in the exam.**

The underlined parts of the recording script confirm the answers.

> 1 company name
> 2 (breakfast) cereal
> 3 direct promotion
> 4 dessert
> 5 (famous/well-known) songwriters
> 6 pop songs
> 7 lifestyle
> 8 downloading
> 9 (strong) emotional connection
> 10 30/ thirty seconds

Recording script ①14

You will hear part of a talk about advertising jingles. For questions 1–10, complete the sentences with a word or short phrase. You now have 45 seconds to look at Part Two.

Today I'm going to consider the history of the commercial jingle. So, first of all, what is it? Well, it's a type of slogan that is set to music. It could be very simple, for example just a <u>company name</u>, if that's the most important message to get across.

Jingles have been in existence since the birth of commercial radio in the USA in the 1920s. It is generally believed that the modern commercial jingle took off on Christmas Eve 1926, when a group of four singers was heard performing a jingle for a <u>breakfast cereal</u>. The product in question had not been selling well but sales increased noticeably after the broadcast.

In the early 1930s, listening to the radio was very popular in the States – there was no television then of course. The rules on advertising did not permit the <u>direct promotion</u> of products during peak listening hours. The jingle was a clever way round this problem, and so advertisers started using them a lot. For example, one long-running radio series called *The Adventures of the Jenkins Family* began with a short rhyming jingle for a <u>dessert</u>. Interestingly, this product was the first of its type to be marketed in the United States, and the catchy rhyme made a big impact on the public.

In the 1950s, jingles became more sophisticated and <u>famous songwriters</u> were often signed up to write them. But by the 1980s, the public had grown tired of listening to jingles like these. Advertisers had to look for something else and they turned to <u>pop songs</u>. In 1987, the Beatles' tune *Revolution* was chosen for a Nike shoe campaign and this marked a revolution in advertising too. Showing a good product was simply not enough any longer – to be successful, a commercial now had to represent a whole <u>lifestyle</u>, which is essentially where we are today. Drawing on the shared cultural experience of music has become the most effective way to sell a product and, with the record industry losing money because of <u>downloading</u>, advertising companies have been very welcome business partners.

Psychologists who study the effects of music on the brain have found that music with a <u>strong emotional connection</u> to the listener is more memorable, and this has become an important area of research at one American university. Apparently, some songs contain a feature called an 'ear worm' – the term comes from a German word. An ear worm is a tiny piece of music of between 15 and <u>30 seconds</u> that gets stuck in your head and tends to repeat itself. Popular examples include Queen's anthem *We will rock you* and the *Mission Impossible* theme tune. The world of advertising is excited by the possibilities here, so we can expect our heads to be full of ear worms before too long!

Unit 10

10.1 pages 66–67

Speaking

1 The photos show (top) a still from the film *Mission to Mars* and (bottom) a conceptual computer artwork of 'spaceboarders' outside a space hotel orbiting Earth with the moon in the background. The hotel is constructed from used Space Shuttle fuel tanks.

Reading

2 Start by reading the title and opening paragraph, as this part of a newspaper or magazine article often holds many clues to the overall subject matter. In Paper 1 Part 6, the first paragraph does not contain a gap, but you should read it carefully for content clues.

NASA is government-owned whereas the SFF is encouraging private enterprise. NASA is seen as elitist, while the SFF wants to open up mass space travel. NASA doesn't share the SFF's belief in space tourism.

3

1 D   2 G   3 B   4 F   5 C   6 E

Vocabulary

4

b settlement   c commercial   d achievement   e endlessly
f inappropriate   g willingness   h affordable
i scientific   j impressive

5 Negative prefixes such as these are tested in Paper 1 Reading and Use of English.

a illegal   b inexperienced   c irresponsible   d immoral
e irregular   f impatient

6

a impatient   b inexperienced   c illegal   d irregular

Speaking

7

Possible answers
a I don't think I'd ever dream of taking a holiday in space because I would miss my family so much. I'd be scared of never seeing them again.
b If space travel was developed commercially, people would be able to travel long distances in a very short time. A drawback might be the additional pollution created.
c No, I don't think it's right for governments to pay for space exploration at the moment, because there are so many other problems in society that require funding.
d Satellites are necessary in the modern world – our communication networks depend on them. I think they will continue to be important for many years to come.

10.2 pages 68–69

Review of future tenses

1

a future simple   b *going to* future   c future continuous
d future perfect   e *going to* future
f present simple – *plans to*
g present simple – *is due to*

2

1 (prediction) a, b, c
2 (planned event) f, g
3 (event that has not yet happened) d
4 (intention) e

3

Both examples use modal verbs to talk about future prediction – *might* is also used in this way.

4

The sentence contains reported speech. David Ashford's words were probably 'Space tourism will begin ten years after people stop laughing at the concept.' This is then reported as 'once said that space tourism would begin ...'. Unit 13 will be looking at reported speech.

5 The photo shows the International Space Station.

a will fall (not a continuous state)
b won't be (prediction rather than definite truth)
c may (prediction of possible future event)
d will carry (future event + verb not tied to an end date)
e am going to (definite plan for the near future; intention)
f would (reported speech)
g will be living (prediction; future truth)
h will have been (anniversary has not yet happened)

6

1 will have risen   2 will have included
3 will have been filled   4 will have become
5 will have taken

Listening

7

Speakers 1 and 2 express negative views; Speaker 3 is positive.

Recording script 1 15

Speaker 1: I find it quite scary actually. Films like *Bladerunner* could really come true. Imagine a city like Los Angeles in twenty years' time. I mean, it's dangerous now, isn't it – remember the riots? People will be living in run-down buildings, too frightened to come out. Oil supplies will have run out, so there won't be any cars. And with global warming and El Niño, the climate is changing, so the lack of sunlight and pouring rain in the film may well be accurate ... what LA weather will be like.

Speaker 2: I'm reading one of his sci-fi ones at the moment. It all happens way off in the future, thousands of years from now. There are human-<u>like</u> characters, but they're a very sophisticated race – we'll never be as clever as them! They live for at least three hundred years and after that they can choose to live on in a different state. And there's no poverty, no war ... For the human race, this seems impossible – there will always be some country at war with another. I don't see a long-term future for the human race ... even if our planet survives in one piece, we'll have wiped each other out or something.

Speaker 3: Things may be different, but they won't necessarily be any worse. We'll just enter a new phase of our culture, our existence. We've always adapted ... I mean, think of the huge changes with the Industrial Revolution ... why should this be any different? And as for the eco-threat, we're going to have to deal with it somehow, aren't we? I think we will. I can't accept that the human race will cease to be. Call me an optimist, but that's what I feel ...

Vocabulary

8 There are many fixed phrases with *at*. It's good to learn these, as they are often tested in Paper 1.

1 B 2 C 3 A 4 B

Writing folder 5 pages 70–71

Paper 2 Part 2 Articles

1 In the real world, articles are usually read for pleasure or for information. They need to be clearly written and interesting to read. An unusual title leading on to a good opening paragraph encourages the reader to continue. In the exam, these features will impress the examiner!

All four titles are short and succeed in attracting the reader.

2 Paragraph B fails to pick up on the idea of a lifelong ambition. The other three link well to their titles.

A 3-2-1 Lift off! **B** A lifelong ambition
C Aliens are coming ... **D** Is anybody there?

3 Look critically at your writing and try to improve what you have done. Varying your vocabulary like this will get you better marks in the exam.

Sample answer
(D, first stage)
On some nights, I open my window and gaze at the stars. It's a wonderful thing to do. Sometimes I stay there for ages, wondering what the universe holds. It makes me feel humble. Space is a vast place. There are so many galaxies apart from our own – so there must be other life?

a adjectives **b** noun phrase **c** quantifiers **d** adverbs

Sample answer
(D, second stage)
On some beautiful, cloudless nights, I open my window and gaze at the twinkling stars. It's such a wonderful thing to do, so I sometimes stay there for ages, wondering what the universe holds. It makes me feel very humble as space is a truly vast place. There are so many galaxies apart from our own – so there must surely be other forms of life?

4 The improvements suggested on page 71 show why the paragraph is a poor attempt.

Sample answer
It has always been my dream to step on board a shiny, silver rocket and be launched into space. An article which I read recently said space travel may be possible for ordinary people soon. Wouldn't it be wonderful to be one of the first to go? I really hope that I am lucky enough to experience this.

5 In-flight magazines are designed to entertain, so the article shouldn't be too serious.

6
a Future forms of transport; future destinations for holidays.
b More than one kind of transport should be mentioned.
c Given the type of magazine, it should be fairly lively and 'easy to read'.
d Probably four: an opening paragraph; one on transport; one on holidays; a final paragraph.

7 The sample answer below contains no mistakes and would score top marks in the examination, as it is interesting to read, has a good title, and starts and ends well. Note the use of modal verbs to speculate about the future.

Sample answer
TRAVEL TO THE STARS
You are probably reading this on board a jumbo jet, but imagine how you could be travelling and where you might be able to get to on holiday in fifty years' time!

By then, planes could be seen as old-fashioned, with re-usable space rockets being used for holiday destinations instead. Or perhaps someone will have invented a completely new form of transport, capable of travelling faster than the speed of light?

If that ever happens, we will be able to go wherever we want to on holiday – not just within our own solar system, but out to other parts of our galaxy, or even to another galaxy further away. A cheap weekend break might consist of a couple of nights on an orbiting space station, watching the world below.

Just sit back in your seat, close your eyes, and dream of your future. Isn't it exciting!

Unit 11

11.1 pages 72–73

Speaking

1 The photos show Tom Hanks and his son Colin, Madonna and her daughter Lourdes, and Will Smith and his son Jaden.

Listening

3 The underlined parts of the recording script confirm the answers.

1 B	2 B	3 C	4 B	5 A	6 C	7 B

Recording script 1 16

Presenter: So, Hannah, what was it like growing up in Hollywood as an only child, and having such a famous mother?

Hannah: Well, I guess I was pretty privileged as I had things most other kids only dream about. For instance, when I was 14 I just loved Harrison Ford films, and my mother arranged for me and a few friends to go to the film set to see him working on his latest film, as a treat for my birthday. I don't think I was particularly spoilt though, even though I was an only child, and I didn't get into trouble like some of the kids I knew did.

Presenter: You, yourself, are an actress now. Did she ever try to put you off acting?

Hannah: Not at all. Just the opposite. She felt I should follow my feelings, I guess in the same way she had done when she was younger. My grandparents hadn't wanted her to take up acting, you know, especially as she had to move from Europe to Hollywood. I don't think her family took her seriously at first and I think she was quite homesick and felt she could have done with a little more family support.

Presenter: Now, you look very like your mother, don't you?

Hannah: Oh, yes. My mouth, the shape of my face, my jaw line is my mother's. My nose too, but only the tip of it, not the bridge – that is unique, like no one else's in the family. My eyes, my forehead, my colouring, my height are different from my mother's but everyone tells me I look like her. When I say everybody, I mean everybody. People stop me in shops, on the subway, in the street.

Presenter: What does your mother say about this?

Hannah: Well, we both looked in the mirror one day and came to the same conclusion – people exaggerate. Then one day I went into a dress shop. I was alone except for another customer. I thought to myself, 'She looks like my mother.' Then I walked too close to her and crashed into a mirror – the lady was me! I hadn't recognised myself!

Presenter: What qualities do you think your mother possesses?

Hannah: Great physical energy. She used to walk fast, and when she wasn't acting she cleaned and organised the house perfectly. She loved acting more than cleaning; she loved acting most and above all. It took me some time not to feel hurt by this. I wanted to come first. When asked what was the most important thing in her life, she got real embarrassed and nervous, but my mother couldn't lie; she had to say 'acting'; though I know for our sake she wished she could say 'family'. She is terribly practical, and I am too. We consider it one of the greatest qualities in people. We give it the same status as intelligence. Practicality is what made my mother advise me to learn to be an accountant. 'If you know how to do it, you know you'll never be cheated out of any money,' she says. I didn't finish the course as I decided I wanted to act.

Presenter: Did she have any personal experience of being cheated out of money?

Hannah: Well, my mother has always been a very generous person to people she likes. I think another actor who she fell out with started the rumour that she is a bit stingy. She does say that I'm a bit extravagant.

Presenter: Now, you don't sound like your mother, do you?

Hannah: Oh no. She still has a bit of an accent. But her voice is definitely an actress's voice – the clearest speech, the most commanding delivery, and loud. The family used to tell her that she didn't need a phone, she could have just talked to us on the other side of town and we would have heard her. She justifies it with 'I picked it up in the theatre. My voice has to reach all the way to the last row.'

Presenter: Thank you for coming in today to talk to us, Hannah, and good luck in your new film, which I believe is released on Tuesday?

Hannah: Yes, that's right. Thank you.

4

a privileged	b homesick	c unique
d embarrassed and nervous		e being practical
f generous; stingy		g clear, commanding, loud

Grammar extra
Don't confuse these two uses of like:
| What's she like? | Friendly and outgoing. |
| What does she like? | Cream cakes! |
A tall, friendly, amusing
B swimming, hamburgers, watching TV, photography

5

Possible answer
I'm an only child and this has never bothered me very much. I had lots of friends of my age to play with when I was small and didn't seem to have as many arguments as some of my friends who had brothers and sisters did.

6

Possible answer
In my family we all wear glasses and have fair skin which
burns easily in the sun.

11.2 pages 74–75

Vocabulary

1   Use an English–English dictionary to help you with this.

a witty   **b** cheerful   **c** optimistic   **d** jealous   **e** bossy
f unpopular   **g** unreliable   **h** stubborn   **i** impatient
j bad-tempered   **k** aggressive   **l** competitive   **m** loyal
n lazy

2   Sometimes an opposite can be formed by adding a
    negative prefix, sometimes another word is required.
    Revise negative prefixes if necessary (see Exam folder 2,
    page 26).

positive: cheerful, loyal, optimistic, witty
negative: aggressive, bossy, bad-tempered, competitive,
impatient, jealous, lazy, stubborn, unpopular, unreliable

Opposites
a witty – boring
b cheerful – miserable
c optimistic – pessimistic
d jealous – contented
e bossy – easy-going
f unpopular – popular
g unreliable – reliable/dependable
h stubborn – obliging/easy-going /flexible
i impatient – patient
j bad-tempered – good-tempered/easy-going
k aggressive – friendly/submissive
l competitive – unambitious / easy-going
m loyal – disloyal
n lazy – hard-working

3

a out   **b** seriously   **c** turns   **d** for granted   **e** after
f charge   **g** off   **h** account of

4   These verbs are usually connected with our senses.

Possible answers
a It sounds romantic/revolting, etc.
b It smells salty.
c It feels scary/quiet.
d It tastes great/delicious.
e It looks interesting/honest/tempting.
f It feels good/expensive.

5   In A *looked* means 'seemed' or 'appeared', whereas in B
    looked means 'directed her eyes towards' – it is an action.

    In A *feel* means 'experience something physical or
    emotional', whereas in B *felt* means 'touched' – it is an
    action.

Suggested answers
a adjective, e.g. delicious
b adverb, e.g. gently
c adjective, e.g. happy, pleased
d adverb, e.g. carefully/quickly
e adjective, e.g. loud/scary/frightening
f adjective, e.g. expensive
g adverb, e.g. meaningfully
h adverb, e.g. suddenly

Past and present participles

6   Read the Corpus spot; -ed and -ing words are commonly
    confused. Check these endings in your written work, using
    the information on page 170 of the Grammar folder.

If Hannah had said her mother 'became quite embarrassing',
it would mean Hannah was embarrassed by her mother.
1 the past participle -ed
2 the present participle -ing

Speaking

7

Possible answers
a My sister is very irritating. Not only does she borrow my
    things, she never gives them back.
b We both feel moved, and we have a good cry together.
c If people tell me I look like my father, I'm quite pleased.
    He's quite handsome.
d That's very depressing news. I'll miss all my friends so
    much.
e My mother finds that quite amusing, but I feel really
    embarrassed.
f I'm shocked and very pleased, of course, and quite moved
    that she remembered us.
g I'm shocked and worried. My cousin can be very irritating.

Exam folder 6 pages 76–77

Paper 3 Part 1   Short extracts

1   Underline key words in both the question and the options,
    like in the sample answers below.

Sample answers
1 You hear a woman calling a friend.
   What is she doing?
   A confirming an arrangement
   B complaining about a delay
   C apologising for her behaviour
2 You overhear a man and a woman talking about a film
   they have just seen.
   What is the man's opinion of the film?
   A It is longer than necessary.
   B It has a weak storyline.
   C Its actors are disappointing.

2   The underlined parts of the recording script confirm the answers.

| 1 A | 2 C | 3 C | 4 B | 5 C | 6 A | 7 B | 8 A |

Recording script ① 17

You will hear people talking in eight different situations. For questions 1–8, choose the best answer, A, B or C.

Question 1 You hear a woman calling a friend.

Woman: Hi, Lizzie. I thought I'd just give you a ring to let you know about this afternoon. I'm actually getting an earlier flight now as I need to get to Frankfurt for a meeting at four this afternoon rather than for tomorrow morning as planned. Honestly, my boss is driving me mad – he changes plans at the drop of a hat. Anyway, <u>I hope we're still OK to meet for coffee this morning.</u> See you then. It won't take me long to get to the airport as I'm already packed.

Question 2 You hear a man and a woman talking about a film they have just seen.

Woman: Well, that was a long one, wasn't it?

Man: Was it? Seemed normal …

Woman: No, no. That scene at the end should have been cut, if you ask me. I thought Jim Franklin was really good though.

Man: Hmm, <u>I've seen him do better … and that co-star was a weak character</u>, wasn't she? What a shame – the book was absolutely gripping and they haven't changed anything, so you can't criticise the story.

Question 3 You hear a woman describing a music festival.

Woman: It's the fifth time I've been to the festival and the programme was the best ever, with some great headline acts. <u>They put on some excellent workshops as well, which cost us nothing</u> – I went to one on face painting and another on African dance. I was rather disappointed that they moved the event this year, though – we had much less room than before, and the camping spots were a joke! Apart from that, we ate reasonably well, even if we had to have much the same thing night after night! There were far fewer stalls to choose from this year.

Question 4 You hear a man and a woman discussing a skiing holiday they have just been on.

Man: Well that was a great week's skiing, wasn't it? The snow couldn't have been much better.

Woman: I suppose so, but I found it quite hard dealing with those conditions for the first couple of days. I'm not quite as good at skiing as you are, remember.

Man: You did fine. What about the hotel though? I'm not sure I'd go back there again. It was a bit too big and impersonal for me, and the restaurant wasn't anything special.

Woman: Oh, I don't know. The rooms were very comfortable and the pool was fantastic. For me, the only bad thing was the airline schedule, having to get up so early both ways. That was a real pain.

Man: You're right there. Well, perhaps we should take the train next time.

Question 5 You hear this conversation in a hotel.

Receptionist: How may I help you, madam?

Woman: I was on the phone to you from my room just now …

Receptionist: Oh yes. There was something wrong with the phone … Is there a problem with the room? You're in 203, aren't you?

Woman: Yes, I am … it's fine. I was actually ringing about room service – <u>it's taken over forty minutes for them to bring me a simple sandwich and a cup of coffee.</u> Well, I was so appalled, I decided to come down here to have a word with you …

Question 6 You hear this radio report about a football match.

Reporter: Well, Grangewood – Trent United has finished one–nil, after a match that was full of excitement. Grangewood took the lead with Bellamy's early goal, a wonderful return for him after his long absence with that broken leg. <u>A crowd of supporters rushed across to Bellamy</u> when the game was over, glad to see their hero back. The referee tried to stop them but in the end it was the whole Grangewood team who walked off the pitch with their delighted fans.

Question 7 You hear part of an interview on the radio.

Interviewer: So, Duncan, you left a well-paid job in Glasgow to move to this beautiful island off the west coast of Scotland. Was it to escape the pressures of city life?

Duncan: Not really. I grew up in the countryside and I know only too well how quiet it can be – I go back to Glasgow regularly, in fact, to enjoy the fast pace again! The point is, I was trying to write a novel while I was working – you know, weekends, evenings – and I realised I couldn't do both. So I quit and <u>came here to cut costs</u> … at the time I didn't even have a publisher's contract, so it was a risky move.

Question 8 You hear a woman talking about an evening course.

Woman: I've started this astronomy course – two hours a week on a Monday evening. Every week the lecturer shows a short film … we've seen one on the Hubble Space Telescope and another about the Sun. It's useful, although I can't help thinking we could watch those over the internet at home. <u>We have to work out lots of calculations in class and I must say that it's terrific!</u> I thought it would be really hard work, but the time goes by really fast and there's always a break – not that the coffee is anything special! I can't wait to get back to my sums!

Unit 12

12.1 pages 78–79

Speaking

1

> **Possible answers**
> *Student A*
> I don't think people could live without electricity. The second photo shows just how hard life was without it. I couldn't live without a washing machine – to wash all the clothes by hand would take too much time.
>
> *Student B*
> I think that the sports car is obviously quicker and more comfortable than the bike. The bike may be greener and healthier but I think it may be dangerous to have a small child on the back in heavy traffic. I prefer the sports car because it looks so cool.

Reading

2 Skim the text quickly to get an idea of what it is about and then to look at the example question before you do the rest of the exercise.

> **1** E   **2** A   **3** F   **4** C   **5** A   **6** D   **7** B   **8** F   **9** D   **10** C

Vocabulary

3

> | a | celebrating – verb | noun: celebration |
> | b | failed – verb | noun: failure |
> | c | hot – adjective | noun: heat |
> | d | fresh – adjective | noun: freshness |
> | e | various – adjective | noun: variety |
> | f | strong – adjective | noun: strength |
> | g | destroying – verb | noun: destruction |
> | h | industrial – adjective | noun: industry |

12.2 pages 80–81

The passive

1

> | a | active – present perfect |
> | b | past simple **passive** |
> | c | active – past simple |
> | d | present simple **passive** |
> | e | present perfect **passive** |
> | f | modal **passive** |
> | g | past perfect **passive** |
> | h | active – past simple |
> | i | present continuous **passive** |
> | j | **passive** infinitive |

2

> The passive is formed as follows:
>
> | Present simple | *am/are/is* + past participle |
> | Present continuous | *am/are/is being* + pp |
> | Past simple | *was/were* + pp |
> | Past continuous | *was/were being* + pp |
> | Present perfect | *have/has been* + pp |
> | Past perfect | *had been* + pp |
> | *Will* | *will be* + pp |
> | Future perfect | *will have been* + pp |
> | *Going to* | *am/are/is going to be* + pp |
> | Passive infinitive | *(to) be* + pp; *(to) have been* + pp |
>
> The passive is used when the action reported is more important than the people doing the action.

3

> **1** could/would be persuaded/encouraged
> **2** were encouraged/persuaded; have been encouraged/persuaded
> **3** were used
> **4** are (often) filled
> **5** can be talked into
> **6** are (being) supplied
> **7** are dissolved
> **8** (can be) dispersed / (are) dispersed
> **9** (can be) / (are) stored
> **10** will be issued / are going to be issued
> **11** is hoped
> **12** can be made up
> **13** are (constantly) being asked

4 It isn't necessary to use *by* when it can be understood from the meaning.

> **Suggested answers**
> **a** by Spielberg.
> **b** *correct* – (obviously by builders)
> **c** *correct*
> **d** *correct*
> **e** *correct*
> **f** deliberately / by children.

5

> **Suggested answers**
> **a** In a canteen.
> **b** In any public building or on public transport.
> **c** On parking spaces or seats at a club. Somewhere where membership is important.
> **d** On a parcel or packet of biscuits, etc.
> **e** As a headline for a newspaper article.

6

Possible answers

a When I was a child my photo appeared in the local newspaper because my school was involved in a project to raise money for charity.

b More work will be done from home because of improvements in computer software and worsening traffic conditions.

c I'm not quite sure, but it starts with trees being cut down and transported to a mill, where wood pulp is produced and refined to make paper.

d My watch was made in Switzerland, the birthplace of many good watches!

e I was given some DVDs, a new jumper and some credit for my mobile phone.

7

a Many watches are made in Switzerland.

b Gunpowder was invented in China.

c Tutankhamen's tomb was discovered/opened by Lord Carnarvon.

d Satellites were first sent into space in 1957.

e The 2020 Olympic Games will not be held in London.

f Togas were worn by the Romans.

8

1 object to their ideas

2 were those chemicals being mixed

3 was made to hand over

4 is supposed to be

5 was informed of my boss's / his

6 would always be hidden

Corpus spot

a I was **given** a leaflet …

b … which **was built** many years ago.

c My laptop **was** bought for me two months ago.

d This brand **was** established in 1980.

e The meeting **has been** cancelled / **is** cancelled.

f It **is** located in a beautiful area.

g My friend **is** called Cecile …

h In your advertisement **it said** (that) there would be more than this.

Vocabulary

9

a 5   b 4   c 1   d 6   e 7   f 3   g 2

Writing folder 6 pages 82–83

Paper 2 Part 2 Reviews

1 Reviews can be written in formal, neutral or informal register, but should be consistent throughout. Remember to include a balance of information and opinion.

Possible answers

The Simpsons Movie
Good points: funny, exciting, cleverly written
Bad points: none!

2

The writer preferred film A.

3

1 frighteningly realistic

2 excellent acting skills

3 interesting locations

4 fascinating storyline

5 historical events

6 shocking violence

7 tremendous soundtrack

4

a I suggest (that) you **see** this film without delay.

b *correct*

c *correct*

d I **would** advise you not to miss this film.

e *correct*

f I **can / would** recommend this film (to you).

5

Possible answers

a The film is directed by (Pedro Almodovar).

b This wonderful story is set (at the end of the eighteenth century).

c All of the costumes were designed by (students at art college).

d The main character is played by (the French actor Daniel Auteuil).

e The supporting cast have been chosen for (their dancing ability).

f Most of the music was composed by (Ennio Morricone).

g A subtitled version will be shown (in a few weeks' time).

h The screenplay has just been nominated for (an award).

7

Possible answers

comedy: jokes, comedian, laughter, humour

documentary: photography, wildlife, facts, interviews

game show: quiz, questions, points, prize

reality show: celebrities, relationships, lifestyle, conflict

soap opera: drama, script, character, plot, story

8

Sample answer
One of my favourite shows on TV is the comedy series *Frasier*, starring Kelsey Grammer. Although new programmes are no longer being made of this long-running series, it is possible to watch regular repeats.

The key to the programme's success is the sensitive and humorous way in which it shows everyday life. Frasier hosts a radio phone-in show, assisted by his efficient producer Roz Doyle. The supporting cast includes his father Martin, a retired policeman, who lives with Frasier; Martin's amusing (and exceptionally well-trained) dog Eddie; Frasier's younger brother Niles, who has gone through many disappointments in love and yet who finally ends up with the woman of his dreams, Daphne Moon; and Frasier's icy ex-wife Lilith and their son Freddy, who appear on the programme from time to time.

The series is set in Seattle and rarely strays far from this city. In fact, the two main locations are Frasier's apartment and his broadcasting room at the radio station. But the programmes are never dull! What makes this series so remarkable is its scripts, which are tightly written and contain some memorable jokes. I highly recommend this show.

Units 7–12 Revision

pages 84–85

1 The photo shows Kim Basinger in *LA Confidential*.

1 in **2** although/though/while/whilst **3** must/would/might/could **4** be **5** All/Most **6** a **7** because **8** This/It

3 The verbs are *get* and *take*.

a getting **b** takes **c** get **d** getting **e** take **f** got
g take **h** take

4

Suggested answers
a cunning (clever; the other three refer to something bad)
b campaign (an advertising campaign involves many activities; the other three are features of advertisements)
c snowboarding (this is a sport which is usually done outside, the others normally take place inside)
d fancy (means that you like someone or something; the other three verbs mean the opposite)
e shallow ('shallow' describes a small volume, whereas the other adjectives refer to large dimensions)
f sports centre (you can find the other three at a sports centre)
g pretend (deceive; the other three refer to the future in some way)
h extravagant (spending more than is necessary; the other three refer to spending less)

5

a looked **b** get **c** kept **d** switching **e** take **f** work
g put **h** broke

6

A 4 (conclusion) **B** 2 **C** 3 (opening)

Unit 13

13.1 pages 86–87

Speaking

1

Possible answer
The classroom on the left is more informal, with students working in small groups or using a computer on their own. They aren't wearing a school uniform. The other classroom is more formal, with students in uniform sitting in rows. Their teacher is walking round the class rather than standing up at the front, which makes the lesson feel a bit more relaxed.

Background information

It is compulsory for children to attend school in Britain between the ages of 5 and 18. There are both state and private schools. For younger children some nursery education is offered by the state and the government has promised more money for this; there is a large private nursery sector.

2

Possible answers
a My secondary school was fairly small by today's standards. There were around 450 students aged 11–18. It was in the centre of Bristol, in a 200-year-old building with beautiful gardens. There weren't many discipline problems and the atmosphere felt quite purposeful – you knew you were expected to work hard from day one.
b There's one history teacher I remember particularly well. She was an excellent teacher and really brought history to life, but it's her appearance I remember so vividly. Her clothes were always colour-coordinated. One day she wore a navy blue suit with red stripes on the jacket collar and skirt, red shoes and handbag, blue stockings and bright red lipstick. For some reason that day she ended up with blue ink around her mouth – so everything about her was either red or blue. It looked so funny.
c Although I'm not terribly good at painting, I really enjoyed spending time in the art room. It was at the top of some creaky old stairs and was a wonderfully light and airy room, where you could be as creative as you liked – the teacher was always encouraging, no matter how daft your ideas were.

d There was one science teacher I didn't get on with at all. She seemed to have it in for me the whole time and, unlike the other science teachers, her lessons were really boring – everybody said so.

3

David said that he wanted to describe what had really happened. He had been inside the classroom during break and he had seen a group of his friends outside. He had gone over to the window and (had) tried to get their attention. He had waved at them but they hadn't seen him, so he had hammered on the window. He said he knew glass was/is* breakable but he just hadn't thought. When his hand had gone through, he had panicked. He hadn't been badly hurt and he had wanted to avoid getting into trouble, so he had put Simon's bag over the hole and had left the room. He said he was sorry he hadn't told anyone the truth until then / that moment.
* Because it is a fact that glass is breakable, the present tense can also be used here.

Listening

4 The underlined parts of the recording script confirm the answers.

a T	b T	c F	d F	e T	f T	g F	h T

Recording script 2 02

Interviewer: With me now are Sandra Wilson and Mike Tripp. Mike is owner of a successful new travel company, Just Trips, and Sandra works for him as Publicity Manager. They were actually in the same class at school, though at that time, they did *not* get on with each other! They met again by chance last year, when Sandra went for an interview at Just Trips and was surprised to find Mike across the table. Sandra, when you were at school, did you think Mike would become successful like this?

Sandra: To be honest, no one thought Mike would get anywhere – <u>he was the original under-achiever! That's why we didn't get on.</u> My group of friends were quite hard-working – you know, we did all the homework, made an effort in class – but Mike was the complete opposite. <u>He was bad news, actually.</u>

Interviewer: Is this true, Mike?

Mike: I'm afraid so. I wasn't the only one though. It was ... uncool for boys to work, a whole group of us were like that. I don't remember being especially horrible to Sandra ...

Sandra: <u>Talk about a selective memory!</u>

Interviewer: Why?

Sandra: Well, he would regularly do annoying things like stealing my ruler or hiding my books. You saw it as a big joke, I suppose, Mike?

Mike: Never thought about it. <u>I can see now that I might have been a bit ... a bit of a nuisance.</u>

Sandra: I've forgiven you though!

Interviewer: And you've done very well since, Mike ...

Mike: Yeah. I got on with my life. Um ... <u>I don't really regret my behaviour back then</u> – obviously I shouldn't have made trouble for you, Sandra – but for myself, it didn't matter ... <u>I've done OK in spite of school.</u>

Sandra: *You* have, Mike, but there are lots of others in your gang who didn't make it.

Mike: Mmm ... I can think of one or two ... But I still think, if you know what you want out of life, you'll get there. I mean, look at me, I didn't pass many exams ... <u>I even walked out of some, like science ... wrote my name at the top of the paper and thought, I can't do this</u> ... oh, what the heck, the sun's shining, I'm off.

Sandra: Incredible! I was totally stressed out during exams, spent hours revising, and Mike managed to fail virtually everything and still be successful.

Interviewer: Should you have been more relaxed at school, Sandra?

Sandra: That's easy to say now. I had a lot of pressure on me to do well. My parents, my brothers ... all my family expected ... the best.

Mike: <u>Same here. But my dad sort of looked beyond school. He knew I'd be OK – he'd left school himself at 14 and he always felt that I'd sort things out for myself, somehow.</u>

Interviewer: And how *did* you get the company started? No careers advice from school, I imagine?

Mike: <u>Careers teachers? They didn't have a clue!</u> I got things started in a small way while I was still at school, actually – I used to help out in a local travel agency, buying and selling cheap tickets on the phone. In my final year, I sometimes spent my lunchtimes checking the internet on the school computer. I found some good deals for flights, that I managed to sell on. Then, <u>when I left school, my dad gave me a bit of money and I set up an office</u> ... and it all ... like ... took off.

Interviewer: So school did help you a little ... or its facilities did?

Mike: Yeah ...

Interviewer: OK, well we'll have to leave it there. One final thing, Mike. Why did Sandra get the job?

Mike: Oh, university education, languages, a good communicator – she's great, just what the company needed.

Sandra: All thanks to school, Mike.

Vocabulary

5 If you try to learn words in word families, it will help you to extend your vocabulary.

a educate	b educated	c educational

6

educational + qualifications, opportunities, standards
(a, c, d)
educated + person (b)
The adjective educational is much more frequent than
educated and can be used with a number of nouns. The
ones included in this exercise are among the most frequent
collocations for educational. Educated is used to describe
people, and can be qualified by an adverb or noun or proper
noun, for example highly/well educated, university educated,
Harvard educated, etc.

8

A Tom Cruise   B Paul Gauguin   C Annie Lennox
D Socrates   E Madonna   F Agatha Christie

9

Useful words and phrases include:
(A) earn/make in a day
(B) have (a) talent for, determination
(C) On leaving school ..., find employment
(D) gain experience, spend x years ..., full-time career
(E) work long hours
(F) take a position, unpaid assistant, qualify in, duties,
a sound knowledge of, extremely relevant

13.2 pages 88–89

Reporting

1 Read the section in the Grammar folder on page 171, if you
   have not already done so.

In **a**, there is 'backshift' in the reported statement. Greg's
actual statement contained a present and a future tense; in
reported speech, the present tense can't has become a past
tense couldn't, and will has become would.

In **b**, there is similar backshift from the past simple to the
past perfect in the reported statement.

In **c**, the reported statement uses the present because the
situation reported continues to be true.

2

a 3   b 4   c 1   d 2

3 Refer to the Corpus spot. Reporting verbs and their various
   structures are commonly tested in Paper 1 Part 4. Also, if
   you use them correctly in Paper 2 Writing, you are likely to
   impress the examiner.

apologise (+ to someone) + for + -ing   e.g. She apologised to
me for forgetting my birthday.
argue + for / against + noun or -ing; argue + that   e.g. The
students argued against wearing school uniform / argued that
school uniforms were unnecessary.
claim + that (optional)   e.g. He claimed (that) the river had
been polluted by factory waste.

deny + that (optional); deny + -ing e.g. She denied (that) she
had taken the money. / She denied taking the money.
explain (+ to someone) + that (optional)   e.g. We explained
(to them) (that) we had lost their phone number.
insist + on + -ing; insist + that (optional)   e.g. They insisted on
paying for our lunch. / They insisted (that) they wouldn't leave
without seeing the manager.
promise + that (optional); promise + to infinitive   e.g. She
promised (me) (that) she would write to me every day. / She
promised to write to me every day.
refuse + to infinitive   e.g. I refused to listen to his excuses.
say + that (optional); in passive, 'is said' + to infinitive   e.g.
He said that he needed a holiday. / He is said to be one of the
world's greatest athletes.
suggest + that (optional); suggest + -ing   e.g. They suggested
(that) we meet at the café. / They suggested meeting at the café.
urge + someone + to infinitive; urge + that   e.g. I urged him
to tell his parents.
warn (+ someone) + that (optional); + (not) to infinitive   e.g.
I warned them (that) it was dangerous to swim here. /
I warned them not to swim here.

Listening

4 Underline key words to help you predict content.

5

1 are   2 need   3 are affected
Speaker 1: statement F

Recording script 2 03

Speaker 1: I'm a retired head teacher and I want to make
two points. First, I know from my own experience that
teachers <u>tend to be</u> female ... and I believe we need to
get more men into all our schools – boys need men
around as role models, from an early age. My second
point is linked to this. There is a growing problem
of broken marriages and one-parent families, which
affects all children but especially boys, because they
usually end up living with their mothers and having less
contact with their fathers. Men are so important to boys'
development.

6 Notice how many different reporting verbs have been used
   in the answers below.

Possible answers
Speaker 2: statement E
She said that when boys and girls start school, they are both
keen to learn.
She complained that parents don't help boys at home.
She insisted that basic skills have to be introduced in the
home.

Speaker 3: statement A
He suggested discussing society rather than just schools.
He explained that as society has changed so much, boys
don't have clear goals any more.
He claimed that girls, in contrast, have a lot to aim for.

Speaker 4: statement H

She explained that girls' brains develop differently to boys' at a young age.

She warned that in Britain education is too formal at the beginning.

She urged that nursery education should be extended to the age of six in Britain.

Speaker 5: statement B

He insisted on the recent achievement by girls being seen as a good thing.

He argued that this was not true ten years ago.

He suggested that this is part of more equal opportunities nowadays.

Recording script 2 04

Speaker 2: Well, I'm an infant teacher and I work with children from the age of four. Both boys and girls arrive at school interested and excited on day one. But I find during that first year that I can't get the parents of boys to help their children at home. They expect their boys to be out playing football after school, not sitting at home reading a book. Basic skills have to be introduced in the home, and because the girls' parents do this, the girls <u>race ahead</u>. Then the boys feel they're failing, so they start <u>mucking about</u>, and things go from bad to worse.

Speaker 3: Can I widen the topic beyond schools? Society has changed radically in the last twenty years and fathers are no longer the <u>bread-winners</u>, necessarily. Indeed, the average boy growing up now may see a lot of men who are unemployed ... and of course he's going to look at that and say, 'What's the point? There's no future for me.' Girls, on the other hand, now see lots of opportunities and they want to get out there and compete, get to the top. We haven't <u>faced up to</u> this, and yet it was obviously going to happen.

Speaker 4: <u>Picking up on</u> what the infant teacher said, I've always understood the brain develops differently in boys and girls, so girls aged four develop quickly, whereas boys take longer to get going. For boys especially, I think we formalise education too soon in Britain. I can find no other examples in the world where formal teaching starts so early. I believe we should <u>extend</u> nursery education to the age of six, so that there is more time for play, for discovery ... and above all, language. Then by the age of six, boys would be ready for formal learning.

Speaker 5: I think we should <u>give credit to</u> what has happened ... I mean, it's a success story for girls, isn't it? OK, so girls are now achieving better results at school than boys ... which is great. It was not the case twenty years ago ... even ten years ago. For the last three years, more girls have gained university places than boys ... good for them. I think this is all part of the wider picture of equal opportunities and we should view it positively.

7 The answers are underlined in the script above.

a tend (to be)   **b** race ahead   **c** mucking about
d bread-winners   **e** faced up to   **f** picking up on
g extend   **h** give credit to

Grammar extra

a why girls are/were gaining more university places.
b in what ways the situation had been different twenty years ago.
c if/whether things would get better in the future.
d if/whether British children should spend more time at nursery school.
e why we hadn't faced up to this problem.

8 **Think about each group in turn and note down some discussion points if you are studying on your own. A few ideas are given below.**

Parents could spend more time reading to young children and encouraging older ones to focus on their homework.
Teachers might offer extra lessons free of charge after school, or attend professional development workshops.
The media could support educational initiatives and publicise examples of best practice.
The government might spend more money upgrading schools and increase teachers' salaries.
Local companies could fund special projects at their local schools or invite students on work experience programmes.

9 **Decide on the two groups and summarise your choices in writing.**

10

1 accused Charlie of putting
2 warned Johnny not to misbehave / warned Johnny to stop misbehaving
3 urged them not to fall
4 (that) she had not / hadn't wasted
5 if/whether they had tidied up
6 apologised for forgetting

Exam folder 7 pages 90–91

Paper 3 Part 3 Multiple matching

1 **Study the example, recording script and explanation carefully.**

Recording script 2 05

You will hear the first speaker talking about his experience of education. Look at the statements A–H and decide which one is true for the first speaker.

Speaker 1: When I started my last year at school, I didn't take it seriously enough. <u>I should've chosen subjects which were useful rather than ones I liked or that sounded easy</u>. By the time the exams came, I'd given up and I did very badly. I knew I'd have to work hard but I wasn't able to catch up with my friends. Because I failed at science, I can't be a teacher, which is what I really want to do. I'm doing a part-time job in order to make ends meet and next year I'll be starting evening classes to get better qualifications.

2 Cover the recording script while you listen and answer the questions.

2 F 3 D 4 H 5 A

Recording script 2 06

Speaker 2: I left school and moved to a college to take my final exams. It was the best decision I could have made. <u>At the college nobody seemed to care about homework and this really motivated me. I had to plan my work myself – there was no one to make you do it and no one to check up on what you'd done.</u> I was still dependent on my parents for money – but that was OK. I learned a lot about real life there – things like getting on with people and organising your time, which has been really useful now I'm working.

Speaker 3: When I left school, I didn't have a particular career in mind so I decided to do Environmental Studies at university, mainly because I'd enjoyed geography at school. I didn't really like the course at university and I did think about leaving, but instead I changed courses, which was easier than I expected. I think university was useful in that I learnt how to live alone and <u>how to budget, and as I'm an underpaid teacher now, that really helps</u>.

Speaker 4: I had no difficulty choosing what I was going to do – my parents are both doctors and ever since I was small I also wanted to do that. They really encouraged me and I did well at school and got into a good medical school fairly easily. <u>It was surprisingly tough at medical school,</u> but I had some good friends and we pulled through together. I think the doubts only began to set in when I graduated and got my first job in a hospital. I began to wonder if I'd missed out because I'd been so focused on becoming a doctor. So now I'm doing some voluntary work in Africa, which I'm really enjoying.

Speaker 5: I decided to take a year off after doing my last year at school. I'd had enough of revising and sitting in a library, so I decided to go off to Australia for nine months and earn a bit of money. I've got relatives there who put me up when I first arrived and found me a job. It wasn't doing anything particularly interesting, <u>but the great part was that I was getting to know people who were completely different to the ones I'd known back home.</u> I really recommend taking a year out, but you need to have a firm plan or it could end up a waste of time.

3 The parts which give the answer are underlined in the script above.

Unit 14

14.1 pages 92–93

Speaking

1 The jobs shown are a restorer of ancient pottery (left) and members of a Formula One technical support team (right).

Possible answer

Well, these are very different jobs – one in motor-racing and the other working in a museum or a university, maybe. Being a member of the technical support team, you'd have to be strong physically, able to work fast under pressure and as part of a team. On the other hand, restoring ancient pottery, as the woman is doing, is very specialised work. It takes a long time, so you would need to have a specialised knowledge of archaeology, and to be patient, have good eyesight and steady hands, and enjoy working on your own – be self-motivated.

I'd like to do the job in motor-racing rather than be shut away in a dusty old museum somewhere. It must be so exciting to work at a Grand Prix!

2

a secure   **b** flexible; adventurous   **c** concerned

Reading

3

1 A   2 B   3 D   4 E   5 C   6 A   7 D   8 D   9 C   10 E

4

Possible answers
a She had been doing the job for too long; her life felt empty outside work; she was getting fed up with the travelling.
b She wouldn't have been familiar with the latest equipment; she wouldn't have been able to handle the financial side of farming.
c She doesn't have a regular salary; she works irregular hours.

Vocabulary

5

a disorganised   **b** impatient   **c** unsuccessful
d dishonest   **e** irresponsible

Grammar extra

All is a very common word in English and is used in many expressions. Try to use the ones given in your writing.

a	= had everything
b	*used for emphasis*
c	= from the beginning
d	*used with a superlative for emphasis*
e	= suddenly
f	= despite
g	= on balance; *used to summarise after different things have been considered*
h	= more than anything

Look at the example and its use of *whole*. Sometimes it is possible to use both *all* and *the whole*, although other words may have to be added to *all* to make the expression fit grammatically. For example, you can say *all the class bought the book / all of the class bought the book / the whole class bought the book* but if you use *all* with a pronoun, you must use *of*, as in *all of us bought the book*.

1 all (of the) **2** the whole (of the) **3** The whole (of the)
4 all **5** all / the whole; all of **6** all (of)
Refer to the Grammar folder on page 172.

14.2 pages 94–95
Perfect tenses

1

Sentence **a** says that the person has sent no emails (neither in the past nor in the present).
Sentence **b** only refers to the past and doesn't tell us whether the situation is still true.
Sentence **c** tells us that the person started to send emails at some point in the past but before that time had never sent any.
Sentence **d** forecasts a future situation at a certain time.
a present perfect
b past simple
c past perfect; past simple
d future perfect

2

1 b **2** f, h **3** h **4** c, e, a **5** a **6** g **7** d

The future perfect continuous tense has not been exemplified. Example: *John will have been driving a taxi for thirteen years next April.*

3

a have been showing **b** was voted **c** has been studying
d will have been working **e** had feared
f will have been launched **g** has made
h had been waiting

Corpus spot

a I felt very sorry after I **had seen** your report.
b Some months ago he **directed** a movie.
c *correct*
d For thousands of years our civilisation **has been making** progress.
e When I left your house in Ljubljana, I **decided** to visit the lakes.
f Some friends of mine **were working** there last summer.
g *correct*
h The Astrid Hotel **has been closed** since last year.

Listening

4 The skills mentioned are given below. Other useful skills or qualifications would be: effective communicator (1), degree in languages/translation and interpreting (2), good at selling (3), life-saving qualification (4), creative/imaginative (5).

The underlined parts of the recording script confirm the answers.

Speaker 1 (office administrator): flexible; (have) commitment; not mind working long hours
Speaker 2 (interpreter): keen on languages; speaks three languages; fluent; dealing with people face to face; a talent for communication; think really fast; confidence; positive
Speaker 3 (shop assistant): dress well; know a lot about ...; handle pressure
Speaker 4 (first-aid worker): get a first-aid qualification; (have) lots of energy; extremely fit; specialise in
Speaker 5 (cook): cope with working at speed; being better organised; staying in control

Recording script 2 07

Speaker 1: There's a big music festival in my town every summer. For the last three years, I've worked in the festival office, doing a whole range of things, from putting leaflets in envelopes to arranging hotel bookings for the various performers. I know I'm <u>flexible</u> – I've had to be – and I've definitely <u>got commitment</u> – <u>I don't mind working long hours</u> as long as there's an end in sight! I really enjoy big events, too – the more people there are, the more enjoyable it is!

Speaker 2: I've always been <u>interested in languages</u>. My mother's from Quebec in Canada, so we <u>speak both German and French</u> at home. I've been <u>learning English</u> since I was 12. By next summer, I'll have been learning it for over ten years, so I'm sure I'll be really <u>fluent</u>. I like <u>dealing with people face to face</u> and people say I've got quite a lot of <u>talent for communication</u>. I can <u>think really fast</u>, which gives me <u>a lot of confidence</u>. Oh, and I'm a <u>very positive person</u> too!

Speaker 3: I've been working in The Gap since I left college last year. I think I <u>dress well</u> myself – that's important when you're in this sort of job. I <u>know a lot about</u> sports and leisure clothing, and I often get asked for advice when people are choosing what to buy. Once you've worked in a busy clothing store you <u>can handle anything</u> – I <u>don't mind pressure</u>, in fact it's usually a good thing – makes the day go more quickly.

Speaker 4: I'm having a year off between school and medical school. At the moment I'm doing part-time voluntary work in a hospital. I've also been going to evening classes to <u>get a first-aid qualification</u>, which I've just managed to get. I've <u>got lots of energy</u> and I like to think I'm <u>extremely fit</u>. My boyfriend thinks I'm obsessed with sport, actually – I swim for a club and I play tennis or basketball whenever I get the chance. I'd like to <u>specialise in</u> sports medicine when I'm older.

Speaker 5: I did a one-year course in catering after leaving school, and since then I've been working alongside one of Edinburgh's top chefs. She's taught me so much – not just recipes and techniques, either. The most important thing I've learned is how to <u>cope with working at speed</u>. It can get very busy some evenings, but through her, I've developed ways of <u>being better organised</u> ... er ... <u>staying in control</u> when it gets really hot in the kitchen.

6

The article is written for office workers.

1. have shrunk
2. has brought
3. have been set up
4. has been growing
5. have ceased
6. have become
7. have been putting in
8. have shown
9. has found
10. will have been given
11. will have been claiming
12. have rambled on / have been rambling on

Writing folder 7 pages 96–97

Paper 2 Part 2 Letters of application

Applications require formal register and a clear layout, with suitable paragraphing. You do not need to include postal addresses, even if they are given in the job advertisement on the question paper. Remember to say at the beginning why you are writing, quoting any reference number or title of the job. It is important to 'sell' yourself to the reader, explaining in detail why you are the right person.

1 Many of these words have already come up in Units 13 and 14.

motivated   committed   determined   cheerful
enthusiastic   energetic   organised   talented
skilled/skilful   confident

2

Skills and qualities include: cheerfulness, energy, self-confidence, fluency in English, some experience of bar/restaurant work.

3

Letter A has covered all the points.

Letter B has omitted to talk about his knowledge of English. The letter is thin on relevant experience and on the reason why he would like the job. It is also thin on personal qualities and what is said would probably irritate the reader. The letter is also inappropriately informal and its tone is too colloquial/chatty.

4

Corrected and improved letter

Dear Sir or Madam

I have seen your advertisement for restaurant and bar staff on your Cool Blue Cruise ships in the Mediterranean and would like to apply. I have travelled around the Mediterranean myself and find its history and culture fascinating. I'm sure I could share my knowledge with your on-board guests, as I am a fluent English speaker.

Although I haven't worked on a cruise ship before, I do have extensive experience of bar work and am able to mix a wide range of cocktails. I have also worked in a beach café, serving meals and snacks. I realise that your own restaurants will probably have a more formal atmosphere, but I am quick to learn new skills and would enjoy working in this type of restaurant.

I have lots of energy, so the idea of working long hours doesn't worry me. My previous employers have always found me cheerful, committed and honest. Finally, I think it is important to tell you that I have never suffered from seasickness.

I look forward to hearing from you soon.

Yours faithfully

Harry Lime

5 Make a paragraph plan before you start writing.

Sample answer

Dear Sir or Madam

I am writing to apply for the job of tour guide with Europewide Coach Tours, which was advertised in 'The Times' last Saturday. I am just the person you are looking for.

I have been studying English for twelve years, so I am fluent. I recently spent three months in London, as part of my studies. I also speak French and a little German.

Although I know many parts of Europe well, I am always keen to visit new places and find out more about them. It would be good to share this knowledge with others.

People say I am a good communicator and I enjoy being with other people. I have a good sense of humour and plenty of energy.

In terms of relevant experience, I have spent the last two summers working as a guide, taking groups of foreign tourists on walking tours around our city. I therefore have a good understanding of the needs of visitors from other countries.

I hope you will consider my application favourably.

Yours faithfully

Unit 15

15.1 pages 98–99

Speaking

1 The photos show

1 tourists at the Pyramid of the Sun (Piramide del Sol), Teotihuacan Archaeological Site, Mexico
2 tourists at Stonehenge, UK
3 tourists in St Mark's Square, Venice
4 a Nepalese sherpa collecting garbage, left by climbers, at an altitude of 8,000 metres during the Everest clean-up expedition at Mount Everest. (In 2010 a group of 20 Nepalese climbers braved thin air and below freezing temperatures in a high-risk expedition to clear around two tonnes of rubbish left behind by mountaineers.)

Possible answers

Yes, I once visited the Pyramids and was really disappointed to find that the city of Cairo is so close. I imagined it being right out in the desert, miles away from civilisation.
I think tourists cause a lot of problems. They drop litter and the streets become overcrowded. Also they wear down paths in the countryside.

Photos 1 and 2
I think that tourists would be unhappy not to be able to climb or touch the monuments. I think that climbing up the pyramid would give you a real feel for the place. However, I understand why Stonehenge is closed off – it's to protect it.

Photos 3 and 4
I would imagine local people are fed up with all the tourists in Venice, even though they benefit financially from them.
Mt Everest is a sacred mountain for most Nepalese, so they are probably horrified by the amount of litter left by the climbers.

Listening

2 The underlined parts of the recording script confirm the answers.

1 northwestern   2 1.6 kms / kilometres   3 1919
4 5m / million   5 free buses   6 air pollution   7 water
8 7 / seven degrees   9 fish   10 (seven/7 natural) wonders

Recording script 2 08

Presenter: Situated in the <u>northwestern</u> part of Arizona, the Grand Canyon is one of the natural wonders of the world. Contrary to popular belief, the Grand Canyon is not the longest, deepest or widest canyon in the world. But it is accessible, and with little vegetation to hide it, it feels big. Nothing prepares you for that first sight of it. From the top it drops <u>1.6 kilometres</u> to the desert floor below. But however vast it seems, it is not big enough to support the millions of people who visit it every year.

When one section of the Grand Canyon was declared a national park in <u>1919</u>, three years after the creation of the National Park Service, visitor numbers were 44,000. Today, with <u>five million</u> visitors a year, the Park Service is finding it difficult to keep the Canyon accessible to the public and to safeguard it for future generations.

The pressures on the Grand Canyon National Park forced the Park Service to draw up a management plan. One of the first problems it tackled was that of the large number of visitors' cars which needed parking space. The Park Service got around the problem by allowing visitors to take advantage of <u>free buses</u>, which take them on a number of routes around the park.

Some of the other problems faced by the park are the result of things happening outside its boundaries. Take <u>air pollution</u>. On summer days, when there are southwesterly winds, the pollution blown in from Southern California can restrict the views over the Canyon.

Then, another of the big problems is the availability of water resources in the park, as, at present, there is a drought. The Park cannot draw water from the river but only from a spring on the north side of the canyon, using a pipeline. If this pipeline is damaged, then <u>water</u> has to be brought in by truck. This last happened in 1995 when floods caused a landslide, which destroyed the pipeline.

The Colorado river, which created the Canyon, looks wild but in fact is managed intensely. Twenty-four kilometres upstream is the Glen Canyon Dam, which has had a profound impact on the river. Now the river flow is about a tenth of what it was previously.

The Colorado used to reach temperatures of 27 degrees in summer. Today, it is a cold <u>7 degrees</u> all year, as water release comes from deep within the reservoir. In addition, the rapids are getting bigger, as the river is too weak to move the boulders washed out of the canyons downstream. As a result of both these problems, some species of <u>fish</u> have become extinct.

Visitors are proving to be powerful allies of the park. Those who once thought that the Grand Canyon was just an awesome hole in the ground soon learn that however big it is, its popularity is in danger of destroying the very qualities that made it one of the seven natural wonders in the world.

Vocabulary

3

> *dam* – a man-made barrier on a river which forms a lake behind it, usually to provide hydroelectric energy or conserve water
> *floods* – a large amount of water covering land which is normally dry
> *rapids* – the place in a river where there are a lot of large stones or boulders and therefore the water flows much faster
> *reservoir* – a man-made lake which is built to provide a source of water for a town or city
> *river* – a large natural stream of water emptying into an ocean, lake or another river.
> A pond is much smaller than a lake.
> A stream is much smaller than a river.
> A canal is artificial (man-made), whereas a river is natural.
> A waterfall is where a river flows over very high rocks and drops to a lower level, whereas rapids are where a river flows between small to medium-sized rocks in the river itself, and so the flow of water is much faster there.

4

adjective	noun	adverb	verb
long	length	lengthily	lengthen
weak	weakness	weakly	weaken
deep	depth	deeply	deepen
strong	strength	strongly	strengthen
wide	width	widely	widen
short	shortness	shortly	shorten
warm	warmth	warmly	warm

5

1 chemical	2 surroundings	3 unwanted	4 poisonous
5 scientists	6 reduction(s)	7 electricity	
8 economical NOT economic			

Speaking

6

Possible answers
a They can separate paper, plastic and glass from their normal rubbish and recycle it.
b The council could ban cars from the city centre to cut down on pollution.
c I don't have a problem with it – some of my favourite outfits are from second-hand shops!
d There could be large fines for dropping litter – but I also think there should be more rubbish bins in the city centre.

e Fairly, yes – I usually take a shower rather than having a bath, and I always switch off electrical appliances when I'm not using them.
f It depends – I like walking, so it wouldn't worry me much, unless I had to get somewhere quickly, or it was pouring with rain!
g That's a hard one! I know we should all try to eat more locally produced food, and I do, but exotic fruit from South America is such a treat, especially in winter.

7

Recording script 2 09
Measurement
thirteen kilometres
thirty centimetres
nought point five kilometres
two point five metres
a hundred and fifty-three kilos
one metre, fifty-three centimetres
a half
a quarter
two thirds
Dates
the first of May, eighteen ninety-nine
the third of August, two thousand
the twelfth of February, two thousand and four
the sixth of September, twenty sixteen
the twenty-fifth of December, nineteen ninety
the fifteenth century
the fourth of the fifth, eleven
Money
ten p or ten pence
one pound forty-five
fifty dollars
twenty euros, thirty cents
'0'
oh one two, three two three, double six, double seven, eight
three nil
forty love
zero or nought degrees Celsius
Telephone numbers
oh one two five six, three double one, three double nine
oh oh four four, three two four, double six seven oh one two
Maths
two plus six equals eight
three minus two equals one
four times four equals sixteen
ten divided by two equals five
twenty per cent
three degrees
the square root of sixteen

15.2 pages 100–101

Countable and uncountable nouns

1   Read the Corpus spot. Always check your written work and remember that *advice*, *information*, *luggage* and *furniture* never have an 's', because they are uncountable.

Countable: note, meal, recommendation, journey, job, coin, storm, verb, vehicle, seat, hairstyle, suitcase, mountain.

These words can be both countable [C] and uncountable [U]:
work: [U] the activities you do as part of your job, e.g. *I've got a lot of work to get through today.* [C] a painting, book, piece of music, e.g. *the works of Shakespeare*
travel: [U] going from one place to another, e.g. *I've always loved travel.* [C] journeys of exploration, e.g. *We learnt about the travels of Marco Polo.*
temperature: [C] *We had temperatures of minus 20 degrees last winter.* [U] *There was a sudden rise in temperature yesterday.*
hair: [U] *She has long, curly hair.* [C] an individual hair on the body or head, e.g. *There was a blond hair on her jacket.*
land: [U] area of ground, e.g. *The land was rich and fertile.* [C] a country, *e.g. the tribal lands of the Maori people*
country: [C] an area of land that has its own government, e.g. *Brazil is the largest country in Latin America.* [U] land which is not in towns and is used for farming or left in a natural state, e.g. *I'd rather live in the country than in a city.*

2   Look at the information about determiners before you do this exercise.

a   How **many** of the tourists actually **realise** the problems they cause?
b   Little of the **soil** can be used for cultivation now the trees have been cut down.
c   A large **amount** of equipment **is** needed to camp at the bottom of the Canyon.
d   Only **a small amount of luggage** can be carried on the back of a donkey down the dirt tracks.
e   A large amount of rainforest **is** being cut down every year.
f   The amount of traffic **is** causing too much **congestion** in major cities.
g   **Many** governments **believe** that nuclear power **is** the key to future energy problems.
h   The Park Ranger gave me **a lot of / a great deal of** good **advice** about camping in the national park.
i   **Few** people nowadays wear fur coats.

3

few mistakes – not many mistakes, = I'm good at English.
a few mistakes – a number of mistakes, = I'm quite good at English, but I still make mistakes.
little time – I'm really too busy.
a little time – I do have some time, but it's not very much.

Grammar extra
Some is used with an affirmative verb, for offers and if the answer to a question is going to be 'yes'.
No is used with an affirmative verb to give a negative meaning.
Any is used with a negative verb and in questions; also when the answer to a question may be 'no'.
Any can be used to mean 'all of them and it's not important which'.

Vocabulary

4

a shower of rain
a slice of cake
an item of clothing
a glass of water
a clap of thunder
a pane of glass
a ball of string
a flash of lightning
a crowd of people
a bar of chocolate

5

a   some; bars
b   any/some; flashes
c   Some / A few / Many / Most / Lots; panes
d   hair
e   some advice/information
f   any coins
g   suitcase; luggage

6

1 few	**2** ago	**3** in	**4** deal/amount
5 Although/Though	**6** of	**7** which/that	**8** one

Exam folder 8 pages 102–103

Paper 3 Part 4   Multiple choice

2   The underlined part of the recording script confirms the answers.

The answer is C. A is wrong because she had enjoyed the journey and was excited. B is wrong because she wasn't worried about changing planes.

Recording script 2 10

You will hear a radio interview with a girl called Lisa Greene, who is talking about her stay at an ecolodge, an environmentally friendly hotel in Costa Rica, Central America. For questions 1–7, choose the best answer (A, B or C).

Interviewer: I'd like to welcome Lisa Greene to the studio today. Lisa, you won a competition in a magazine to stay at an ecolodge – an environmentally friendly hotel – in Costa Rica, didn't you?

Lisa: That's right. I had to write an article about recycling and why it is a good thing for the planet.

Interviewer: You hadn't travelled outside of Europe before – how did you feel about the journey?

Lisa: Well, I flew to Costa Rica from London and then had to take a small plane to an airport very near the ecolodge. I was then picked up at the local airport by the ecolodge manager in an electric car. <u>It all took a bit longer than I was expecting</u> but then I was only used to short journeys within Europe. Anyway, I was so excited I didn't care about having to change planes or travelling by myself for the first time.

3 The underlined parts of the recording script confirm the answers.

| 1 C | 2 B | 3 A | 4 C | 5 B | 6 A | 7 B |

Recording script 2 **11**

Interviewer: I'm told the site of the ecolodge is amazing. You must've seen quite a few animals and birds?

Lisa: Yes. It's high up on a mountainside with incredible views of the surrounding forest and the sea. It has an observation gallery, where you can sit and look over the rainforest. <u>I particularly liked it when the parrots, which were amazingly gentle and unafraid, came and sat by me, hoping for a piece of fruit.</u> There were also monkeys in the forest but they were too shy to come up close. People are often disappointed that I didn't see any large animals like jaguars – but these are actually quite rare now.

Interviewer: What was your accommodation like?

Lisa: There were 16 small, really nice bungalows built around the central building. As it's environmentally friendly, there's no air conditioning, but the bungalows each have a roof which shades the outside of the building. Another good idea, especially for me, is that if you leave a light on accidentally, it will automatically switch itself off after 20 minutes. I also really liked the outdoor shower <u>but was really puzzled at first when I got back all hot and sweaty to find there was only cold water to wash in.</u> This was because all the water is heated by solar power and when the hot water is finished you just have to wait for the sun to heat up some more!

Interviewer: So what did you do while you were there? Did you go for walks through the forest?

Lisa: Yes. You can hike through the forest with one of the local guides or you can choose from 13 different well-marked trails and go by yourself. Each one takes all day and <u>you do need to be in good shape</u> as the paths aren't always very easy. It's really worth it though, just to hear the noise the birds make and to catch glimpses of them flying through the trees.

Interviewer: What about swimming – did you manage to do that?

Lisa: I went to the beach a few times as it's only a thirty-minute walk away. It's a beautiful sandy beach, and the sea and beach are absolutely clean – no litter or anything to ruin it. <u>Another day I went swimming in a natural pool under a waterfall. It was a real highlight of my trip.</u> The water was really cold and refreshing. As you can imagine, I didn't miss the fact that there wasn't a swimming pool at the place I was staying.

Interviewer: Now one reason for your trip was to see the conservation centre in action, wasn't it?

Lisa: Yes. The centre supplies the ecolodge with organic food but this is just a minor part of what they do. <u>What the centre was built for is to develop green construction techniques using local materials and teach young people in the area how to use them.</u> The people there were really friendly and I learnt a lot about their area. It's not really set up for tourists, so I was very lucky to be invited to visit.

Interviewer: It must have been sad to leave. Are you going to write up your experience for the magazine?

Lisa: Yes, I have to send the magazine another article – this time on my trip. It needs to be at the magazine by the end of November <u>so it can be in the January edition.</u> I know it'll be online from February, if you want to read it and can't afford to buy a copy.

Interviewer: Thank you, Lisa. And next week …

Unit 16

16.1 pages 104–105

Listening

1

Possible answers
Breakfast: cereal, yogurt, toast
Lunch: sandwich, fruit, chocolate
Dinner: pasta, salad, cheese, fruit

2

Possible answers
Japan: sushi, rice, noodles
Alaska: fish
California: junk food

3

Akiko
Breakfast   soup, rice, fish
Lunch   noodles, hamburgers
Dinner   pasta, soup
Also eats vegetables.

Kunu
Breakfast   cheese sandwich, orange juice
Lunch   raw fish
Supper   reindeer, fish
Hardly ever eats sweet food.

Gayle

Breakfast	omelette
Lunch	sandwich – tuna, tomato paste, non-fat bread
Dinner	grilled fish, chicken

Does not eat fat.

Recording script 2️⃣ 12

Speaker 1: My name is Akiko and I was born in Hiroshima in Japan. I moved to England with my family when I was three but my mother always makes us traditional Japanese food. For breakfast we have soup, rice and fish. For lunch I eat noodles, but I also love hamburgers. It's very common for Japanese people to mix traditional and Western food. I'm conscious of healthy eating and I eat a lot of vegetables, but I don't worry about my weight! In the evening I'll have pasta or some more soup.

Speaker 2: My name is Kunu, and I grew up in Alaska, where meals are central to Inuit life. I moved to Seattle when I was seventeen, and became physically ill because my body rejected Western foods. I do eat some Western food though. For breakfast I always have a cheese sandwich with orange juice. Lunch is usually raw fish, and for supper I have reindeer or fish. I hardly eat any sweet foods and I exercise five times a week.

Speaker 3: Everyone calls me Gayle. I exercise for about half an hour before breakfast, which is usually an omelette. For lunch I'll have a sandwich – a mixture of tuna and tomato paste on non-fat bread. I eat a lot but I never eat fat. If I go out to eat, I always ask the waiter to miss out the cream or cheese or oil. People are used to it in LA. I keep a journal every day to say what exercise I've done and exactly what I've eaten. In the evening I'll have grilled fish or chicken.

4 Thinking about the answers to the questions should help you with the text you are going to read.

Possible answers
- Yes, it's ripe and probably juicy.
- No, it's not ripe.
- No, it's probably stale. / I prefer crunchy biscuits.
- No, it's mouldy.
- No, it will taste awful. / I prefer sparkling lemonade.
- No, it will probably be raw.

Reading

5

1 F	**2** A	**3** D	**4** E	**5** C	**6** G

6

Possible answers
a I think they're fascinating. It's surprising how our senses can be influenced by each other.
b On the whole, yes, because there are so many laws and government checks about food safety these days.

c My diet is fairly healthy – I eat lots of fruit and vegetables, and plenty of oily fish like mackerel, but I also love chocolate, which is not so healthy!
d I think I could cut out meat but not fish. I love pasta and some of my favourite pasta recipes are vegetarian, in fact.
e I hate cherry jam because it reminds me of when I was ill as a child. Just the thought of it makes me feel sick!

Vocabulary

7

a rich	**b** off	**c** tough	**d** ripe
e mild	**f** rotten	**g** weak	**h** bad

16.2 pages 106–107

The article

1

singular countable = waiter, lunch (a, the)

Normally, we talk about 'a' or 'the' waiter. We can use lunch with 'a' or 'the', but when we are talking about it in general terms, we don't use an article: *What time are we having lunch?* (This is the same for all meals.)

plural countable = noodles (nothing, the)

uncountable = fish, cheese (nothing, the)

2

a 4	**b** 6	**c** 7, 9	**d** 3, 9	**e** 8, 2	**f** 10, 1	**g** 1, 5	**h** 9
i 10, 11	**j** 5						

Background information

In Japan, and in many other countries, customers can get an idea of what to order from looking at plastic replicas of the food available. This article is about fake food in Japanese restaurants. These plastic replicas are called *sanpuru*.

3

1 –/the	**2** –/the	**3** a	**4** the	**5** –	**6** –	**7** a	**8** a/the
9 The	**10** –	**11** a/the	**12** the	**13** the	**14** –	**15** –	**16** a

4 Using an article or not can change the meaning of some English expressions. For example:

I went to the hospital to see a sick friend.
I went to hospital because I was sick.
They go to church every Sunday.
We visited the church to look for my great-aunt's grave.
Her brother is in prison for burglary.
Our drama group sometimes puts on plays in the prison.

Also you *play football*, but *play the violin*.

a the	**b** –	**c** the	**d** –	**e** the/–	**f** –	**g** –	**h** –	**i** –
j a	**k** –	**l** –	**m** the	**n** the/a	**o** the		

Possession

5

a My husband's father (person)
b restaurant window (kind)
c *correct* (position)
d a cookery magazine (kind)
e *correct* (kind)
f *correct* (time)
g *correct* (object)
h a cup of coffee (a container with something in it)

Corpus spot

a (written) I am coming **on** 24th June. (spoken) I am coming **on the** 24th of June.
b So cycling **in** the rush hour / **at** rush hour is nearly as fast as driving a car.
c Young people have a nice time **at** (US **on**) the weekend.
d We had to wait **a** long time for lunch.
e **In the** evening / **During the** evening she made a cake.
f **On** the first day of my holidays, I was afraid because I was alone.
g In **the** afternoon we could go for a burger.
h I played tennis **for** seven years.
i The man is coming **on** Tuesday morning.
j I should arrive **at** 3 am in London.

Choosing the right preposition can be difficult! Remember these rules:

at for times and holiday periods – at 9.30, at midnight, at Easter

on for days and dates – on Tuesday, on New Year's Day, on 14 June

in for months, years, centuries – in May, in 1979, in the 15th century

Writing folder 8 pages 108–109

Paper 2 Part 1 Essays

1 Informal language is underlined.

This essay discusses the advantages and disadvantages of cycling to work in an urban environment. It considers traffic congestion, the dangers to cyclists and the savings that can be made by using two wheels instead of four.

Nowadays there are loads of cars and trucks on the roads, causing long queues of traffic, especially during the rush hour. For drivers, the stress of waiting in a traffic jam must be unbelievable. So why don't they leave their vehicles at home and cycle instead?

Well, perhaps. Some people argue that it is healthier but I don't agree! You end up breathing in car fumes and risking your life every single day – cycling in cities can be incredibly dangerous and you can get seriously hurt.

On the other hand, it is much cheaper to use a bike. You don't have to buy petrol or pay for many repairs. I guess for this reason it is preferable to cycle to work, but only if you can avoid the busy main roads and follow more pleasant routes.

In conclusion, yes, we should cycle wherever possible. However, not enough is being done to encourage people to leave their cars at home and this needs to be addressed urgently.

2

Possible rewording

loads of – substantial numbers of

unbelievable – considerable

So why don't they – Therefore, isn't it more sensible for them to

Well, perhaps – The answer to this is not straightforward.

I don't agree! – This isn't necessarily the case.

You end up – As a cyclist, you have to breathe in … and risk

I guess – (omit)

yes – it is certainly true that

3

Suggested answers

Possible solutions: **a, c, e, f, h**
a The key to reducing the number of cars on the road is to impose higher taxes on motorists.
c It is essential to restrict the opportunities for parking in the city centre.
e One of the biggest challenges in the short term will be how to persuade people to take public transport but with lower speed limits for private cars, that might become a more attractive option.
f The key to reducing traffic is to raise petrol prices substantially, so that driving becomes the less obvious choice.
h It is vital that the number of cars in a city is restricted, so issuing driving permits for use on certain days seems a good policy to adopt.

4

a What is of high priority is the introduction of tighter laws on older vehicles, whose exhaust fumes cause greater pollution.
b In the short term, it is essential to consult the public, whose concerns have never been fully aired.
c Instant action is needed to reduce the volume of cars in our cities, while in the medium term, further research should be carried out on alternative forms of transport.

TRAFFIC IN OUR CITIES

The volume of traffic in most cities has reached an unsustainable level and urgent action is needed. This essay considers the importance of public transport and suggests other ways of restricting the use of private cars.

Any city needs to have an efficient and reliable public transport network . This requires regular investment, but funding is not always available. In addition, as fares are so high, it can be more cost-effective for people to drive themselves.

It is clearly vital to find ways of reducing the numbers of cars on the road. The key to this may be to impose higher taxes on motorists, or to restrict parking in cities. Furthermore, if petrol prices were raised substantially, driving would become the less obvious choice.

Finally, people should be persuaded to think twice before making an unnecessary journey. More companies are supporting staff wishing to work from home rather than commuting, and with online shopping, fewer trips to the supermarket should be necessary.

In conclusion, improvements to public transport are only part of the solution to reducing traffic. As a society, we need to look at other ways of minimising the use of private cars, including lifestyle changes.

(197 words)

Unit 17

17.1 pages 110–111

Speaking

1 The first photo shows a collection of shells; the second shows a sizeable collection of pin badges and patches worn on the waistcoat of an Aston Villa fan. Aston Villa is a football club in Birmingham.

Read the information about Part 2 of the Speaking test on page 8. Then, using Student A's notes, record yourself doing the task. Try to speak for a whole minute. Make sure you cover both the benefits and the problems of collecting the things shown.

When you listen to your recording, note down any errors in grammar and vocabulary, for example subject–verb agreement, tense choice, plurals of countable nouns.

Remember that the other candidate has to make a brief comment.

2 Do the same thing, this time as Student B. The photos show a woman with her collection of hub caps and a woman whose hobby is making jewellery.

3 Here are some examples of each type of hobby.

Collecting: stamps, postcards, shells, beer mats, posters.

Making things: model planes, science fiction warriors, jewellery, hats, furniture.

Listening

4 The picture at the bottom of the page shows slot-car racing. The underlined parts of the recording script confirm the answers.

1 B 2 C 3 B 4 A 5 A 6 A 7 B 8 C

Recording script 2 13

You will hear people talking in eight different situations. For questions 1–8, choose the best answer (A, B or C).

Question 1 You hear a woman talking about making jewellery.

Woman: 2003 was the year my passion for jewellery making began – there was a fantastic art teacher at school who made earrings and bracelets out of copper, and I thought, I want to do that one day too! I found an evening class, where I learned a lot of useful techniques for working with gold and silver. I've never considered using the former for my own jewellery because it's outside my price range, but <u>I can afford the latter and in fact I've made several things with it</u> recently.

Question 2 You hear two friends talking about postcards.

Man: Here are those cards I bought for you in Oxford, to add to your collection. I hope you don't think they're too tatty – they must be at least fifty years old.

Woman: Thanks. The condition they're in doesn't bother me. And actually, looking at the stamps, they're older than you say, which is brilliant because I haven't got many from the 1930s.

Man: Oh, so you're looking for cards from a certain period?

Woman: Well, I collect all sorts, but <u>I'm on the lookout for older ones that have text on the picture</u>. Like this one, which says: 'Thinking of you in St Ives'.

Question 3 You hear a radio talk about wooden objects.

Woman: I knew someone once who had an absolute passion for making things out of wood. He spent hours and hours on his hobby – whatever the object was, he always took great pride in doing it well and <u>making it unique, by choosing a special wood. He never chose the same kind twice.</u> He would make all sorts of things – a new handle for a fork, with a pattern cut into it; enough models to fill several glass cases ... He even made an electric guitar, which he painted designs on – something he didn't normally do. One piece I remember well is a polar bear. The way it was carved really captured the look of the animal, walking heavily through the snow.

Question 4 You hear a man talking about his hobby.

Man: People think it's a bit odd that I spend my weekends dressed up in anything from metal armour to old uniforms, out in the open air. But it's good fun! The group that puts on these events was only formed about four months ago. I joined in April and <u>we've already performed five battles!</u> You learn a great deal about history, because everything is researched properly – from the costumes to the actual battle tactics. My girlfriend's not too pleased with me at the moment. I'm going to have to miss her birthday 'cos we're doing the Battle of Naseby. That's not the reason she's mad at me though. She wanted to come too but I wouldn't let her!

Question 5 *You hear a girl talking about collecting beads.*

Interviewer: This is Radio QB, the phone lines are open and we want to hear about *your* hobbies. And here's Eleanor, from London. What are you into, Eleanor?

Eleanor: Beads. I've got several hundred, in all shapes and sizes – glass, metal, plastic ones ... They're from all over the world, too: I've got a handful of beautiful wooden ones from India and some very unusual African ones carved out of bone. A few of them I've made up into earrings and necklaces, but what I really like doing is collecting! Especially coloured glass ones, which I've got loads of.

Interviewer: And you say you've got several hundred – how long has it taken you to get so many?

Eleanor: Not that long, really ... I had lots of plastic ones when I was a kid, but I gave those away, so they don't count! I suppose I got serious about beads three years ago. Since then, my family have given me tins of beads as presents, and I spend most of my pocket money on them too.

Question 6 *You hear part of a conversation in a radio play.*

Man: Well, I've rung them twice already and they said I must take the matter up with you. It's clearly your responsibility as I got the model kit from you in the first place. It was sealed when I got it too. No, I'm quite sure. I buy a lot of your kits, you know. Do you want me to contact *Model Makers* magazine and tell them about what's happened? You have all my details, so I suggest you sort it out!

Question 7 *You hear an interview with a girl who collects pebbles.*

Interviewer: I'm with Jenny Braintree, who paints the whole world in miniature on small stones she finds at the seaside. Jenny, you took up this hobby four years ago ...

Jenny: Er ... it was four months ago, in fact. I was on a beach holiday with my parents and I collected loads of nice smooth pebbles. When I got home, I started to paint tiny images of beautiful places like the Swiss mountains and the Brazilian rainforest. I've done 89 so far.

Interviewer: Amazing! These pictures are no more than five centimetres across and yet they contain so much detail! So what's the reason behind this, Jenny? Do you earn anything from all your hard work?

Jenny: Dad thinks I could sell them but I'm not interested in that and anyway they're too special to me. My real aim is to get better at painting because that's what I want to do when I'm older. And although I haven't been to the places I illustrate on the pebbles, it can be really good fun finding out about them on the internet.

Question 8 *You hear an interview with a boy whose hobby is slot-car racing.*

Interviewer: Jamie Eagle, who is the outright winner of today's slot-car racing, is with me now. Congratulations, Jamie, and this is now your tenth win! So where did it all begin? I know your father was also racing here today. Did he know what he was doing when he persuaded you to take up such a time-consuming hobby?

Jamie: Erm, actually, it was *me* who persuaded *him* – he's only been racing this year. He's pretty hopeless at it, too! No, it was my cousin who's to blame. He used to take me along when he went to race meetings – I was five at the time – and I thought it was just brilliant!

Interviewer: And if your father's racing his own car, who do you have as back-up today?

Jamie: I've introduced my friend Ian to slot-car racing – at the moment he's free to help me, though next year he hopes to have a car of his own.

5

Possible answer
Speaking personally, the hobby that would interest me least is making model planes and so on. I just wouldn't have the patience to sit down and stick all the bits together, let alone paint the model afterwards!

Vocabulary

6

Possible answers
1 **A** a doctor   **B** a plumber   **C** a mechanic
2 **A** sew   **B** cook   **C** translate
3 **A** a coastguard
   B a detective / the police
   C an accountant / a business person
4 **A** shiny and expensive   **B** dark brown   **C** dull and grey
5 **A** a doctor   **B** a gardener   **C** an MP / the city council
6 **A** ... these bank charges are completely unreasonable!
   B ... you can't stay up to watch that programme on TV.
   C ... my private life is my own concern.
7 **A** reason(s) why the proposal was turned down
   B new facts about the crime
   C practical information such as visa requirements and likely living costs
8 **A** someone was crossing the road
   B a big wave was about to hit you
   C a pot of paint was in danger of toppling over
9 **A** his older brother or sister
   B a professor
   C the head chef
10 **A** reaching the finish
   B seeing his/her family
   C going away for a long weekend

17.2 pages 112–113
Relative clauses

1

a Only some of the children were tired, so not all of them went to bed. (defining relative clause)
b All the children were tired and all went to bed. (non-defining relative clause)
c They wanted a hotel with a pool, so they probably passed several which didn't have pools before they came to one that did. (defining relative clause)
d They stayed at the very first hotel they came to and, fortunately, it had a pool. (non-defining relative clause)

2

a has a non-defining relative clause
b has a defining relative clause

c which N   d who D   e who D   f whose N
g (most of) which N   h that D

3 The relative pronoun *which* or *that* would go after 'those cards', because it refers to them. Read the section headed **Relative pronouns** in the Grammar folder.

Here are those cards **which/that** I bought for you in Oxford.
a that/which I wanted to buy
b who/that I really looked up to
c that/which I can't stand about Harry
d who/that you met at John's party
e that/which we stayed at

4

a where   b when   c who   d which

Relative pronouns

5

a The collector from whom I have bought many rare film posters lives in Paris.
b The weird millionaire for whom my sister worked expected her to …
c Wetherby, with whom I went riding, was always …

6

a The singer, whose art collection is now worth millions, has always been a fan …
b Maria, whose hobbies include skydiving and collecting antiques, works in a bank …
c The hot air balloon, whose first flight was made in 1783, was designed by the …
d Collectors, whose number has doubled over the last decade, form an increasingly large part of the buyers at local auctions.

Vocabulary

7

a delight   b elegance   c exception   d mass
e remark   f substance

8

emphasising attractiveness	delightful, elegant
emphasising extent	massive, substantial
emphasising rarity	exceptional, remarkable

9

1 more	**2** which/that	**3** whose	**4** as
5 from	**6** ought	**7** not	**8** would

10

Possible sentences
It's a delightful painting of a young girl playing in the sand with her brother.
Jackie is an elegant woman, whose clothing always looks extremely stylish.
The race will be an exceptional challenge for everyone taking part in it.
He collects postcards on a massive scale and has over 1000!
The shopkeeper has a remarkable memory for faces.
This essay needs a substantial amount of rewriting, I'm afraid.

Exam folder 9 pages 114–115
Paper 1 Part 6   Gapped text

Remember that each question is worth two marks. You need to spend enough time on this difficult part of Paper 1.

1 B   **2** G   **3** D   **4** A   **5** C   **6** E

Unit 18
18.1 pages 116–117
Reading

1 The illustration shows two people fishing from a small boat in a quiet lagoon. The book is mainly set in a group of tiny islands known as the Sundarbans, which lie in the Bay of Bengal. The word 'Sundarban' can be translated from Bengali as 'beautiful forest' and the Sundarbans are a UNESCO world heritage site, with the largest area of tidal mangrove forest in the world.

Background information
Amitav Ghosh is an Indian writer, born July 11, 1956 in Kolkata (Calcutta). *The Hungry Tide* was published in 2005. His next book, *Sea of Poppies*, was shortlisted for the 2008 Man Booker Prize. Amitav Ghosh has also written non-fiction books and essays.

2

Possible answers

The first review talks about adventure, so the novel could have an exciting plot. It also refers to personal identity and there's a love story, it seems, as well as some historical references.

The second review praises the author for being able to develop a plot from very little – so the book might be about ordinary people, I suppose?

3   Remember that it is not necessary to understand every word in a text.

Answers

The action in this extract takes place on a train that has recently left Kolkata (Calcutta) in India.

The main character, a young woman called Piya, is mentioned in the second line of the opening paragraph and it is clear that she is travelling with a lot of luggage (she has more than one backpack). You are unlikely to know the word *arrayed* but you can probably picture the scene, with Piya's luggage spread out around her.

4

Answers

1 D   2 C   3 A   4 B   5 C   6 B

Detailed explanation:

1   Multiple-choice questions at this B2 level will often require some inference, as here. The answer (**D**) comes from two places in the first paragraph: *an unexpected stroke of luck presented Piya with an opportunity to go for a seat beside a window* and *she had been sitting in the stuffiest part of the train compartment, on the edge of a bench*. **A** is wrong because she was already sitting down. **B** is not suggested in the text beyond the distraction of *the train had stopped at a station called Champahati*. **C**, although plausible, is not stated, so we don't know whether there is more room for her backpacks or not.

2   The answer (**C**) comes from *somehow, in the ten days she had spent in India she had developed an unexpected taste for milky, overboiled tea* and *there were no spices in it for one thing, and this was more to her taste than the chai back home*. **A** is wrong because the chai is different from what she drinks in Seattle. **B** is wrong because although the Indian chai mentioned has no spices in it and could therefore be described as 'bland', Piya is not 'disappointed' by this fact, as she finds it more to her taste. **D** is not suggested by the text.

3   The answer (**A**) comes towards the end of the fourth paragraph, in the words *she had been struck by the self-satisfied tilt of his head and the way in which he stared at everyone around him …* **B** is wrong as he didn't know any of the people he was looking at, but was *taking them in, sizing them up, sorting them all into their places*. **C** is not suggested by the text and **D** does not reflect Piya's initial reaction when she had first seen the man on the platform. It is important to read each **question** carefully, not just the options.

4   This question requires some reading between the lines of the text to work out Piya's thoughts and behaviour.

The answer (B) comes from text immediately before the quoted *But how did you guess?* – *Piya had no wish to get into an argument so she let this pass. Instead she opened her eyes wide and, in an attempt to restore peace…* and her strategy is also confirmed by the later statement *This seemed to do the trick*. A and C are plausible but not true to the text. D is wrong as the man had already acknowledged her apology.

5   The answer (**C**) is confirmed by Piya's implication that she knows what is ahead of her *I'll do what I usually do … in my line of work there's not much talk needed*. **B** and **D** are ruled out because of this (she doesn't need to communicate much to do her job, either in English or in the local languages). And **A** is wrong because she is relaxed and confident about the work.

6   The answer (**B**) comes from the adverb *sharply* and the fact that he interrupts her to say that he knows what the term means. **A** is wrong because although he understands the basic meaning of 'cetologist', the text doesn't suggest that he knows 'quite a bit' about it. **C** and **D** are plausible but not stated in this extract.

Vocabulary

5   These are examples of two- and three-part phrasal verbs, the meanings of which are given below

Answers
go for – try to get
come out with – say something suddenly and unexpectedly

a come up with   **b** go ahead   **c** went up   **d** went by
e came out   **f** came across   **g** went through   **h** gone off

18.2 pages 118–119

Listening

1

A play   **B** biography   **C** science fiction   **D** historical novel
E non-fiction   **F** crime novel

2

1 D   2 E   3 B   4 C   5 F

Recording script 2 14

Speaker 1: All of her books are really well researched and they're full of amazing details about what daily life used to be like, so you learn a lot about that period. It's extremely imaginative, the characters are very realistic and, as the title suggests, there's a murder mystery too. This is the seventh one of hers I've read and I can't wait to get my hands on another!

Speaker 2: I found the book fascinating, but at the same time it's more than a little depressing. We're so dependent on these creatures! The writers consider the planet's future, suggesting what might happen if they died out completely. It's a really scary possibility actually, because their disappearance would affect the food chain dramatically – in only four years, apparently.

Speaker 3: I don't normally read lengthy books of this kind, but I'd enjoyed several of his novels, so I was interested to find out more about the man himself. It's certainly comprehensive and thoroughly researched, but I have to admit I found it a little hard-going in places – the writer's own account of his experiences is so much more colourful. Still, it's worth keeping on the shelves to revisit one day.

Speaker 4: A friend lent me the first book written by this author, which I enjoyed, but this one is loads better. It's the same character from the previous story but he's a lot more developed somehow. It's set a few centuries ahead of now, and the vision of how a society so different to ours might operate is really powerful. I got completely carried along with the storyline, and the dialogue is fantastic too. Yes, a great read!

Speaker 5: Once I started it, I just couldn't put it down. The plot is quite complicated and it moves along at a really fast pace. What I like best about it is the two main characters – they have such different personalities. The private investigator himself is quite jokey and upbeat, while his business partner is a rather mysterious figure. He's an ex-police officer, who says very little but is always there to provide backup when things get tough. This is the ninth title in the series, but I haven't read them all yet.

enough, too, very, so, such

3

Yes, the writer does believe the book has a future. Reasons (in second paragraph): people have more leisure time to read in; the book has a strong tradition; it's very practical.

1 as **2** would **3** besides **4** why **5** used **6** from
7 not **8** be

4

a enough reasons
b small enough
c This is the extra statement – common expressions of this type are: *funnily enough, strangely enough*, etc. For example: *Funnily enough, my friend had bought the same book for me.*
d too dismissive; too much
e and by other technological attractions, too
f very badly injured; very strong pull
g so effective
h the last hundred years or so
i If that is so,
j such alternatives to books as
k such a practical tool

5 Refer to the Corpus spot on page 118.

a enough time **b** large enough **c** enough books
d had had enough of **e** not enough people
f got enough to **g** quite enough about
h Funnily enough

6

1 such cold weather (that) we
2 too little time to give
3 so well (that) you should/could
4 is very good at getting
5 takes such a lot of / takes such a long
6 (this is) so, a refund

Writing folder 9 pages 120–121

Paper 2 Part 2 Reviews

1 The mistakes are highlighted.

The book 'Marcovaldo', by Italo Calvino is one of the jewels of 20th century fiction. It is actually a series of twenty short stories, all focusing on the same caracter – Marcovaldo – who lives with his large family in an unnamed city in the north of italy. Each story is set, in a diferent season: there are five about living in the city in summer, and so on.

Many aspects of modern life are described, such as advertiseing and pollution of the enviroment, though the book is not completly true to life. This is perhaps it's greatest strength. It has a unique mixture of realistic events and bizzare ones, which often take the reader by suprise.

One particluar story features the publicity campains of rival soap powder manufacturers. Marcovaldos' children and their frends collect hundreds of free cartons of washing powder, which they hope to sell to people in the neibourhood. In the end, they have to get rid of everything quickly and so throw the cartons into the River. The story closes with a memorable descricion of soap bubbles being blown over the city their whiteness competing with the black factory smoke. Black wins.

Corrected version
The book 'Marcovaldo', by Italo Calvino, is one of the jewels of 20th-century fiction. It is actually a series of twenty short stories, all focusing on the same character – Marcovaldo – who lives with his large family in an unnamed city in the north of Italy. Each story is set in a different season: there are five about living in the city in summer, and so on.

Many aspects of modern life are described, such as advertising and pollution of the environment, though the book is not completely true to life. This is perhaps its greatest strength. It has a unique mixture of realistic events and bizarre ones, which often take the reader by surprise.

One particular story features the publicity campaigns of rival soap powder manufacturers. Marcovaldo's children and their friends collect hundreds of free cartons of washing powder, which they hope to sell to people in the neighbourhood. In the end, they have to get rid of everything quickly and so throw the cartons into the river. The story closes with a memorable description of soap bubbles being blown over the city, their whiteness competing with the black factory smoke. Black wins.

2 B is the most suitable.

3

Characters: ambition, attitude, determination, enthusiasm, loyalty, manner, mood, reputation, sympathy, temper

Events: action, adventure, chaos, impact, incident, mood, theme

Mood and *reputation* can apply to both characters and events.

4

a	loyalty	**e**	impact
b	sympathy	**f**	manner
c	chaos	**g**	theme
d	reputation	**h**	incident

5

Sample answers

Started early, took my dog by Kate Atkinson

This wonderful novel is one of a series featuring Jackson Brodie, who is a private investigator. Kate Atkinson has developed Jackson's character across the books and in this particular novel, we feel quite sympathetic towards him, as he has a rather complicated and not totally successful life.

We learn a lot about Jackson from his actual words and the author is brilliant at writing sharp and amusing dialogue. I can recommend the novel to anyone of my age with a sense of humour and I guarantee you will laugh out loud at times.

Another interesting character in the novel is a retired police officer called Tracy Waterhouse, whose life is turned upside down by a chance event and the decision she makes as a result. We get to know Tracy through her inner thoughts on how she sees the world around her. The contrast between Tracy's life and Jackson's is fascinating.

There is a whole cast of other characters to enjoy, not to mention more than one dog, as suggested by the title. Read this book soon!

(185 words)

The Old Man and the Sea by Ernest Hemingway

For me, the most memorable episode in this novel is when the fish first appears. The description of the great purple marlin emerging from the sea has an enormous impact and the rest of the story will centre on the relationship between these two 'characters' – the old fisherman and his catch.

This is the biggest fish that the old man has ever come across, and he has doubts about whether he can physically land it in his small boat. Hemingway describes this struggle in considerable detail and we live each moment with the old man.

In short, this is a tale that will hold your attention and move you as well. The style that Hemingway uses is quite different from anything I had ever read before, and it has made me think about the art of storytelling. I believe everyone at college should read this unique work of fiction, for although it was written several decades ago, it remains strangely relevant today.

(171 words)

Units 13–18 Revision

pages 122–123

2   This is exam practice for Paper 1 Part 1.

1 A	**2** C	**3** B	**4** C	**5** C	**6** B	**7** C	**8** D

3

a There is too much traffic in our town.

b I have such a lot of / so much work to do, I don't know where to start.

c The Netherlands and Austria are both countries in the European Union.

d Her house, whose roof is thatched, is twelfth century. / Her house, the roof of which is thatched, is twelfth century.

e John plays the piano and he also plays football, whereas his brother prefers playing chess.

f Let me give you some advice / a piece of advice – don't go on a journey/trip without checking whether you need a visa or not.

g There's a man over there who has been watching us for about half an hour.

h I have lived in Las Vegas for ten years and I still find it exciting.

i By this time next year, I will have taught / will have been teaching for twenty years.

j He asked me where the police station was.

k I saw a flash of lightning when I was out in the garden.

l Have you got enough information to object to the factory noise?

m He's the one to whom I gave the book. / He's the one who I gave the book to.

n My eldest son, who lives in Paris, is a physicist.

4

a 5	**b** 3	**c** 7	**d** 4	**e** 1	**f** 2	**g** 6

5

1 B an operation, a relationship that's ended

2 A someone's career, the market for e-books

3 B an idea, a plan, an answer, an explanation

4 C an adventure

5 A at an airport

6 B e.g. hours, days, months

7 A

8 C sugar, chocolate

9 A a meeting, something you've arranged to do but don't want to

10 A interest rates, the number of students going to university

Unit 19

19.1 pages 124–125

Speaking

1 *An apple a day ...* is part of the British saying *An apple a day keeps the doctor away.*

Modals 3

3 The section in the Grammar folder on page 174 lists the structures of advice and suggestion. Note the following:
You should + infinitive without *to*
If I were you + *I would* + infinitive without *to*
You ought + *to* + infinitive

Mostly As
You are fairly healthy and have a good attitude to life. You should try to watch what you eat a little more, and if I were you, I'd try to do a little more exercise. Too much work and not enough play isn't good for you! I think it's about time you thought about your diet.

Mostly Bs
You are obviously in the peak of condition! I recommend you relax as you ought to get some rest even if you don't need much sleep. Overdoing things can lead to illness! Why don't you try doing more reading, or go on holiday – or have you ever thought of playing a musical instrument?

Mostly Cs
Oh dear! It's time you took a good look at your lifestyle. Missing meals and not getting enough sleep and exercise are very bad for you. My advice to you is to start right away – you'd better join a gym. I also suggest cutting down on coffee and drinking more water and fruit juice. Too much caffeine will keep you awake!

Suggested answers
a You ought to see if you're allergic to something.
b You should run it under the cold tap immediately.
c Why don't you do extra cycling practice?
d If I were you, I'd go straight to hospital.
e You'd better check if you need any injections.
f What about putting your head between your knees?
g I recommend you put some vinegar on it.
h My advice to you is to see your doctor.

4 Refer to the Corpus spot. The expressions *It's time, It's about time* and *It's high time* are often tested in the exam.

Suggested answers
(You could also use *he* or *she* in your answer.)
a It's (about / high) time you gave up smoking.
b It's (about / high) time you walked a bit more.
c It's (about / high) time you read a book occasionally.
d It's (about / high) time you applied for another one.
e It's (about / high) time you ate something healthier.
f It's (about / high) time you bought your own house.
g It's (about / high) time you had it mended.
h It's (about / high) time you bought your own.
i It's (about / high) time you got up earlier.
j It's (about / high) time you bought a new one.

Vocabulary

5

a jaw   b wrist   c eyebrow   d elbow   e chest   f waist
g thigh   h knee   i ankle

6 There is more than one right answer here.

Suggested answers
If I broke my leg, I'd have it put in plaster.
If I had a headache, I'd take an aspirin.
If I cut my knee badly, I'd have stitches.
If I grazed my elbow, I'd get an elastoplast / a plaster.
If I sprained my ankle, I'd put a bandage on it.
If I had flu, I'd go to bed.
If I had a cough, I'd take some cough medicine.

7 Prepositional phrases are often tested in Paper 1.

a on average   b on behalf of   c on purpose   d on duty
e on condition that   f On balance   g on offer

19.2 pages 126–127

Listening

1

Background information

Homeopathy – a method of treating disease with small amounts of remedies that, in large amounts in healthy people, produce symptoms similar to those being treated

Osteopathy – therapy based on the assumption that restoring health is best accomplished by manipulating the skeleton and muscles

Reflexology – a therapeutic method of relieving pain by stimulating specific pressure points on the feet and hands

Herbal medicine – a medicine made from plants and used to prevent or treat disease or promote health

2 Acupuncture is a type of treatment that has been used in Chinese medicine for over 4500 years. It is now an important part of alternative medicine in many parts of the world. Acupuncture involves controlling the body's flow of energy, known as chi, in this way encouraging the body to heal itself.

3

Possible answer
I think the man may feel a little nervous about the needles going into his face but he seems happy. The person having reflexology is probably feeling very relaxed if they like having their feet massaged. Personally, I think that the main difference between the treatments is that acupuncture is medically proven to work whereas reflexology isn't.

4 The underlined parts of the recording script confirm the answers.

1 C   2 B   3 A   4 B   5 A   6 A   7 B

Recording script 2 15

Interviewer: Good morning. On the programme this morning we have Dr Sylvia Carpenter, who is a family doctor. Dr Carpenter, you're a great believer in Chinese medicine, aren't you?

Doctor: Yes, I am. When I was a medical student <u>I spent a wonderful month at a hospital in Hong Kong, where they use acupuncture as well as Western medicine, which is, of course, what I was studying.</u> I saw how effective acupuncture could be, especially for people with digestive disorders, asthma, back pain or stress.

Interviewer: Now, you're not qualified to practise acupuncture yourself, are you?

Doctor: Oh, I'm just an ordinary GP or General Practitioner. I work in a small community, with about 3,000 people on my list. In the past we only referred patients to specialists at the local hospital for treatment – you know, to have their chests X-rayed or have a blood test done. Now I <u>often suggest they see an acupuncturist as well,</u> if I feel it would be of benefit. <u>I can't actually recommend one specifically, but I keep a list of qualified ones.</u>

Interviewer: So, say I go to see an acupuncturist about my backache. What would happen to me?

Doctor: Well, first of all <u>the acupuncturist will ask you for very detailed information,</u> not just about your medical history, but about your lifestyle, what you eat, what sort of exercise you do, how much sleep you get. The treatment you need is then decided and he or she will insert needles in various parts of your body. If you have a back pain, you won't necessarily have a needle in your back, though. It might be in one of your limbs – maybe in a knee or a wrist.

Interviewer: How often would I have to go?

Doctor: It depends on your problems. For some conditions, one or two treatments a week for several months may be recommended. For less acute problems, usually fewer visits are required. There aren't usually any side effects. You might feel worse for a couple of days, but that just means the treatment is working. <u>It's quite common to feel exhausted after the first treatment,</u> and this can be overcome with a bit of extra rest.

Interviewer: Now, the big question. Does it hurt?

Doctor: <u>Well, it'd be wrong to say 'No'. It depends where the needles are inserted.</u> Some areas are more sensitive than others. <u>Once the needles are in place, there's no pain at all.</u>

Interviewer: Are any positive benefits all in the mind, do you think?

Doctor: <u>No, not at all. Acupuncture has been successfully used on cats and dogs. These animals don't understand or believe in the process that helps them to get better.</u> A positive attitude towards the treatment may reinforce its effects, just as a negative attitude may hinder the effects.

Interviewer: It's a relatively new type of treatment, isn't it?

Doctor: Only in the West. It was first discovered in China in 2696 BC! In 1671 a French Jesuit priest wrote about his experiences in China and was the first Westerner to see acupuncture in use. In 1820 acupuncture was actually being used in a Paris hospital! Acupuncture received a lot of publicity in the West when James Reston, a reporter for the *New York Times*, was covering the visit of President Nixon to China in 1971. Reston developed appendicitis and <u>his appendix was removed using acupuncture as the anaesthetic.</u> He felt no pain during or after the operation because of acupuncture. But, in some ways, your question was right. Acupuncture is still a fairly new subject in the West, but growing all the time.

Interviewer: Thank you, Dr Carpenter. Now we're …

Grammar extra

Note that *get something done* is more informal than *have something done.*

You have something done because it is something that you don't normally do yourself and you need someone else to do it for you.
a to have your clothes cleaned
b to have your hair cut/styled
c to have your car serviced/repaired
d to have a dress or other item of clothing made/altered
e to have a suit made/altered
f to have your nails done/polished
g to have your teeth checked / a tooth filled
h to have some furniture repaired/made

5

1 A   2 B   3 B   4 D   5 B   6 A   7 B   8 C

Vocabulary

6

a believer   **b** specialists, treatment   **c** medical
d effective   **e** various   **f** sensitive   **g** successfully
h operation

7

a sweat   **b** surgery   **c** ward   **d** scar   **e** bruise
f examination   **g** bug   **h** symptom

Exam folder 10 pages 128–129

Paper 1 Part 5 Multiple choice – fiction

In Paper 1 Part 5 there is sometimes an extract from a novel or short story. The advice for fiction and non-fiction is exactly the same. There is no difference in how you should approach the questions.

> 1 C 2 B 3 D 4 B 5 A 6 C

Unit 20

20.1 pages 130–131

Speaking

1 The five photographs show clues in a police case and are (left to right): a fingerprint, a hair being removed from an item of clothing, a tyre track, a glass with fingerprints and some liquid in the bottom, and a DNA analysis.

2

> **Possible answers**
> a Many crimes today are drug-related. Addicts need money to buy drugs, so they steal or commit other crimes.
> b I don't think this can be proved either way, but there are certainly more violent TV programmes and films than there used to be.
> c Criminals change in prison and many come to realise that what they did was wrong. Some prisoners with life sentences should be released early as they are no longer a threat to society.
> d It depends on the crime committed. Voluntary service in the community can be a successful alternative for minor offenders.

Reading

3

> a a forensic scientist b the proof c guilty
> d genetic code e evidence; the suspect
> f to cover your tracks g taken to court

4 The article is about detecting crime. It is practice for Paper 1 Part 6.

> 1 G 2 F 3 C 4 A 5 E 6 B

5

> **Possible answers**
> I think DNA profiling is an excellent idea. It means that it is much more likely you can catch a criminal and have real proof that they were the one who committed a crime.
>
> I think there should be an international database as long as there are safeguards. It is quite worrying that there is the potential for it to be misused.

6 This exercise practises back reference, which is often tested in Paper 1 Part 5.

> a the traces of evidence
> b the old techniques
> c an item
> d the dusting of surfaces

20.2 pages 132–133

Listening

1 You are going to hear a true story about a man in the USA who committed a robbery but who was caught through DNA evidence.

The underlined parts of the recording script confirm the answers.

> a 72 months
> b in a car park
> c so he could take his friends on holiday/vacation
> d when he was working near the bank
> e He wanted a lot of people who were all dressed like him to be outside the bank because it would confuse the police.
> f He pretended to work as a landscape gardener outside the bank.
> g on a tyre/raft down the river
> h because a lot of people were wearing the same clothes as the robber
> i Curcio had left some things when he had been rehearsing the robbery and they were found by a homeless man and given to the police.
> j DNA on a bottle that matched DNA on a mask

Recording script 2 **16**

Good morning. Here is the news. Anthony Curcio, 28, of Monroe, Washington, was sentenced today to <u>72 months</u> in prison for robbing an armored car in Monroe. Curcio, a former star athlete in high school, who earned college scholarships in basketball and football, carefully planned the robbery over nearly a year. Curcio was arrested <u>in a car park</u> following a spending spree at a shopping mall. At the trial, Curcio stated that he had needed the money from the robbery <u>to pay to take his friends on an 'all expenses paid' vacation to Las Vegas.</u>

According to records filed in the case, Curcio first came up with the idea of robbing an armored car <u>while working for his parents' landscaping company</u>. They were doing some work near the Monroe branch of the Bank of America and Curcio studied the deliveries that the armored car made every week. At the same time, he decided on the best ways to escape after the robbery. He manufactured a disguise with clothing that could be easily removed, and even strung a cable in a nearby river so that he could use an old tyre as an inflatable raft and pull himself down the creek away from the scene of the crime.

Curcio decided to use an open WiFi network to put an advertisement on the internet offering men a potential job. The open WiFi was to enable him to post things on the internet without the police being able to trace him. Applicants for the job were told that they had to stand outside the Bank of America in Monroe at a certain time on a certain date and wear specific clothing. This was to consist of a blue shirt, yellow vest, safety goggles and work shoes. They were told that there was construction work available for whoever turned up.

On the day of the robbery, Curcio wore a wig, safety goggles, work boots and a tear-away blue shirt <u>and he pretended to be a landscaper cutting weeds outside the bank</u>. When the armored car arrived, it stopped outside the bank to unload the money and the delivery person got out. Curcio stopped working and then sprayed the delivery person in the face with pepper and stole a bag containing approximately $400,000. Curcio remembered to remove his wig, face mask, work clothes and hat and threw them in bushes before <u>making his escape on the inflatable raft down the river</u>. What initially confused police was <u>the group of people at the scene all dressed in the same clothing as the robber</u>.

However, the FBI and Monroe Police were soon on Curcio's trail. According to police, three weeks before the robbery took place, <u>a homeless man had seen Curcio trying out his ideas for the robbery. Curcio had arrived in a wig and gone through what he would do on the day of the robbery. Before leaving in his car, he had then dropped the wig and an empty bottle behind a trash can at the bank. The homeless man had reported Curcio's license plate number to police and given them the items he had found behind the trash can</u>. The police found out that the car was registered to Curcio's wife. Nothing was done at the time as there was no crime to connect it to, but the police had kept the items.

When news came of the attack on the armored van at the bank, a police sergeant remembered getting the earlier report. Investigators retrieved the drink bottle from storage and found it had a sample of DNA on it. They then compared it to the DNA from the face mask and wig left by Curcio a short distance from the scene of the real robbery. <u>The DNA from the bottle matched the DNA from the items left at the scene.</u> The police then began following Curcio and finally arrested him in the car park.

Some $220,000 of the stolen money was recovered following Curcio's arrest. He pleaded guilty to all charges. In asking for a five-year sentence, Assistant United States Attorney Bruce Miyake said that, and I quote, 'All robberies are inherently violent and serious. This robbery stands out for its boldness, level of planning, and its ingenuity. As has been seen, Curcio was obsessive in his planning. This, however, led to his ultimate downfall.'

2

> you stop to do something = you stop in order to do something
> you remember to do something = you remember that you need to do it and then you do it
>
> you stop doing something = you finish doing something
> you remember doing something = you remember something now that you did in the past

Gerunds and infinitives 2

3 Read the Corpus spot and the section on page 174 of the Grammar folder to check on the difference in meaning.

> **1a** I tried to stop the thief taking the woman's bag but I failed. *I made an attempt to do something but it didn't work.*
> **1b** The burglar tried climbing through the kitchen window when he couldn't break the door lock. *He thought of a way of doing something.*
> **2a** The detective stopped at the top of the hill to look at the footprint. *His intention/purpose was to look at the footprint.*
> **2b** Tom stopped working for the police last year. *He doesn't work for them any more.*
> **3a** Pete regrets leaving his car unlocked. *He is sorry about something in the past.*
> **3b** We regret to inform you that your stolen bicycle has been found in the river. *A formal expression referring to the present*
> **4a** I remember our house being broken into when I was six. *I remember something in the past.*
> **4b** You must remember to get travel insurance tomorrow. *not forget to do something – here referring to the future*
> **5a** Cycling without lights will mean getting a fine. *It will result in a fine.*
> **5b** Sally means to write her first detective novel this autumn. *She intends to write it.*
> **6a** The police officer, after discussing personal safety, went on to talk about car crime in the town. *He changed the topic.*
> **6b** Lucy went on talking about having her suitcase stolen all evening. *She continued talking about the same topic.*

4

> **a** fitting   **b** reading   **c** to inform   **d** walking
> **e** to hurt   **f** to pay   **g** telling
> **h** drinking and driving / to drink and drive
> **i** to keep   **j** to talk   **k** to do up   **l** running

5

1 to make off	2 to be	3 to fasten	4 checking
5 to see	6 to avoid	7 carrying	8 to put
9 reporting	10 lead	11 know	12 to sign

Vocabulary

6

Possible answers
a hang – all the others are to do with freeing
b illegal – all the others are adjectives which normally describe a person
c arrest – all the others are forms of crime
d jury – all the others are guilty
e trial – all the others are places
f offence – all the others are what happens after you are caught
g commit – all the others are what the legal system does to you

Writing folder 10 pages 134–135

Paper 2 Part 2 Emails

1 Your own answers

2 All areas are covered.

3

Phrasal verbs: stick to, cutting out, checking out, giving up, work out, going for

Prepositional phrases: between you and me, in (great) shape, in fact, (keep) in touch

Adverbs: radically, more regularly, incredibly

4

a temporary
b expect
c understand
d disappearance
e unbelievable
f recommendation
g passionate
h carelessly

5

Sample answer

Hi Nicky

Sorry to hear you are facing a bit of a problem with unwelcome guests! I know how tiny your apartment is and I guess it must be really difficult sharing such a small space. If it was me, I'd never have invited them to stay in the first place. You're too nice, you know!

Anyway, I'd say you have to get tough with these people – they're really taking advantage of your good nature! Give them a deadline and make it clear they'll have to have found somewhere else to live by that date.

In the meantime, make sure they help out with the cleaning, and insist they cook a meal or two as well. You're out at work all day, so it's rather unfair of them to expect you to play the perfect host when you get home.

Above all, you shouldn't worry about hurting their feelings – after all, they're not close friends, so it doesn't matter if you fall out over this, does it? They sound as though they are behaving totally unreasonably.

Let me know how you get on.

Love,

(184 words)

Unit 21

21.1 pages 136–137

Vocabulary

1

Buildings
property value, construction work
Leisure facilities
art gallery, shopping mall, community centre / shopping centre
Services
rubbish collection, road maintenance, street lighting
Transport
traffic jam, congestion charge, residents parking

Speaking

2 The photos show (1) a street in Greenwich Village, New York, and (2) a suburb in Melbourne, Australia.

Listening

3

The expert is an architect – the profession is architecture.

Recording script 2 17
Part 1
My name is Julia Banks and I'm here today to defend modern, high-rise architecture. Those who criticise this type of living accommodation claim that it is unnatural – the argument goes something like this: If we were meant to live up in the sky, we would have been born with wings! Well, as an experienced architect, I obviously challenge this view. The fact is that many people have to opt for high-rise accommodation, and our profession has a responsibility to design homes that are fit for them to live in.

4 The underlined parts of the recording script confirm the answers.

Possible predictions
1 a person/organisation
2 a word that collocates with *regulations* e.g. official
3 a type of housing, e.g. *flat*
4 something connected with new buildings, e.g. *bricks*
5 an example of an environmental requirement
6 something that means the same as *urban sprawl*
7 something that collocates with *facilities*
8 something relating to architecture in a city centre
9 something that might exist downstairs in a building, e.g. *shop*
10 something in cities that may make people unhealthy, e.g. *pollution*

Answers
1 government   2 planning   3 tower block
4 material(s)   5 heating   6 suburb(s)   7 out-of-town
8 skyscraper(s)   9 jazz club   10 (heavy) traffic

Recording script 2 18
Part 2

There's no doubt that things have improved over time. We look back to the high-rise buildings of the 1960s, where people were sometimes uprooted from established communities and forced to live in ugly concrete blocks against their will. Yet we should remember that this was a time when many people wanted to be rehoused because their living conditions were so bad. And this was a policy upheld by government, rather than decided by architects.

So, the situation has changed for the better. It seems that lack of consultation over new buildings is rarely an issue with the public nowadays. The fact of the matter is that there are much tougher planning regulations in place than was previously the case.

I should underline my personal experience here. For six years of my childhood, I was in a tower block in quite a run-down part of Bristol, so I do know what it's like. That's largely what drove me to become an architect, actually. Yes, some 60s architecture is poor, but the point is, if it hadn't happened, we would be making similar mistakes today, whereas, as it is, we have been able to learn from it and move on.

For one thing, the buildings being put up today generally have better materials than in the past, certainly in comparison with the 1960s. A lot more thought goes into this aspect, with the upside that new buildings look more attractive as a result.

Then there are the environmental considerations. We have to design buildings that are efficient, so for us in Britain that means paying particular attention to things like heating. Of course, that particular requirement wouldn't be an issue for architects in southern Europe.

Something that does trouble me is 'urban sprawl', by which I mean the endless suburbs. And their existence is at a huge cost to the tax-paying public in terms of upkeep – basic services like drainage, road maintenance, that sort of thing. City expansion isn't very good news for the countryside either. At the same time, there's sometimes appalling decay in the middle of our cities as a direct result of this move outwards. Shops in the centre have closed because of out-of-town facilities, and people are forced to drive when once they bought locally. That's not sustainable, is it?

What I believe in – and what many architects are trying to work towards – is the regeneration of our city centres, but this can only happen if we think vertically – design skyscrapers, in other words. There's no space to do anything else! It's a really exciting development that could breathe new life into our cities.

Imagine if your building was a multi-use one, where you just go downstairs to a jazz club, or across the street to pick up some late-night shopping ... this is the upmarket housing of the future, where no one will need to own a car.

In a recent radio phone-in, 67% of callers thought that the car should be banned altogether from central London. I truly think people are ready for this. They understand that traffic is slowly killing us. Living in the city has to become a healthier and more acceptable option.

5

a	T	She says: *It seems that lack of consultation over new buildings is rarely an issue with the public nowadays.*
b	T	She says: *For six years of my childhood, I was in a tower block in quite a run-down part of Bristol, so I do know what it's like. That's largely what drove me to become an architect, actually.*
c	T	She says: *City expansion isn't very good news for the countryside either.*
d	F	She says: *What I believe in – and what many architects are trying to work towards – is the regeneration of our city centres*
e	T	She says: *In a recent radio phone-in, 67% of callers thought that the car should be banned altogether from central London. I truly think people are ready for this.*

6

a 3   b 5   c 1   d 2   e 4

7

a 2   b 1   c 1   d 2   e 3   f 2   g 1   h 3
d is too direct for a discussion and might give offence. Other non-verbal strategies for directing a conversation include nodding or shaking your head; making eye contact; raising a hand; leaning forward.

21.2 pages 138–139

Mixed conditionals

1 A 'mixed conditional' is a conditional structure that does not follow the standard types but uses different tenses. The mixed conditionals here are formed with one second conditional element and one third conditional element. See Grammar folder page 175.

2

Possible answers
a … would look much worse.
b … wouldn't be starving now.
c … would be less well-informed.
d … wouldn't be stuck in this traffic jam.
e … would still be living at home.

3

Possible answers
a would have chosen to live in them in the first place.
b would have finished your essay by now.
c wouldn't have been so high for the last 20 years.
d would have gone out at 3 am this morning to buy you some paracetamol.

4

a 5 b 3 c 6 d 1 e 2 f 4 (mixed conditional)

5

Possible answers
a Given a lack of basic supplies, people would have to get used to having less choice of food and growing their own vegetables.
b In the absence of any proper control of pollution levels, you would need to be really careful about going out, and when outside, you would have to wear a mask over your face to protect yourself.
c Without electricity at certain times, you would need to be well prepared – buy lots of candles and get some nice food that doesn't need cooking.
d In the absence of a proper banking system it wouldn't be possible to keep your money safely anywhere, so you would need to guard your home from thieves!

Vocabulary

6 The photo shows the central dome of the Reichstag, designed by Norman Foster.

1 C 2 C 3 B 4 A 5 D 6 A 7 C 8 B

7

structure, construction
enlarge, expand, extend
enormous, extensive, huge, vast

8

rebuild; reconsider/reconsideration; regenerate/regeneration; reopen/reopening; repay/repayment; repossess/repossession; rewrite

a regenerated b reconstructed/rebuilt c reopening
d reconsider

Exam folder 11 pages 140–141

Paper 1 Part 7 Multiple matching

You might find it useful to use a highlighter pen to highlight the parts of the text with the answers in.

1 D 2 A 3 B 4 D 5 C 6 B 7 A 8 C 9 B 10 A

Unit 22

22.1 pages 142–143

Speaking

1 The two photos show an open air music festival and a special event where 2,740 young musicians played in the Birmingham Symphony Hall.

Suggested answer
The basic similarity is that both pictures show music being played. The two types of music seem very different – in the open-air concert there's a rock or soul band performing on the stage, while the other photo shows young people playing classical music and it may not be a concert at all. I've never seen so many cellos under one roof!

2 The recording is an example of the 'long turn' – Paper 4 Part 2. One candidate, Carmen, speaks for about a minute, and then the other, Jurgen, is asked to make a brief comment for about 20 seconds.

Jurgen prefers taking part, whereas Carmen says she enjoys being part of a large audience and listening to music.

Recording script 2 19

Examiner: Carmen, here are your two photographs. They show a lot of people in one place. Please let Jurgen have a look at them. Carmen, I'd like you to compare these photographs, and say how you would feel in each situation. Remember, you have only about a minute for this, so don't worry if I interrupt you. All right?

Carmen: Yes, fine. Well, the pictures have two things in common. The first, which you mentioned, is the huge number of people. The other is that they both show music taking place. This one is at a major rock festival – it's outdoors, of course. The other one is indoors and it looks like an enormous orchestra. There must be hundreds of performers there, I mean er … there are over a hundred cellists taking part! I don't know where it is but all the musicians are quite young, so maybe it's a concert organised by several schools?

The main difference between the two scenes is that in the first one, there is an audience – people are watching a band on stage – while in this one, everyone is a performer. I really like being part of a large audience, sitting back and relaxing to the music.

Examiner: Thank you, Carmen. Now, Jurgen, which situation would you prefer to be in?

Jurgen: Oh, the orchestra, definitely. I'd rather participate than watch music. I actually belong to a large choir and we sing as a group of about a hundred and twenty. It's really good fun, and because there are so many of us, it doesn't matter if you make a mistake sometimes.

Examiner: Thank you.

Vocabulary

4

> *Perform*: take part, participate
> *Performers*: musician, orchestra, cellist, choir
> *Performance*: concert, festival

5

> **a** violinist **b** pianist, piano player **c** drummer
> **d** saxophonist **e** trumpeter **f** flautist

Reading

6

> A tribute band is a group of musicians who play the music of a famous pop group and pretend to be that group.

8

> **1** F **2** B **3** G **4** D **5** E **6** A

9

> **Possible answers**
> **a** I think tribute bands are gaining in popularity because people want to hear the music of 'old' bands like Pink Floyd and Abba, who don't play any more.
> **b** It is perfectly possible for a cover version to be better than the original song – or at least different from it.
> **c** Yes, I'd pay something, especially the reasonable prices of Glastonbudget!
> **d** Perhaps they have – there is certainly a lot of selling that goes on at festivals nowadays. But you can find interesting and unusual things to buy, so it's not necessarily a bad thing.

22.2 pages 144–145

Concessive clauses

1

> The underlined words introduce information that contrasts with that in the main clause.
> **1** c **2** e **3** b, d **4** e **5** a, e **6** a

2

> **Suggested answers**
> **a** Although the concert was supposed to start at 8.00, it actually started at 9.30. OR The concert was supposed to start at 8.00, although it actually started at 9.30.
> **b** The group did a lot of dancing on stage, though it was very small. OR Though the stage was very small, the group did a lot of dancing (on it).
> **c** Despite still being a member of Blur, Damon Albarn is in the band Gorillaz. OR Damon Albarn is in the band Gorillaz despite still being a member of Blur.
> **d** Even though I can't get to many gigs, I manage to keep up to date by watching YouTube. OR I manage to keep up to date by watching YouTube even though I can't get to many gigs.
> **e** While you are allowed to use the school instruments in the music room, they should not be taken away from there.
> **f** Even if we miss the first band, we'll still get to the festival in time for Arctic Monkeys. OR We'll still get to the festival in time for Arctic Monkeys, even if we miss the first band.

3

> Putting the reason first makes for a more cohesive and logical piece of writing.
>
> Example **a** starts with a conjunction.
>
> Other conjunctions used in this way are *because* and *since*.

5

> *Although I like almost everything about music* starts with a concessive clause – highlighting a choice.
>
> In the sentence *Seeing blues or soul bands in concert is one of the things that I really enjoy*, the underlined extended noun phrase is put at the beginning to give it particular emphasis.
>
> The adverb used three times is *really*. Other adverbs that could be used instead: *especially, particularly*

6

> **Suggested answers**
> **a** Since it was late, we decided not to stay for the final band.
> **b** Beautifully made by hand and reddish brown in colour, the cello has an excellent sound.
> **c** Having learnt the recorder for three years, Ellen then went on to the flute.
> **d** Despite its technical brilliance, the trumpeter's playing has neither energy nor emotion.
> **e** Due to the conductor's mistake, the soloist had to miss out a whole verse.

7

> **1** B **2** D **3** D **4** A **5** D **6** B **7** C **8** D

Writing folder 11 pages 146–147

Paper 2 Part 2 Reports

Remember to write reports in a consistently neutral or formal register. Do not start or end them as though they were letters.

> **a** Add something to make it clear what the report is about, for example *on last year's festival*.
> Add a concluding sentence, for example, *I hope you will find this information helpful.*
> **b** The site
> Catering facilities
> **c** The underlined parts of the answer are too informal.
> To the festival organisers
> People were forced to go from one end of the site to the other when buying food and drink, which they were not pleased about.
> This would give the festival useful additional funds.
> It is clear that a bigger site and improved catering are needed, as well as some changes to the timing of the event.
> **d** Even though there was some car parking, many people had to park ...
> Although there was some choice of catering at the site, very little vegetarian food was offered.
> People seemed to enjoy the performances, so perhaps each band ...
> Since several members ... thought the tickets were unusually cheap, the price could be raised next year.

3 This exercise is designed to make you think about the target reader of the report, which will inform your answer.

> **Suggested answers**
> **1** f, h, i **2** a, d, j **3** c, e, j **4** b, d, g

4 Before you write the report, do exercises 5 and 6, which will provide you with some useful language.

5

> | | | | |
> |---|---|---|---|
> | **a** competitive | **b** bargain | **c** fortune | **d** purchase |
> | **e** economical | **f** savings | **g** budget | **h** expense |
> | **i** brand | **j** stock | | |
>
> The adjectives are *competitive* and *economical*.

6

> | | | | |
> |---|---|---|---|
> | **a** brands | **b** competitive | **c** stock | **d** budget |
> | **e** fortune | **f** bargains | | |

7 Make a paragraph plan before you start.

> **Sample answer**
> This report covers the main shopping facilities in Newtown.
> **Food**
> There are two supermarkets: Coopers, selling luxury brands of food, is only five minutes from the college and has a large car park; Shopsmart, on the edge of town, is bigger and usually has the most competitive prices, but is difficult to get to. It is best to buy fresh fruit and vegetables in the market, which is held every day apart from Sunday.
>
> **Study materials**
> In Bridge Street, there are four bookshops, where you'll find a good range of dictionaries in stock. For those on a tight budget, there is a huge stationery shop in the main square, where you can buy everything from files and pens to software. There is a small bookshop on the college campus, which also sells basic stationery items like paper.
>
> **Souvenirs**
> Newtown doesn't have as many souvenir shops as London, but the castle has its own shop, and so does the museum. Additionally, things on the market stalls won't cost a fortune, so your students can hunt for bargains there.
>
> I hope this report will be useful for your students and I wish them a pleasant stay.

Unit 23

23.1 pages 148–149

Speaking

1

> | | |
> |---|---|
> | **1** | volcano – c |
> | **2** | lightning – a |
> | **3** | floods – b |
> | **4** | earthquake – d |

2

> **Possible answers**
> **a** No, I haven't, and I hope I never will.
> **b** Of course. I watched the coverage of the Japanese earthquake and tsunami, which was horrible to see.
> **c** It is possible to build up sea walls and construct buildings that will stand up to earthquakes, but you can only do so much, can't you?

Listening

3 The underlined parts of the recording script confirm the answers.

Background information

The talk is based on a true story of what happened when Mount St Helens in Washington State in the USA erupted in 1980.

> **1** forest fire   **2** smoke cloud   **3** silent   **4** handle
> **5** the tent   **6** (some) (tree) branches   **7** shirts   **8** (hot) ash
> **9** rotten/bad eggs   **10** radio

Recording script 2 20

Liz: Thank you for asking me here today to talk about what happened to me and my brother Dave when we went on a camping trip.

On the morning of May 18th, 1980, we were camping about 18 kilometres from Mount St Helens in Washington State in the United States. I was making coffee over a wood fire and Dave was fishing down in the creek. I saw him look up at a small black shape on the horizon. He shouted that there must be a <u>forest fire</u> – it couldn't be a storm as we knew that rain wasn't forecast. Within 30 seconds the thing was absolutely enormous and then it just kept getting bigger and bigger and coming at us faster and faster, and it became very dark.

All I could think was that I wished I were somewhere else! It wasn't like a <u>smoke cloud</u>, it was as if it were alive and it was massive and dense, and very black. It was the strangest thing you can imagine. It was totally <u>silent</u> until it got down into the canyon where we were and then there was a huge roaring. I remember looking at the fire and the wind just blew the flames low along the ground, and watching <u>the handle</u> of my coffee pot just kind of melt in the flames, and then this awful cold – it just surrounded us. The funny thing was that the spoon inside the pot was just fine.

I wasn't just frightened by then, I was absolutely petrified, and so was Dave. Well, we started to run back towards <u>the tent</u>. Stupidly I thought that if only we could get in the tent, we'd be safe! Then the thing hit us. It was … it was like a bomb going off and I fell over backwards and was covered with dirt. I remember wishing it would stop and almost immediately it did, and then Dave reached over to me and asked me if I was OK. We got up and realised that there were trees all around us. In fact, we'd fallen down into a hole left by the roots of a tree and then <u>some branches</u> had covered us. Dave tried to climb out of the hole but it was too hot. Then, when we did get out we were met with such a scene of total destruction. Everything had happened so fast. When we set off it was difficult to breathe, so we took our <u>shirts</u> off and wrapped them around our heads. There were flashes of lightning across the sky at that point too. Wet towels would have been better, but needs must as they say.

It was really hard to get out of the valley because the <u>ash</u> was nearly a metre deep and it was so hot underneath you could only stay in it for a short period of time. Then we had to get up on a tree stump and take our shoes off and unroll our pants, but within a few minutes they would be filled up again. There was a terrible smell – like <u>rotten eggs</u>, not smoke or burning wood. Anyway, we were really lucky. We could easily have been killed. I wish now that we'd taken <u>a radio</u> with us, then maybe we would have had some warning. Even a couple of hours' warning would have helped. I had my cell phone with me but there was no signal in that valley. We went back a few days later and found the site where our tent had been. Thank goodness we fell in that hole!

Vocabulary

4 These phrasal verbs all have *off* as the adverbial particle.

> **1** going off – exploding
> **2** took off – removed
> **3** set off – began the journey
>
> **a** Tom *told* the boys *off* for throwing stones at the windows.
> **b** The Prime Minister's visit to Australia has been *called off* because of the floods at home.
> **c** Anne *sent off* fifty job applications before she got an interview.
> **d** The excitement of living in New York soon *wore off* and then I felt homesick.
> **e** The village was *cut off* because of the flooding.
> **f** My sister *broke off* her engagement to Pete yesterday.
> **g** The thief was *let off* by the magistrate as it was his first offence.
> **h** I *logged off* (my laptop) and went to bed at about midnight.

5 Use an English–English dictionary as you work through the sentences.

a in the end **b** invaluable **c** nowadays **d** raised **e** Lie
f Tell **g** cook **h** stolen **i** injured **j** sympathetic
k sensitive

The differences can be explained as follows:
a we say *at the end of the story/film/book*
in the end = finally
b *priceless* = so valuable it has no price
invaluable means very useful and is usually used about something abstract like help or advice
valuable = worth a lot of money
c we use *nowadays* when we talk about something that is happening currently
actually = in fact
d *to raise* – transitive – takes an object
to rise – intransitive – no object
e *to lie* – takes no object
to lay – takes an object – *to lay eggs, to lay the table, to lay your head on a pillow*
f to tell someone something
to say something to someone
g *a cook* is a person
a cooker is a machine
h *to steal something from someone*
to rob somewhere or someone of something
i *to damage something*
to injure someone
j *sympathetic* = kind and understanding if you have a problem
friendly = pleasant and sociable
k *sensible* = full of common sense
sensitive – used about someone who feels very deeply

6

1 in **2** without **3** over **4** called/named **5** the
6 which/that **7** was **8** this

23.2 pages 150–151

I wish / if only

1 See the section in the Grammar folder on page 175.

Possible answers
I wish we had realised the mountain might erupt.
I wish there had been a cave nearby.
I wish we had left the area before the eruption.
I wish we had never decided to go camping.
I wish it hadn't happened to us.

2

Possible answers
I wish I could give up work and move to a tropical island.
I wish I were still in bed – I'm so tired!

3

Possible answers
I wish the teacher would stop giving us so much homework.
I wish my parents would send me some more money.

4

a I hope the rain stops soon.
b I hope you can come to my party.
c I wish I could speak Arabic.
d I wish Peter would finish writing his book.
e I wish I had remembered to bring the sleeping bags.

Corpus spot
a I wish I **had known** it two days ago.
b I wish you **had been** there with us.
c I hope you **can** give me some more information. / I **wish you could** give me some more information.
d I **hope** you can come to Japan. (it's possible the person will be able to go to Japan) / I **wish you could** come to Japan. (it probably isn't possible for the person to go to Japan)
e I **hope** (that) you have a good time.
f I **wish** I could help you out a little bit. (the speaker doesn't think they will be able to help) / I hope I **can** help you out a little bit. (the speaker thinks they will be able to help)
g I wish I **hadn't** said that.

Note that the alternative sentences don't have exactly the same meaning.

5 a The use of the past tense after *as if / as though* is for hypothetical situations – they express unreality.

b *Would rather* has a similar meaning to *would prefer to*.

Suggested answers
a I'd rather go for a Chinese meal.
b I'd rather do economics.
c I'd rather lie on a beach somewhere hot.
d I'd rather you taught me Japanese.
e I'd rather you bought me a new mobile phone.

6

1 wish (that) I had taken
2 would/'d rather the children stayed
3 only we had seen some
4 wish (that) I lived / could live
5 wish (that) you wouldn't
6 would/'d rather you didn't

Vocabulary

7

> **Possible answers**
> **a** a knot, shoelaces
> **b** a cardigan, a jacket
> **c** a knot, shoelaces
> **d** a parcel
> **e** a secret, a clue
> **f** a Roman coin, treasure
> **g** a belt, a seat belt, a hair clip
> **h** a door, a suitcase, a cupboard
> **i** a ball of string

8

> **a** tornadoes **b** tropical **c** boiling **d** forecast
> **e** freezing **f** poured **g** hurricanes **h** drought
> **i** damp, humid

Exam folder 12 pages 152–153

Paper 1 Part 5 Multiple choice – non-fiction

1 This article is about a woman who goes on a painting holiday to Africa.

2 The questions are always in text order, with the global question, if there is one, at the end.

> **1** D **2** C **3** A **4** B **5** B **6** B
> **1** Although I can make a try at it with words, trying to paint it in my sketch book is another matter altogether.
> **2** I certainly don't want a man capable of such things looking at my own awful brush-strokes.
> **3** To begin with, it seems that he considers me a fellow artist.
> **4** I grew up in places like that, and I connected with it immediately.
> **5** wonderfully organised; reclaim the land; rebuild farmhouse; lay foundations; etc.
> **6** The answer is **B**. The holiday wasn't totally unsuccessful. Although the woman meets another artist, there is nothing about learning to work with others. The article isn't really about travel.

Unit 24

24.1 pages 154–155

Speaking

1 Photos 1 and 2 show Mr Bean (actor Rowan Atkinson), and a scene from the Wallace and Gromit animation film *The Curse of the Were Rabbit*.

Photos 3 and 4 show clowns performing in a circus tent and a street performer on a tiny bicycle cycling through a ring of fire.

Record yourself doing each long turn, aiming to speak for one minute each time. Check your accuracy of grammar and vocabulary when you play the recordings back.

Reading

3

> **1** B **2** A **3** D **4** C **5** A **6** D **7** B **8** D **9** A **10** C
> The relevant words in the texts are given beside each answer.
> **1** B he found he only had about £5
> **2** A he'd dropped a metal milk crate on its head
> **3** D paid no attention
> **4** C the petrified couple tossed all their money at him
> **5** A rushed off to hospital to have their stomachs pumped
> **6** D carried on puffing
> **7** B go home or get a quarterpounder
> **8** D ignoring the company's no-smoking policy
> **9** A disguised the damage with ... lemon and cucumber
> **10** C a note saying: 'I'm real sorry ...'

5 Difficult words in the exam texts should not cause you problems, providing you look at the surrounding words to help you guess the meaning.

> **a** loomed **b** retained **c** bewildered **d** tossed
> **e** shooed ... away **f** all the trimmings **g** settled
> **h** scruffy **i** fleeing **j** crates

Grammar extra

Rather is a very useful word in English, but you need to learn how it is used. See the Grammar folder page 176.

> **a** 1 than **b** 3 would; not **c** 2, 4 quite

24.2 pages 156–157

The grammar of phrasal verbs

1 The grammar of phrasal verbs is summarised in the Grammar folder on page 176.

d and **g** contain intransitive phrasal verbs.

2

b no change possible
e also possible: He put down the snack ...
f no change possible
h no change possible
i no change possible
j no change possible

3

1 d, g
2 f, j
3 b
4 c, e – h is an exception (we do not say 'put a fight up')
5 a, i

4

Possible answers
a turn off the TV   **b** get it over with   **c** made out a car
d has put me off   **e** picked up Swedish   **f** look them up
g worked out the answer   **h** faced up to the problem

Corpus spot

catch up on some sleep
come up with some good ideas
keep up with the international news
live up to his expectations
put up with your bad news

5

a 10   **b** 7   **c** 15   **d** 9   **e** 4   **f** 13   **g** 2   **h** 8   **i** 11   **j** 5
k 1   **l** 12   **m** 6   **n** 14   **o** 3

6

1 during/in   **2** at   **3** though   **4** up
5 be   **6** most   **7** for   **8** since

Writing folder 12 pages 158–159

Paper 2 Part 2 Articles

2 The errors are highlighted below.

> **Eddie Izzard – a man of many talents**
>
> Eddie Izzard has been a stand-up comedian for over 30 years and regularly sells out the biggest venues, included the Hollywood Bowl. I've seen one of his live show and they are hilarious. He loves experimenting with language and delivers also whole performances in French. The touring show *Force Majeure* has taken him to 25 countries around the world.
>
> Not only that, but he has acted in much films and plays, and often appears in TV. The most impressive thing about him is the way he raises money for the charity. For example, for Sports Relief, he spent seven weeks running marathons, covering more then 1100 miles across the UK with only one day off each week! Even though he had very few training beforehand, he somehow managed to keep going, in spite of be in pain at times.
>
> That's why I respect him so much. Nothing is too challenging for him, from facing a huge live audience to the physical strain of marathon running. He received an Outstanding Lifetime Achievement Award from Harvard University, there he was described as an outstanding member of global society.

3

> **Corrected version**
>
> Eddie Izzard has been a stand-up comedian for over 30 years and regularly sells out the biggest venues, *including* the Hollywood Bowl. I've seen one of his live *shows* and they are hilarious. He loves experimenting with language and *also delivers* whole performances in French. The touring show *Force Majeure* has taken him to 25 countries around the world.
>
> Not only that, but he has acted in *many* films and plays, and often appears *on* TV. The most impressive thing about him is the way he raises money for ~~the~~ charity. For example, for Sports Relief, he spent seven weeks running marathons, covering more *than* 1100 miles across the UK with only one day off each week! Even though he had very *little* training beforehand, he somehow managed to keep going, in spite of *being* in pain at times.
>
> That's why I respect him so much. Nothing is too challenging for him, from facing a huge live audience to the physical strain of marathon running. He received an Outstanding Lifetime Achievement Award from Harvard University, *where* he was described as an outstanding member of global society.

Sample answer

Flight of the Conchords

Flight of the Conchords is a comedy act consisting of two immensely talented guys from New Zealand – Bret McKenzie and Jemaine Clement. As well as being great comedians, they are excellent musicians and write extremely funny songs. I first heard them on the radio, but they have since made American TV series and appeared live worldwide. Their best performances are on YouTube.

The one that never ceases to make me laugh features the song *Issues* (*Think about it*), which sounds a serious topic but is in actual fact hilarious! Part of the reason why their act is so successful is their ability to keep a straight face, even when they are saying the most ridiculous things. For example, in the chat they do before performing this particular song, Bret expresses concern for the future of his children and his wife, who are then revealed by Jemaine as imaginary people!

Both performers have a background in music and are able to copy different styles, making fun of them in a gentle way. Their lyrics also display a special sense of humour. Bret and Jemaine are without doubt the funniest musical comedy duo ever – check them out soon!

(200 words)

Units 19–24 Revision

pages 160–161

2

1 C	2 A	3 C	4 B	5 C	6 B	7 A	8 B

3

illness or injury
1 sprain **2** cough
volcanoes
3 eruption **4** ash **5** lava
musical instruments
6 oboe **7** piano **8** guitar **9** flute
crime and punishment
10 robbery **11** court **12** burglar **13** trial **14** fine
parts of the body
15 eyebrow **16** waist **17** jaw **18** knee **19** elbow
20 thigh

a flute **b** waist **c** eruption **d** sprain **e** fine

4

1 calling up **2** taken on **3** taken aback **4** bring in
5 work out **6** ended up **7** put off
8 miss out on

5

1 not	**2** few	**3** enough	**4** up
5 than	**6** at	**7** being	**8** if

Speaking folder pages 162–163

The section on the Speaking test on page 8 gives information about the timing of each part.

Think about the advice given on page 162 and then record yourself doing each part of the test. Check the time taken as you play back your recording.

The Part 2 photographs show:

First turn: Uma Thurman at the Cannes Film Festival premiere of *Pirates of the Caribbean: On Stranger Tides* and Sir Paul McCartney being mobbed by fans after attending a ceremony at the Liverpool Institute of Performing Arts, which he founded

Second turn: A street in a village in Nepal and traffic in a European city centre.